Terrible Terry Allen

Terrible Terry Allen

Combat General of World War II—
The Life of an American Soldier

Gerald Astor

PRESIDIO

Ballantine Books • New York

In memory of our beloved Andy, a tower of integrity and a wonderful soul,
and for my brave Sonia.

A Presidio Press Book
Published by The Random House Publishing Group

Copyright © 2003 by Gerald Astor

All rights reserved under International and Pan-American Copyright Conventions. Published in the United States by Presidio Press, an imprint of The Random House Publishing Group, a division of Random House, Inc., New York, and simultaneously in Canada by Random House of Canada Limited, Toronto.

Presidio Press and colophon are trademarks of Random House, Inc.

www.presidiopress.com

All photos courtesy University of Texas at El Paso Library Special Collections Department

Grateful acknowledgment is made to Doubleday, a division of Random House, Inc., for permission to reproduce the map of the invasion of North Africa, by Rafael Palacios, from *Crusade in Europe* by Dwight D. Eisenhower, copyright 1948 by Doubleday, a division of Random House, Inc.

Library of Congress Control Number: 2004093591

ISBN: 0-89141-834-2

Manufactured in the United States of America

First Edition: April 2003
First Trade Paperback Edition: July 2004

1 3 5 7 9 10 8 6 4 2

Contents

Acknowledgments

I am greatly indebted to all of those who graciously allowed me to interview them, and their information is credited to them within the text of the book. There were some individuals who were particularly helpful in this regard. Consuelo Allen and her two sisters, Mary Francis and Alice Genevieve, not only gave me their recollections but also pointed me to people who could aid me. Claudette McGovern produced genealogical information on the Allen clan. Retired Brig. Gen. Jim Shelton was a source on Terry Allen Jr. and supplied leads on his experiences in the Vietnam War.

Through the University of Texas at El Paso, in the persons of Claudia Rivers and Thomas Burdett, I gained access to the Terry de la Mesa Allen papers and the photographic collection. The Eisenhower Library in Abilene, Kansas, produced other relevant documents. Tim Nenninger and Mitchell Yockelson at the National Archives in College Park, Maryland, aided my quest for material from World War I and II and patiently answered questions on terminology and events.

At the U.S. Army Military History Library in Carlisle, Pennsylvania, the head of the archives, Dr. Richard J. Sommers, pointed out some highly relevant material on the general's pre-World War II activities. Suzanne Christoff and Suzanne Lintelmann of the U.S.M.A. library provided access to records for the Allen men during their times at West Point. Major Kirk Frady, chief of public information, located photographs that dealt with their cadets days. Lieutenant Colonel Julian Olejniczak, vice president for publications of the U.S.M.A. Association of Graduates, steered me to the appropriate sources at West Point.

Colonel John S. Wetherell, U.S.M.A. Class of 1952, was kind enough to offer names of Terry Allen Jr.'s classmates at West Point and New Mexico Military Institute and to print a notice of my interest in *Assembly*, the academy's alumni publication.

Dr. John Votaw of the 1st Division association in Cantigny, Illinois, gave me advice on possible sources and Glen Lytle head of the 104th Division Association, and Peter Branton, webmaster for this organization, spread the word of my interest in their former commander. I also made fertile use of the 104th's web site with its "War Stories." Retired colonel Warren Lacy, editor of *The Retired Officer Magazine*, provided me with a copy of an informative article from the publication.

Carlo D'Este, whose own histories of campaigns and military figures are exemplary, encouraged me to pursue the topic, offered advice on sources and information. Kevin Hymel assisted me by locating maps.

The manuscript benefitted from the editing and expertise of E. J. McCarthy and Bob Kane from Presidio as well as the sharp-eyed diligence of copy editor Netty Kahan. Last but not least, I am indebted to Ted Astor for his help with the computer, and scanning of maps and photographs.

Preface

The Greatest Soldier

During World War II—a "just" war suffused with virulent patriotism—the media of the day printed hardly a discouraging word about any senior military man. Only one flagrant offense brought censure, the breach against the code of conduct committed by Lt. Gen. George S. Patton Jr. in slapping soldiers afflicted with battle fatigue. For the most part, generals enjoyed immunity from criticism and often were painted in a near godlike image. Of all who led troops in the field, none received better press than Maj. Gen. Terry de la Mesa Allen. In 1943, when Allen was in command of the 1st Infantry Division, a *Time* correspondent wrote of him, "He is a gentle man. He does not like the fact that men will be killed carrying out his orders, but he has accepted the inevitability of it. He will spare or spend his men as military necessity demands; while they live he will see that they get every comfort and consideration. That is one reason why the spirit of the 1st Division is second to none in the U.S. Army."

Quentin Reynolds, who covered World War II for *Colliers*, broadcast a radio tribute to Allen on 8 June 1944 in which he said, "If I had ten sons I'd be proud and happy to know that they were serving in the Fighting First, under this wiry, little, smiling-eyed man." Reynolds was unaware that Allen was no longer with the 1st Division as it landed on the D-day beaches. On another occasion, Reynolds gushed, "Never in my life have I seen a man so worshiped as Terry was and [he] is not only loved by his men . . . but by every war correspondent who has ever come in contact with him. As far as I am concerned, Terry Allen is the greatest leader of men and the greatest tactical general in our army."

Other reporters also sang the praises of Allen. Ernie Pyle of the Scripps Howard newspaper chain—who ordinarily preferred the company of the lesser ranks—said, "Major General Terry Allen was one of my favorite people. Partly because he didn't give a damn for hell or high water; partly because he was more colorful than most; and partly because he was the only general outside the Air Forces I could call by his first name. If there was one thing in the world Allen lived and breathed for, it was to fight. . . . Allen's speech was picturesque. No writer could fully capture him on paper; because his talk was wonderfully profane it couldn't be put down in black and white."

Curiously, notwithstanding the veneration from the media of his day, Allen privately expressed a low opinion of newspaper people.

One might harbor suspicions about the adulation of Allen by reporters who sometimes elevate a person only because he is colorful and accessible. But professionals who fought the war also revered Allen as a soldier of the highest caliber. In the words stated, fifteen years after Allen had retired, by Brig. John Corley, a 1938 graduate of West Point who served under Allen in North Africa and Sicily and earned a staggering array of medals (a Distinguished Service Cross, five Silver Stars, a Legion of Merit, four Bronze Stars and a Purple Heart): "There's no question about who was the greatest soldier in the war, Terry Allen."

Early in the 1960s, Brig. Gen. James Shelton, then a young officer on the staff of Gen. Don Clayman, heard his superior remark on the excellence of Gen. Ben Harrell as one of the best soldiers he ever observed; Clayman then added, "There was only one other greater soldier, Terry Allen."

Great Britain's Gen. Sir Harold Alexander commanded the Allied ground forces in North Africa and Sicily, where Allen led the 1st Division. Although Alexander had a low opinion of most of the American military, he rated Allen as among the finest division commanders he had observed in two world wars.

Major General Samuel W. Koster, a 1942 graduate of the United States Military Academy (U.S.M.A.), who served under Allen with the 104th Division in Europe, said, "He was a very good commander, very much seen around the battlefield. He was such a genuine person, with sincere interest in people. He made you feel part of what was happening and that is how he sold the men on him."

George O'Connor, who entered World War II as an enlisted man and finished as a lieutenant colonel, recalled, "There was a time when a battalion from the 413th Regiment [O'Connor's organization] was badly torn up after heavy casualties. I had become the executive officer and [Allen] gathered groups of men in cellars. He got up on a box and talked to them in that reedy voice, sometimes a whistling noise because of his wound in World War I. I couldn't tell you what he said because I was way in the back but when he finished, these guys were all ready to go back to the fight. He was that kind of leader."

At the bottom of the military pyramid, the enlisted men respected, or in Reynolds's word, "worshiped" Allen. John Rheney went to Europe with the 104th Infantry Division a private, first class, and returned to the States as a staff sergeant. He said: "Whether we had personal contact with him or not he was admired by all of his troops. We trusted General Allen because while we knew that he would attack where ordered, he would make use of our extensive night training where at all possible because of the lower casualty rates."

As Rheney suggested, from ranks of the common privates through the upper echelons of officers who served under Allen's authority, the remarkable fondness for him approached adoration. Major General Norman "Dutch" Cota, who was on Allen's staff early in the war, landed on Omaha Beach on D day, and later commanded the 28th Infantry Division, explained the extraordinary affection of the soldiers for Allen: "It's because he's so damned honest."

Yet, Allen had his detractors. The voice-over for a television documentary on the 1st Division described him as showing up disheveled and drunk to meet with the top brass in Sicily. The commentary also labeled him "not a team player." Author Leonard Mosley, in a biography of Gen. George C. Marshall, called Allen "a rip-roaring drunk." In 1943, when writer Clark Lee told Dwight D. Eisenhower's chief of staff, Lt. Gen. Walter Bedell "Beetle" Smith, that Allen made the 1st Division one of the best in the army, Smith shouted, "Made the 1st Division! He ruined the 1st Division. He started out to make it a rough, tough outfit that would win battles. He thought it was enough to win battles, to have battlefield discipline. He didn't realize the importance of discipline when the troops are out of the line."

The differences of opinion about Allen and his handling of the men he commanded raises the issue of what is the role of a general. What makes one high officer superior to another? How should a commander be judged—by strategic moves, leadership, or as Smith indicated, by discipline imposed on his subordinates?

The 1st Infantry Division under Allen's generalship was recognized by his peers as the best foot soldier outfit in the North African campaign. When Patton—long a sometime friend and competitor—was in charge of the American effort for the invasion of Sicily, he insisted on having Allen and his division under his command. The 1st Division spearheaded the ground forces in the conquest of the Italian island. Yet, Patton would acquiesce to Allen's subsequent relief from his post and his transfer in semidisgrace back to the United States. Nonetheless, Allen "rose from his ashes" to return to Europe as leader of the 104th Infantry Division and successfully campaign to the Elbe River, where he and his troops met the Soviet forces.

Although the *Time* writer used the word "gentle" when describing Allen, the general claimed to the *New Yorker* magazine's A. J. Liebling that during World War I he shot a subordinate in the buttocks who balked at an order. Allen told Liebling, "If I hear anybody talking that way in my division now, I'll shoot him and not in the behind, either. I'm getting tougher as I go along."

He had been blooded along the Mexican border and participated in the U.S. punitive adventure that invaded Mexico in 1916. As a member of the American Expeditionary Force in France, Allen incurred bullet and shrapnel wounds while piling up a heroic record. He returned to the States for the twenty-year period during which the American military—still an alien culture in a democracy devoted to material gain—all but starved. The Great Depression would pinch the armed forces even further.

Most newspaper and magazine accounts of Allen paint a portrait of the traditional professional soldier, hard-bitten, profane, and combative. To many he fitted the stereotype of the Irishman: boisterous, fond of storytelling, and most comfortable on a bar stool. The impression given is that of a man with limited dimensions—a person who, unlike the citizen soldier, falls outside the common American experience. However, although Terry Allen, an army brat born at the time the frontier vanished, operated within the ordinarily tight, hierarchal confines of his profession, he disdained the "book." Mercurial, a maverick from childhood, he showed scant interest in the academic aspects of the institutionally schooled soldier, yet time and again he demonstrated that, not only did he know how to wage war, but also he was a master of strategy, tactics, and ordnance.

He was less than adept with any language other than English. While his letters correctly spelled the names of foreign villages and natural formations, he habitually mangled pronunciation when he spoke. Kenneth Downs, an aide who served with him in both North Africa and in Europe, said, "The general's idiosyncrasies tickled his men. He had a fine disdain for foreign names and rarely got anything less well known than Paris or Berlin straight. So the staffs learned early they would have to keep up with his private glossary for name places as well as the official codes' names. They had to know that 'Weisenheimer-or-whatever-the-hell-they-call-it' meant Weisweiler and that the 'Irk' was the Erft [River] . . . that 'Boozy-Bar-or-whatever-the-hell-they-call-it' was an unpronounceable Arab town in Algeria and 'Nicodemus' was Nicosia, Sicily."

Allen never was all gun and no heart. Unlike many of his contemporaries, he was a man of extraordinary compassion even as he directed the bloody business of America's greatest war. Although he grew up on army posts, played with the rough-hewn children of soldiers, associated with the crude, hard-drinking, often illiterate enlisted men, and as a young officer was a zealous carouser, he was as devoted a family man as one could find. As he approached his thirtieth birthday, his letters from the trenches of France to "my dearest Mama," and "Papa" were filled with affection and filial respect. He adored his wife, Mary Fran, and doted on his son, Terry junior. And while deeply engaged in wartime operations, his position did not isolate him from the vicissitudes of money problems and family crises.

Terry Allen was the middle man in a military saga that stretches for nearly a century. His is a tale of fathers and sons: His sire, Samuel E. Allen, graduated from the U.S.M.A. in 1881. And, Terry Allen's son, Terry Allen Jr., followed the family vocation to meet his destiny in Vietnam. As a family of West Pointers, professional soldiers, husbands, and fathers, genetic fingerprints mark the three Allens; but within their commonality, they were nourished by very different climates. The nineteenth-century military academy of Samuel Allen was not the same as that attended by Terry senior. Forty years later, Terry junior spent his four years at an even more markedly different institution. The army in which Sam Allen served barely resembled that which occupied his son from 1912–1945, and in the post–Korea and Vietnam era, Terry Allen Jr. confided to a friend, "My dad could never have survived in the army of today." Terry junior "adored his father," according to his closest associates. When he chose to follow the path of a father who is the stuff of legends, he embarked on an exceedingly rough road.

Beyond their personal experiences, the lives of the Allens also cover the passage of the U.S. Army from the first decade of the twentieth century through World War II, the Korean War, and into the Vietnam War. These are accounts of change, success and failure, America's wars, triumphs and shattering losses—the very essence of the nation's biography.

1 : Sam Allen's West Point

Samuel Edward Allen, a nineteen-year-old youth with "coal black hair" and "beautiful white teeth" (in the words of a fellow plebe), traveled by railroad from his home in Posey County in Indiana to Cold Spring in New York, on 15 June 1877—he was bound for West Point. According to research done by Susan Zinniker (Sam Allen's step-great-great-granddaughter), two brothers—Robert and John Allen—had emigrated from Armagh, Ireland, in 1736 to settle in Virginia. Robert Allen died in 1769, and John Allen joined the local militia, ultimately serving as a major during the American Revolution. While Zinniker could trace a line of Allens from 1791 to 1856, she was unable to distinguish the exact line to Sam Allen, who was born in Indiana as the son of A. P. Allen.

After graduating from high school, Sam Allen worked for local commercial establishments before he received an appointment to the U.S.M.A. from the Eighth Congressional District in his state. Sam Allen became one of eighty-one admitted as members of the class of 1881— only fifty-seven would survive to graduate.

Following his first year as a cadet, Sam Allen scored twenty-seventh in the order of merit, which ranked cadets on an overall basis that included final grades in academic work and discipline (conduct). He finished well down the list in the latter, but his achievements in math raised his standing. The next year, he continued to excel in math, improved in French, and did well enough in drawing to attain seventh place. Again, his record

1

in discipline fell below average. In his third year, Allen neared the top of the class in natural and experimental philosophy, chemistry, tactics, and drawing. With only five members of the class who rated worse in discipline, he dropped, this time to tenth. In his final year at West Point, Allen posted impressive grades in the sciences, mathematics, drawing, engineering (which dealt with the civil as well as military aspects), and law. He excelled in ordnance and gunnery. But he climbed only to eighth because of his continuing problems with discipline. In that respect he scored worst of the top seventeen cadets.

When one pores over the legal-size, leather-bound ledgers in which cadet delinquencies are inscribed in a fine penmanship, the young Sam Allen's character becomes a bit clearer. He received his first demerits shortly after he reported for the summer encampment in 1877 because his shoes were improperly arranged in his tent. Notations over the following months cite a twisted belt, an incorrect laundry list, an overdue library book, appearing improperly shaven, and responding slowly to a command "carry arms." Over the years, reports on failings in appearance declined; but with familiarity, Allen took other liberties. He was gigged for lateness at reveille, missing a class parade, idling while at the gymnasium, and above all, for violating the restrictions on tobacco. Throughout his time at West Point, black marks appear for "smoking at inspection," "smoking in barracks," and "odor of tobacco in quarters."

Another common complaint about him—which, however, undoubtedly made him popular with his colleagues—was his protection and indulgence of fellow cadets. As a cadet first sergeant, he was handed four demerits because he failed to report two cadets absent from a formation. He was observed marching a guard detail to its post too slowly, and he was chastised for allowing applause and unnecessary noise while in command of a table in the mess. During a cavalry drill while serving as chief of a platoon, he permitted loud talking and laughing as members of the unit were leaping hurdles.

The one element that set Samuel Edward Allen somewhat apart from his fellows was his Roman Catholic religion. The academy was predominantly Protestant, and attendance at chapel every Sunday morning was compulsory. However, the campus had no Catholic chapel. The Catholics attended mass at a church located in Buttermilk Falls.

Williston Fish, Sam Allen's classmate, wrote in his memoirs of four years in which "we had been drilled and scorned and ordered about, and as Burns says, we had in a way, been 'huffed and scuffed and disrespekit' but we were a class like other classes." Rather than a particularly tortur-ous ordeal, the experience sounds much like that of students at con-temporary civilian colleges where hazing in various degrees from verbal abuse to brutal, sadistic depravity also prevailed. Indeed, a time came when the heads of the Ivy League schools, like U.S.M.A. superintendent John M. Schofield, felt obliged to dampen the excessive harassment in-flicted upon freshmen by more senior students.

The "files" as Fish and his contemporaries referred to themselves, took note of those who could not "go with us all the four years through." In the seasons of "snow and ice and fierce blasts . . . we put on gray trousers for armor against winter, and five times we happily donned the white to rejoice in summer."

Fish described Allen as a congenial sort and said there was "no one quicker on a joke." He also said that Allen always looked "as if he were joining in songs, jokes, quips and comments at an evening roundup; or he looked as if he were about to go to the board [in a classroom] light of heart, write down 'Allen' in his easy and unsurpassed way, make his drawing like Apeles [a Greek painter] and recite in a sober way so as to be respectful, without any worry or anxiety."

For all the lightheartedness suggested by Fish, life at the academy dur-ing the time of Sam Allen could be arduous. The ancient barracks, nearly forty years old by the time Allen arrived, were cold, dark quarters. Al-though the mess hall's kitchens (erected in 1851) were equipped with hand pumps delivering water to the sinks (so the residents were not re-quired to haul water in buckets from outdoor mains), it was only in 1904 that pipes were installed to bring running water inside the barracks. La-trines were located in a separate building until that year, when toilets and bathing facilities were placed in the basements of the barracks. Before this amenity was added, cadets walked to a nearby building to bathe.

An 1876 graduate, Edward Farrow, who published *West Point*—a short book describing life at the academy—reported that reveille awoke the cadets from between five and six in the morning, depending upon the season. After roll call, they policed their quarters, cleaned arms and var-ious accoutrements for inspection, or studied. Following breakfast at seven o'clock, a guard-mounting ceremony, and "recreation" time, a class parade preceded class sessions. Cadets received formal instruction or su-pervised study from Monday through Saturday, usually starting at eight in the morning and finishing at four in the afternoon, with an hour for "dinner" between one and two.

Plebes (first-year cadets) were fed an academic menu that consisted solely of mathematics and French. The only other courses of instruction for fourth classmen covered subjects such as fencing and bayonet drill. Third-year cadets were taught French, which was alternated from day to day with Spanish. They learned drawing, both topography and figures, using lead pencils, ink, and color. The artwork alternated with two hours of equitation.

Second classmen endured what was listed as "natural and experimental philosophy," a kind of basic science. Chemistry, which included what was called "chemical physics," alternated with riding, while further learning in drawing alternated with instruction in military tactics. The men in the uppermost class studied civil engineering six days a week from September through January; they learned "military engineering and the art of war" the remainder of the academic year. Ethics and law, mineralogy and geology, and ordnance and gunnery occupied them on a rotating schedule with two hours on horseback as part of the interchanging daily mix. Conspicuous by their absence are such subjects as English, Latin, history, geography, politics, philosophy in its more theoretical vein, and a host of other liberal arts topics. A candidate for the academy was assumed to have already learned the rudiments of mathematics and American history.

A host of regulations circumscribed appearance and behavior from reveille to lights out and then an inspection at 10:00 P.M. Cadets were tightly disciplined by the officers at the Point as well as by upperclassmen. All students were to wear their hair cut short, "cropped" was the term employed by Farrow. Whiskers and mustaches were forbidden, as were tobacco in any form, the tools of any "games of chance," duels, and non-regulation dress. A cadet was forbidden from leaving his room without permission during the hours of study and between tattoo (the signal for the end of the day) and reveille. They could visit with relatives and others, at the Thayer Hotel, only with written approval. The cadets were prohibited from receiving newspapers or magazines without special permission from the superintendent—and in any case, no cadet could subscribe to more than two newspapers. Any cadet found drunk was liable for expulsion. Hazing that bordered, and even crossed over, the line into brutal was tolerated. The four-year ordeal had one positive effect: Like many extended shared hardships, it bonded the files for life. The ring that signified graduation became a talisman of brotherhood. At the same time, it set West Pointers apart from officers drawn from other circumstances.

As a good student, Sam Allen completed his West Point sojourn number eight in his graduating class of fifty-seven. Twenty-four of those who entered with him were either "turned back" (forced to repeat a year) or "found" (dismissed entirely). He was assigned to the 5th Field Artillery, which was based at Fort Hamilton, New York. An outpost on the extreme southeastern tip of Long Island, Fort Hamilton overlooks the Narrows, a strategic entry into New York harbor.

Sam Allen rose to first lieutenant in 1886. During the period of 1890–1892, he attended an artillery school. Those years were followed by a stint with the 5th Artillery and then promotion to captain in 1899, after which Allen served on the staffs of both Maj. Gen. Winfield Scott Hancock and Lt. Gen. John M. Schofield. As commander of the Department of the East, Hancock operated out of Governors Island, New York, and was credited with establishing the Military Service Institution of the United States and also military journals that helped professionalize the army. Schofield served as Commanding General of the Army from 1881–1895.

While stationed in New York at Fort Hamilton and Governors Island, Sam Allen met and courted a Brooklynite, Concepcion Alvarez de la Mesa. She was the daughter of Carlos de la Mesa (a native of Seville, Spain, born in 1828) and the former Mary Frances Taft. According to John Van Pelt Lassoe Jr., a grandson of de la Mesa, Carlos actually came to the United States to fight on the Union side. He spoke no English but enlisted in the 39th Infantry from New York, which included an international assortment of volunteers known as the Garibaldi Guards. They were splendidly outfitted in the uniforms of the Italian Bersaglieri.

Shortly after he arrived in the States, de la Mesa became entranced by a young woman, twenty-year-old Mary Frances Taft, who allegedly was a descendant of *Mayflower* passenger John Alden. A letter from Lassoe reported, "He [Carlos] courted Mary Frances Taft in French because he spoke no English and she no Spanish." Lassoe also reported that de la Mesa apparently was wounded at Gettysburg. Supposedly, his wife collected a stretcher and four litter-bearers to carry him off the battlefield.

Carlos de la Mesa recovered from his wounds only enough to qualify for service with the Invalid Corps. Ultimately he held a post with the Freedman's Bureau, set up in the South to assist the newly liberated slaves. In 1865, a daughter, Concepcion, was born in Washington. De la Mesa died in 1872 at Saint Elizabeth's Hospital in Washington, D.C. In the words of Lassoe, "I gather [he succumbed] quite mad when he died, presumably as a result of wounds received at Gettysburg—although I

seem to recall learning someplace that it was the result of general pare-
sis." His widow then wed Charles A. Terry in 1872 and became known as
Mama Terry.

Lieutenant Sam Allen married Concepcion in a Brooklyn church in
1885. Their first child, a baby girl, was born in New York in 1887; they
named her Ethel. Shortly thereafter, Allen received a posting to Fort
Douglas, Utah, which had been established in 1862 to protect the over-
land mail and to control the Mormons in the vicinity. On April Fools'
Day in 1888, while Sam Allen was stationed there, Conchita (the name
by which Concepcion was less formally known) bore a son. They baptized him Terry in honor of the current family surname of Conchita's
mother, and they tacked on "de la Mesa" for his grandfather.

The family moved from Fort Douglas to West Point where Allen was
stationed from 1892–1896 as an assistant instructor in the Department
of Natural and Experimental Philosophy. The academy had continued
its practice of staffing most of the faculty with graduates. Led by a handful of professors with a creditable educational background, the teachers
were supplemented by assistants drawn from the ranks of graduates. The
officers chosen, while generally known from their cadet days as good students, had not attended institutions of higher learning.

For Allen, the experience was somewhat disquieting. Fish said he
asked him how he felt about being "the chill and lofty instructor instead
of the warm-hearted and hopeful cadet, and he said 'it seemed all right.'
And then he said, 'Well, no; it didn't seem all right either. It did not seem
so very good.' He said that all the time he was seeing the Plain, the old
Barracks, the River and the hills–he was seeing them looking just as they
used to look but they seemed to look as they used to look all in vain and
to no purpose, because the files were not there. It was very lonely. He
said that it got more lonely as time went on and that finally he was glad
to have his tour over, and to go away. But then Allen remarked, 'And still,
I like to go back, and look again and remember.'"

Whatever misgivings Sam Allen had about his four years as an instructor, young Terry, from age four to eight, was exposed to the glam-
orous aspects of the long gray line: the parades, the smart uniforms, and
the developing enthusiasm for intercollegiate sports and competition as
the rivalry with the midshipmen at Annapolis flowered.

It was Sam Allen's fate to never come under enemy fire. After his term
as an instructor at the academy, he took up station at Fort Monroe, Virginia, in 1897. He was there when the Spanish-American War began. Like

any career army officer would, he obviously regretted missing the action. In a jocular note to Fish, he mentioned a pair of classmates who had not been involved in Cuba, and he remarked: "I was not in it either. I am and have been Q.M. [quartermaster] here ever since the first gun was fired. I have sent off shiploads of soldiers and have seen them come staggering back down the gangplank, apologizing almost for being alive, but so happy to set foot on native soil again."

The closest Sam Allen came to the "splendid little war" against Spain was the great victory parade through the streets of New York. When the hero of the Battle of Manila Bay, Adm. George Dewey, sailed into New York harbor following his triumph, some claimed the salvos of welcome consumed more ammunition than the U.S. fleet fired in the Philippines. At the parade on 30 September, Admiral Dewey, Pres. William McKinley, Sen. Mark Hanna, and New York state governor Theodore Roosevelt headed a 35,000-man parade. Among those in the line of march was Capt. Sam Allen. He wrote to Fish inviting him to see the sights in New York, "for instance, the kinetoscope exhibit at Keith's [a theater] where I am told they make daily exhibitions of myself riding at the head of the brigade (just in rear of the General commanding) at the Dewey celebration."

As an officer stationed for a number of years in New York and a participant in such revels, Allen undoubtedly met many of the city's more illustrious figures, including Theodore Roosevelt—who had preceded his exploits in Cuba and election as governor with a stint as a police commissioner vigorously pursuing Tammany corruption. That acquaintance would play a significant role in the destinies of the Allens.

2: Terry Allen's West Point

Sam Allen settled into the role of a garrison officer without the credentials conferred upon those who actually went to war or commanded troops in the field. After his tour at Fort Monroe during the Spanish-American War, he served at a number of field, and then coast, artillery posts, which became a separate branch in 1907. He oversaw coast artillery units in the harbors of Boston, New York, and Pensacola; slowly he rose in rank. In 1901, the Allens had their third child, Mary Conchita de la Mesa Allen.

Terry Allen's acquaintance with West Point began with his father's tour as a teacher. Between the ages of three and seven, he feasted on the panorama of smartly uniformed young men amid a citadel that crowned the scenic splendor of massive fortress-type buildings ensconced on the shores of a magnificent river. There was pomp and circumstance aplenty to seduce the imagination of a boy, and over the years Samuel Allen undoubtedly transmitted to Terry his nostalgic affection for his life as a cadet.

When the family then moved to a series of army posts, the child indulged himself in a passion for riding. As an artillery officer, Samuel Allen frequently pursued his duties while in the saddle, and it was natural for his offspring to emulate his style. In her fading years, his mother, Concepcion Allen, recalled her small boy in the saddle, proudly riding off to accompany his father on maneuvers. By age ten, Terry felt totally comfortable in the saddle.

Sam Allen—the somewhat free-spirited, joking, dancing, gregarious cadet and young officer captured in the memories of Fish and in his own letters—had become a more reserved man with considerable respect for the dignity and discipline of the army. Terry Allen recalled that while his father was a captain he refused to have a telephone installed in his home. "I don't want to telephone my seniors and I won't have my junior officers calling me." But, for all of the parent's concern for decorum and the code of "an officer and a gentleman," the enlisted personnel of the day were cut from a different cloth, and their children likewise.

The rough-and-tumble lot of youngsters Terry's age, many of them the spawn of enlisted personnel, were his natural playmates. Even at an early age he showed signs of leadership, coupled with a reputation that was less than salubrious. Allen reported that he once came across a contemporary in tears, and the boy explained that his mother had just spanked him. When Allen inquired why, his companion explained, "Because I was playing with you." According to Liebling, Allen said, "My opinion of myself went up like a rocket." Aside from his adventures with other army brats, Allen spent considerable time with the lesser ranks stationed at the camps, giving him a lifelong empathy toward enlisted men, not to mention a taste for some of their habits. He informed Liebling that along with horsemanship, he had learned at a tender age how to smoke, chew, cuss, and fight. He also surely became aware of how much the soldiers favored drinking.

Terry never doubted the kind of career he would follow. Having lived at West Point for four years and enjoyed his life at army bases, he expected to follow in his father's footsteps. While he took for granted that as the son of a graduate and a colonel on active duty he would receive an appointment, he apparently had not foreseen that the U.S.M.A. demanded a disciplined behavior and a certain academic proficiency.

Undoubtedly, the young Allen was oblivious to all the controversy about the quality of a U.S.M.A. education and the caliber of the students. His own questionable academic background indicates that the evaluation of the student body by a 1902 board of advisors that criticized the scholastic credentials of the cadets was well on the mark. At the time he hoped to enter West Point, Sam Allen was stationed at Fort Snelling, in the heart of Minneapolis—where Terry had attended Central High School for two years and compiled a mediocre record. On his application to the academy, he summarized some of his academic credentials, including one year each of Latin and French. The candidate noted, "I graduated from that school [1906] and in my senior year I took higher algebra, trigonometry, surveying, English literature, mechanical drawing physics and shop work." He might also have proffered his proficiency as a horseman. A 1905 story in the *St. Paul Pioneer Press* reported that he won a "tilting contest" in a local horse show, competing against an army lieutenant and other older riders.

After seven months at the University of Minnesota, on 15 June 1907, at age nineteen, he received an appointment at large to the U.S.M.A. Because of his dubious academic standing, and despite his lineage, Terry required the intercession of the nation's chief executive. Somewhere along the line the Allens had met Theodore Roosevelt, police commissioner from 1895–1897, and then governor of the state following his triumphant return from Cuba. Concepcion Allen managed to have tea with him at the White House and successfully pleaded the case for her son.

Subsequently admitted with 141 others, plebe Allen was a youth of modest height and weight, certainly well under six feet. Along with his weak educational credits, he stammered. In classrooms that featured recitations by the cadets, this would certainly be a handicap. His contemporaries for the Class of 1911 included a fair spectrum of White America: sons of farmers, lawyers, merchants, salesmen, bankers, a livery stable manager, a shoemaker, planter, mail carrier, and even one with "no occupation." A number were, like Allen, offspring of army officer fathers.

Restrictions upon cadets had loosened little since the days of Sam Allen. Fairly quickly, it became obvious that Terry found it difficult to abide by the rules. Within little more than a week's time during the "Beast Barracks" (the oppression of newcomers by those more senior) of the July encampment, he was cited five separate times for "not turning safety lock to 'safe' on his rifle." He piled up additional demerits for failing to brush his cap before breakfast, for spots on his blouse, and for oil on his gun, as well as for dirty fingernails and shoes not properly shined at Catholic chapel formation. He missed formations and was accused of inattention, such as appearing at an inspection of the guard without his rifle. He was caught taking a bath a midnight, and he was gigged for various forms of improper dress—including an unbuttoned raincoat and appearances in the company street in his underclothes; for being out of bed at taps, late for breakfast, late for dinner, and late for supper; and, for not turning in required written exercises in mathematics and English. He smiled in ranks, yawned during a class, and was marked distracted during a recitation. What's more, he showed up late for reveille, for classes, and for chapel. A week did not pass without the register of delin-quencies recording a number of his sins. Many classmates required six months of infractions to roll up as many demerits as Terry Allen did in a single month. Somewhere along the line, his natural exuberance earned him nicknames like "Terry the Terror" and, in recognition of his speech defect, "T-t-t-tear around the mess hall Allen." If anything, the gre-garious gene that flowed through Sam Allen's veins flourished even stronger in his son.

Allen's insouciance extended into the academic areas. He managed to stay afloat until, as a third classman in January 1909, he was "found"—declared deficient in mathematics and turned back. Under the academy's system, he reverted to the status of a fourth classman and thus a member of the group scheduled to graduate in 1912.

His new status changed nothing in his ebullient deportment. A steady stream of ink listed violations in the ledger record including his absence from a formation only two days after he was turned back. His breaches of the rules covered almost every possible transgression up through a form of insubordination—failing to salute an officer. He was habitually tardy and sloppy; he socialized at inappropriate times, was dilatory in his studies and preparation for classes, smiled in ranks, and went into debt to buy a silver cup. He was cited for loitering in a sweater, talking when entering the academic building, yelling during a fire drill, making un-necessary noise in the mess hall, and hanging his head while marching. While other cadets made efforts to conceal their misdemeanors, Allen seemed almost to delight in committing his offensive acts openly. One anecdote reports on a time that a puppy suddenly appeared during a drill: While his startled sergeant looked on, Allen whistled and then broke ranks to pet the dog.

Undoubtedly, he drew his share of hazing. But at no point in his life did he ever refer to any deviling. Having lived among the roughs of mil-itary camps, he was immune to the oppression by upperclassmen.

With his companions, he spent an inordinate amount of time in close order drill and parades, and they devoted many hours to the study of drill regulations. Most of the direct military instruction occurred at summer camps where the youths fired the weapons of the day and practiced ar-tillery drills. Allen definitely enjoyed one feature of cadet life—the enor-mous number of hours devoted to equestrian skills at the riding hall. One of the mantras of the day was "It is the pride of the cavalry to be bold and dashing." The young Allen did his best to personify that ethos.

In the classrooms, the cadets received a smattering of foreign language instruction and a single course in world history. They learned to draw freehand, took courses in astronomy, geology, mineralogy, and chemistry, and explored the subject taught by Sam Allen—natural philosophy (which had more to do with physics than with the meaning of meaning). Engineering courses still focused on fortifications.

The young Allen was an enthusiastic participant in sports. Not big enough for football, he boxed, wrestled, played lacrosse and baseball, and of course, pursued any activity that involved horses. Throughout his life, he sprinkled his conversation, even his discussion of strategy and tactics, with terms taken from sports. And he developed a signature greeting, a left hook thrown more or less gently at the jaw.

As a member of the Class of 1912, his grades were roughly average, although he stood a commendable twentieth in French. He was above the norm in English and history, but below in conduct. His overall order of merit (which included his demerits) placed him eighty-eighth among the fewer than 150 fellow cadets. As a third classman from 1909–1910, Allen remained eighty-eighth, even though the complement of his 1912 class had steadily shrunk through dismissals and resignations. His generous accumulation of demerits continued; he was at his best in French and drawing.

Years later he related a desperate scheme to save him from flunking out: Facing failure in several courses, he drank a concoction of chalk dust and pencil shavings. Almost immediately he began to vomit, and the authorities hospitalized him. While restricted from the normal pursuits of a cadet, he crammed for tests in the subjects for which he was deficient and passed the exams. This solution to his problem teetered on the edge of an honor code violation. Like all such systems, the honor code leaked. Had Allen simply feigned illness, he would have crossed the line, lying to gain an advantage. But, in this instance, he actually required medical treatment, albeit for purposely ingesting an insult to his digestive tract.

The maneuver to maintain academic standing worked—but it was a "temporary stay of execution." Sinking lower and lower in the order of merit, Allen seemed unable to cope with the demands of the academic program. At best, he appeared determined to finish at the bottom of the heap, as, in the argot of the academy, the goat. In May of 1911, however, while a second classman, Allen was found in the widely scorned subject of ordnance and gunnery, known among the cadets as ignorance and gummery. That course also happened to be the one in which his father had excelled. The academic skills gene never reached Terry. He was dismissed from the academy for his deficiency. Many years later, Allen began a letter to members of the Class of 1912 with the words, "As the last goat to be found in our class . . ."

Sam Allen was neither amused nor forgiving enough for his son to come home and seek a career in the civilian world. For that matter, neither was Terry willing to surrender his ambition to wear an army uniform. He enrolled at the Catholic University, in Washington, D.C., and in 1912 earned a bachelor of arts degree. With degree in hand, the twenty-four-year-old took an examination for a commission in the Regular Army and received his gold bars as a second lieutenant as well as an assignment to the 14th Cavalry.

3: The Cavalryman

In 1912, the internal combustion engine and the automobile with their inevitable child—mechanized military transport—had yet to persuade the U.S. Army that the era of the horse was passing. Consequently, newly brevetted as a second lieutenant in the U.S. Army in November of that year, and an expert horseman, Terry Allen naturally gravitated toward the cavalry. On 3 March 1913, he joined Troop D of the 14th Cavalry Regiment at Fort Clark, Texas, where he patrolled the uncertain border with Mexico.

A graduate of the U.S.M.A. Class of 1912, John T. McLane recalled that the train from San Antonio dropped those destined for the 14th Cavalry at a stop known as Spofford, "a hot dusty little town consisting of a few houses, a water tank and the other adjuncts of a tank stop." From Spofford, the newcomers boarded a wagon and amid clouds of white dust jounced ten miles to Fort Clark.

McLane reported that his first assignment was to return to Spofford, again in a wagon (the automobile had not been enlisted by the army for duty at Fort Clark). He was to pick up sixty thousand dollars in quartermaster funds. In his words: "The troops assigned to me for this mission were one private of Troop D, armed with rifle and ball cartridges. I had heard about what a wild and wooly country Texas was and how every so often the trains were held up; the journey was therefore a very serious one for me on the threshold of my career. This feeling was intensified when I saw the train stop, and two Wells Fargo [& Co.] Express guards

armed with sawed-off shot guns turn over the money to the station agent."
McLane returned with the funds to Fort Clark without incident, but his
tale indicates the ambience experienced by cavalrymen serving along the
border.

At the time, the cavalry found its use as a weapon for modern warfare
was a reluctantly sinking sun. Second Lieutenant Terry Allen reported
that year to the 14th Cavalry Regiment. Stationed at Eagle Pass and Del
Rio, Texas—a stretch of turf running down the southernmost prong of
the state—the troopers watched for interlopers crossing the Rio Grande.
For nearly four years the unit patrolled the turbulent Mexican border,
in the wake of that country's 1910 revolution. It was perhaps one of the
few occasions in which soldiers on horseback still served a useful purpose.
Mexicans, described as either bandits or rebels (depending upon who
is writing the history), frequently operated in mounted groups along the
ragged line that separated the two nations. Their raids challenged American settlers and jurisdiction. Only cavalry units could hope to cover the
largely roadless turf and pursue the offenders. However, one of the major values of such troops, that of reconnaissance, had already been challenged by the airplane. It was 1911, a mere eight years after a pair of Ohio
bicycle repairmen, the brothers Wright, took off in the first controlled,
power-driven craft to skim a few hundred feet over the sands at Kitty
Hawk, North Carolina. And now a U.S. Army plane flew one hundred
miles along the border south of Laredo on a scouting mission. Not with-
standing that while returning from its patrol the airplane crashed in a
river—thereby eliminating one-fifth of the entire U.S. air armada—the
reconnaissance role played by cavalry had been challenged.

The hundreds of miles of border were impossible to guard, and for-
ays from the south were frequent. In 1912, just west of Del Rio, a railroad track worker discovered ten Mexicans loaded with explosives. The
interlopers, who probably intended to blow up the rail line and loot a
train, fled, dropping their bombs and dynamite. Similar attempts of ban-
ditry kept the American cavalry busy.

According to Allen, on 13 September 1913, he with six troopers pursued and captured what A. J. Liebling labeled "the band of rustlers from
across the border." The official description of the affair says that Allen
led his men to apprehend a band of "ammunition smugglers" near San
Ambrosia Creek. Allen's most pungent memory of the occasion was of a
good horse shot from under him. Supposedly the Americans seized more
than twenty prisoners.

John McLane recalled that the 14th Cavalry troopers passed most of their time in the field around Eagle Pass and Del Rio from 1913–1915. For short intervals, they returned to Fort Clark to engage in target practice. "Nothing out of the routine of 'border service' occurred, except for a little brush with Mexican bandits near Carrizo Springs, Texas, in which Terry Allen and I were involved."

The stage was set for a more open conflict with Mexico by events that began in 1912. Democrat Woodrow Wilson won the election for president when William H. Taft, the incumbent Republican, lost a bid for re-election, and Terry Allen's benefactor, Theodore Roosevelt, drained away votes through a third-party campaign for the White House. Only a few weeks before Wilson's inauguration in 1913, Gen. Victoriano Huerta engineered a coup that culminated with the murder of the duly elected Mexican president, Francisco Madero. As an apostle of democracy, the overthrow of democratic rule shocked and offended Wilson. He refused to recognize the new leader and now another military man, Gen. Venustiano Carranza, established a rival claim to the leadership of the country. Most of Europe and not a few U.S. industrialists—anxious for the free flow of Mexican oil—scorned Wilson's policy. They perceived Huerta as a dictator with whom they could do business. There was talk of a new election, pitting the two generals against one another.

Wilson remained adamant, throwing his support behind Carranza while arguing that Huerta should not be permitted on the ballots. Huerta responded by arresting 110 members of the country's congress, which he dissolved, and then to the surprise of no one, he was elected. Unwilling to concede, the American president lifted an arms embargo previously applied to Carranza's forces. The Germans, observing the clouds of war approaching, offered aid to Huerta: If the general would promise to cut off oil to the British in the event of war, they would deliver the arms necessary to defeat Carranza. Four freighters in Hamburg soon began loading rifles, ammunition, and other armaments.

The testy relationship between the United States and Mexico boiled over during a minor confrontation in the port of Tampico. Huertistas temporarily detained a U.S. Navy detail before returning the sailors to the ship, with apologies. Unsatisfied, the American admiral on the scene demanded a twenty-one-gun salute to assuage the national honor. Huerta refused to accept this humiliation and a minor contretemps now escalated into a full-blown contest of national egos. Wilson, hoping the affair might convince Huerta to quit, issued an ultimatum: Unless the Mexicans acquiesced, the American navy would blockade and occupy the country's largest port, Vera Cruz. Huerta stuck to his guns. When word reached the White House that a German-owned ship, the *Ypiranga,* was bearing ammunition and expected to dock soon at Vera Cruz, the president asked Congress for a resolution enabling him to use force to obtain redress for "affronts and indignities" to the United States. He presented the issue on the basis of American honor, rather than the munitions being delivered. A debate ended without any statement from the legislators.

In the early hours of the following day, Wilson was awakened from his sleep by a telephone call that confirmed the scheduled arrival of the *Ypiranga* at 10 A.M. After a discussion by linked phones with Secretary of the Navy Josephus Daniels and Secretary of State William Jennings Bryan in what became known as the Pajama Conference, Wilson ordered the navy to seize Vera Cruz. As American marines and sailors, armed with rifles and fixed bayonets poured ashore, Mexican military and civilians opened fire. The navy responded with shells from an offshore ship. When the shooting stopped, 19 Americans and 126 Mexicans had died. In addition, 71 of the invaders and 95 of the residents were wounded.

In the wake of the senseless slaughter, the *Ypiranga* slipped down the coast and off-loaded its cargo to Huerta troops. The Americans were forced to apologize to the Germans for interfering in the freedom of the seas. Much of Latin America, and particularly Mexico, seethed with anti-Yankee sentiment. Mediation by Argentina, Brazil, and Chile eased the crisis. Huerta lost out to Carranza, who returned from temporary exile in Spain.

The Carranza regime sorely disappointed Wilson's hopes for a stable, friendly government across the border. Private armies—notably that of Emiliano Zapata and Pancho Villa—as well as forces who pledged allegiance to the departed Huerta, convulsed the country. During the following few years, Allen and the cavalrymen of the 14th Regiment confronted armed Mexicans four times in what he described as "sharp skirmishes."

The most troublesome figure for Americans was Villa, the legendary rebel-patriot-bandit, formerly an ally of Carranza, who regarded the tacit support of the Wilson administration for Carranza as an affront. In 1915, Villa's irregular horse soldiers murdered seventeen U.S. citizens who were traveling on a Mexican train chugging toward a mining town in the state of Chihuahua. Although the action infuriated Americans, they could visit only sound, but no fury, on their neighbors to the south.

Meanwhile, in 1916 Allen left the 14th Cavalry for a brief respite that brought him to the Mounted Service School at Fort Riley, Kansas. In January while he was there, Pancho Villa crossed the border and attacked the hamlet of Columbus, New Mexico. A post-action report, by the commandant of the 13th Cavalry stationed at Camp Furlong, in Columbus, stated there had been talk of the Villistas prowling the vicinity. He noted that, as a precaution, he increased patrols on the outskirts of the town. Either they were less than vigilant or the commander's account was an attempt to cover up his failure to put his troops on full alert. A large number of Mexicans—broken into small groups—infiltrated into Columbus after the moon set, but before daylight. A furious battle erupted, leaving eighteen Americans dead, including ten soldiers. The troopers in turn claimed to have killed one hundred of the raiders, wounded seven, and captured one.

When Terry Allen was fighting the Axis forces in North Africa a quarter of a century later, he claimed that the defenders in Columbus were totally unprepared and the soldiers, caught without their rifles, had fought the interlopers with rocks. (It is difficult to believe the Americans could have slain one hundred of the enemy with stones; the body count for the Columbus affair is as dubious as the figures for later conflicts such as Vietnam.) In any event, Allen would dismiss risky propositions from his staff with the comment, "To hell with that. We don't want any Columbus massacres here."

Whatever the correct number for the Villista casualties and the circumstances of the attack on Columbus, public and official indignation of the offense on U.S. territory forced Woodrow Wilson to retaliate. He instigated a punitive expedition over the border to pursue Villa. Negotiations with Carranza brought an agreement that the Americans could trod the sovereign turf of Mexico as long as they limited their incursion to the state of Chihuahua. Wilson named Brig. Gen. John J. Pershing to head up the American forces, by virtue of his years spent on frontier skirmishes to control Native Americans, his participation in the Spanish-American War, his role suppressing the Philippine insurrection, and his work as an observer in the Russo-Japanese War. To his task, Pershing brought knowledge of both war and diplomacy.

Pershing marshaled a force of infantry, cavalry, field artillery, engineers, and the eight-plane 1st Aero Squadron to chase Villa. The students at the Fort Riley cavalry school had immediately returned to their regiments following the incident at Columbus, and Allen with the 14th Cavalry became part of the punitive expedition. As a sign of serious intent, 110,000 National Guardsmen were mobilized for duty along the border. At the time his son rode into Mexico with Pershing's 6,700 force, Sam Allen held command of a provisional infantry brigade stationed in Texas—which like its leader never saw action.

As the hunt for Villa stretched four-hundred-miles deep into Mexico, in July 1916 Allen became a first lieutenant. Whatever other adventures he had during this brief series of skirmishes are unrecorded, but another youthful cavalry officer, George S. Patton Jr., achieved fame. While Patton led a fifteen-man detail to a ranch near the town of Rubio, a trio of mounted horsemen suddenly approached and opened fire. Patton pulled his revolver, killed two of them, and shot a third rider off his horse. He, too, was gunned down while trying to escape.

Several sharp encounters followed between the expedition and the Villistas but without a decisive battle. Inevitably, the Americans also confronted elements of the Mexican army, with casualties on both sides. For ambitious young bloods like Terry Allen, the skirmishes with the neighbors across the border were almost a lark. Except for a few occasions of ambushes or an unwise penetration that exposed them to superior forces, the Americans' greatest danger lay in the terrain, climate, and disease. Pershing set up a base camp at Dublan where dust, flies, and boredom tormented the troops. Baseball games, boxing matches, and hunting provided healthy recreation. The men also engaged in considerable gambling, which Pershing tolerated, and wholesale patronage of prostitution, which he controlled. To avoid the ravages of venereal disease upon his contingent, Pershing placed the whores behind a barbed-wire stockade surrounded by guards. Any visitor to the enclosure was required to show he had the money to pay, and upon leaving the compound he was compelled to take a prophylactic treatment. The measures kept sexually transmitted illnesses to a minimum.

4: Terry Allen Goes to War

Following the assassination of the archduke Franz Ferdinand on 28 July 1914, Austria-Hungary declared war on Serbia, which triggered a parallel series of falling dominos: Germany lined up against Serbia. Russia and France backed Serbia. Belgium was overrun by Germany en route to France. And, thereby, Great Britain—which had pledged to support the Belgian neutrality—was drawn in. Initially, the United States proclaimed itself strictly neutral. Sympathies lay with the Triple Entente, which at first was Great Britain, France, and Russia, with Italy subsequently replacing Russia. While people had an affinity with the democracies, when they were confronted by the Central Powers monarchies of Germany, Austria-Hungary, and the Ottoman Empire, their attitude was mitigated by pacifism and isolationism.

Freedom of the seas became an instant issue as the Royal Navy blockaded Germany and barred U.S. ships from bearing cargoes for Germany. American commercial interests were mollified by the sharply increased purchases of food and munitions from the States by the Entente. The Germans struck back in 1915 with torpedoes from submarines that sank ships bound for their enemies' ports. The first incident occurred on 1 May 1915, when a U-boat blasted the American tanker *Gulflight*. Germany apologized for this "unfortunate accident," but six days later another submarine, without warning, fatally struck the Cunard liner *Lusitania* within sight of the Irish shore. Among the more than 1,100 who lost their lives were

128 U.S. citizens. Outraged Americans denounced Germany, and a deepening hostility marked attitudes toward that country. A number of influential people, including Theodore Roosevelt, called for intervention on the side of the Allies, and others enlisted in organizations such as the Lafayette Escadrille and the American Field Service (AFS) to aid the beleaguered British and French forces. Slowly the country adopted programs to build military strength.

The Germans attempted to quell the worsening climate in the United States. To avoid offending the States, if a merchant ship sailed into the war zones, U-boat captains were instructed to surface and challenge it on its registry and destination. Crews would be allowed to abandon ship before the vessel was sunk. But that tactic denied a submarine its underwater cover and exposed it to the guns now mounted on many freighters. Nevertheless, with the British blockade seriously affecting the country's power to wage war—while American freighters freely carried supplies to England and France—early in 1917 the Germans decided to declare open season on all vessels bound toward enemy ports. That was one of two actions that charted a collision of Germany with the United States.

The second factor involved Mexico. The border strife that had ignited with Wilson's distaste for Huerta struck the Germans as a prime opportunity for serious mischief. Anxious to deflect any moral and material support given by the United States to the Allies, the Germans plotted to occupy American energies with Mexico. Engaged in a continuing strategy to detour American action away from Europe, in 1915 the kaiser's government appropriated some $30 million to return General Huerta as head of Mexico. Historian Barbara Tuchman has suggested that an international conglomeration of oil, copper, mining, and railroad tycoons believed they would profit if the deposed president restored order to his country. Diplomatic documents unearthed after World War I indicate that Huerta made extravagant promises to his patrons and vowed to use money and arms for an attack upon the United States once he regained power. Whether he truly intended to make such a disastrous attempt or was only conning his benefactors is unknown.

Huerta had traveled from Spain to the United States and engaged in innocent activities such as taking in a baseball game in New York City and buying tickets to a policemen's ball before embarking on a railroad trip for San Francisco. American agents kept track of his movements. When he left his train in Kansas City and bought passage to El Paso on the Mexican border, Washington was alerted. Taken into custody with some of his supporters from across the border, he was detained first as an honored guest and then as a prisoner at Fort Bliss in El Paso, a site that would become most familiar to both Terry Allen senior and junior. For weeks, the United States dithered over what to do with Huerta, who enjoyed strong support from partisans in his country. He solved the problem on 16 January 1916 by dying of yellow fever at Fort Bliss.

Loss of this partner did not dissuade Germany from its manipulation of Mexico. The resentment toward its northern neighbor had been steadily fueled. In pursuit of Pancho Villa and others considered a threat to U.S. citizens and property, some twelve thousand soldiers under John J. Pershing, including Terry Allen, remained across the border in 1917.

In a subtle pas de deux after the death of Huerta, German diplomats planned to woo Venustiano Carranza, still the head of government although he and the chaos that enveloped his country had long alienated Woodrow Wilson. The German foreign minister, Arthur Zimmermann, on 16 January 1917 dispatched two telegrams to the imperial minister in Mexico. Unfortunately for the Fatherland, the cables (which became known as the "Zimmerman telegram") were intercepted by British intelligence, and they slowly deciphered the text.

Message number one announced: "We propose to begin on February 1 unrestricted submarine warfare. In doing this however, we shall endeavor to keep America neutral. If we should not succeed in doing so, we propose [with Mexico] an alliance upon the following basis joint conduct of war, joint conclusion of peace. Your excellency should for the present inform the President [of Mexico] secretly that we expect war with the U.S.A." There was also a suggestion that Mexico might persuade Japan to abandon its support for the Allies and join with Germany and Austria-Hungary. Even more inflammatory, another section the decoders subsequently interpreted included a promise by Germany to help Mexico "regain by conquest her lost territory in Texas, Arizona and New Mexico."

Coupled with discoveries of espionage, attempts to foment labor union strikes, and sabotage at munitions factories, the activities of the Germans and their associates forced Wilson's hand. On a warm rainy night, the president, flanked by a cavalry honor guard, traveled the short trip from the White House to Capitol Hill to address the Congress. His speech on 2 April 1917 pronounced that "The world must be made safe for democracy," and he asked the legislators for a declaration of war. By the sixth of the month, both houses had passed the resolution. Despite efforts to increase military preparedness, the Regular Army numbered only 5,791 officers and 121,797 enlisted personnel. Supplementing this force were 80,446 mobilized National Guardsmen and another 101,174 guardsmen still under state control. The armament was equally deficient—with a shortage of Springfield rifles and the War Department still vacillating over which machine gun ought to become standard issue. While an Army War College and a few advanced military schools such as the cavalry program that Allen had attended until Villa's attack on Columbus had been established, few officers had either experience or theoretical knowledge of contemporary warfare. Neither the hit-and-run battles against the Mexicans nor the efforts to suppress the Philippine insurrection resembled what would be faced on France's western front.

Almost immediately, the overseas allies dispatched their experts to confer and advise on the best means to involve American forces. They proposed the quick insertion of soldiers into their established organizations rather than creation of a large independent U.S. army. Such an arrangement would have eliminated the need to create the vast administration and backup by noncombatant support troops. The British and French believed their new partner woefully weak in officers and staff and the men already in uniform poorly trained, unskilled, and inexperienced.

While the proposal would have more swiftly filled the ranks in France, it would have subordinated Americans to French and British commands and reduced the army to a sterile feeder of cannon fodder rather than a fighting organism. National pride alone would not permit such an amalgamation nor could ambitious professional soldiers hope for advancement while serving under another nation's flag.

Two months earlier, having "papered over" his disagreements with the Carranza government, Wilson yanked Pershing and his troops out of Mexico after their futile pursuit of the elusive Pancho Villa. Terry Allen and other cavalrymen were in garrison at Fort Bliss when the United States formally entered World War I. With the scant education in history and global politics provided at West Point and a tour in the boondocks of the border and the wilds of Mexico, Allen probably had little understanding of the machinations that had occurred. He never showed any signs of being a student of international politics. Yet, the state of war and the urgent expansion of the army almost instantly brought promotions down the line. On 15 May, Allen—along with numerous graduates of his former 1912 class—pinned on his captain's bars.

Although he was woefully ignorant of the trench warfare of the western front, Allen had gained some valuable knowledge during his tour on the border. He had learned how to lead and to command men. He knew what it was to engage in a firefight and, having acquitted himself well, could be confident that he would perform under pressure.

During his years as the son of an officer at different encampments, he mingled freely with the rough-hewn enlisted men and their children. Even then he held no rigid distinctions—favoring neither those who commanded nor those who followed. When he was on active duty with the 14th Cavalry, he lived in the field with the troopers, isolated from the niceties of a well-established army post, and his appreciation of fellow soldiers regardless of rank could only have been enhanced.

For little more than a year, Allen languished in Texas army camps as the recruits poured in. He availed himself of the opportunity for polo, quickly developing a reputation as an expert player. His gregarious personality widened his circle of acquaintances, and when he realized that he might be doomed to spend World War I training cavalrymen in the States, he scouted about for a transfer. While he would have preferred an outfit destined for combat, the best he could wangle was assignment to the 315th Ammunition Train, a self-contained organization attached to the 90th Infantry Division and responsible for transporting artillery ordnance to the front. While delighted to be bound for the American Expeditionary Force, Allen wrote home, "I cannot understand my good fortune to jump over the heads of quite a few fellows who rank me. Am in the artillery now and though I hate to take off the crossed sabers it's anything to get to France."

On 10 June, from San Antonio he wired his father, who was now stationed in the Seattle headquarters for the Pacific Coast Artillery, "Promotion As Major National Army [the designation for the wartime force] Just Received. Assignment 90th Division. Pulling Out Full Hack On Wednesday. Cannot Understand It As Promotion Is Out Of My Turn. Best Love And Good Luck To You All." The promotion officially occurred 7 June.

Command of the 90th Division was vested in Maj. Gen. Henry T. Allen—no relation to Terry—a sartorial dandy with credentials as an attaché in Berlin and Moscow as well as combat duty in Cuba and the Philippines. His tour in Cuba had earned him the favor of Theodore Roosevelt, who had unsuccessfully attempted to siphon him off for duty with a division of volunteers that Roosevelt tried to form in 1916.

Henry Allen, who graduated from the U.S.M.A. in 1882, a year after Sam Allen, had a cavalry background. In army and government circles he was regarded as a thoughtful man whose abilities ranged beyond military strategy and tactics. In 1901, he had a major role in shaping the Philippine constabulary, a national police force trained and organized along military lines. His experience with government would come into play again and involve Terry Allen. Significantly, a polo enthusiast, the commander of the 90th Division knew Terry Allen through the game. Along with the 315th, the division embarked by train for New York, and Allen's command halted at Port Jervis, a New York hamlet located near the borders of Pennsylvania and New Jersey about eighty miles from New York City.

On the stationery of the Hotel Mitchell, which boasted "Running Water in All Rooms," Allen, in a full-flowing hand wrote: "My dearest Mama, We expect to arrive at Camp Mills, Mineola, Long Island tomorrow. Just when we will embark is uncertain as we have to get quite a little equipment. It may be weeks, then again it may be days. . . . Am in command of 315th Ammunition Train, 90th Division, which is really a Lt. Col's command as it comprises 13 organizations total strength 1,301 men and 26 officers."

That was the complement listed in the army's table of organization, but the unit that traveled from San Antonio numbered far fewer personnel. "The 14th Cavalry say that the reason for the War Department's [transfer] (I was assigned straight from War Dept.) was that Gen. Allen wanted to organize a division polo team abroad. Maybe my energy in polo is now standing me in good stead. The present dope is that we will get to England first to complete our training and will be in the thick of it before long. We had an excellent trip. The Red Cross treated us very well, giving us all sorts of receptions on the layovers. The greatest difficulty was in convincing the conductor, civilian officials, etc., that I really was a major in command. There are 4 old cavalrymen of over 15 years service who are captains under me and look more fitted to command than I." It was one of the few notes of uncertainty sounded by Allen.

He added information about the storage of his belongings in San Antonio and instructions for his mother to pay any bills. "By the way I won another polo cup the day before we left Texas. It will be sent to Papa. Please keep it for me as they mean many a hard-fought game." He reassured Concepcion, "Am fairly well equipped, have enough to get by on financially, am in very best of health and spirits so please don't worry about your n'er-do-well son." He closed with his best wishes for his sisters, Ethel and Mary, and Papa. Because of a hurried departure from San Antonio, Allen sold his horses at what he called "a sacrifice" and entrusted his cavalry saber to an officer from the 14th Cavalry at Fort Sam Houston.

While at Camp Mills, Allen dispatched a long letter to his "dear Mamma and Papa." "I hope you will pardon my delay in writing but you can't imagine the way you have to keep hustling around this place. We are being filled up to our required quota now and I now have 770 men, almost 55 percent. The rest we hope to get on the 30th [of June]. It may be that the train will embark before then, possibly the 28th. But now that we have opportunities of getting such high-class men, I would rather stick around and go over full strength. Got 200 men yesterday, all college men from Purdue University. The camp inspector said that my outfit was the best disciplined and best equipped he had seen for some time. In fact, Major March gave me authority to conduct all further embarkation inspections myself."

He chatted about his social life, mentioning dinner with a fellow officer and his wife: "She is as rich as the devil but not much to look at although she's very nice. Have been flying high. Have had luncheon and dinner with a J. P. Phipps, at Westbury, L.I. He is one of the wealthiest men in N.Y. and is an international polo player and his wife and kids are as humble and unaffected as can be. They have a wonderful place here, about 6 butlers, 30 horses, his own polo fields, etc. Harry Payne Whitney [another wealthy sportsman, five times rated a 10-goal player and whose stable of racehorses won top money during the 1920s and early 1930s] was there at luncheon also. They all laughed when I said I had a pony in Texas named S.O.S. who could skin anything they had. Saturday night they took me to a Red Cross . . . dance. You can imagine what it was like, the proceeds were $60,000."

Even in this heady atmosphere, Allen remained coolly observant of the class distinctions. "However, I realize that they have only taken me up because I can play a little polo and men are scarce around here. Have discovered that the men who bootlick and fawn [with] these people are regarded with the greatest contempt. None of them entertain any more or better than you, Mama.

"I hate to think of little S.O.S. doing duty in a cavalry troop, but I suppose they will take good care of her, and I may see her again. She's the best friend I ever had in the Army and the best little animal that ever lived. Some day I hope to buy her back.

"I will pay back the $107.68 I owe you as soon as possible. One hundred borrowed and $7.68 borrowed on my storage. With my heedless ways you know how it is to settle up." Throughout his military career, Terry Allen was hard-pressed for money.

Allen's letters show a good grasp of grammar and spelling although he consistently substituted the possessive "its" when he intended to use "it's." He also had a habit of beginning sentences with a verb, leaving out the first-person subject.

Although officially he was an artilleryman, now it appears that Allen had something else in mind for the future. He informed his parents, "Am busy as the devil studying up Infantry Drill Regs [Regulations], Ordnance and all the latest dope. I know that I have a big job ahead and it will take a whole lot to learn it." He continued to muse over the haphazard promotions that brought him his majority, noting that while the commander of another ammunition train held a colonelcy, a former 1911 classmate remained a captain.

In the New York area, Allen was visited by family relatives, including Uncle Curtin (who was involved in shipping), as well as by officers whose paths had crossed those of Sam Allen and accordingly sent their regards. He spoke of a former navy officer once stationed at Brooklyn Navy Yard who "asked very cordially after you both. He married a very wealthy Miss Grace and lives on her money."

He continued to fret that the big show would end without his participation. "I believe our first destination is Salisbury Plains. Brig. Gen. [J. P.] O'Neil [assistant division commander] says the unit when fully equipped may be sent over to France for full duty very shortly and promises us plenty of action. Don't mean to be unpatriotic but I hope the war lasts long to give us a good hard crack at them." He closed on an affectionate note to his sisters, adding, "Tell Mary I expect to see her a very accomplished young lady some day."

The giddy whirl among the New York upper crust, occasional visits with his local kin, and the press of duties packed Allen's final letter to his mother before he embarked for Europe. He spoke of dinner dances at the homes of the Clarence Mackays (another family engaged in the shipping business) and at "Harrimans" (the railroad and banking dynasty). A Mrs. C. C. Rumsey, whose husband also was an international polo star, took him to dinner at the Ritz and then to a show entitled *Kitchy Koo*.

Allen reiterated his understanding of the hospitality extended by stating, "I presume, however, that the scarcity of men is responsible for my having such a good time."

Allen had a number of relatives living in the New York area and he said he dined with his Aunt Lila and Uncle Curtin. He remarked that his efforts to reach his Aunt Lila had been unsuccessful and their son Carlos had been in France since January. "She has a very modest room at the Morrison House in Brooklyn and I guess is pretty hard up. Uncle Will you know is living by himself. Uncle Curtin got him a job on the docks. Mama Terry [for whom he was named] is still at the sanitarium and Aunt Lila is very well pleased with the way she is situated."

He reported that a colonel from a new National Army cavalry regiment advised Allen he had asked for him as a field officer, but Allen responded, "I didn't wish him any hard luck but preferred to stay where I was." Although he rejected that offer because he was uncertain when and if the organization would ever leave for France, Allen remarked, "It is hard to realize that I am now in artillery but I hope to get back when they use the cavalry abroad."

The son commiserated with his mother over an apparent snub of his father. "I saw by the paper that Papa had again been overlooked [for promotion]. You can't realize how badly I feel about it. Of course there are lots in the same boat but none as deserving as he is and every one says the same thing too."

Allen sailed for the British Isles in July for an uneventful trip and boasted to the folks at home that he had not suffered a single moment of seasickness. He spent only a short time in England before reaching the continent. "My dear Papa: We are here at last and are up to our ears in work. You have no idea how the French people fairly worship the Americans over here and how the American troops are all on their toes. They all seem to feel that they have a whole lot to live up to.

"We have been here a short while getting outfitted and have been promised that we will get into the game very shortly. We are a self-contained unit now and go right up into the front line. Am going off on a long auto trip tomorrow to one of the largest French towns to see about our trucks and horses."

From a French outpost of the YMCA, on stationery that urged, "To The Writer: Save By Writing On Both Sides Of This Paper. To The Folks At Home: Save Food, Buy Liberty Bonds And War Savings Stamps," Allen advised his dear Papa of a significant change. "Expect a transfer to the

90th Division Infantry. I know that sounds funny coming from me but there is no doubt of them receiving first invitation to the ball [combat]. There is no particular news at present and what I do know, I can't talk about. They are awfully particular about dress and appearance here and we all have to keep spruced up to beat the band." From his first demerits at West Point throughout his entire career, Allen had problems with the look of his uniforms. But on the eve of his admittance to the "ball," the demands for sartorial exactitude could hardly diminish his enthusiasm.

5: At the Front

When the United States entered World War I in April 1917, its allies on the western front had already been engaged with the enemy for close to three years. Their chief adversary, Germany, began the conflict with several important advantages: Beginning in the last half of the nineteenth century, every physically able male was eligible for military duty and large numbers of them had put on uniforms for several years and after discharge remained members of a trained and ready reserve. With a smaller population, France was already handicapped and its reservists were much inferior to those of the foe. Unlike the French who were soundly defeated by the Prussian-led armies in 1870 and the British whose last conflict, the Boer War in 1899–1902, brought no glory, the German officers shared an extremely high esprit de corps.

The Germans also started out ahead of the game in terms of artillery, particularly the heavy howitzer, and with a better—if not full—understanding of the machine gun's potential. (In contrast, the United States had not even decided which version of the machine gun its army should use when Wilson asked Congress to declare war.) The quick-firing French 75mm field gun gave that country a powerful asset, but its quality could not compensate for many other deficiencies in armament and strategic thinking. The British army had long been subservient to the faith in the Royal Navy. Small in size in 1914, its experience lay in the limited engagements required to maintain colonial power.

Working on a plan developed by Graf von Schlieffen, chief of the German general staff in the 1890s, but modified by his successor, the armies of the Reich crossed the Belgian frontier only a day after a formal declaration of war against France. This invasion had brought England, a guarantor of Belgian neutrality, into the fight. The tiny lowland nation resisted briefly before the weight of the German forces overwhelmed them and approached the French border from the north. Meanwhile, as a counterbalance, the French committed themselves to an offensive against their territory lost in 1870, Alsace-Lorraine. When this adventure crashed into the heavyweight defenses of the Germans, the nature of World War I revealed itself: huge masses of men and materials slugging it out with machine guns, artillery shells that exploded in fragments of metal, and weapons of exponentially increased lethality. Tanks crept onto the battlefields, airplanes strafed and bombed hapless troops, and poison gas choked the lungs of those in the field. Names like the Marne, Verdun, Somme, Ypres, and Passchendaele became shorthand for slaughter. While large aggregations of soldiers had confronted one another during the nineteenth century at Waterloo or Gettysburg, the killing machinery was far less effective. None of the warring armies had trained for this sort of thing, nor were Allen and his contemporaries well prepared.

President Wilson and Secretary of War Newton Baker both were impressed by John J. "Black Jack" Pershing, West Point 1886, who had led the 10th Cavalry's Black troopers against Native Americans and had served in Cuba and fought uprisings in the Philippines before leading the Punitive Expedition into Mexico. They chose him to lead the American Expeditionary Force to France. Among those on Pershing's staff when it arrived in England in June 1917 was Captain George S. Patton Jr. and a chauffeur, Sfc. Edward V. Rickenbacker. Several months later, when Patton learned that the AEF would mount a tank corps, he volunteered. Following his training, he would lead a light-tank brigade in combat nearly a year later. Rickenbacker, a former auto race champion, applied to the Army Air Corps and subsequently became the leading ace with twenty-six victories.

By the time the first American soldiers reached the continent in June 1917, millions of the young men opposing one another in France had been killed or wounded. While the front lines shifted occasionally, the war was essentially a stalemate amid endless trenches, barbed wire, mud, and shell holes. On both sides, poor intelligence, errors in judgment, and incompetence wrought fearful slaughter. Sir Douglas Haig, the British commander in France, referred to casualties as "wastage"—which indicates both a lack of concern and a pigheaded obstinacy. The French were already so war weary that they faced mutiny by some troops and a lack of resolve among senior commanders. The attitudes of their allies confirmed to the American military leaders that under no circumstances should their men serve under foreign commanders. The one exception would be soldiers from the segregated African American 92d Infantry Division, handed off to the French.

The Regular Army 1st Infantry Division, the initial fighting component of the American Expeditionary Force to arrive in France, paraded some units through Paris before settling in to learn their trade in combat. French veterans tried to teach American infantrymen from the 1st Division about tactics in trench warfare. U.S. artillerymen learned about the French 75 and 155mm cannons with which they would shell the enemy. Among those being schooled and serving with the 26th Infantry of the 1st Division was battalion commander Maj. Theodore Roosevelt Jr., son of the former president. Another student was Lt. Clarence R. Huebner, commander of Company G, 28th Infantry. Both would become involved with Terry Allen some twenty-five years later.

In late October and early November, one battalion from each of the 1st Division's four regiments moved into trenches in the Sommerviller sector, about ten kilometers northeast of Nancy. Shelling and German patrols cost eighty-three officers and enlisted men—killed, wounded, or captured. After a few weeks of this initiation, the Americans returned to the training area.

"The winter of 1917–1918 was godawful" complained Clarence Huebner, a young infantry officer who rose through the ranks. The doughboys continued to condition themselves with long marches—in the rain, snow, and chill—bearing full field packs.

On 15 January 1918, the 1st Division headed for the front. Again the scene was quiet under the French who commanded the Ansauville sector, a portion of the Saint-Mihiel salient. Things were so inactive here that the troops, facing each other across a no-man's-land spanning from fifty to five hundred yards of barbed wire and pockmarked ground, often stood upon the parapets and hung up their laundry. When Brig. Gen. Robert Bullard, the 1st Division commander, assumed responsibility for action, he understood the Allied Expeditionary Force (AEF) chief John J. Pershing's wishes. "He is looking for results. He intends to have them. He will sacrifice any man who does not bring them."

Bullard's initial attempt to fulfill Pershing's desires began with an American sniper taking a potshot at a German one thousand yards off, who was putting up his wet clothes to dry. The outraged enemy responded with a burst of artillery. American gunners upped the ante with a daily dose of one thousand shells a day and then triple that amount the following month. About one out of every ten missiles contained cannisters of phosgene and mustard gases that choked and stung the U.S. soldiers. Raiding parties inflicted death and injury. During the six weeks before the National Guard's 26th Division relieved the 1st, it counted 549 casualties. Soon after its training period, the 42d "Rainbow" Division, another National Guard outfit, whose chief of staff was Col. Douglas MacArthur, underwent a baptism of blood. Next up on the line went the 2d Division, composed of two brigades of each, army and marine—the 9th and 23d Infantry Regiments and the 5th and 6th Marine Regiments.

Despite the infusion of these four oversize organizations—the "square" American divisions with four regiments, plus all the supporting units, each fielded 28,000 men—a German offensive in the spring of 1918 heightened the need for more U.S. troops. The Russians' withdrawal after the revolution in 1917 plus a crushing defeat of the Italians at Caporetto that same month enabled the Germans to bring greater forces to bear in the West.

To the dismay of the Allies, the German drive in May 1918 carried its armies perilously close to Paris. The French government made plans to move to Bordeaux. In response to the pleas from the French field marshal and chief of staff, Ferdinand Foch, Pershing committed two divisions. On 31 May, two companies from the 7th Machine Gun Battalion, which was part of the 3d Division, a Regular Army organization, rode 110 miles in trucks in a twenty-two-hour journey to protect the bridges over the Marne River at Chateau-Thierry. The machine gunners—who had not even received the indoctrination training period granted troops from the 1st Division—nevertheless were credited with bolstering the French resistance sufficiently to prevent a crossing of the Marne.

Simultaneously, Pershing deployed the 2d Division to meet the enemy in an area known as Belleau Wood, northeast of Chateau-Thierry, on the left flank of the 3d Division defenses. After a long trip by truck and then a march over miles of dusty roads clogged with refugees bearing pots, featherbeds, clocks, and even birdcages—along with retreating, dispirited, beaten French infantry and artillerymen hauling their field pieces—the components of the 2d Division reached their positions. On the line now stood the 9th and 23d Infantries and the two regiments of the 4th Marine Brigade.

On 6 June, waves of marines, supported by doughboys from the 2d Engineer Battalion and the 7th Infantry, attacked, once at 5 A.M. and again twelve hours later. They advanced across the poppy fields into a cross fire of machine guns as they stormed the woods. Supposedly, GySgt. Dan Daly, twice decorated with the Medal of Honor, shouted to his platoon, "Come on, you sons of bitches. Do you want to live forever?" The marines stormed into Belleau Wood, capturing parts of it, but losing 1,087 men, which was the greatest number of casualties for a single day until twenty-five years later on the beaches of Tarawa. For twenty days the battle over Belleau Wood raged, with both sides exchanging fierce artillery and gas barrages, fighting hand to hand, suffering from shortages of food and water along with epidemics of diarrhea and influenza. Eventually, it was the Germans who quit the scene.

Subsequent analyses suggest that the decision to attack into the heavily defended woods was dubious strategy further handicapped by a lack of accurate maps, intelligence, and poor communication. A German general explained to his beaten forces, "It is not a question of the possession or non-possession of this or that village or woods, insignificant in itself; it is a question whether the Anglo-American claim that the American Army is equal or even the superior of the German Army is to be made good." If that were the issue, the settlement of the question was a bloody, costly one. Belleau Wood could have been neutralized with artillery and gas while foot soldiers bypassed it. The mistakes of Belleau Wood would be repeated a quarter of a century later when GIs breaking the German West Wall entered a slaughterhouse known as the Hürtgen Forest.

General Erich von Ludendorf, battered but unbowed, continued to think in terms of attack. Americans from the 3d, 28th, and 42d Divisions, who were fighting alongside the French to prevent further advance, blunted the offensives. The all-Black 92d Division, parceled out to serve under French generals, also helped stem the enemy tide. Its 369th Regiment endured 191 days at the front—more time than any other similar unit in the AEF.

By the time Terry Allen was in France, the American contribution amounted to twenty-nine infantry divisions as well as numerous other ground force organizations. Fighting alongside French poilus, the U.S. 1st and 2d Divisions rolled back the enemy at Soissons in mid-July, albeit at a high cost in dead and wounded. The Allies had halted Ludendorf's final advances with the climactic blow to the German hopes administered early in August by the British at Amiens. With the foe staggered by these defeats, the Allies prepared to smash forward. For the first time, the sector commander would be an American, "Black Jack" Pershing. He would field his own separate troops, the newly formed First Army. Its objective would be the elimination of the Saint-Mihiel salient that poked a disturbing bulge in the Allied lines.

In August, from a hotel in Dijon, Allen wrote to his mother: "Have been shifted again, two days ago, having received orders to quit the Am[munition] Train and report to Gen. Allen. Am on the way now. Do not know what my assignment is but believe it is either a staff job or a job with the doughboys. Spent the day in Paris yesterday and it was very amusing with the Boche shells from their big Berthas dropping every 15 minutes. 4 American soldiers were killed near me. They say it is very noisy where I am going."

Having given his mother the less-than-reassuring news, Allen turned to a more mundane subject, his troubled finances: "Uncle Curtin gave me a letter to the White Star representative in Paris and he was very nice to me indeed. It happened I needed help as I had been banking with American Express Co. and owing to congested mails, they had not received my check for July. . . . The Am. Train officers presented me with a silver safety razor and a wrist watch when I left them. Considering I had only had the train a month I thought it was very nice of them."

He followed up with more details several days later. "Am a full fledged doughboy now, in command of a battalion of doughboys in 358th Inf. We have a fine regiment recruited [draftees] from Oklahoma and Texas." Years later Allen noted that the junior officers were largely native Texans, graduates of the University of Texas and Texas A&M. They had graduated from the officer candidate school at Leon Springs, Texas. The division also included a strong sprinkling of Mexicans and Indians among the enlisted personnel, and Allen remarked, "Most of them made fine soldiers."

To his mother he confided, "This division is made up largely of ex-cavalrymen, so I hope my lack of experience with infantry will be overlooked until I get my bearings. Gen. H[enry] Allen is in command and Gen. [Francis C.] Marshall [not George C. Marshall, the World War II chief of staff who during World War I served as operations officer of the 1st Division and then G-3 (operations officer) for the entire First Army] and Col. Leary has the artillery. Could have received a Lt. Colonelcy by staying with the Am Train but would far rather have present assignment, especially as Gen. O'Neil asked for me.

"Have been billeted for a few days in a wonderful old chateau, where I had a room that seemed like a Waldorf bedroom. The old lady gives me all the chocolate cake I can eat and is always bringing up something good to eat at bedtime. She says she lost a boy at Verdun. . . . Her daughter-in-law has also been teaching me French.

"Last night after maneuvers, Capt. Henderson of headquarters and I started the first polo game of the A. E. F. . . . Had a lot of little garçons kick out the balls that ran into the canals and had a great time.

"Am leaving today for a big staff school established by A. E. F. where I will take a get-rich-quick course of 15 days and then will rejoin the regiment. By that time they will have moved and they will not move south [meaning they would advance toward the enemy]."

A fortnight later, on 26 August, he reiterated his pleasure in having transferred to the infantry regiment even though it cost him a quick promotion. "The doughboys are doing the dirty work now and it's [more] fun to shoot ammunition than to load it. Have completed the course at the Get Rich Course for Field Officers at the big school center and tomorrow night to join my battalion of the 358th In. which is now very much on the job. Do you understand can not say more without violating censor staff. Have been assigned a battalion recruited from Texas and Oklahoma. They are a hard-boiled lot, cow handlers and range riders, all of them as big as a house and are sure to give the Boche merry hell. Strange to say, one of the cooks runs a little luncheonette in Eagle Pass, and he surely feeds me well. The sheriff of Spofford, an old sidekick of mine, is also a sergeant in the battalion. My future seems to be completely tied in with Texas and the border. It seems rather funny to command men I once associated with intimately. You can see what a select circle of friends I have had and I'm always expecting someone to call me Terry but they go to the other extreme in their efforts to be military.

"You'd surely be proud of the American soldiers if you could see them over here. They are so far superior to anything else that there's nothing to it. And their morale is wonderful." He compared their willingness to get on with the war's demands to the lack of spirit in the "lousy foreigners." That the local people had endured three years of war—like the old woman in the chateau, losing son or husband or brother—seems not to have diminished his pride in his troops.

Although he would spend considerable time in Europe during World Wars I and II, Allen did not show any interest in classic culture. He appears not to have visited museums, attended plays or concerts and little interest in the antiquities. Although he never attempted to describe in detail the countryside, the towns, or even the glories of Paris, Allen admired the scenery. "This is a wonderful sort of country in a way but one devil of a place to live in. Am keen to stay here until the shivaree is over but also want to catch the first boat home after it's over. In the first place, baths are as scarce as hens' teeth. The sanitation is frightful and the morals in the same class. The French femmes may set the styles for the world, but they surely ought to brush their teeth more.

"The various old ladies with whom I have been billeted have treated me like a king, with tea, cake and every thing, but they all think I'm crazy for taking my daily exercise and for demanding a daily bath, even if under a hydrant.

"Can't express my feelings about the way Papa has been left out. It has hurt me terribly and disillusioned me a lot. The old stiffs needn't hand me any more of their guff about the disinterestedness of selection. Of course I shall always give the best I've got, but my ideals in one way have been certainly shattered and I don't fail to express my opinions when I care to."

The letters home demolish one of the legends that later enveloped Allen. A 1943 article in *Time* claimed that Allen, while in France, arrived the day before a class for infantry officers was about to graduate. "He lined up with that class," reported *Time*. "Said the commandant, passing out certificates: 'I don't remember you in this class.'

"'I'm Allen—why don't you?' Allen brazenly replied. He got his certificate and as temporary major he led a battalion of the 90th Division into battle. . . ."

His correspondence home indicates he attended a training class for two weeks; and, his concern that his lack of infantry experience would be overlooked until he got his bearings suggests that he knew full well his ignorance of foot soldier warfare. Even though he passed off the instruction as "the Get Rich Course for Field Officers," he was too good a soldier to have skipped an opportunity to gain knowledge of the deadly game he was about to play. Finally, in his letters Allen speaks often of the many old friends and acquaintances he saw. It would have been most unlikely for him to have possessed the anonymity to permit him to fool those in charge of the school.

Initially, according to Allen, his 3d Battalion of the 358th Regiment relieved soldiers from the 1st Division in the Saizerais sector, north of Toul on 22 August. The area remained quiet but on 3 September, Allen—unable to restrain himself—ventured forward. He reported to headquarters of the 358th: "At noon I went to the outpost trenches . . . to look over the forward trenches. I first reported to Bn. P.C. [one abbreviation for "command post"] and there picked up Lieut. Culp. With him I proceeded to the frontline trenches, and while in the trench, . . . we met a patrol of two men who reported a 37 mm gun then in operation just N.W. of Fey. At this time Lieut. Betts, with Lieut. Woods, reported with 4 men. We picked up Sgt. Batiste, Co. G, and 2 men who were then on outpost duty, and approached Fey from west. . . . We surrounded the supposed location of this gun and found that it was not there.

"Having a strong patrol of 13 men I then decided to investigate the German front lines. We crept up . . . N.W. of Fey as far as point 370.4-236.2 [map coordinates]. While we were at this point, 8 minutes after leaving Fey, our place of departure from Fey was shelled by 77 mm shells for several minutes. . . . I left 3 men and started north with Lieuts. Betts, Culp and Woods and 6 men. We crept north until we found ourselves under aeroplane observation and a little later were fired on by trench mortars. We changed our course to east. . . . Here we were again fired upon by trench mortars and therefore changed our course. . . . When close to German wire . . . we were fired upon by a machine gun. . . . This may have been an anti-aircraft gun in operation.

"Entered German wire at approximately point 370.7-236.5 and entered the German first line trenches opposite that point at 8:00 p.m. While in the German trench, discovered an outpost of 2 men, 30 yds on our right. Made dispositions to surround these men, but failed to complete same in time to surround them. Did not open fire for fear of drawing fire from surrounding M.G.s. Continued our investigations and then started back. Here the patrol became separated and I found myself with 2 men. Leaving them outside the wire, I proceeded east along the German trench approximately to point 370.8-236.5. Here I found a trap in the wire. At this time the enemy sent up star shells, which exposed us, and another machine gun opened fire. I saw what appeared to be another outpost near point. . . . I then returned to the 2 men I had left behind and we returned toward Fey. Entered a communication trench . . . and followed that trench to outpost system. Reached Bn. P.C. at about 11:15 p.m."

Allen turned in papers collected in the German trenches and then detailed information on the disposition of the opposing troops, the location of some machine-gun nests. He remarked, "Enemy appears nervous. He has good aeroplane observation and scatters minenwerfer shells on the slightest pretext. Saw one drop in our rear [that] closely resembled a G.I. can." He described the terrain in terms of slope, firmness, shell holes, and the feasibility of tank movement. He reported "The wire outside trenches is very dense and is very difficult to pass through." He had spent more than eleven hours in this reconnaissance and obviously brought back worthwhile intelligence.

To his father he wrote, "Things are picking up. Took a patrol through the Boche first line the other night and to within 45 yards of the second line. Happened to be in the first line one day when the location of a hostile 37 mm was located. Took a patrol out and surrounded the supposed location but found they had left, leaving only a small slice of bologny and an odor. . . . Knowing that some definite dope was needed, we continued our way, and after crawling 3/4 of a mile under aeroplane observation, we reached the Boche wire at 8 p.m. It took all the afternoon as we had to zigzag a good bit, having been observed and were under shell fire 4 times and m.g. fire 3 times. We wormed through their wire after dark, and after laying in wait in the tall grass, slipped in between the outposts. Located m.g. nests, got some documents out of a trench dugout and the lay of the land of their lines and brought back some pretty good dope. The colonel seemed to be glad to get it, but said it was no place for a field officer. But mission was accomplished.

"The infantry game is great business these days but I shall be glad to return to the cavalry if they use them on a large scale. Am in excellent health and getting along fairly well. We get fine grub now, jam 3 times a day, and if we only had shower baths this war would be a picknick [sic]."

The area remained quiet until what was labeled the St. Mihiel Offensive: The 90th, along with seven other U.S. infantry divisions, plus several French organizations, began to chew up the salient. The full offensive had commenced on the night of 12–13 September. In a scribbled field message carried by a runner to the regimental commander, Col. E. M. Leary, Allen said, "Am going forward with battalion. Held up by m.g. nests in draw." Another field message from a 3d Battalion officer named Philip Gallagher tersely reported, "Have not seen Major Allen all day but have heard he is here." Subsequently, Gallagher advised Leary, "Major shot through neck. Capt. Leftwich is in command." In that

first day of fighting, Allen's 3d Battalion listed seven of its twelve officers as casualties.

But his absence was brief; on 15 September Allen informed Leary,
"Have reconnoitered position and most logical situation is left of line,
s.w. of Vilcey. . . . Please have barrage plans conform."

The confusion generated by the fury of the guns is indicated by another message from Gallagher. "All agree that volunteers cannot be gotten to secure them [four bodies atop a hill] and that if volunteers are secured their mission cannot be accomplished, that the place where any
bodies may be is in such a network of machine guns that nothing can
pass through without intense artillery preparation, day or night."

Days later, Allen detailed his experiences to his father: "Have been fortunate enough to have helped start the big all-American offensive [the
U.S. divisions advanced along a fifteen-mile line from the southeastern
approach to the Saint-Mihiel salient]. Can't tell you where we are but my
battalion was one of the assault battalions. We had a little hard luck, having been shelled in the woods as we left for our position. We lost a few
and then got some of that dastardly gas. The confusion was fierce but I
finally got them all in their jump-off trench. Just before zero hour, went
out to reconnoiter No Man's Land and got knocked clean over by the
shrapnel. When I came to, my field glasses and knapsack were blown away,
but aside from minor scratches, I was intact and O.K. Finally got started
with a portion of my own battalion and a lot of casuals. We were fortunate enough to have reached our objective and somewhat beyond it.

"In the meanwhile we had some pretty good sport in the woods. Our
ammunition ran a little low and we took one strong point with fists and
clubs. My only regret is that a couple of my dearly cherished back teeth
were knocked out by a machine gun bullet. Spent 24 hours in a base hospital, but with the help of one of the doctors got released and am now
back with the organization. These hard-boiled doughboys 'with the dirt
behind their ears' are doing splendidly. It is the greatly despised American buck private who is winning this war." Throughout his long career,
Allen would express his faith in the lowliest of soldiers.

He closed his account with reassurance, "Am in the best of health and
doing fine. Don't worry as they have not got my number."

The letter masked omitted details with a touch of typical Allen
bravado. Clark Wright, who commanded a machine-gun company attached to Allen's battalion, recalled, "Major Allen was wounded by shell
fire just before his battalion jumped off west of Fey-en-Heye. He was re-

ported killed to me, but was not, having merely [been] knocked unconscious and slightly wounded. He was evacuated to a dressing station, and tagged for evacuation to the rear. On regaining consciousness he left the dressing station while still dazed and weak and followed his battalion. En route he organized stragglers and loose individuals, led them forward and engaged enemy machine [gun] nests. These nests were in the Bois-d-Pretre, north of Fey-en-Heye, and holding up the advance of the 2d and 3d Battalions, 358th Infantry. He engaged these machine gun nests with his detachment in hand-to-hand fighting and knocked them out. At one stage he used his fists in the fighting, so closely were they engaged. The removal of these nests aided materially in the advance of the 358th Inf. Major Allen was shot in the jaw in this fighting and was evacuated to a Field Hospital at about noon, before he could reach his own command post.

"He left the Field Hospital on September 13th and rejoined his battalion by motorcycle. He was again evacuated by direct order of the regimental surgeon on September 14th." (Wright's statement errs on the date as a field message from Allen bears the notation of 15 September.)

Another account of the action says, "When he came to in an aid station, he tore off his first-aid tag and ran to catch up with his troops." After noting the hand-to-hand battle with enemy machine gunners, the report continues. "The major, missing some teeth and with his face covered with blood, paused to pick up one of the German identification tags and then resumed his search for his battalion. Before he could find it, some soldiers from another regiment stopped him. Like other officers, he had removed his insignia prior to the attack, so when these Americans searched him and they found the German ID tag, they thought he might be an enemy in disguise. Eventually Allen convinced them of his proper identity, but by this time, he was so weak that they sent him back to an aid station."

Three weeks later, Allen advised his father he was still at the hospital but expected to be discharged within a few days. "My wounds have done very well, the jaw injury healed and my teeth fixed up." In fact, the result of the machine-gun bullet strike to his jaw and the loss of several teeth was that it all but eliminated Allen's tendency to stammer. In later years, only when he became intense did he have any hesitation when attempting to speak.

He spoke of "three little abrasions," on his neck, hand, and side that the doctors were still treating. "But am feeling so well that I've been knocking off almost ten miles in the hills every day and been taking cold showers every day. That helps a lot to tone me and I really am feeling O. K." Nearly fifty years before America discovered jogging, Terry Allen was nearly fanatical in his devotion to that form of exercise.

"Am really anxious to get back to my battalion as they really are a fine lot. Tell Mama not to worry in the least as the Boche naturally have not got my number and besides battalion commanders lead a very sheltered existence, comparatively speaking. The American troops are showing a fine spirit here and you'd be surprised to see how these foreigners are beginning to 'bootlick' our troops. The Germans seem to feel that there is something fatalistic about the Am. Troops as the prisoners say they simply breeze along in spite of opposition."

He was being cared for at Base Hospital 20, located in Châtel-Guyon, which he described as "a beautiful little town, a typical French resort. They have all kinds of spring water here to drink. Have tried them once in a while but they all make me sick.

"We are supposed to go to Nice to convalesce for two weeks after leaving here, but am going straight back to my regiment. Would like to take in England for a week or two though, before coming back. But nix on these French resorts, they're rotten. . . . The doughboys here have a song now that they call 'Heaven, Hell or Hoboken by Xmas.' But I believe they are very optimistic. However, things are certainly coming our way.

"Tell Mary that there's not much doing in the line of souvenirs. Of course there are stacks and stacks of helmets and all sorts of stuff in the salvage piles but it is very difficult to send anything home, and then a fellow is so busy that you have to leave the souvenir hunting to those in the rear. Iron crosses are rather nice to pick up but I hate to take decorations from the poor devil.

"Very funny things happen over here sometimes when you have time to laugh afterwards. As usual my striker is quite a character but he does take awfully good care of me. When he saw his first Boche, he threw 6 grenades at him before I could stop him, and the Boche resembled a corn beef hash. Later in the day we had a little hand-to-hand stuff in the woods and he amused everyone on one occasion by jumping up and down and yelling, 'That's the way, Terry old kid,' when I happened to swing and catch a Boche noncom square on the jaw. His ideas of discipline are very vague but he's a darn good striker and besides lots of amusement."

By late 1916, the civilians responsible for the military, such as Secretary of War Baker and Secretary of the Navy Josephus Daniels, realized that the growing number of men in the armed forces would stimulate commercial vice. During the mobilization along the Mexican border where Allen had served, saloons, brothels, and gambling flourished, catering to the soldiers during off-duty hours. Although many officers regarded the condition as inevitable, Baker directed an associate, Raymond B. Fosdick, to investigate and propose a solution that would protect the troops from the consequences of liquor and whores. As a stopgap tactic, Baker threatened to shift soldiers away from vice-ridden towns.

After the United States entered the war, Baker—with the aid of Fosdick—concluded the army must sponsor wholesome, organized recreation and facilities to divert soldiers from pursuit of whiskey and women. On behalf of the navy, Daniels concurred. The draft act included sections that prescribed vice-free zones around the training bases and prohibited sale of liquor to men in uniform. The commission, through its law enforcement division, shut down 116 red-light districts across the country, notwithstanding two visits by the mayor of New Orleans to Washington to protest the ban. Baker created a Commission on Training Camp Activities, headed by Fosdick. It supervised the recreational facilities on military posts and encouraged a host of agencies—the Red Cross, Salvation Army, YMCA and YWCA, Knights of Columbus, and Jewish Welfare Board—to meet the desires of servicemen without recourse to alcohol or sex. The commission operated the post exchanges where one could buy candy, cigarettes, razor blades, or other amenities. The Ys provided places for men to relax and write home, as Allen did on its stationery.

In the United States, civilian and military police supported by public morality could exercise control over the purveyance of vice, but overseas it was different. American authorities abroad relaxed on the matter of drinking as long as the troops kept their imbibing within limits. Prostitution, however, was another matter, not only as an affront to the American sense of morality, but also because it spread venereal disease. During the summer of 1917, the British Expeditionary Force reported twenty-three thousand men hospitalized because of sexually transmitted diseases. The French army listed one million cases of gonorrhea and syphilis since 1914. Pershing had been able to control the problem in Mexico with his military preserve of prostitutes, but there he had a relatively small number of men concentrated in one area. That would not work when two million Americans tramped through the villages, towns, and cities of France.

When the Americans first arrived, Pershing—aware of the statistics piled up by his allies—studied daily the venereal report on his men. When he inspected a unit, he invariably inquired about its cases, and if it seemed high or on the increase, he demanded an explanation. General James Harbord, chief of staff to Pershing for a period, said, "There was no subject on which more emphasis was laid, throughout the existence of the American Expeditionary Forces."

To prevent an epidemic among the AEF, Pershing issued orders and directives that stressed to the doughboys that they should avoid sexual intercourse, but that if they failed to resist temptation, they must avail themselves of prophylaxis. Anyone who came down with gonorrhea or syphilis could expect a court-martial and appropriate punishment.

The host country regarded the U.S. policy as repressive and ineffective. Prime Minister Georges Clemenceau even wrote a letter to Pershing criticizing the American approach, and he volunteered to establish licensed houses of prostitution. The general passed a copy to Fosdick, who in turn handed it to Baker. The Secretary of War allegedly exclaimed, "For God's sake, Raymond, don't show this to the President or he'll stop the war."

In fact, the U.S. effort, spearheaded by surgeon and urologist Dr. Hugh Young, worked rather well. Young arranged for medical care of French civilians in areas where Americans were billeted and brought treatment of venereal diseases to the level of regimental facilities rather than clogging transportation and hospital beds with this non-combat-incurred disability. As a consequence, the venereal disease rate among the doughboys in 1918 was less than one case per thousand.

In his letters, Allen makes no mention of this delicate subject, but he obviously availed himself of the respectable facilities provided by the volunteer organizations. From his hospital bed in Châtel-Guyon he observed, "We all take off our hats to the Red Cross here. They are doing wonderful work and the men appreciate it too. For instance when you are sent to an evacuation hospital and all your equipment and uniforms and toilet articles are lost, stolen or destroyed, they give us all a complete toilet set, underwear and hand-knit socks. So we at least shave and brush our teeth. I shall never tease the ladies again about their Red Cross activities.

"Tell Mama tomorrow is Sunday and I shall try to get down in time for Mass, provided the Butcher Wagon comes around in time. The attending surgeon comes around to dress our wounds every morning and the nurse always wheels a little medical cart, which I call the Butcher Wagon much to her disgust. However, the name has stuck."

Allen's reference to attendance at Catholic services was not simply to reassure his mother. Throughout his life he remained dedicated to the faith in a quiet fashion, going off by himself to pray or showing up for mass without publicizing his presence.

Released from the hospital, he managed to have only a few days before requiring further medical care. "Am now back in the hospital again," he wrote to his mother, "as the regimental surgeon would not let me remain in the field with my battalion. I am incapacitated for the time being. Was fortunate enough to have rejoined in time to be with my outfit when they helped drive back a feeble attempt the Boche made to counter-attack. But a couple of my shrapnel wounds looked a little angry and the doctors were afraid to let me stay.

"This is a beautiful little French summer resort. All the countesses and dukes and the rest of the French silk stockinged aristocracy are here in full force. They are taking fine care of us here. It's a Univ. of Penn unit, the best doctors in Phila. They are making quite a case of me; it seems that I am the victim of some sort of dastardly poisoned shrapnel the Boche threw over. In addition, am having a couple of my missing teeth replaced by very pretty gold ones. The dentist here, a big practitioner in Philadelphia, is really a wonder. He says I sure must have a hard face when a machine gun bullet can ricochet off my jaw and only knock out two teeth. No other damage done. Hope to rejoin about October 1st. Unfortunately will have to replace a large part of my equipment. You should have seen me traveling through France with half a shirt, part of my breeches, a tin hat and no blouse. My new trench coat got full of mustard gas and the hospital authorities buried it all.

"Don't worry about me as they haven't got my number. Am worried now for fear I'll be detached from the regiment. Where is Ethel [his older sister]? Would like to get in touch with her. For heaven's sake don't worry about me." After the recitation of what happened, it is difficult to understand how he could urge his mother not to be anxious.

Her fears could not have been calmed by his next message. "Am just passing thru Paris en route to my regiment. Was given classification 'A' at the hospital,which means fit for active service, so I am perfectly O.K. again. It looks as if the Boche were beginning to throw up the sponge, but he still has a lot of punishment coming. Can't say where I'm going but my outfit is very much on the job."

During the respite after the baptism of fire, the 90th Division soldiers underwent training that concentrated upon company maneuvers against machine-gun nests. Terry Allen was bemused by replacement lieutenants, "decked out in a regalia of trench coats and other equipment that made them ornate compared to the veterans." General Henry Allen visited the troops, and Terry Allen recalled that he "stressed he did not want to hear any complaints about unprotected flanks or undue complaints about lack of supplies, manpower or imaginary obstacles. The men realized their commander was not an imaginary figure who ruthlessly ordered them out on impossible missions and who neglected their needs and safe-guards. On the other hand they knew he was an inspiring leader, one who had organized and trained them and had already led them on one major offensive and was ready to lead them on their next drive and share their dangers and hardships."

The general's performance stuck with Allen. More than a dozen years later, he paused during an account of the actions of his battalion for a digression on the effect of such personal leadership.

The AEF now geared up for the final strike, the Meuse [River]–Argonne [Forest] offensive. The 90th Division would play a central role. On the night of 21 October, Allen and his battalion headed toward the front by bus. He remembered, "The movement was handled by a French motor convoy. The busses were American ammunition trucks, difficult to drive at best. The truck drivers were Chinese soldiers in the French Colonial Forces and the convoy was supervised by French NCOs. The Americans could speak little if any French, the French could speak no English, and the Chinamen could speak neither. A touch of hilarity was added . . . some of the doughboys had succeeded in trading their white bread for a liberal supply of pinard [wine] from some accommodating poilus."

According to Allen, "The roads were terrible, mud was heavy with in-termittent shelling. While positions were marked on maps, landmarks had been obliterated." The villages consisted of rubble and broken rock. The men bivouacked in the Bois de Cuny, a site grievously wounded by the conflict. "The very atmosphere," wrote Allen, "the ground itself seemed to stink of the violence of warfare. The battalion was scheduled to relieve elements of the 11th Infantry from the 5th Division in the Bois des Rappes, north of Cunel. The doughs carried a loaf of French bread, cans of corn willy, and goldfish and a reserve ration. The march forward occurred without incident other than intermittent shelling.

"Lack of guides hampering movement," Allen advised regiment. "Few casualties from shell fire marching up. Nothing serious. Did not receive pigeons [for messages]." According to him, a soldier claimed that the pigeons flew out of their baskets while they were being brought forward. He noted, "Will need 25 men to carry wire [for telephone lines]. Had to use one day's reserve rations today. Badly need 50 thousand rounds ammunition for M Co., 2000 grenades, 100 picks, 100 shovels. Litters are with wagons. Runner chain has already been established. [Regimental] Chaplain to be notified of Lt. Ridley and other casualties."

Allen and his adjutant went to the 10th Brigade's headquarters, where the commanding officer informed them that a defensive barrage would stop an expected counterattack. Allen said, "We protested against the necessity for this barrage, knowing that the resultant counter-barrage might react to our disadvantage, against our machine gun carts still en route. But this was what occurred. Our early prediction was amply proven."

The battalion moved forward in a column of fours. The L Company commander was killed leading his unit into position. Heavy artillery fire rained down upon them causing numerous casualties. The Germans had control of the air and their planes drizzled machine-gun fire, "a continual annoyance," said Allen. His battalion was short on rations but an obliging NCO from the departing forces donated enough food for a hot meal." To guard against a fiasco like the Columbus raid by the Villistas, he stationed twelve men in front as a cordon of snipers. Meanwhile he reported that fifty enemy aircraft flew overhead firing their machine guns, wounding two of the men.

The foe's barrages intensified. Allen reported, "Violent artillery fire. High explosives and shrapnel coming from points north of the PC and north of Aincreville. The pummeling from the big guns was followed by a half-hour gas attack. Our patrols to Aincreville met with considerable resistance, machine guns and snipers more active on our right flank. Enemy aerial activity increasing. Enemy artillery very active. Not much counter-battery work."

His message of 24 October read, "Need 2 squads of litter bearers. Several men still left. Am occupying front 300 meters of which I gave coordinates of center. Sniper actions on our front and flanks. Am entrenched with 357th on our left. Started a filter toward north Aincreville-Bantheville road. Have M Co. held in readiness northern edge Bois des Rappes. Please arrange for several squads of litter bearers. Have located strong machine gun nests. I am preparing to filter north."

A staff officer at the regimental command post, after chatting with Allen on the telephone, informed his commander, "He got within 100 yards of his objectives when a great mass of fireworks broke loose. He will send in sketch showing positions. States there is considerable confusion where he is and wants litters." The iteration and reiteration of the need for stretchers indicates the growing number of wounded.

He telephoned his superior to report, "We are now prepared to advance forward provided we can receive information as to whether our artillery will support us. Have sent out patrols and established liaison with 357th on our left. Can advance but am awaiting information on whether our advance north will be interfered with by our artillery. Have sent in 5 prisoners. Have received about 20 casualties." He passed along word of the death of the Company M commander while on a patrol that produced no useful information.

As the 90th readied itself in anticipation of the order to go over the top, Allen noted, "Some apprehension was felt." Years later, he wrote down what occurred and referred to himself in the third person: "Therefore, it was decided to make a personal reconnaissance toward Aincreville. Command of the battalion was turned over to Captain Clark Wright of the Machine Gun Company. The Battalion scout officer was ordered to take a patrol to the northern edge of the [forest]. The patrol worked its way north through an old trench system and reached a point on the Andon River, 400 meters southwest of Aincreville.

"An enemy machine gun nest and sniper post was observed and they opened up. The Germans in Aincreville began shooting. The patrol seemed 'on the spot.' Two men were wounded and they took refuge behind a manure pile.

"At this stage a most interesting situation developed. The Germans seemed to disclose themselves on the front and on both flanks. Apparently, the patrol had been allowed to pierce their front line. At least 10 machine gun nests were spotted.

"American artillery fire was increasing and it was as worrisome to the patrol as it was to the Germans. In confusion, the patrol withdrew with the wounded, returning by 5 p.m. The command post in a rock quarry had been hit with several casualties. Battalion records were strewn all over the forest."

Clark Wright, who had taken charge of the battalion while Allen led the patrol, noted that the members of the group were all volunteers. A runner from Allen had returned with information on the enemy disposition, which led to the American artillery barrage that almost inflicted friendly fire on the patrol.

Allen now drafted a plan "for the capture of A" [obviously Aincreville] which he sent by runner to Colonel Leary: "Suggest that this movement be a surprise movement executed by two cos. of infantry with 2 M.G. platoons and 1 Co. of support. Enclosed sketch shows Cos. I, K, and M in position just south of Bourrut-Aincreville Road, echeloned with Co. K in front and Cos. I and M in support along creek bottom with Co. L and two platoons [from] Co. D, M.G. Bn in support in Bois des Rappes. One platoon of M.G. Co is now supporting Co. K.

"The assault on the town should be delivered from a point just south of the town with Co. M in the first echelon and Co I in the second echelon. Co. F should approach along the creek bottom and be ready to support the attack. Co. K should hold its present position and extend its front 200 m. to right. Co. I should be supported with an M.G. platoon on either flank."

Allen urged what he considered the most important aspect of the plan. "The approach to the attack formation should be made during the night and the attack be delivered just before dawn." He would never waver in his belief that the cover of darkness was one of the strongest weapons available to a soldier. His plan, with precise notations on the map, then outlined how the troops should proceed toward the objective. Allen predicted considerable opposition from enemy artillery and machine-gun nests overlooking the town, but argued that a U.S. artillery barrage should be delivered only if he asked for it. "This would necessarily have to be a surprise movement to insure success." Allen added that a gas attack occurred on the previous night and some fairly heavy—"very accurate"—artillery fire all day caused some casualties. "Use of telephone draws art. fire. Suggest that this be done in Spanish by Lt. [Rapheal] Garcia when use of the phone is necessary."

Based on the intelligence and knowledge gained by the scouting mission, Allen thus organized an attack to begin at 2 A.M. on 26 October. He had twenty-three officers and more than eight hundred men in what was a reinforced battalion. After first briefing all the company commanders, he held back the usual advance scouts to add to the element of surprise. "The success of the attack would depend entirely on whether all units could be located in the dark, the direction maintained, and above all, straggling had to be eliminated. [It] depended upon the initiative of

NCOs and company officers and discipline of all concerned. Intervals and distances were decreased because of darkness and depleted ranks. There was heavy rain and constant shelling during the night.

"The two companies jumped off in the dark. At first there was not a sound to disturb the advance. An enemy machine gun opened up as the leading wave crossed the Andon River—really only a brook—but [the mg fire] was not effective. Enemy were killed or captured and the advance proceeded until the battalion crossed the highway from Aincreville to Bourrut, but with daylight, further advance was suicidal. Conditions were precarious. There was a problem from a machine gun bypassed during the night attack. An NCO crawled forward, dropped two rifle grenades in and the Germans not killed, surrendered." Allen remarked on the effectiveness of the rifle grenades as weapons.

Subsequently, he added more information. "I have personally reconnoitered the Andon Brook from our left . . . and do not believe the creek to be actually fordable. It has steep sides, 3 to 4 feet deep. It averages 24 feet wide. But the ground is firm and it would be easy to construct a pontoon bridge at any point. . . . There are remains of partially destroyed bridges strong enough to support artillery. The foundations are partially intact, half the piles still being in place. I believe the [pontoon] bridge . . . could be completed by engineers in 30 minutes."

Wright noted, "Word was received from regimental headquarters for Maj. Allen to cross the Andon Brook and seize the ridge between Aincreville and Bantheville.

"The attack was made with two companies and one machine gun platoon to save casualties. Maj. Allen led the first wave in person, reaching his objective at 4:00 a.m. The support company followed the next day. His position was under constantly heavy m.g. and shell fire. In fact rations could not be sent to him for nearly 48 hours."

Summing up this adventure, Allen noted, "It is questionable whether it was proper for the battalion commander [himself] to have personally conducted the reconnaissance. However, control of the battalion was not lost and the information proved of inestimable value." Probably of at least equal value was the unspoken message to the troops that their leader would not ask them to perform any action he was not personally prepared to do himself. "Personal reconnaissance is a great factor to success," said Allen. "Information is a big help and the knowledge to the men in ranks that they are not taking a leap in the dark is a big help in boosting their morale. Night attacks for a comparatively short advance can be accomplished under the worst conditions. The surprise effect saves lives."

In subsequent claims about the efficacy of action in the dark, Allen asserted that while he had orders to attack in daylight, the night attack near Aincreville was done on his own initiative. He related the events of the evening to A. J. Liebling: "I had one goddamn company commander who was a pessimist. 'This is suicide,' he said. I pulled out my revolver and shot him in the behind. 'There. You're out,' I said. You're wounded. He was glad to get out of it and I sent a second lieutenant up to take the company and he did fine. We took the position with about twenty killed, and if we'd done it by day we would have lost 300." Allen later said to Liebling, "We took about fifty German prisoners and they were whining as if we didn't have the right to attack by night. Acted as if we should fight by their rules. The German is arrogant in victory and servile in defeat."

The battle continued with an enemy counterattack but it dwindled away. By the end of October, Allen's battalion had lost three officers KIA, four more were severely wounded, and another three were hurt less seriously. The casualties among the enlisted personnel were proportionately high. The effort, however, had straightened out the line, as the Americans geared up for further assaults.

On 1 and 2 November, the 180th Brigade, with the 358th as one of its two regiments, again attacked the enemy. Allen dourly remarked, "The orders were vague. As it turned out, the regimental command post was too far to the rear and rapidly lost touch with the battalions in their advance. Cohesion broke down as the regimental CP [command post] didn't move up to coordinate advances of regiments and battalions. Heavy infantry losses Nov. 1–2 might have been avoided by liberal use of smoke," and again he criticized the failure of those above to come forward and "eliminate breakdown of communications." After remarking on the "helter-skelter movements of the battalions when the opposition collapsed," Allen saw a role for his old specialty: "Properly led cavalry could have made the German retreat a rout."

He was notably less cheery than earlier when he dashed off the words to his beloved mother, "Ethel and Mary have the benefit of my insurance in case I get bumped off." Actually, he had divided the military insurance of ten thousand dollars among his sisters and his mother and bought an additional two thousand dollars' worth, which was payable to Concepcion. "Our men are doing splendidly but are fighting under terribly hard conditions. The weather is strictly terrible and living in the mud with very little food, polluted water.

". . . We are just beginning to realize now how the casualties have hit some of our friends. Do you remember little Timothy at the Catholic University who I used to see so much of. Well, Tim was killed at the head of his company of marines in Belleau Wood. John Hatch [from Allen's original U.S.M.A. class] went back with consumption contracted in the Argonne. Seery [sic] [Edward] Hayes who broke me in beast barracks, lost his arm, and there are numerous other cases. So I feel I was extremely lucky with two little bullet holes and a superficial shrapnel scar.

"I'm back on the job with my battalion and in addition am divisional musketry instructor. We hear rumors of going home in a few weeks but of course we do not know [how] true they are. Am going to try to get to the school at Leavenworth [the Command and General Staff School] when I get back. Gen. Allen has been trying to get me on his staff, principally to play polo I believe, but so far have been unable to leave the division."

To his father on 5 November he reported, "We had 18 hours rest from our last time at the front in which my battalion was congratulated by the Div. Comdr. And we just got back in time to get in on this last big American show. Am writing now in a dugout which was in German hands a few hours ago. Am using a German artillery officer's paper, am wearing his socks and have just shaved with his razor.

"It's bound to be over very soon now. At any rate I shall certainly appreciate the ordinary comforts of life after this." He tacked on a postscript, "Guess I told you I was recommended for promotion and have already passed the exam, but do not expect any results as the vacancy does not exist in the division and this selective promotion is by divisions."

On 11 November, Colonel Leary sent a memorandum to all of his commanders: "Hostilities will cease at 11 o'clock today and no troops will pass beyond the line occupied by them at that hour. All communication with the enemy is absolutely forbidden and any lack of vigilance in this respect will be reported and punishment administered to the person offending. . . . Every emphasis will be laid on the fact that this is an Armistice and not Peace. . . . Troops must be prepared at any moment for further operations."

Allen wrote to his father on 11 November—which would become Armistice Day—"Well this has been a great day at the front, with the war practically 'fini.' We got the news to call off the game at 11 a.m. and it seems queer as the devil to be able to walk around in the open without dodging or carrying an infernal gas mask.

"Last night I led my gang across the M——e [obviously the Meuse River and a weak attempt to avoid censorship], and this morning we were prepared to go over the top again with the remnants of my battalion, about 50%, when Gen. Allen sent word to sit tight and eat our rations (rather rubbing it in as we had nothing to eat). However, am sitting on the world tonight, sleeping in a German barrack, with a belly full of stolen German sausage and canned potatoes and with a German feather bed if you please."

Although the 90th Division received the word and halted its operations, some other U.S. combat units were not notified to stand down. The 2d, 81st, and 89th Divisions all had men who continued fighting, bleeding, and dying well after the 11 A.M. cease-fire supposedly took hold.

The sudden cease-fire along the western front led to melancholy in some quarters: Most troops were described as too tired to cheer; and now that the guns had stopped, they could mourn their losses. Allen wrote, "I haven't become as hardened to this game as some of the fellows. I don't mind pulling the blanket off of a dead man's pack, having a couple of Boche pulled out of a dugout before occupying it, but I can't help but weaken when I look at the size of some of my companies. Some of them cut down to 40% and only 3 officers left who went over the top with me at St. Mihiel. Am using my 3d adjutant now. Two of them were killed, poor fellows.

"Don't expect to get my promotion now, as the vacancy has never occurred, but I at least have had the recommendation. It would have seemed queer with 2 colonels in the family, wouldn't it?

"Am well and in great shape physically. Got a touch of that infernal mustard gas at Aincreville, but am all right now.

"We are wondering what dispositions will be made of us all over here. I suppose it'll be border duty on the German border for a while. Have had several invitations [for] England on the way back and may try to get a short leave before returning. We all think it will take at least five or six months to get all our troops back.

"It is hard to realize that Mary is growing up so rapidly. . . ." He made no mention of his sister Ethel who would fade from his life after her marriage to a man named McGovern. Mary, however, would be of concern to him for many years.

6: Occupation Duty

The end of the war came as the Allied armed forces broke down German resistance and that country's supreme command urged negotiations. The civilian political parties had challenged the imperial government's right to rule, and the kaiser—along with his heirs and other members of the royal family—agreed to dissolve the monarchy. When the Allied commanders met with the representatives of the German government in early November, they demanded that not only must its army evacuate all of the territory held in the West but that all of the troops must withdraw to the east of the Rhine River. The peace treaty signed at Versailles in 1919 specified a fifteen-year occupation of Germany up to the west bank of the river.

At the time of the armistice, the Allied troops, still deep in France, held a front 120 miles from the Rhine as it flowed through northern Germany. The conditions of the cease-fire required a neutral zone six miles deep on the east bank of the Rhine. British and Belgian troops would move into Cologne, and the American forces would set up headquarters farther south at Coblenz. The French were to occupy a sector around Mainz, below the Americans.

As Allen had predicted, he did not advance any further in rank. The War Department halted promotions on Armistice Day. However, while Allen retained his rank as a major, others were less fortunate, some were broken back to much more junior levels or even forced into retirement.

Less than ten days after the armistice of 11 November, Allen informed his mother, "This division has been selected for one of those to go into Germany as part of the Army of Occupation. I suppose it's more or less an honor but hope it will not drag out the way the Mexican Border duty dragged along. Probably it will seem strange to the Boche to see our troops in Germany, 18 months after we declared war. We may move any time in the next 10 days. . . .

"I have enclosed a little letter of commendation that Gen. Allen issued the four doughboy regts. of the division after the last drive. It's all I can send you for a Xmas present . . . but hope to do better later. . . . I was especially fortunate to have effected my transfer to the Inf. as my old outfit, the ammunition train, never got enough horses to get to the front, in fact none of our artillery brigade got into it at all. Am going to try to get a few days in which to renew my equipment. . . . At present am wearing a soldier's uniform and a chauffeur's coat. Fortunately, my striker rustles enough blankets to make up for my lost bedding roll which has gone astray with everything else I own. This is a great life if you don't weaken in the first 100 years. When I see some of the French people in their condition, I realize that my losses are small in comparison."

In earlier mail home Allen had frequently mentioned financial problems, debts incurred while stationed in the States and the costs of outfitting himself. Through his parents, an American named Heffernan had learned that Allen was strapped for money. Heffernan apparently attempted to send an instrument for money overseas, which the family reported to Allen. His letter to his mother reveals his ambivalence about his would-be patron. "In regard to the Heffernan draft, I certainly appreciate the gentleman's kindness exceedingly but I have never received it. But just what is the idea, Mamma? Is it a form of charity? Of course it would be more than acceptable in view of all my property that has been salvaged during the last two drives. But I do not exactly wish to be an object of charity. Nevertheless I do not wish to be churlish about it and wish you would thank the gentleman sincerely for his kindness, but I have not received it as yet."

Even as he expected to become part of the occupation troops, Allen cast his eyes longingly home. "We are all wondering now what is to become of us when we return to the States. No doubt it will be a grand mixup for a while. After all the mustering out is over, of course, I should like to return to the Cavalry, as my heart will always be with them." Aside from his fondness for horses, Allen remained—as did so many soldiers—loyal to his first assignment. He wobbled between gloom and hope. "Although with my equipment scattered about and my horses gone, prospects do look a little dim. . . . However, Col. S. P. Adams, who used to be in the 14th Cavalry and who now has a cavalry regiment in California, has always said he would have a berth for me in his regiment, so I'm going to count on maybe eventually getting to California. Normal post life would sure be a welcome duty after 5 years on the Border followed by 6 months or more in France. One never realizes what a cinch a fellow has sometimes."

Under the terms of the armistice, the Americans assigned to occupation duty headed for German territory. The soldiers of the 90th Division were directed to proceed with full field equipment, one blanket, an overcoat, a raincoat, a single change of underwear, three pairs of socks, and two days' worth of rations. In a note to his father, Allen remarked that his unit had traveled thirty-one kilometers in a day, which he labeled "a fairly good hike for doughboys." With the Coblenz area as the ultimate destination, the Americans faced a month on the road.

He remarked on his regrets that Gen. Henry Allen had left the division because he was appointed corps commander. By virtue of his experiences with civil government while in the Philippines and his service at embassies, General Allen would assume responsibility for the entire U.S. occupation force, some sixteen thousand soldiers.

Terry Allen expressed mixed feelings about his own situation. Although he regretted that he would not soon return home, he believed the division's assignment was an honor. The troops had departed so swiftly that Allen reported his equipment "still pretty thin," and cancellation of leaves prevented him from collecting a pair of new uniforms made up for him in Paris.

He asked Samuel Allen to mail to the storage company the receipts for all of the items warehoused when he left San Antonio. Once the company received them, he could retrieve his gear. He was particularly keen to reacquire his saddle.

By 29 November, he was writing from Belgium while still marching toward Germany. He complained that although others had obtained leave, he had not managed to get away. "Am afraid the M.P.s will arrest me if I don't get some new clothes soon."

The good news was that the long-missing and mysterious "Heffernan draft" arrived. He explained to his mother, "It seems so unexpected that I can hardly understand it, but I appreciate his kindness immensely and will write immediately to thank him. If I ever get ahead for a few days and a chance to repair my outfit, his offering will certainly be most acceptable, having lost two complete sets of equipment. Shall use it for that purpose and wish you would thank him most sincerely in the event my letter is delayed."

He related the details of a Thanksgiving Day celebration at regimental headquarters. "It was a real feed even if we [ate] canned potatoes and camouflaged corn willy in place of turkey. The dining room was one of the most beautiful rooms I've ever seen, in an old French chateau, and the old French lady presented us with two dozen bottles of champagne for our dinner to help out the corn willy."

He continued, "Now that the war is over they are getting over[ly] generous with their citations and much to my surprise they stuck me in on the Division list [of those receiving commendations from the commander]. The Sgt. Major sent me over a copy of these and I almost tore it up by mistake but managed to save part of the first sheet. It was a great surprise to me, especially as it was entirely undeserved. There were hundreds who did more than I did, and as for my being an inspiration to everyone, that is a joke. I believe old Col. Tillman [Samuel E., West Point 1869, one of his first commanders] would turn over in his grave at that."

Allen earned three Purple Hearts in France, medals issued routinely for any wounds from enemy action. On the surface he appears to have been low-key about commendations for himself, which in addition to the citation by the division commander included a Silver Star. Allen was ambivalent about honors. While he referred to his achievements with modesty, on several occasions he spoke wistfully of the possibility of a Distinguished Service Cross.

Chatting about the unavailability of souvenirs, he announced, "Personally, I don't wish to be reminded of the beastly, rotten Germans. They lived like perfect beasts and fought us in a most unsportsmanlike way that cannot be described." Those who experienced the carnage of France from 1914–1918, including Allen, despite his reference to sportsmanship, had realized that war was not some sort of "game", a word that appears frequently in his early letters.The trek east toward his destinations in Germany continued into December. He advised his mother, "[I] am getting my first taste of real doughboy hiking. I don't mind scrapping with the doughboys but am not so keen about hiking with them. We are short on horses for transportation and consequently battalion commanders have to hoof it with the rest of them. . . . We are going through Luxembourg now and cross into Germany tomorrow. . . . We are the heart of the Army of Occupation and expect to see something of Coblenz when we stop." He still hoped for a promotion because the division had requested an extension beyond the freeze imposed on Armistice Day. He had learned that his name was again forwarded for advancement.

On 11 December, writing by candlelight, he reported to his father that the occupiers were now well inside the German border, en route to Coblenz. "The Germans have been exceptionally cordial to the Americans so there has not been any trouble at all but they are such a hypocritical bunch they probably realize what side their bread is buttered on. Last night I had a whole suite of an apartment for a billet, sitting room, bed room and even a bath. Coffee and toast was served in my room, a hot bath prepared in the morning. With my mud-stained trench coat and pair of shoes, I did not feel up to such grandeur. It was all because I happened to be in command of my section of the town, but the German burgomeisters all insist that I am too much of a youth to be dealing with them. Guess I'll have to grow a mustache or a bay-window or something.

"The corps inspector gave my battalion the 'once over' the other day and gave us a very high rating in march discipline and appearance. He happened to be an old friend of mine and took particular delight in kidding me because I had to hoof it." The inspector's comments belie the notion that arose particularly during World War II that Allen was too lax about the appearance of men in his command. But in fact, where it seemed appropriate, he insisted upon proper dress and grooming. His son once reported to a friend that his father was a stickler about shaving every day, on the grounds that it boosted morale.

During his traipse toward Germany, Allen received word that early in June he had been approved for a commission as a major in the cavalry; he now held a majority in all three major branches of the army—infantry, artillery, and cavalry. While continuing to protest his allegiance to the cavalry, he reiterated that his experiences with other organizations had broadened his outlook—and most certainly his experience as an infantry officer had given him a new appreciation of the life of a foot soldier.

Although he had lived most of his early life elsewhere, Allen increasingly considered himself a Texan. The 90th Division had been issued a brassard with the insignia of a "T" intertwined with an "O." "It is supposed to signify Texas and Oklahoma troops," he observed. "My adjutant heard a violent discussion the other day between some of the Texans and Okla. orderlies. The Texas delegation claimed the T and O meant 'Texas Only' and the Oklahoma delegation claimed it meant 'Oklahoma Toughs.' But they finally agreed on calling it, 'Terry's Own.'

"Except for a slight tendency to beat up troops from other divisions, they are remarkably well behaved and have acquired a fine reputation as they took all their objectives and were never forced back. Now that it is over, we can tell tales out of school and there is one division over here whom we kid unmercifully, because on one occasion in the Argonne offensive, we took one of their objectives and sent back word for them to come ahead as we had left a detachment to hold it for them."

It was a hallmark of his career to draw pride from the units with which he served. But more significantly, those whom he commanded seemed habitually to consider themselves "Terry's Own," a testament to his ability to lead and simultaneously win deep affection.

Even as Allen reached a destination thirty-five miles west of Coblenz and believed he would be settled down for a while, speculation—so integral a part of military life—ground out possible alternatives: "We hear constant rumors about going home. In fact the latest dope is that three officers are to be detailed to go to the port of embarkation very shortly to make the necessary preliminary arrangements. But that sounds too good to be true." And it was.

He voiced the soldier's common lament about his unit condemned to "a lot of dirty work while the other outfits have been resting back in France." He drew solace from the "satisfaction in having been part of the Army of Occupation." Christmas was approaching, and he remarked that the cooks and mess sergeants were scouring the country for hogs and chickens but these were quite scarce. "Want to feed my battalion up if possible."

As ever, he thought of where he might land upon his return to the States. "Am hoping to be lucky enough to draw a fairly good post when I get back after over 5 years on the Border and then 6 months over here. A decent post would look good for a change. But I imagine that I'll be chased from pillar to post for some time. Have heard from 2 cav. cols. saying they would ask for me after the war, providing they held their regiments."

George S. Patton Jr., his contemporary, had quickly recognized that the tank and the motorized vehicle doomed an equestrian cavalry, but Allen continued to cling to the horse as a viable instrument for warfare. In his defense, his sector of combat may have seen little armor deployed, but to boot, his insights probably were clouded by his love of riding. And while he most definitely was a career soldier, Allen—unlike Patton—was more inclined to pursue pleasure than immerse himself in activities that might advance him.

While Allen began his tour with the Army of Occupation, Samuel Allen in Seattle readied himself for his own new assignment as "Commander of the Department" in the Philippine Islands. The son was dismayed: "Hate to think of your going to the Philippines now and think it would be a crying shame after your good work in Seattle and in training artillery. Am sure your work had its effect out here, because we always had supreme confidence in our own artillery—always felt a little better knowing we were getting an American barrage. . . . Maybe one of your regiments replied when I used to call up near Aincreville and ask for counter-battery fire. At any rate it was always effective.

"I certainly hope it will turn out that you are all settled at a good location in the States when I return and hope you don't get a change of station, as I have been looking forward to a few weeks leave when I get back. Nothing would please one more. Am afraid Mama would still find me as hard to feed and she would have to pick up after me as much as when I used to come home from the Point. . . .

"It is hard to realize that just 7 years ago now I was hopelessly plugging away for an exam down there at Pensacola [one of Sam Allen's posts] and now am commanding a regiment of infantry in Germany with 2 attached machine gun cos. You may be surprised to hear that I was relieved of my battalion last night and placed in command of the regiment. Col. Hacker was sent over to take over the 357th which seems to have needed a change for some reason and I now have the whole outfit for a more or less indefinite period."

Position had its privileges, and he moved from his spartan quarters to a "swell joint," with bath and electric lights, that formerly was the property of a member of the Reichstag. The local people apparently were nonplussed that such a youthful-looking officer [Allen was thirty] governed the area; but he explained, "Fortunately, I have an excellent adjutant, who has enough gray hairs to give dignity to the regimental staff.

"My striker is greatly worried now, as he says the men are worried for fear my being regimental commander will keep me from working out with the squad, which is training for the Division boxing meet." Despite his rank and responsibilities, Allen seems to have had no qualms about putting his jaw on the line with the lowliest private.

On Christmas Day 1918, Allen informed his mother that his command of the regiment appeared to be "an indefinite proposition." The unit had shifted to a sector encompassing Daum, Hillesheim, and Gerolstein, with headquarters in Daum. He had the use of an automobile, a motorcycle, and a horse, "and manage to keep all 3 busy." Even in snow or rain he tried to squeeze in a few hours in the saddle. He commiserated over the departure of the family from Seattle, where he had hoped to visit them while on a leave. "However, it's all in the game and I realize it's back to the Border for me when this mess is over."

He was bemused over a dinner scheduled that night for his division commander and a visiting superior, and he wrote, "It will seem odd for me to be presiding at the table with two generals present. Gen. O'Neil [the 90th's commander] . . . was responsible for my temporary transfer to the doughboys and says I'll have to stick now but I'm determined to get back to the cavalry in the final shakeup, rank or no rank.

"You'd be surprised to see my present quarters. We just moved into our new town of Daum the other day and I am billeted with some count or something. Have a bedroom, sitting room, bath with all carved-oak furniture and oil paintings. But all this grandeur doesn't help much on Xmas Day. We are all fairly comfortable without a great deal to do except to keep up a fairly stiff training schedule and it's a lot better than living in the trenches and dodging shells."

A day later he reported the regimental banquet a great success. Perhaps his pleasure was influenced by O'Neil's remarks after the dinner: "He said that I had been recommended by the Board for the Distinguished Service Cross and that the division commander had endorsed the application as strongly as possible. Can't imagine their reasons as I never did anything out of the ordinary."

The particular engagement for which he was nominated for the DSC involved the advance of two of his companies from the woods with instructions to make contact with the allegedly retreating Germans. "Their information was not correct as proven later. . . . We went over the top at night and bit into the German lines about 1 or 2 kilometers. Then morning came, we found the Boche on three sides of us, 8 m.g. nests in front, 5 on right flank and 2 behind us. When the 5th Division then went forward to take Aincreville they were driven back and that left our right flank still exposed. However, the Bn dug in and stuck it out for 5 days, until the whole line moved forward Nov. 1st. In the meantime, Div. Hqtrs. used to call us up every day to see if we were still there. That seems to be their excuse for it [his proposed DSC]. I probably will not get it, not having done anything individual that warrants a reward."

The question of a reward for Allen's valor wandered through the occupying army's bureaucracy. The regimental adjutant informed him that the recommendation for a DSC had been returned from division headquarters with a certificate to raise the citation to a medal of honor. Allen protested to his mother that he did not deserve anything on that order for what he called "a reconnaissance to the extreme limit of the neutral zone."

In March of 1919, he noted a trip into the interior of Germany where "I got mixed up in a hot little revolution, which reminded me of the old Argonne days." There were scattered outbreaks of violence in Germany because of severe shortages of food with rationing based upon one thousand calories a day—barely more than half of a normal day's intake. Civil disorders rattled an already unstable government.

With the occupation forces, Allen attended a school for field-grade officers and sneered, "Seems funny to be learning the game after the war is over, from a lecture on grenades from a chemical expert who never saw Boche toss a potato masher." The division engaged in maneuvers along the edge of the neutral zone, using both of its infantry brigades and the auxiliary troops. Cavalry soldiers simulated a regiment of horse-borne troops before Allen's admiring eye.

The 90th Division soldiers saw a parade of top-level military leaders, acting as escorts first for Field Marshal Ferdinand Foch, then for Gen. Sir Henry Wilson, the British chief of staff, and finally for the Belgian army leader. General Henry Allen dispatched his namesake to Frankfurt to examine prospective entrees for a coming summer horse show. The emissary related to his father, "Frankfurt is well into the interior, beyond the neutral zone and Americans were about as popular as the devil is with holy water." He and a companion had not yet completed their business when the local people took to the streets to protest their deprivation. "We decided to take a chance and Capt. Brumbaugh and I threaded our way through all their demonstrations and crowds from the hotel to the depot. We were fortunate in bluffing our way through and we sort [of] surprised them into leaving us alone."

The reductions in rank finally reached him. "I managed to hang on until the last minute but am down to my regular grade as every one else over here is now. You would laugh and I know Col. Ruggles would have a fit to know that I've been sitting on an ordnance board which is testing German munitions [the course in gunnery and ordnance had been his downfall at West Point]. Am the only line officer on the board. . . . They needed a line officer with personal combat experience and I got chosen."

With all of his duties, Allen talked of buying a horse. "With the low rate of marks, they are fairly cheap now and the extra pay we then get as a captain makes it a good investment." The son assured his mother he had not become enamored of Europe. "I'll be damn glad to get back to Texas as I've had my fill of the stupid Dutchmen and the idiotic French with all their queer ideas and loose morals."

After the Russian Revolution (in 1917), the Communists, in what had been imperial Russia, had overthrown the republican government. They solidified their rule in the face of opposition from White Russians who were supported by a small contingent of British, French, and American forces that landed in Archangel and Siberia. Allen commented, "The Bolsheviki situation begins to look like the Mexican situation." He subsequently wondered whether he might be among the U.S. soldiers ordered to fight the Communists; but, American support for another huge expeditionary force never materialized.

Allen increasingly engaged in diversions from standard military duty. He mentioned participation in a fencing tournament sponsored by the AEF in Strasbourg and rode in a horse show and steeplechase against British soldiers in Cologne. And he traveled to England to inspect their care of horses.

As the occupation dragged on, the 90th Division—with its soldiers and reserve officers—boarded ships to return to the United States. Regular Army men like Allen, however, stayed on to carry out the American role as expressed in the armistice. He continued to attend courses for officers and even engaged in some field maneuvers. His only solace lay in a transfer back to a cavalry unit, but even there his feelings were ambivalent.

Increasingly, his letters revealed a homesick spirit. Apologizing for his neglect in writing, he told his mother, "It's not because I don't think of you all frequently and often wish that I was back with you again. However, I suppose I should be satisfied to be here now, where the whole army is having to serve. Am back to my old job now of commanding a troop of cavalry and it's not so bad, although I often yearn for the old days when I had a battalion of doughboys in the old A.E.F. days. I suppose those times will never come again, but it was great while it lasted. Everything seems sort of let down now, nothing seems worth while."

Although he sounded melancholy with nostalgia themes, Allen was beginning to gravitate to some of his old pleasures. "During my absence for a few days, they elected me captain of the cavalry polo team. . . . What with that job and sitting on an examining board am fairly busy. It's rather an awkward situation to run the team as most of them are far more experienced than I am. . . . An order has come from the War Dept. authorizing an American team from [American forces in Germany] to play polo in England during the month of June. . . . It would be a great trip as we'd play some of the best teams in England; but it's all more or less tentative. It seems quite lucky for a player with the little experience I've had." He noted that the polo team might be in several major tournaments that would have royalty in attendance, but he cautioned, "The whole scheme is uncertain and they may not want it too widely advertised in the states as Congress is set against these junketing trips."

He was also engaged on another athletic front. "The French and Belgian officers have asked me to join their fencing club, and I'm taking lessons from a very wonderful instructor. Am rather glad of the opportunity.

"On the whole, it is a particularly unsettled sort of life. You are here one minute and off the next. Europe has ceased to have any interest. I only wish you and Papa or all of you could come over while I'm here but things are so darned uncertain that one never can tell where you are for five minutes at a time. Please write and tell me the news. . . . You don't know how good it seems to see U.S. mail, especially from home."

A few weeks later, Allen was hospitalized for a dislocated shoulder and two cracked ribs that he suffered when his horse fell during a polo competition. Upon recovery, he returned to the sport and happily reported that his squad had beaten one fielded by the British Army of Occupation, 7 to 3. "I was lucky enough to have scored four goals for the American team." While on a visit to Koblenz, he wrote to his father that he had met another well-known cavalry officer, Jonathan "Skinny" Wainwright, who was the assistant G-3 of the U.S. Third Army. "Eagle Pass might even be a relief from Koblenz." Polo had now become a staple of Allen's life; he was playing three times a week against Britons. Sam Allen was on the verge of retiring, and his son condemned what he described as a "raw deal."

The Distinguished Service Cross possibility cropped up again in a letter, yet Allen complained, "Staff officers who never heard the shells crack, much less who never went over the top" were receiving decorations. For his part, he wrote letters to the mothers of the six officers in his command who had been killed.

The letters home suggest a sedate, dull life, but a number of tales suggest that Allen availed himself of the opportunities afforded through his equestrian skills. He partied enthusiastically with all comers. One tale of his escapades says that he arrived late for a soirée and missed the introductions with some of the British guests. He and a charming English officer hit it off, swapping stories while downing drinks into early morning. The next day, someone asked Allen if he knew who his convivial companion was. "No, who?" replied Allen. "The Prince of Wales," was the answer, and Allen could only manage, an "Oh, my God."

The story goes that the prince enjoyed Allen's company so much that he invited him to another gathering, but Allen demurred, feeling he had disgraced himself. The prince insisted and Allen attended—reverting to his usual bon vivant mode.

As the occupation dragged on, the desire of the French for vengeance and reparations threatened to set off open opposition from the defeated people. The United States, which had agreed only to name an observer, Pierrepont D. Noyes, to the Rhineland High Commission, ultimately sent a message to the State Department in which Noyes reported, "Two sinister purposes are developing with Allied occupation as basic: first determination to effect separation of the Rhine territory from Germany. Second, plan to use local disturbances or German dereliction in fulfillment of impossible reparations demand as an excuse for invading and occupying the Ruhr."

Even before Noyes dispatched his discouraging report, the Germans had shown marked reluctance to allow the victors the right to occupy the Fatherland. Allied soldiers advanced deeper into the conquered country to reaffirm their rights under the armistice. Allen informed his parents, "Just what the outcome will be 'quien sabe.' It feels familiar to get under a tin hat again." The contretemps subsided, however, and the Americans, like Allen, retreated to their former occupation turf.

In September 1919, Allen again briefly occupied a hospital bed—on this occasion for a "bum knee" and "blood poisoning" from his wound scars. He continued to bemoan his location. "Fraternization with the Germans is now permitted," but he pronounced himself unimpressed with "their overfed women and beer-fed men."

He became one of the stars for the American squad in a series of matches in England. The team scored a great triumph whipping the hosts

9 to 5 in London at the Foxhunters Ranelagh Club, and a newspaper account praised his horsemanship. The Roehampton Club's managing director sent a note to the U.S. military attaché at the American embassy in London expressing the pleasure of serving as competitive hosts for the American army polo team. "They played polo as it should be played and we all miss them greatly as their keenness and love for the game was delightful to see." In turn, the military attaché advised Gen. Henry Allen of the team's contribution toward "the Anglo-American Entente."

Allen himself met the king and queen at a tea tended by the opposition polo squads, and he witnessed the English Derby. Polo was slated to be one of the events in the 1920 Olympics, and the U.S. Army team won the right to represent the country. By the time Allen and his mates reached Antwerp for the Olympic Games, they had played an exhausting schedule. They were eliminated early, and as Allen explained, "The horses were very jaded."

The glow of the Olympics had faded by mid-September, and Allen renewed his duties as a soldier. He led two troops of cavalry as a personal escort for Foch and the French premier while they stayed in Koblenz. "After dragging them about and horsing around with the big bullfrogs, we made another forced march to catch up with the doughboys at maneuvers." Allen relished the war games. "I took a couple of husky lieuts. and two platoons and went on a real old-fashioned [trench] raid. We managed to break through their lines, grabbed off a half dozen prisoners and kept their whole front lines in a turmoil. All in all it seemed quite like old times.

"Last night I went into Cochem to lay out Monday's maneuvers. Stayed overnight in Cochem Castle where a couple of the "Rhineland Commission" officials are billeted. It's one of the most famous castles in Germany. You'd have laughed to have seen a couple of muddy Americans, dining in state in a wonderful old dining room called the Hall of the Knights, surrounded by the most wonderful tapestries and paintings. I slept in a room supposed to have been reserved for Mary Garden [a famous actress of the day] during the crown prince's house parties. Contrary to most castles, there was a good bath, which was the best part of the whole show."

Although he longed for home, he remarked that one advantage of staying in Europe was the depreciation of the German mark. "We can all live very reasonably and at the end of a couple of months will be able to regain all my savings that the Polo Trials ate up."

He spoke of his hopes for a promotion or at least being put near the head of the captain's list. And a friend had told him that he could probably get a berth at the cavalry school at Fort Riley because, as Allen wrote, "It seems that they are trying to develop some strong polo teams there and seem to think they need my services. That at least would be better than Border Service."

For the first time, he expressed some doubts about his career as a soldier. "It would not take much persuasion for me to resign if I could be sure of getting something on the outside, that might be better than being in the Army. I would like to be in a position to do more [for] you and Papa than I can on Army pay. As it does seem that I should be doing more for you than I am. At least there'll be no harm in looking around."

7 : Stateside Duty

Terry Allen returned to the United States in September 1920, having been promoted to the permanent rank of major in July and as a member of the 2d Division stationed at Camp Travis, Texas. In place of the often-mentioned Distinguished Service Cross, his valor in France had earned him a Silver Star and a citation. A DSC, however, went to the regimental commander, Col. E. M. Leary.

The year also saw the retirement of Samuel Allen as a colonel, after his final assignment as the commanding officer of the coast defenses at Manila and the Subic Bay in the Philippine Islands. Probably through family connections, he went to work for a New York–based shipping company and became a resident of Brooklyn.

Major Allen left the 2d Division for the 4th Cavalry Regiment in March 1922. Brigadier General E. M. Lewis officially notified him of his transfer with a highly complimentary letter: "During your comparatively short tour of duty with this division, you have displayed qualities most essential to officers in our service. Your excellent horsemanship, proficiency in the game of polo and true sportsmanship have been an example to our younger officers. . . ."

While still with the 2d Division, on 13 January 1922 Allen entered into a bizarre competition. He recalled, "I was summoned to the office of Col. [Philip] Corbusier. He said that both Tex Austin, a rodeo promoter, and the Cattlemen's Association president wanted to put on a riding contest between a cowboy and a cavalryman. I said it sounded like an interesting idea.

"'Who will represent the Army?' I asked.

"'You will,' the colonel replied, adding quickly, 'We expect you to win.'

"That took the wind out of my sails for a minute," said Allen. "But I knew of course that I'd ride the race. It was a challenge worthy of any horseman."

The contest called for a three-hundred-mile trip over a five-day period, using a single horse. Allen and the cowboy, Key Dunne—a one-time wagon boss and celebrated figure on the range—started from a different location. Allen's route was from Dallas to Waco to Temple to Austin to the remount station in San Antonio. Dunne would saddle up at Fort Worth and from there travel to Waco to Temple to Austin to the finishing point in San Antonio. The race generated intense interest, capitalizing on the deep rivalry between the two main horse-borne groups. Adherents bet large sums of money. Newspapers played up the story with Allen being described as "a Brooklyn man." The *Brooklyn Eagle* actually covered the event.

Allen said, "I was allowed to choose any mount from our regular Army stable. I chose a big black horse named Coronado who was a combination of quarter horse and thoroughbred, one of the finest breeding combinations. The quarter horse is quick, very fast for a short distance, and very trainable; the thoroughbred has magnificent speed and stamina."

He noted that he and Dunne were roughly the same size but "I've always thought I had an edge because Sergeant Linden, the man who had charge of Coronado, was the best horseman I've ever known."

Large crowds, rooting for their favorites and hoping to cash in on wagers, packed the streets for the start on a Friday morning. Allen dressed in a cavalryman's uniform, stiff-brimmed hat, regulation shirt and breeches, polished leather boots, and plain leather gloves, and he used an army issue saddle. He was clearly outshone in appearance by Dunne, who sported a bright plaid shirt and kerchief, fine chaps, a Stetson hat, fancy boots, and used a Western saddle and bridle trimmed with silver. Dunne's choice of steed was a small Texas mustang.

The major set a brisk pace once he left his starting point in front of the Adolphus Hotel, racking up 51.9 miles before he and Coronado bedded down for the night. Dunne chose a more leisurely pace and fell behind. Along the way, the inhabitants of small towns turned out to shout encouragement. On Saturday, during the second lap, Allen halted at a restaurant for a breakfast of ham and eggs. Unaware of the identity of his customer, the proprietor, who was accustomed to serving army men traveling cross-country, stopped to chat about the famous race between the cowboy and the soldier. According to Allen, he drawled, "Course, Major Allen don't have a chance to beat Key Dunne. That cowboy will wear out the Army officer; he's too strong for him. That Army horse hasn't a chance to stick it out with a mustang in a 300-mile race."

Allen said he replied, "I can't say as to the outcome of the race yet, but I'm Major Allen and I'm out in front at the present time and still in good condition. Up to the present, the joke is on you so hurry with the ham and eggs."

Taken aback, the restaurant owner responded, "The joke is not only on me, but the ham and eggs as well. So go to it. Good luck and more power to you!"

On Sunday, a torrential downpour doused the riders. Allen recalled, "I had huddled down in the saddle all day, cold, wet and miserable. Coronado slid and splashed through mud and water on roads that for the most part were unpaved. During the afternoon, after the sun began to shine, we rode by a small house where a Mexican woman was preparing to wash. Several kettles and tubs of hot water were waiting for her washboard when I rode up and stopped. I offered her three dollars for the hot water and some rags to rub my horse down and she accepted with alacrity. After giving Coronado that good hot bath and rubdown, I got back into the saddle and my horse pranced down the muddy road with the energy and enthusiasm of a young colt. I think it was the best bargain I ever made."

Contemporary accounts also credit Allen with an act of sportsmanship. Dunne had run into a problem in obtaining hay for his horse. When Allen heard of the problem, he arranged for fodder to be shipped to the cowboy by automobile.

Although Dunne began to make up time, Allen, having husbanded Coronado's strength, let the big black horse out on the final day and beat his opponent by seven hours. After the judges checked the condition of the two mounts, he was officially declared the victor. Allen modestly shrugged off praise, insisting he profited because of "luck and Sgt. Linden's training of Coronado."

For a brief sojourn, Allen moved to Fort McIntosh, Texas, and then he was posted to the 61st Cavalry Division, a reserve organization in New York City. The 61st apparently represented an attempt to plant the cavalry guidon in an area where it might draw support from the horsey set around the city. Its headquarters eventually was placed in a suite in a downtown office building. The assignment gave Allen an opportunity to be near his beloved parents. It could hardly be considered a career move, to shunt oneself off to what essentially was a backwater of the army, even if located in New York City. But the army was now entering a long period of low appropriations, extremely slow ascent up the ladders of command, and a general decline in prestige among Americans—who were hurling themselves into the frenzy of the 1920s, a stock market out of control, and in some circles a flapper society. For Allen, who took up residence at the Army and Navy Club in Manhattan, the duty allowed him to indulge himself in polo and partying.

In January of 1924, Allen attended the six-month advanced course at the Fort Riley Cavalry School in Kansas. The U.S. Army steadfastly supported horse-borne forces despite World War I's demonstration of their obsolescence, although a small number of officers had begun to concentrate on mechanized troops. In his faith in the traditional cavalry, Allen was hardly a maverick. George S. Patton Jr., who had led tanks during World War I, still strode about in the breeches of a horseman. Any hopes the ambitious Patton harbored for a future in armor were dashed when the nascent Tank Corps—instead of achieving independence—became a fief of the infantry. Patton, like Allen, had returned to the cavalry. More adventurous souls, for example followers of the discredited Gen. Billy Mitchell, pursued opportunities in the Air Corps.

In 1924 Allen also took what seemed like a more serious step toward a higher responsibility, entering the Command and General Staff School at Fort Leavenworth, Kansas. One of his fellow students supposedly grumped, "Why in the hell are we training cavalry officers in peacetime when they won't use them in wartime." Allen, drawing upon his own experience, is reported to have snapped, "Because they make the best infantry-division commanders in wartime." However, while this institution was a prerequisite for any officer thinking of his future in the army, Allen approached it with a breathtaking insouciance. On his very first day at the school, Allen brushed off a tactical problem: "It was all full of silly questions like, 'What are the enemy's intentions?' I wrote, 'The enemy didn't tell me' and beat it. I was already five minutes late for my tennis date [with the daughter of a senior officer]."

His attitude on the first day led the head of the school to declare Allen the most indifferent student ever enrolled. At the end of the two-year

session, Allen graduated 221st out of the 241 in his class. The top grades
went to a 1915 West Point alumnus who had never commanded troops
in the field, Dwight D. Eisenhower.

On 12 January, while Terry was playing hard and studying lightly at
the Command and General Staff School, Samuel Allen finished a day of
work and headed for his home. As he started up the walk at 231 Gates
Avenue, he collapsed and died of a heart attack while his wife watched
his approach through a window—he was sixty-eight years old. The family arranged for burial at Arlington National Cemetery after a Catholic
mass. During the period Terry was at the Command and General Staff
School, he frequently visited New York City, and he made the *New York
Times* twice. Once was on 11 July 1925, when the society page reported
that Mr. and Mrs. John A. Manning of Loudonville, New York announced
the engagement of their daughter, Miss Edith Manning, to Maj. Terry de
la Mesa Allen of the 61st Cavalry. The notice said that the prospective
groom "was in the class of 1912 at West Point," delicately skirting the fact
that he had been dismissed, and it concluded with "The wedding will take
place next Spring." It did not.

How long the engagement lasted is uncertain, but in 1926 the *Times*
carried a short news item with the headline, "AIDS ARMY MAJOR WHO
LED HIM 'OVER THE TOP.'" Allen, while living at the Army and Navy
Club, had appeared in traffic court on the charge of driving an automobile without carrying his identification card. There was a second
charge, that of disorderly conduct charged by a traffic cop who had arrested Allen. The genesis of the incident was a fender bender with another vehicle at Fifth Avenue and Sixty-seventh Street after which the
other driver pursued Allen through Central Park until a patrolman
halted both vehicles at Sixty-fifth Street. Said the *Times*, "The disorderly
conduct, according to the testimony, was based on the Major's having expressed his opinion of the arresting officer in the police station."

In court, Allen pleaded guilty on both charges and was fined five dollars for his remarks in the police station. However, he protested to the
magistrate over his treatment. He claimed the cops had not permitted
him to telephone friends to raise five hundred dollars bail and insisted
he was a reliable individual.

The judge inquired how the accused could prove his identity. "Major
Allen," the *Times* reported, "hesitated and then Patrolman [Henry]
Bauer who happened to be in the courtroom, spoke up. 'I can vouch for
him,' said Bauer. 'He led me over the top many times. He always brought

me back safely, too.'" Bauer had been a private in the AEF, and the magistrate promptly suspended sentence.

Armed with his diploma from the Command and General Staff School, Allen joined the 7th Cavalry, George Armstrong Custer's organization at Fort Bliss, El Paso. In an era that predated iconoclastic history, the fiction of Custer's bravery, rather than the fact of his foolhardy bloodthirstiness, gripped Allen. He celebrated the fallen at Little Bighorn. "Custer didn't ask what price bookies were laying, did he?" Allen said to A. J. Liebling. "He fought, didn't he? And he got killed, and after he got killed Congress had to buy the cavalry repeating rifles. And the cavalry cleaned out the Indians, and Custer is up in heaven thumbing his nose at those damn Indians now."

The colonel in command of the 7th Cavalry was a legendary figure with a penchant for binges. On more than one occasion, Allen, as executive officer, was obliged to remove the elderly officer from the scene of what could have developed into an embarrassment for the cavalry. Allen later admitted, however, that sometimes he entered into the spirit of the colonel's revels.

The years at Fort Bliss provided several turning points in Allen's life and career. Anita Whelan—born in Mexico, but an American citizen who grew up in El Paso—became acquainted with Allen during this period. "I met him through Mary Frances Robinson who would later become his wife. Mary Frances and I had been childhood friends, grew up together and were in the same circle in our late teens. A lot of our social life after graduating from high school and college was centered around Ft. Bliss. The people there were very close to the civilians in El Paso and they encouraged their young lieutenants to meet girls from El Paso.

"During the 1920s before the stock market crash [1929] the girls in our circle were dating and socializing with the officers of Fort Bliss. It was peacetime and Ft. Bliss offered more fun than civilian places. We had dates there every week and they'd have dances too. If you didn't have a date there you felt out of it. About 20 girls or so were very privileged at Ft. Bliss. They had special riding classes to teach us, we were allowed to swim in their pool, entertained in the homes of the commanding general and the colonels of the 1st Cavalry Division. We went to all of their functions and parties, a wonderful time for us.

"The 82d Field Artillery was also there and they too had their bachelors. We liked the cavalry better. They seemed to be more social, they played polo and were sort of the jet set of the Army at that time. [Although Prohibition had dried up many parts of the country, El Paso had a ready source of liquor from across its border with Mexico.]

"Terry Allen was known as somewhat rambunctious, very colorful, a great polo player, dynamic, wonderful personality and everybody loved him. He was a very eligible bachelor when he first came to El Paso and had other girls before he met Mary Frances. He wasn't handsome, not beautiful, not very tall but he had an interesting face."

"Tall, stately, typically old Army," was how a woman who had been an army brat herself described Mary Frances during her later years. When Allen met her, Mary Frances Robinson was beautiful and young, nearly twenty years his junior. William Robinson, her father, had been a popular mayor of the city, but when Mary Fran—as her familiars referred to her—was only about three, Robinson had left a church mass to attend a fire raging in his city. When he tried to aid a trapped firefighter, the wall of the building toppled over, killing him. She was educated at the El Paso School for Girls and the Bronson School in New York. With her family, in the tradition of the times she had made an extended tour of Europe. And, she was an accomplished horsewoman who had been featured in local society pages.

The courtship lasted for well over a year before Mary Frances and Terry Allen were wed in 1928 at El Paso's Saint Patrick's Cathedral. She was attended by a bevy of formally attired bridesmaids. A platoon of uniformed officers waited on Allen, forming an archway of sabers as the couple exited the church. They honeymooned in Santa Fe. A year later, the marriage produced a son, Terry junior. At the time, the army still had minor problems with bandits from across the border, and the cavalry often patrolled the frontier at various points. According to Liebling, while Allen was celebrating the birth of his son, he was summoned to headquarters and ordered to entrain his squadron for a place where it would start a sustained march toward a suspected trouble spot. He directed subordinates to get the troopers and horses aboard the train while he returned for further festivities in honor of Terry junior's appearance. After two more hours of fun, Allen caught another troop train and, with his knowledge of the territory, disregarded his superior's instructions of a route to follow and instead followed a shortcut. He covered himself with a wire that stated, "Circumstances make it necessary to disregard your orders." Allen arrived at the designated place in time to prevent a possible Columbus-style raid. The State Department congratulated the corps-area command for Allen's preventive action.

While Mary Fran was familiar with the military ambiance, their personas were markedly different. In contrast to her husband with his rough-hewn, gregarious style, she was the epitome of a well-bred Texas belle, always showing up in public carefully dressed and groomed. In public, people regarded her as "reserved" in the presence of her husband. However, an acquaintance recalled that "when he got carried away and let out a 'hell' or 'damn,' she would remind him to tone down his language—and he did."

Anita Whelan remembered a typical manifestation of the contrast between husband and wife: "Terry had met many interesting people through polo and he was friendly with Will Rogers [the famous humorist and performer of the 1920s and 1930s]. Rogers came to El Paso while on a tour and we went to see him at Liberty Hall. He looked up Terry and said he wanted to play polo and Terry agreed to arrange a game.

"The game was a comedy. Rogers used a western saddle which was strange to real polo players and he wasn't very good at the game. Terry invited a number of people to come to the Allens' quarters at Fort Bliss after the game. Mary Fran was delayed a bit and Terry reached their home first. He started to get things ready for drinks and he couldn't find the right kind of glasses. Mary Fran arrived and was horrified to see him serving drinks in jelly glasses." In fact, Mary Fran would often remark about her need to hurry home and prepare for guests before her husband would bring out the jelly glasses.

Allen continued to play polo and tennis while in command of his cavalry unit. A newspaper account described a polo match of his Fort Oglethorpe squad against a Fort McPherson team. The report mentioned "the brilliant shooting of Major Allen who scored 6 times in a 15–7 win" after spotting the Fort McPherson team three goals.

Far more important, in that same year of 1931 he enrolled in the advanced course of the Infantry School at Fort Benning, Georgia. According to Robert W. Porter, U.S.M.A. 1930, who would serve with Allen in the cavalry and later be his intelligence officer, the efficiency report from the head of the academic board at the Leavenworth Command and General Staff School had badly tarnished Allen with negative comments. It stated, "Allen has a brilliant mind, but I would not give him a command in time of war. He will not make a good staff officer." Porter claimed that when this assessment hit the chief of cavalry's office, a friend warned Allen that his future was at risk. He would be denied an opportunity to command troops. Desperate to make amends, Allen accepted a position as cavalry instructor at the Fort Benning Infantry School.

The assistant director, and guiding spirit of the institution, was Lt. Col. George C. Marshall—who had served as Pershing's chief of operations with the AEF in France. In response to a question from Marshall's biographer Forrest C. Pogue in 1964, Allen said that Marshall was "greatly interested in the athletic schedules there, including the Officers, Polo Tournaments and the Enlisted Men's Baseball Schedules. When I reported to him . . . he wanted to know if I came there to work or to play polo. I said to him that I hoped to do both."

Given an opportunity to demonstrate his understanding of strategy and tactics rather than a command of abstract textbook or field-manual information, Allen dazzled Marshall. In the efficiency report covering the period of 1 September 1931 to 1 June 1932, Marshall personally rated Allen as "superior" in physical activity, endurance, tact, judgment, leadership, and consideration, as well as in sensibility dealing with others, initiative, and "force in carrying out with energy and resolution what is believed reasonable, right or duty." He wrote "excellent" for the category of intelligence. The one less-than-outstanding grade, a "satisfactory" was his rating of Allen's "military bearing and neatness."

Marshall described Allen as "highly qualified for the war college" and said that he "exercised excellent influence in his class." Marshall's concluding statement said, "By training, experience and temperament, highly qualified as a leader . . . qualified as of now as commanding officer of a regiment and in wartime a division."

The future chief of staff of the U.S. Army did more than write a highly complimentary efficiency report on Terry Allen. He also inscribed him in his small black notebook, a ledger in which Marshall carefully noted those officers he deemed held special promise. Besides Allen, some other noteworthy entries were Eisenhower, Patton, and Bradley.

Marshall's fondness for Allen was once explained by biographer Pogue as a weakness for a "swashbuckler." While it is readily understandable that Marshall might be impressed by a charismatic officer like Allen, it should also be noted that Marshall had an aversion for heavy drinkers. In one instance, an officer was denied promotion because Marshall confused his name with that of a man known for high alcoholic intake. In another instance, he cautioned a corps commander to investigate gossip about a senior officer drinking heavily. How much Allen imbibed is questionable, but obviously he was discrete enough not to have given Marshall any anxiety about this aspect of his personality. Apart from what he demonstrated at Fort Benning, Allen also bore a reputation as a solid infantry commander during World War I, and Marshall had been in a position to be aware of his achievements in France.

In late 1932, Allen was back at his post with the 7th Cavalry at Fort Bliss. In 1927, he had borrowed money to invest in a business with a New Yorker named Howard Okie who subsequently surfaced for a period in Washington, D.C. Okie apparently absconded, and Allen had become increasingly desperate trying to locate him. Unsuccessful in finding Okie, Allen had enlisted his mother who now lived in Washington to see if she might find him through an Okie parent. The best she could furnish was an address for Okie's brother who worked for the New York Steam Corporation in Manhattan.

Allen wrote to the brother with the "hope you will not misunderstand my motive . . . and that you will accept this letter in the spirit in which it is written.

"I am anxious to secure some information concerning . . . Howard. Have been unable to get in touch with him through any of his former addresses, for the past two years. . . . Please do not consider this letter of mine as being anything in the nature of a hold-up. Am only doing this as a last resort, and would not do so even now if it were not absolutely necessary for my own self-protection."

Allen went on to say that as a result of his involvement with Howard, "he incurred a considerable indebtedness, part of which included funds expended for [Howard's] personal needs and part of which included money tied up with him in a business way."

Noting that he had been unable to contact the missing man he continued, ". . . this is a matter which is highly embarrassing to me. It happens that my own personal obligations have considerably increased since I incurred this indebtedness"—referring to his marriage and child. "If such were not case I would not think of subjecting myself to the embarrassment of presenting this matter to you. As you may know our pay and allowances in the Army have been considerably decreased this year, whereas our expenses involving changes of station, upkeep, etc., have not decreased.

"I am heavily in debt and am slowly getting on my feet, and in the meantime this state of affairs has not made matters any easier for my family. It happens that when debts are incurred by an Army Officer, these obligations have to be met.

"Up to now I have kept my credit good. But I find it increasingly difficult to carry the load caused by incurring this indebtedness. And it is vitally important to me to preserve my standing in the Service. If that were not endangered, I assure you this letter would never have been written."

In his petition to R. H. Okie, Allen mentioned a two hundred dollar payment that Okie's mother had made on behalf of her son; he explained that after the departure of Howard for New York, the entire sum was used "to pay expenses, etc. incurred by Howard, probably which he does not remember or even knew of at the time, and which I did not care to list [in an enclosed statement detailing the money spent]."

A week later, Allen received a crushing response from R. H. Okie: "It was with a great deal of regret that I learned of your financial dealings with Howard and I appreciate very much the help you gave him. Howard, from his childhood, was always very irresponsible and was always getting into one scrape after another and while he never did any intentional wrong, he caused embarrassment to many including his family."

R. H. Okie explained that the family was struggling to support itself and any impression Howard gave of a wealthy family was erroneous. "Mother's sole income was from a small trust, all of which went to Howard upon her death. Howard, upon receiving his monthly check from the trust, immediately spent it for liquor and consequently his debts mounted considerably.

"I had not seen Howard for about a year until last week when I was called on the phone by his landlady in whose apartment he had a room, telling me he was very ill. I went right up but was too late—he had died in the meantime. His death was induced by complications brought on by drink. His sole beneficiary of his estate was his landlady, a Mrs. McKinstry of 542 W. 112th Street, N.Y.C. [a Harlem neighborhood], which consisted of a $1,500 life insurance policy assigned by him to her which he had taken out a few months ago for her to pay his funeral expenses and to repay her for money she had paid out to his creditors. I understand this is all eaten up.

"It is a pitiable situation but it looks as tho your loss must be credited to a misplaced faith in poor Howard."

Reading between the lines it seems fairly clear that the deceased had been a drinking companion of Allen and the soldier had indeed made a serious mistake in investing with him. The piled-up debts would bedevil Allen for nearly twenty years.

A modest improvement in his fortunes followed the bad news. With the imprimatur of Marshall upon him, in August 1934 Allen entered the Army War College in Washington, D.C., and together with about eighty colleagues graduated the next June. During this period at Fort Humphreys, his group studied topics such as army school systems compared with those of other nations, plans of the War Department for processing enlisted personnel in a general mobilization, and intelligence accounts on the European situation.

Allen's group also conducted a paper war game that dealt with a possible second World War. The assumption was based on a conflict that pitted Nazi Germany, Austria, Hungary, and Japan against France, Italy (the study group posited a coup that overthrew Mussolini), Great Britain, and eventually the United States. The Germans and their associates, it was said, would instantly revert to unrestricted submarine and air raids. It is interesting to note that the officers foresaw a pact between Germany and Japan, which indeed came to pass. However, the crystal ball clouded over when it came to the Soviet Union, which in this exercise was a neutral.

The estimates of the relative military strengths also were wildly inaccurate, with the French being given credit for a far more formidable army and air force than would actually enter World War II four years later. To be sure, the Germans had only recently renounced the disarmament imposed after World War I and begun their intense mobilization. However, the study did make an effort to present the economic and political strengths and weaknesses of the various countries: The treatise they produced was replete with statistics and tables. Allen also drafted a report on the political objectives of Austria and their relationship to pertinent international treaties.

With reference to the United States, the scholars analyzed psychological aspects of American participation: "Affront to national dignity is no longer felt to be sufficient cause for war. Public support can be won only by convincing people they will benefit. . . . The American public is essentially selfish, unaccustomed to making sacrifices or enduring hardships except for immediate personal gain." For that reason it would be necessary to have conscription.

The cynicism of Americans, the study observed, was apparently fostered by the Depression, which caused a loss of faith in traditions and ideals. The western states were supposedly well aware of an influx of Japanese immigrants and cognizant of the "Yellow Peril."

Allen also submitted a paper concerning the "Adequacy of the present system of formulating, publishing and issuing combat orders in a war of movement." His survey went under the assumption that "the present trend towards motorization and mechanization will result in making our next war a war of movement, determining whether our present system of formulating, publishing and issuing combat orders can be expected to prove adequate in such a war," along with recommendations that might be advisable for changes in current doctrine.

One of his conclusions was "the necessity for brief, clear and concise combat orders." While accepting the standard form of five-paragraph field orders, Allen declared, "The padding of the paragraphs is a matter of common error." He then outlined the habitual mistakes made: inclusion of previously accrued information, too much detail, and micromanagement (although that term had yet to be invented). "How to accomplish the mission is an ingredient of the prerogatives of the subordinate commanders." The brevity of Allen's field orders was often remarked upon subsequently during World War II. He also argued that the increased mechanization placed a premium on "the principle of surprise." That too would guide him in the future.

Two months after he completed his term at the Army War College and after fifteen years in grade, he pinned on the silver leaf of a lieutenant colonel. In a continuing demonstration of the army's obduracy, he received the post of instructor at the Fort Riley Cavalry School, where the horse remained the vehicle of choice.

Polo remained high on his priorities, but here he also demonstrated his insight into perfection of tactics. His regimental polo team surprised the experts by reaching the finals of an army tournament in Texas. It was assumed the Allen squad would fall before the better competition. But for a week prior to the critical match, Allen directed his players to practice with the polo goalposts set only a yard and a half apart instead of the standard eight yards. In the actual match, his men had only eight chances to score; and on every occasion, they knocked the ball through for a goal. The opponents—with their superior skills, strength, and ponies—had forty shots on the goal and scored only seven times.

During his service at installations between the wars, Allen secured his reputation as an officer who looked out for his men. Whereas his father had refused to have a telephone in his quarters on grounds he did not want his juniors to bother him, Terry Allen's phone must have rung frequently. He had established a policy that those in his command should not languish in civilian jails for minor crimes committed off post. Consequently, he was often awakened at night with word of a soldier who had been arrested. "My men never keep me waiting," he would say. "I won't make my men wait for me." He had extended the code of the cavalry that stressed "first take care of the horses" to include the soldiers who served under him.

He remained, however, adamant in his attitude toward what he considered information of no practical value. While at Fort Riley, the *Cavalry Journal* asked him to review a West Point textbook on ordnance and gunnery, the very subject that had cost him whatever hope he had for graduation from that institution. He wrote that the material at hand was less intelligible and worth less than an earlier manual. "All you want to know about guns is how to kill people with them and that book was all full of mathematics beyond calculus."

Allen's superior with the 7th Cavalry, Lt. Col. W. H. Gordon, wrote a glowing efficiency report describing his Regimental S-3 (operations officer) as "excellent" in performance of his prescribed assignment, "superior in physical action, endurance, initiative, intelligence." He was "excellent" in "tact, force, judgment, and leadership," but only "satisfactory" in "military bearing and neatness." At Fort Riley, Allen served also as chief of the Department of Weapons and Material; he contributed heavily to a manual for cavalrymen produced there.

It was at Fort Riley that Porter, a recent graduate of the U.S.M.A., first met Allen. "He was very busy. We were rewriting a lot of manuals because armor instructions were beginning to be needed for the officers going to the armor force. He was a perfectionist in working on manuals. He would call you up at 2:00 or 3:00 in the morning. He had been working at home, and read a sentence to you over the telephone to see whether you understood it. Frank Merrill, who went on to lead Merrill's Marauders, had been in the regular class with me and he was the other man who Terry would call up in the middle of the night. Frank used to get so mad that the next morning he would be fit to be tied. He would come in and ask me if I had been called and I would say, 'Yes,' and he would say, 'What did you tell that damn Terry?' I would say, 'I just would tell him whether I understood it or not and I would hang up and go to sleep.' He said, 'I couldn't get back to sleep because of the stupid questions.'

"Allen was director of the Weapons Department. He did a very fine job but anything he took on to do, whether it was to write a simple exercise for field firing or anything like that, he thought that was number one priority. He used everybody who was in his department to help. He got them in, talked to them about his project and tried things on for size.

You had to do your work in addition to being his consultant. I liked Allen a great deal. He was a very sensitive person.

"He and Patton were arguing all the time. They didn't seem to agree on much of anything and yet they did. But it was their approach to things. Patton was inclined to be more direct and very abrupt. Terry tried to cajole people into doing things by saying, 'This is the way we ought to do it. Don't you think so?' Patton said, 'Do it!' and that was the difference. My office was right in back of theirs. I would hear these violent arguments. Suddenly both of them would appear and they would say, 'Which one of us do you think is right?'"As director of instruction, Patton technically was Allen's boss. Said Porter, "I would listen to their argument. Then Patton would say to me, 'All right, in 10 minutes you come and tell me what you think of what we just said.' And Terry would say, 'After you get through with Patton, come in and see me.'

"I would weasel out. I would say, 'I'm just a young lieutenant. I have no way of settling this. If you would take your two ideas and put them together you would have the perfect solution. Normally that was the way the thing would come out. But it was curious the way they would argue back and forth. Patton was quite a disciplinarian and he had a wonderful mind, but he was very conventional too.

"Terry was impulsive and he had a brilliant mind; suddenly a solution would appear to him and the logical steps of how he got to that solution were pretty difficult sometimes to construct. He had been at Bliss before he came to Riley. He had been on a field exercise where there would be one squadron against another. He commanded a squadron. They would be out on a maneuver that was supposed to last two or three days. They had to be careful what they did with Terry and his squadron because he would have the maneuver finished in about eight hours. . . . If they put Terry on reserve, on one side of the maneuver, he would analyze what was going on, and the first you know there would be an infiltration and the key terrain would be in Allen's squadron's hands long before the problem planned for them to get there. He was a disruptive force to the tacticians for that reason. Later, I was his G-2 [intelligence officer] in the 1st Infantry Division and that was his way of dealing with the Germans too."

The U.S. military continued to rely heavily on the potential of horse-borne troops. Other major powers in the world also seemed quite dependent upon cavalry, according to a 1938 paper by Maj. Gen. John K. Herr, the U.S. chief of cavalry. He conceded an increasing mixture of horse cavalry with mechanized forces among foreign powers. (Not until 1940, did the U.S. Army establish armor as a separate branch.) The British, for example, fielded 5 regiments on horseback and 17 mechanized regiments. France had 41 equine-driven regiments and 6 mechanized ones but planned to add another employing armored cars. With the invasion by Germany but a year away, Poland expected to face the panzers of the Third Reich with only mounted troopers. In the Soviet Union, out of 112 regiments, 90 were composed of horsemen. According to Herr's intelligence, Japan had no armored contingent, but had 25 traditional cavalry regiments.

Considering Japan's deployment of tanks within a few years, Herr's information is questionable. Far more dubious was his advocacy of a role for the soldier on horseback: "In general it may be said that horse cavalry has greater tactical mobility and is better adapted to a self-contained and sustained action but has not a strategic mobility or tactical mobility on favorable ground for mechanized cavalry. [Nor does it have] the same volume of firepower."

He theorized on the potential to exploit the pursuit of a defeated foe—as Allen had at the close of World War I. "With the air, the mechanized and horse cavalry combining in relentless pursuit, we envision a real victory of destruction. The beaten enemy, struck successively by air, motor and horse will have little chance to reorganize."

Herr called for an increase in the mechanized component of the U.S. cavalry; but, in recommending four cavalry divisions, he suggested that only one be composed of motorized vehicles. He concluded that any new wars would be "wars of movement in the U.S., South America or elsewhere," and the idea of another "Western Front" (à la World War I) be discarded because of "well nigh impregnable defense systems," meaning the French Maginot line and the German Siegfried line.

Terry Allen also still believed enough in his branch to draft a memorandum spelling out ways to enhance its value. For a war strength cavalry troop, he argued for an allotment of three squads with six machine guns to supplement three platoons of riflemen. Allen said his proposed table of organization provided the advantage of close supporting fire, but he admitted that the presence of led animals (bearing the machine guns) reduced mobility. To lessen the drag on a cavalry unit so equipped, he suggested development of a new-model, light machine gun weighing between twenty-two and twenty-six pounds, with a tripod mount capable of supporting antiaircraft fire. He had not forgotten how German planes bedeviled his battalion during World War I. Allen and others who kept the cavalry faith were not so foolish as to think in terms of a thundering-hooves charge. Instead, they theorized that horses could transport soldiers over terrain inimical to wheels, and at the battle scene the men would fight dragoon style, dismounted, which would be the only possible way to deploy machine guns.

Although Allen built a reputation as a field officer limited at best to tactical theory, and myopic as he was to the demise of horse-borne troops as a weapon of war, on a number of occasions he demonstrated an understanding and insight into wider military matters such as ordnance, discipline, and leadership. For example, his 1939 memorandum dealing with the cavalry and its firepower analyzed machine guns in terms of bipods and tripods, gun barrels, the ammunition loads suitable, and the crews. He also evaluated the newly adopted M1 rifle and gave it high marks. He included remarks on the best tactics for deployment of cavalry in wooded areas, emphasizing the necessity for accurate and extensive reconnaissance.

While at Fort Riley, Allen sent a copy of the cavalry manual that he had partially authored as well as his paper on "Methods of Combat for Cavalry" to Marshall, who was then in command of the 5th Brigade of the 3d Infantry Division, stationed at Vancouver Barracks, Washington. Allen's letter accompanying his text said, "It has always seemed to me the service schools neglect instruction in methods of execution. It seems that instruction in methods of execution is equally as important as instruction in making tactical decisions. . . . By debunking the mystery connected with combat, by avoiding generalities and by stressing the needs of simplicity, I believe we have evolved a text, the intelligent study of which will enable any smart corporal to lead a squadron in battle. As a matter of fact, this *same* text is now being used for N.C.O. Classes, Regular Classes, National Guard and Reserve Classes, Extension Courses and as a reference by cavalry units. . . . I trust I may not seem troublesome in asking for your opinion on our innovation in school instruction. As a matter of fact, I was actuated largely by what I learned at Benning in evolving the changes that we introduced here."

Marshall responded, "I am very much interested in glancing over what you had produced for the cavalry along this line. The procedure of the presentation impresses me very favorably because I have come to believe that one of the most important considerations for all military training is brevity in the manuals, coupled with expeditious methods for accomplishing the training. . . . I am very glad to hear from you, as I am always much interested in your military progress. Give my warmest regards to Mrs. Allen, in which Mrs. Marshall would join me if she were present at this dictation."

Certainly, Allen flattered the senior officer who had promoted his standing with the glowing efficiency report for his term at the Fort Benning Infantry School. But there was no way that at this point Allen could have perceived how valuable Marshall might prove to his career. The future head of the army was only a brigade commander, and as a graduate of Virginia Military Institute—rather than West Point—not a particularly promising star upon which to wish. And during his thirty-nine years in uniform, Allen never quite stooped to abject sycophancy.

Although the odds had seemed against it, George C. Marshall—who had been in Washington, D.C., as deputy chief of staff—ascended to four-star rank as U.S. Army chief of staff on 1 September 1939, the very day Adolf Hitler sent his troops over the Polish border. Marshall, chosen by President Franklin D. Roosevelt, probably on the advice of his counselor, Harry Hopkins, vaulted over several senior contenders and began a major project in building up both the army and its semiautonomous air corps.

Shortly after Marshall pinned on his fourth star, Allen chose two horses from the stock at Fort Riley and arranged for them to be shipped to Washington for the chief of staff's use. Marshall pronounced himself "delighted with the animals." Writing to his predecessor, Gen. Malin Craig, Marshall noted, "Fifteen minutes after I leave the office I am in riding clothes and on a horse and have been getting in an hour's riding practically every day. . . . The riding has done me a world of good and I am able to keep things in focus and shed almost all worries."

Allen's sometimes-friendly rival, George S. Patton Jr., surpassed him when it came to currying favor with Marshall. In July 1939, he urged the then–deputy chief of staff on his arrival in Washington, D.C., to live with him. A grateful Marshall responded, "I have just found your letter . . . with its hospitable invitation for me to 'batch' with you while I am getting my house established. . . . I will be glad to accept. . . . You are very kind to invite me."

An exuberant Patton wrote to his wife at their permanent home in Massachusetts, "I have just consummated a pretty snappy move. Gen. George C. Marshall is going to live at our house!!! He and I are batching it. I think that once I can get my natural charm working I won't need any letters from John J. P[ershing] or anyone else. Of course it may cramp my style a little about going out but there are compensations."

In February 1940, Marshall passed along his good impression of Allen to his chief of infantry, Maj. Gen. George A Lynch: "He [referring to another officer], Terry Allen and one or two others, there are very few of them, are of that unusual type who enthuse all of their subordinates to carry through almost impossible tasks."

The death knell for the cavalry—whether mounted or as dragoons—sounded in the spring of 1940 during maneuvers held by the Third Army in Georgia and Louisiana. Patton had been appointed as an umpire during these war games, and he had a ringside seat when an improvised armored division smashed horse cavalry forces. The army's top staff grasped the implications of the confrontation of equine soldiers and motorized wheels and tracks. Brigadier General Adna Chaffee was named to head up the I Armored Corps. Patton, among the converts to armor, contacted Chaffee, and Chaffee quickly recruited him for the 2d Armored Division mobilized at Fort Benning.

Even after the Nazi blitzkrieg, which was propelled by tanks, had rolled through Poland, driven through the low countries and France to the edge of the English Channel, and defeated the homebred cavalry by armor less than a month earlier (in July 1940), Fort Bliss conducted a seventeen-day course for reserve officers assigned to the cavalry. The troopers were to devote more than thirty hours to horsemanship: "basic equitation, basic schooling, jumping low obstacles, cross-country training." Another twenty-seven hours would be spent on "horsemastership": care, grooming, shoeing, stable management, and disease prevention. Instruction in cavalry techniques would teach extended order drill and how to approach and attack a target. At least the material on map and photo interpretation and also on training with light machine guns and other weapons would be useful if they were assigned to other kinds of units. But even here, the bias toward a future on horseback was evident, because they would practice more with the .45-caliber pistol than with the M1 rifle, the weapon for infantrymen.

The events in Europe demanded a swift expansion of U.S. forces, including an increase in general officers. In September 1940, Marshall named two new brigadier generals, and the Senate confirmed the appointments a day later. One was Col. George S. Patton Jr., who at the time commanded an armored brigade at Fort Benning, Georgia. The second was Terry Allen, who was at Fort Bliss with the 7th Cavalry. His selection elicited astonishment and rancor from those who considered him an undisciplined lightweight. Allen not only was the first general from the West Point class with which he failed to graduate, but also he leaped over the heads of more than nine hundred senior men. A rumor held that only Allen's promotion enabled him to escape disciplinary punishment for some infraction of the rules. Marshall was well aware of resentment toward Allen. A letter to retired Maj. Gen. Frank McCoy said, "I learned indirectly from Mr. Stimson [Henry L., Secretary of War], that you had done a great deal in securing his full acceptance of the list of 'makes' [promotions] submitted the other day. It might interest you to know that my own people have been pressing me this morning to scratch off Terry Allen's name because of the depressing effect on other officers to such an advancement. I have left his name on the list."

Patton dropped a note saying, "My dear Terry: Congratulations!!! The ARMY HAS CERTAINLY GONE TO HELL when both of us are made [promoted].

"I guess we must be in for some serious fighting and we are the ones who can lead the way to hell with [out] too much thinking.

"There is little more that I can say because you know I am tickled to death. Give my best to the lovely lady. Yours."

According to a story in *Time*, a bartender friend congratulated Allen on his promotion. "Allen pointed to his star and said: 'You know who is responsible for that—the enlisted men, that's who.'" It was a nice stroke of modesty; but more likely his success was due to his achievements beginning with World War I and his performance at the infantry school course run by Marshall.

Richard L. Stokes, Washington correspondent of the *St. Louis Post-Dispatch* reported, "Joy over Allen's promotion was unconfined among junior officers and enlisted men. Only strong measures from above prevented non-commissioned officers and privates at Fort Bliss from throwing a party in his honor. Among felicitations received the one he most prized was scrawled in pencil on rough paper. It read, 'Us guys in the guardhouse want to congratulate you, too.'" There is an air of apocrypha to the properly punctuated poor grammar, but the tenor of Stoke's reportage confirms the esteem in which Allen was held. Stokes maintained that the promotion of Allen signified an end to the stifling military caste system and an opening of the door for talent.

Allen had now passed his fiftieth birthday, but he still fancied himself a competitive polo player. Harold Gambrell, who began his military career as an officer with the 9th and 10th Cavalry Regiments, set aside for African Americans (except for white senior officers), drew an assignment to Fort Riley in 1940, where Allen was in charge of the 3d Cavalry Brigade. "My father who had been a major in the medical corps during World War I was in France with Terry. When I went to Fort Riley, he said, 'Look up Terry. He was a darn good officer, a little bit wild at times but he was a soldier's officer, a great officer."

Gambrell recalled, "His men, all the enlisted men thought he was God as far as they were concerned. Whenever they would stop to bivouac, the officers might get together and have a little party. Terry would get a bottle of booze and go down to the enlisted men, sit down and have a few drinks with them. They just idolized him.

"One day at Ft. Riley, there were a bunch of 2d lieutenants out on the polo field, kind of playing around and here came Terry. While his brigade headquarters was there, his two regiments were off in Arizona and he didn't have a great deal to do. He had just returned from Fort Robinson, a remount depot, and picked up a bunch of horses, 14 of them." Gambrell laughed, "By chance, all of them happened to be polo ponies."

"He came on the field and asked, 'Mind if I join you?' 'Of course not, general. Whatever you want, sir.'

"We started scrimmaging a little bit. Of course, when he'd get on the ball, why a bunch of brand new 2d lieutenants would back off and give the general all the room he wanted, more than he wanted. Terry noticed it.

"He held his mallet up and said, 'Assemble. Gentlemen, on the polo field there's no such thing as rank.' Yessir, all right sir. We got to playing again. About that time my good friend, Lt. John Norton who was from Waxahachie, and who was killed in Italy, and me had Terry sandwiched in between us, banging him. He went up out of the saddle about two or three feet it seemed, then bounced back down. Young men don't have any fear, don't think you can get hurt if you fall off a horse. But as you get older, you realize you can get hurt. Terry held his mallet up again and said, 'Gentlemen, rescind that last order.' He did not want a bunch of young 2d lieutenants killing him and I don't blame him."

The rank of general then put him in command of the 2d Cavalry Division, which included two black regiments, under white officers. He advised Marshall that the pair lagged behind their white counterparts because of delays in organization and a lack of a trained cadre. His tenure was too short to effectuate change. He moved to assignments as a deputy commander for the 36th and 4th Infantry Divisions. Marshall harbored no illusions about any future for mounted troopers. He looked for people to lead foot soldiers. Concerned about several generals who appeared not up to the task of commanding a division, he ruminated to Lt. Gen. Hugh A. Drum, the First Army's chief, "I have several men on a tentative list that I think have special qualifications. Omar Bradley, now Commandant of the Infantry School, who is outstanding for any job in the Army. Terry Allen of the Second Cavalry Division, who is now attached to the 4th Division to learn more of the Infantry game. He took the Infantry School course, was weapons instructor at Riley, in fact wrote their pamphlet on this subject, and is outstanding as a leader. And his work in this regard during the recent maneuvers was so notable as to excite comment. He can do anything with men and officers, though unprepossessing in appearance and apparently casual in manner."

As the United States entered the shooting war on 7 December 1941, Allen was completing his re-education in the arts of the infantry. All he required was a theater in which to demonstrate his mastery.

8: Going to War Again

Terry Allen's familiarity with the infantry had carried him to Camp Bowie, Texas, where he was deputy commander of the 36th Infantry Division. While he studied his trade, the British and American forces staggered through a series of defeats. The Japanese, having battered the U.S. Navy at Pearl Harbor, had conquered the Philippines, occupied the American possessions of Guam and Wake Islands, moved close enough to invade Australia, and overrun the British and French holdings in Southeast Asia—while digging ever deeper into China. The Nazi armies in Europe, having defeated France, controlled all of the land mass west of the Soviet Union with the exception of Switzerland, Spain, and Portugal; they also held the strategic Mediterranean island of Crete and were threatening to evict the British from their North African colonial turf. Enemy submarines ravaged hapless freighters, tankers, and ammunition ships sailing to the British Isles and to the embattled Soviets with the stuff of war. In England, where the country had been engaged in the war for more than two years, people clamored for American troops to dam the tide. And the Soviet Union, desperately fending off the Nazi war machine, demanded its allies open up a second front that would relieve the pressure upon it.

Great Britain's Prime Minister Winston Churchill and President Franklin D. Roosevelt agreed from the beginning to make Europe the priority, while fighting off further advances by the Japanese largely through the navy, by air, and with small commitments of soldiers and U.S. marines. Concerned that the Soviet Union might stack its arms because of its horrendous losses and allow the Axis forces to devote their full attention to the West, top American strategists plotted actions to keep the Communists in the war.

In a wildly unrealistic scenario, the U.S. Joint Planning Staff drew up Sledgehammer, a scenario for a land attack across the English Channel in the summer of 1942. The Americans recognized that their own troops would not be ready that soon and that the British would need to field the majority of the combat soldiers. British strategists agreed that retention of Soviet participation in the war was critical, but further study convinced everyone that a summer adventure in 1942 onto the French shores was doomed because of a lack of shipping, trained troops, and supplies.

Marshall and his war department associates then proposed a scheme that became known as Roundup. Bombers would batter the Germans from the air during 1942 and then the Allies would mount Sledgehammer in the spring of 1943. Initially, the British cousins, right up to Churchill, seemed favorable. But that prospect too evaporated. Not enough American bombers and crews were available to make a serious impact upon the ability of the foe to defend the continent. Franklin D. Roosevelt—perhaps influenced by Churchill—was dubious, and the U.S. Navy felt it could not detour its assets away from the task of halting the Japanese in the Pacific.

The debate remained in full voice as May slid into June in 1942, when German advances in North Africa placed in jeopardy all of Egypt and the Middle East with its vital oil. Tobruk fell to the Afrika Korps under *Generalfeldmarschall* Erwin Rommel. That news along with word of brutal beatings absorbed by the Soviets in the Caucasus and other fronts demanded a more immediate response to the Axis forces.

On 19 June, Marshall saw to it that Allen received a second star; and with it came the responsibility to serve as a major general with the mission to command what was considered the foremost U.S. infantry organization, the 1st Division. Regiments from the "Big Red One," a nickname derived from the distinctive red "1" on the shoulder patch, had fought in the Civil War, the Spanish-American War, Pershing's incursion into Mexico, and World War I. In the ranks of this regular army unit were men who, like Allen, were veterans of the AEF of 1917–1918, as well as enlistees who joined up during the Great Depression. Beginning in 1940, the complement had been augmented by draftees. At the moment Allen assumed command, the Allied strategy remained a matter of debate.

Winston Churchill now put forward an alternative to Sledgehammer named Gymnast. As a joint invasion of North Africa, it would squeeze the Axis armies between the assault from the west and the British Eighth Army attacking from Egypt. Success would preserve Africa and the Near East for the Allies and open up a launching pad for attacks on Sicily and then Italy, the reputed soft underbelly of Europe. Marshall opposed the idea; like many Americans, he suspected that the British agenda was to rescue their troops and real estate. His assistant chief of staff of the War Plans Division, Brig. Gen. Dwight D. "Ike" Eisenhower, could not in good conscience argue for tactical success by Sledgehammer as early as 1942. But he, too, opposed Gymnast as neither a useful preliminary for Roundup nor of much value in reducing the Nazi assault in the Soviet Union.

Yet, with a mandate for some sort of decisive action, the Americans were effectively boxed in: The strike against North Africa was the only possibility. Roosevelt gave his approval to Gymnast—which drew a new moniker, Torch. American troops and material had already begun to arrive in the British Isles, and in January 1942, the first contingent of combat soldiers, the 34th Infantry Division, debarked in Northern Ireland.

Even as Torch left the drawing board and began taking physical shape, in June, Rommel smashed into the key British bastion of Tobruk in Libya, capturing thirty-three thousand troops as well as vast stores of fuel and other supplies. Rommel's Afrika Korps pushed into Egypt, only sixty miles from the critical port of Alexandria.

Torch began resembling a desperation gambit, a second front against Rommel that would prevent the enemy from sweeping the Allies out of North Africa. The strategy—regardless of the situation for the British troops besieged by Axis soldiers—posited an attack through the French colonial countries of Morocco, Algeria, and Tunisia. When Germany had conquered France, it left a puppet government in Vichy to govern the unoccupied portions of the nation in Europe and the remnants of French imperialism in North Africa. Under Gen. Charles de Gaulle, a Free French military had been recruited to fight to free their homeland from the Nazis. The Allies pondered whether the Vichy-controlled soldiers, sailors, and airmen in North Africa would remain loyal to their government and resist an invasion or whether they would opt to join the movement to liberate France, under de Gaulle or some other leader.

Any open commitment from the French in North Africa in advance of the landings would necessarily tip off the enemy and jeopardize Torch. Therefore, clandestine diplomatic negotiations involved American civilians in the foreign service with representation in Vichy as well as in North Africa and representatives on the armed forces, most notably Eisenhower's deputy, Gen. Mark Clark. Meanwhile the strategists plotted invasion sites, uncertain whether the troops coming ashore would be greeted with flowers or bullets.

The final plans for Torch specified a joint task force of a little more than 105,000 American and British ground forces, supported by the navies and air forces. The Vichy government and its satellite in North Africa under Adm. Jean Darlan were fiercely hostile to the British. The Royal Navy had attacked a portion of the French fleet in the North African port of Mers el-Kébir for fear it would be seized by the Germans; the British compounded their sins, in the eyes of their former ally, by combining with the Free French in a futile assault on the West African seaport of Dakar. Because of the expected antagonism of the French to the British, the Americans would be the facade of the invasion. They would target three major sites, Casablanca in French Morocco, Oran, and Algiers in Algeria.

With his army committed to a joint invasion of North Africa, Marshall now chose those people who would command and those who would fight. Eisenhower, already high in Marshall's esteem for his work on war plans, by dint of his close involvement with the British, and for being in Churchill's good graces, was chosen to lead U.S. forces. He set up shop in London 24 June 1942, quickly received a third star, and then assumed command of Torch. His deputy commander would be Mark Wayne Clark, a good friend of his.

Marshall and Eisenhower then consulted about which officers and units should be assigned. The chief of staff nominated Maj. Gen. Lloyd R. Fredendall to head the II Corps in North Africa, whose initial mission as the Center Task Force was Oran. Patton was chosen to lead the Western Task Force destined for Casablanca. He would have at his disposal the 3d Infantry Division and the 2d Armored, which he once commanded, and he would sail directly from the United States to North Africa. An often-bitter enmity existed between Fredendall (formerly the commander of the 4th Division at Fort Benning) and Patton when he commanded the 2d Armored Division. Major General Charles Ryder, the commander of the 34th Infantry Division, which was already in England, had responsibility for the Eastern Task Force, the one intent on capturing Algiers. Once the Americans were established, the overall field command would go to Lt. Gen. Sir Kenneth Anderson, of the British First Army.

Having designated the leaders for Torch, the strategists selected the other organizations that would participate in the invasion. The choices from American forces were limited: The first peacetime draft had only begun in November 1940, and many of the earliest recruits and volunteers opted for specialized training or the Air Corps. The federalized National Guard divisions too often had spent years under the leadership of those with political and social clout rather than military skills. Poorly equipped, and inadequately trained, for the most part the guardsmen were not ready for battle. The units with the most credentials for combat were mainly Regular Army, such as the 1st, 3d, and 9th Infantry Divisions, and the 1st Armored Division. Torch also called for deployment of airborne troopers and the 1st Ranger Battalion.

The 1st Division and elements of the 1st Armored drew the task of subduing Oran. The order of battle for the 1st Division, the Big Red One—which had fought long and hard twenty-five years earlier in France—was composed of the 16th, 18th, and 26th Infantry Regiments. In World War I, it was a "square" organization with four infantry regiments. But in 1939, the mode became triangular, and the 28th Infantry shifted to the 8th Division. Four field artillery battalions (5th, 7th, 32d, and 33d) were assigned to the 1st Division along with the 1st Engineer Combat Battalion, the 745th Tank Battalion, the 603d and 703d Antitank Battalions, and the 103d Antiaircraft Battalion, plus assorted service and support units.

On 19 June 1942, Major General Allen assumed command of the 1st Infantry Division. Its previous chief wrote a "Dear Terry" letter: "I want to tell you that I don't know anyone to whom I'd rather turn over the division. It is really a superb outfit and not one easy to leave but . . . it is a genuine pleasure to know that you are the man who will take over."

In his biography of Marshall, Leonard Mosley asserts that Eisenhower hesitated before accepting Allen with his 1st Division as one of his units. Mosley commented, "It was said that 'his [Allen's] fondness for fighting made enemies in peacetime but friends in battle.' Unfortunately, as Ike well knew, Allen in peaceful moments was apt to get bored and become restless; at such times he often went out looking for a fight, not necessarily against the enemy." That judgment simply does not hold up. The criticisms of Allen as quarrelsome when not engaged in battle all erupted *during* the campaigns in North Africa and then Sicily and, therefore, could not have been a reason for Eisenhower to doubt him before Torch began. If Eisenhower harbored misgivings about Allen, they more than likely harkened back to the period when both men attended the Command and General Staff School where the future leader of Torch starred while his subordinate in North Africa tendered short shrift to the instruction. The popular image of Ike was that of a friendly, outgoing, self-effacing man; but, beneath his exterior was a believer in strict discipline with a volatile temper and a burning ambition. Allen's surface manner, slapdash and seemingly careless about his career, could not have gained favor with Eisenhower.

When Allen took over the 1st Division, he accepted as his deputy commander Brig. Gen. Theodore Roosevelt Jr. It was an association of two men from opposite ends of the American spectrum—Allen, the son of an almost anonymous officer from the nondescript heartland, and Roosevelt, the offspring of a former president and descendant of a distinguished family of manufacturers, merchants, and bankers. Ted Roosevelt had graduated from Harvard in 1908 while Allen, of course, had flunked out of West Point in 1912. While Allen was hustling after Pancho Villa in the wilds of Mexico and struggling to pay his bills, Ted Roosevelt had a brief fling in the carpet trade and then ventured into Wall Street where he conquered bulls and bears to amass a $7 million fortune.

Their paths crossed in World War I. Spurred by the influence of his father who early sounded a call for military preparedness, in 1915 Ted Roosevelt organized one of the Citizens Military Training Camps, which was held each summer at Plattsburgh, New York. When Congress heeded Woodrow Wilson's call for a declaration of war on Germany, Roosevelt—armed with a commission as a major—sailed overseas as a member of the Big Red One's 26th Infantry.

Like Allen, he put himself in harm's way, supposedly telling a friend, "We're officers, aren't we? I always thought an officer's job was to lead his men, not follow them." That attitude brought him two wounds, gassing and hospitalization after the savage fighting near Cantigny and the Meuse-Argonne offensive. He, too, went AWOL from the hospital to rejoin his unit. His exploits received far more recognition than Allen's did—the DSC, a Silver Star with an oak-leaf cluster, the Purple Heart, the Croix de Guerre, and the Legion of Honor. No one disputes Roosevelt's courage, but as the son of a former president and the brother of Quentin Roosevelt, who was killed when his plane was shot down, he was more likely to be noticed than others.

Roosevelt left the service after the armistice. He dabbled in politics and in expeditions to far off places, in the style of his father; he served in governmental posts in Puerto Rico and the Philippines as well as in a number of civic organizations, such as the National Association for the Advancement of Colored People. He continued his connections with military training, although he was a stalwart opponent of American involvement in World War II.

Nonetheless, he yielded to the inevitable, rejoining the army in the spring of 1941, eight months before Pearl Harbor, and receiving command of the 26th Infantry.

He brought several credentials to his association with Allen. As a veteran of combat, he was like his new boss—devoted to the welfare of his troops. In his dress, he never put the notoriously unpressed Allen to embarrassment. Roosevelt's aide, Lt. Marcus O. Stevenson, said, "He was the most disreputable-looking general I have ever met. Half the time he'd forgotten his helmet, which he didn't like to wear anyhow and in his combat fatigues . . . he looked like the most beat-up GI you ever saw." And he also liked his whiskey, probably far more than Allen did. Both men, despite their lofty ranks, felt comfortable associating with the lesser files, even though privates were occasionally awed by generals who casually struck up conversations. They also were alike in their concern for the well-being of their soldiers, whether it was Allen fretting over the shortage of socks or Roosevelt pestering mess sergeants to check whether they had adequate baking powder. In contrast, though, while Allen never demonstrated any keenness for reading, Roosevelt habitually tucked poetry anthologies, mysteries, and works on anthropology (a favorite subject of discourse) in his bed roll.

During the Great Depression of the 1930s, the army offered a refuge from bread lines, soup kitchens, and the dust bowl. Until selective service added personnel, the 1st Division provided succor mostly to young men east of Ohio, with a great many drawn from the Northeast. One of them was George Zenie, the son of immigrants from Beirut, Lebanon. He said, "My father had actually joined the U.S. Army, serving from 1913–1914, at which time he was honorably discharged. He worked at a series of jobs, sales, delivery and as a street car conductor. But he was killed in an accident in 1920 when I was only eight months old."

As a seamstress, Zenie's mother supported the family—which included another boy and Zenie's grandmother—in a cold-water flat. At age seven, Zenie made liquor deliveries for a grocer to bring home seventy-five cents a week plus tips and lunch. "It was during Prohibition and he felt no one would suspect a young boy," remarked Zenie. In high school Zenie took jobs in a music record store and behind a soda fountain, and he also delivered newspapers. When he graduated, he found positions in the lingerie business and a sweater factory, but he was let go.

"Since I had no luck finding employment, I enlisted in October, 1940. Because I requested a post close to home, I was sent to Fort Hamilton, Brooklyn [Sam Allen's onetime post] where a new unit was being organized, the antitank company of the 18th Infantry Regiment in the 1st Infantry Division.

"When I enlisted, my original company officers, and indeed the officers of the 1st Infantry Division, were for the most part West Point graduates. They ran their outfits by the book, but we expected that and respected them." Zenie—who remained with the Big Red One throughout the war—obviously was on hand when Allen took over: "Our division commander, Maj. Gen. Terry Allen, and Brig. Gen. Teddy Roosevelt, Jr., the assistant commander, were revered. Our noncoms were also old army. They enjoyed telling us what a sad state the army had come to, to have people like us in it. They drilled us and worked us very hard. Later in North Africa, Sicily, France and Germany, I thanked God they had pushed us."

Another New Yorker, Fred Erben, was a native of Brooklyn, who grew up in the shadow of the borough's huge navy yard. "I dropped out of high school after three years and joined the Civilian Conservation Corps," said Erben. "We built roads, cut down trees, planted new ones. We also fought forest fires. The pay was a dollar a day, more than I got when I enlisted in the army in January, 1941, as a private at twenty-one dollars a month. I was seventeen years old, and I joined the 16th Regiment of the 1st Division to train at Governors Island [another port of call for Sam Allen]."

A third New Yorker, Bronx-born Bill Wills, said, "When I graduated from De Witt Clinton High in 1938, I worked part-time at the A & P, a gas station, at the New York Botanical Gardens [where his father was the chief engineer] and even on a farm in upstate Sullivan County.

"I was twenty-one when I enlisted in the regular army in October, 1940. I was assigned to the 1st Engineer Combat Battalion, part of the 1st Division, at Fort Dupont, Delaware. We lived in a tent city for about three weeks while receiving shots, clothing and equipment, some of which dated back to World War I. There was never a real boot camp training program. Instead, you were put in a squad and a corporal taught you close-order drill and similar stuff. Then we went into the field and received on-the-job training in bridge building, demolition—we blew up the old fort's gun emplacements.

"We did a lot of marching and exercising to get into shape. We qualified on the rifle range with the Springfield '03. [The M1 Garand was actually adopted in 1939]. There was only one .30-caliber, water-cooled machine gun available, and it was passed from company to company. The outfit shipped to Fort Devens [Massachusetts], where the entire division got together for the first time. Training intensified, emphasizing bridge building, river crossings, and weapons."

According to Wills, the instruction had one major omission: "We did not have much mine training in the States. I never saw a Teller Mine or a Bouncing Betty [the German S mine which when tripped, a small charge boosted the device into the air before it exploded] until North Africa."

John Hanlon, a native of a Boston suburb—whose Irish-immigrant father was a policeman—attended the University of New Hampshire, played football, and enlisted in the ROTC. After graduation in 1940, he was granted a Thomason Act commission, which required a year of service and then afforded an opportunity for a permanent rank.

"I was assigned to the 26th Infantry, at Fort Devens. Teddy Roosevelt was the regiment commander. He was a great leader. Our equipment was all right; we had Springfield rifles but the ROTC had been a joke. I knew nothing. Our regiment had a lot of West Pointers and old-timers like our first sergeant. He had nine re-enlistments, all with the same company. He scared the shit out of everybody, including the junior officers like me. My platoon sergeant was another old timer who knew what the army was about. I learned something about military procedure from them and when I completed that year I knew something about being a soldier." Hanlon left the 26th Infantry to become a paratrooper with the 101st Airborne.

The draft introduced a wider mix of Americans to the 1st Division. When his number was called in August 1941, Bill Behlmer, a twenty-two-year-old South Carolinian, traveled to Camp Croft in his home state for thirteen weeks of basic training. "I loved every minute of it," said Behlmer, "manual of arms, close-order drill, long hikes, marching, even the food. We were issued blue denim fatigues and no one advised me to wash them first. After a day in the sun I was purple for three days."

He remembered being on KP on 7 December 1941, peeling potatoes while awaiting assignment: "We were listening to music played by Sammy

Kaye [a bandleader of the day] when the news broke about Pearl Harbor. We were immediately issued rifles and live ammo and then walked guard duty around the camp. Before, the rifles were always locked up. Attitudes changed, those of the civilians and us. Before then, civilians would not speak to soldiers on the street, ignoring us completely. Now, they became friendly and treated us with respect."

Behlmer received a ten-day furlough, and when he reported back to Camp Croft, he learned most of his companions had already been shipped out. "The CO [commanding officer] said the 1st Division needed replacements immediately and they would be one of the first units shipped over. About five hundred of us went by troop train to join the 1st Division at Fort Devens.

"When we arrived, the regular army treated us coldly, because we were draftees. I was issued an M-1 rifle, live ammo, and a pair of skis. I had never seen a pair before and that made me nervous. But after about a week, we turned in the skis.

"The 16th Infantry Regiment was a spit-and-polish outfit. The regulars taught me how to shine my shoes, iron creases in shirts, polish brass buttons. I ate it up. It didn't take long for the regulars to realize that us draftees were going to be good soldiers and pretty savvy. They began to warm up to us and take us under their wings. When I sewed on my 1st Division patch and put the 16th Regiment insignia on my uniform, I stood tall and proud. I was where I belonged. One of the regulars even let me wear his dress blue uniform to a dance on the base. It was the only dress uniform I ever saw.

"Most of our officers were West Pointers and very knowledgeable. Our CO, 1st Lt. Charles Denholm, a West Pointer who made captain shortly after I arrived was one of the finest soldiers I ever met. He really cared for his men; we called him Mother Denholm."

Siegmund Spiegel was not even an American citizen when he became a member of the 1st Division. In his words, "I came to the United States on a Polish passport late in 1938, although I was actually born in Germany. I was not quite 19 and shortly after I came my parents [still in Germany] were deported to Poland. From 1940 on I had tried to enlist because of what happened to my parents but was told I could not because I wasn't a citizen.

"Finally, in November 1941 I was allowed to volunteer for the draft and from Camp Upton on Long Island, four or five of us with the similar origins were sent to Camp Croft. After basic training I went to radio school but I was under surveillance because they were not sure they could trust us. I went to the 18th Regiment at Camp Blanding, Florida. I was hardly there three or four days before they called me to Division Headquarters, because of my 201 file [a GI's background report—his indicated he knew the German language]. They decided I should be in G-2 [division intelligence]."

His first task as an expert in the enemy's language carried him to a special school in Texas where he trained soldiers in the ways to issue commands to German prisoners of war. "I drilled people, drilled them in German commands for four weeks. I was now a T-4 [equivalent of a sergeant] and returned to division headquarters shortly after maneuvers at Fort Benning. I had met Gen. Allen in the G-2 section, but other than a hello, I had no conversation with him."

As the 1st Division moved toward its rendezvous with combat in North Africa, Spiegel traveled along with other GIs from Fort Benning to Indiantown Gap, Pennsylvania. "I was all ready to embark with the rest of the men when suddenly I was put under arrest. An MP brought me to the G-2 office, where [Lt.] Col. Porter [Robert W.] said, 'Sergeant, the general insists you come with us but you are not a citizen.' There was an FBI agent present. He asked me a few questions and said I was okay. The next thing I knew a major, a captain and I were on our way to get me sworn in as a citizen, by command of Gen. Allen."

As Spiegel indicated, the 1st Division now had its orders for overseas. At Indiantown Gap, the troops removed the Big Red One shoulder patch and regimental insignia that Bill Behlmer had so proudly sewn on. The precaution proved unnecessary because German intelligence was extremely well organized and the movement of the division could not have escaped notice. In July 1942, much of the Big Red One, along with soldiers from other organizations—about sixteen thousand men, boarded the former Cunard luxury liner *Queen Mary*. Just before the ship pulled away from the dock, the officers gathered in a lounge. On hand was Allen, as well as the ship's captain. The general introduced the skipper of the *Queen Mary*, who delivered a casual lecture on procedures for abandoning ship. He remarked that there were too few lifeboats for all of the men but that the life rafts could support those unable to pack into boats, as long as the men simply clung to the sides of the rafts rather than climbing onto them.

That discouraging news was followed by a speech from a British general who warned how tough the enemy was. Allen expressed his faith in the division in a few muted words. The meeting ended and one lieutenant recalled, "It wasn't a morale builder."

On the jam-packed vessel, the troops slept in shifts, ate two meals a day in shifts, and became frustrated with the salt water used for shaving and washing. Apart from practicing the "abandon ship" procedures, the men listened to lectures on the British military and the monetary system. The *Queen Mary* traveled with a destroyer escort a short way from New York before steaming toward the British Isles on her own, in the belief that she had enough speed to avoid a fatal encounter with a U-boat. Near Ireland, British aircraft flew overhead to protect the big ship against undersea attack. On 16 August, the *Queen Mary* reached the harbor at Gourock, Scotland, and the troops disembarked before boarding a train bound for Tidworth Barracks (a former British cavalry station).

The 16th Regiment sailed from New York on the British *Duchess of Bedford*. On board, assistant division commander Roosevelt informed the troops of their destination. As the soldiers assembled at Liverpool and prepared to board a train, the Company G mascot, a mixed-breed dog known as "Whitey," gamboled along the platform. He had been smuggled, against all regulations, aboard the *Duchess of Bedford*. Ted Roosevelt heard the commotion when the men whistled and called to Whitey, endeavoring to sneak him onto the train. According to an interview that author Edwin Hoyt had with John Moglia (a private, first class, with G Company at the time), Roosevelt smiled at the sight of the animal. Someone yelled, "Hey, get that dog out of sight. Here's the general."

"Look at that English dog," Roosevelt said, pointing. "He seems to like us."

"Hey, that's Whitey. He's not English."

"Nonsense, soldier," said Roosevelt, "he has to be an English dog. He barks like an English dog. Somebody pick him up. We'll take him with us." Roosevelt had seen Whitey on several marches in the States and the mascot had even trotted alongside the general. Roosevelt cared less about animal quarantine regulations than he did about the morale of his people.

The hasty departure of the 1st Division for England left many men without the proper Class A uniform required when off post. Several GIs subsequently were picked up by military police for being improperly dressed while they were in town. Roosevelt interceded, telling the MPs not to bother the 1st Division soldiers because of their clothing—only if they misbehaved. For better or worse, the Big Red One was setting a pattern that would continue to create trouble.

On 1 August 1942, shortly before leaving for overseas, Allen wrote the first of many letters to his wife. "I did so hate to see you and little Sonny leave yesterday. Don't know when I ever admired you or loved you more. You really took it like a soldier.

"Joe Pennisi [the corporal who served as his orderly], is taking wonderful care of me. He is like a nurse, valet and orderly combined."

From England, on 21 August, Allen brought his wife up-to-date and referred to a cloud on his career horizon. He began with his regular salutation, "Dearest Mary Fran," and continued, "Am sending this by George Patton, who is making a quick return trip. . . . I have spent most of my time running about to attend all sorts of conferences with all sorts of people, including the top big shots in the British Army as well as the Americans.

"Mark Clark and Eisenhower have been most cordial and highly complimentary regarding our entire involvement. . . . Apparently the worrisome reports of incidents etc. just prior to our departure have been entirely wiped off the slate. . . . We are in fine shape and are now again undergoing very intensive training. There have been a few alarms and one or two very slight air raids in our training center but nothing serious.

"I do not anticipate our doing anything but intensive training for a very long time. So do not worry as we are really quite safe in every respect. If mail is delayed it does not necessarily mean anything."

Allen mentioned payments he had made on loans from a bank and reported, "The Abercrombie bill is practically paid in full." He concluded, "You are *always* in my thoughts, Mary Fran, and I want to assure you I've acted accordingly. Things may happen but my luck will always hold. Have never admired or loved you so much as when you showed what *real* nerve you had when you left."

Along with a steady stream of messages to his wife, Allen regularly wrote his son. The father expressed his concern over a recent illness but pronounced himself "very much relieved that you are so much better now.

"Cannot tell you how much I miss you and your mother. I miss being with you while you are growing so rapidly. You and I had lots of fun together and will do so after the war. You will be hard to win that tennis set from me." As he would do so often, the senior Allen advised, "You must try hard to get the best marks you can because your foundation will help you a lot later. I will assure you that we'll send you to Roswell [home of

New Mexico Military Institute (N.M.M.I.), then a prep school and two-year college] as you so much want.

"Take good care of your mother, Sonny. You must be her helpmate and protector now. As you grow older, always be fine and decent as you have been as a little boy and your dad will always be proud of you." He signed off, "Best love, Pops."

Joe Pennisi became a source of information for Allen's wife and son. He wrote chatty, almost intimate, letters, such as one to Mary Fran that said, "General Allen is a pretty busy man, now, travels very much on business for our division, also General Roosevelt and Col. [Norman "Dutch"] Cota [Allen's chief of staff], and at times he comes back very tired and I could tell he needs a rest too. Liquor is very scarce here, no ice cubes for anybody, even the mess and kitchens do not have ice, but we are getting along fine." (This was possibly an oblique way of saying Allen was not drinking heavily.)

"We still have blackout, every night and every day something new turns up where General Allen is always bothered. But he can take it with a smile. We are still holding out with our supplies you gave us, cigarettes, matches, soap, etc. I lock everything up when he is not at his quarters.

". . . Gen. Allen still takes his exercise. I started too. He got his boots fixed and his shoes he uses when he runs; the shoemaker did a pretty good job. . . . He did not use the heavy wool socks yet; it is not so cold here, but will be next month. The gray overcoat he claims he will not use, but from what I hear he will use it next month. We are living in a brick house with no stove, no refrigerator, toilet separate from bathtub and we keep a little stove going with hot soft coal for hot water. Toilet paper is not like you wanted to give us, which you had the right idea, ours is stiff and smooth—you don't mind me writing this, do you? It will be a military secret just between you and I so do not laugh out loud.

"Laundry and tailoring we manage alright. Meals is (*sic*) not so good, but fair. Women is (*sic*) out of our line; we forgot them as they are all working for their country, and not so pretty either. I'll match every girl from America one by one, and they must come very good to beat you and Angie [Pennisi's pregnant wife] so don't worry about us with women, we are too busy for that, and I advise you to keep writing to General Allen because he misses you. How about sending us your picture? I will give it to him." The orderly closed with regards to Mary Fran's mother and "Sunny." He signed off as "Your friend."

Pennisi did not neglect Terry junior. To the boy he wrote a four-page letter explaining that his father had very little time for himself. The corporal related a visit to the Hershey, Pennsylvania, amusement park and other incidents at Indiantown Gap.

He remarked that one of the younger officers had given him a snapshot of the Terry Allens—father and son. "I put it in his identification book where he sees it every day. He is taking his exercise every other day, and is fine only they bother him so much. He is so good to everybody that he nearly gave all his cigarettes away until finally I took the key from his footlocker and stopped him. He still has 5 cartons left. Hershey candy he still has except he gave 3 bars away but from now on I'm going to break a couple of bars so he will eat it himself."

In another letter to Mary Fran, dated 6 October, Allen returned to the subject of "worrisome incidents" from an earlier message: "I sent you a very formal communication from our friend George. [The reference was to Chief of Staff Marshall.] My reply was equally as formal. After the incidents of last August [while the division staged at Indiantown Gap] it is hard to ever feel the same towards him. It all seemed so unnecessary, uncalled for and undeserved. But in these times of stress, it is necessary to forget one's own troubles when there is so much to be done." What triggered the apparent rebuke of Allen by his patron is unknown, but obviously the junior officer felt the criticism unjustified.

In that same letter, he apologized—as he would so frequently—for not writing more often; he explained that he was so busy he could not attend to his own needs. "Have had to maintain three headquarters, one in Scotland one in London and one in the South. . . . I have been out with the Prime Minister for dinner, with Averell Harriman, the American Ambassador and with various big shots in the British Army and Navy. But as I have said, it's all because of my job."

He mentioned payments made for obligations at home and promised to try and increase her monthly allotment by another fifty dollars. She apparently was having a difficult time because of the absence of her husband. "I do hope that things will seem better for you, when next I hear from you. It is so disheartening to hear nothing at all but bad news all the time.

"There has been an awful lot to do and obstacles have had to be overcome that at first seemed insurmountable. In spite of these difficulties of one sort or another, the division is really in fine shape and should do well in whatever it may have to do. Most of the men seem so young and are dependent upon the few of us that I lay awake at night hoping that everything that could have been done for them has been done."

Training for Torch quickly occupied the American arrivals. Fred Erben with the 16th Infantry recalled, "While we had originally trained with the Springfield bolt-action rifles, we had been issued the M-1 Garand just before leaving the States. We trained with the British who showed us the rights and wrongs of beach landings." Similarly the 18th and 26th Regiments drilled in amphibious maneuvers, guided by British commandos.

Allen issued orders that every member of the division, officers and enlisted men, were to qualify as combat soldiers. Cooks, supply sergeants, and clerks all went on sustained marches to condition themselves. Like the riflemen, they practiced with weapons.

An old acquaintance, Chaplain L. C. Tiernan, dropped a note to Mary Frances. He had been at a restaurant in London and told her, "Terry blew in and had dinner with us. . . . You would be proud of Terry if you could see him now because he looks so well and is in splendid condition. He was actually well dressed and his hair was combed."

Terry had made one last stab at improving his appearance, visiting a British tailor who made up a uniform for him. It was not quite standard issue, a greenish hue rather than the conventional olive drab or brown, and the jacket was longer than the standard issue. That was more than likely the last time Allen concerned himself with his sartorial look.

On 19 October, the 1st Division climbed onto transports and engaged in a war game that put them ashore on Scottish beaches. On hand to observe the operations was their supreme commander, Dwight Eisenhower. In the dark of night, with rain pelting down upon them, the GIs and their officers attempted to demonstrate what they had learned. Companies milled about; columns of soldiers passed one another going in opposite directions. Confusion and disorder reigned. The show received dismal reviews from Eisenhower, who perceived failures at the battalion and company levels. Allen responded with more intensive training exercises and a generous shuffling and replacement of officers, mostly at company level. Just three weeks remained before Torch would light up and Allen's Big Red One would scramble ashore.

He did not share his concerns about the readiness of his people with those at home. Instead, in a letter to Terry junior he wrote, "You may rest assured that as soon as we get Hitler and his gang on the run and finish this argument that we will be together just as we were before." While encouraging the boy in his studies, he confessed he probably could no longer offer much help, since the youngster was probably now "past what I have learned."

The Iago of loneliness apparently filled the porches of Mary Fran's mind with tales of American soldiers engaged in bacchanalian revels on the British Isles. He wrote to her, "Do not be disturbed about what you hear of the gay American life in London. It only applies to some loungers that exist at every big headquarters."

Shortly thereafter a distressed Allen pleaded, "I know that you have the impression that I have been in a mad social whirl. I assure you that such is not the case. I have met some friends of mine and have been asked to one or two formal functions because of the fact that I happened to command the First Infantry Division. I was asked to the Lord Mayor's for dinner and took Mrs. Churchill in as my dinner partner. The King of Greece was there. I asked how to address him and he said, 'Just call me George, Terry.' I have enclosed the invitation which I received. It is rather stained because I carried it in my back pocket during very wet and muddy maneuvers when in Scotland." Judging from subsequent correspondence, Mary Fran's suspicions about revels in England were not allayed.

In the same letter, he responded to one of hers dealing with "Sonny's needs for uniform shirts for his ROTC and your need for a trench coat. We are quite distant from London and are quite out of touch. So I wrote to Abercrombie and Fitch and explained what I want. Told them to send Sonny two ROTC olive drab shirts . . . and to send you a tweed coat, gray or brown, size 16. You may exchange or return them."

Again he urged her "not to think that I am not doing all in my power to keep you informed. At times it is just not possible to get mail off. When such intervals do arise, please remember that I am thinking of you and Sonny all the time. You are foremost in my thoughts.

"Do not worry too much . . . and remember that my luck will always hold. Am in the best of health . . . have been jogging about 3 miles a day and swinging Indian clubs which I got at the YMCA.

"Joe Pennisi continues to take very wonderful care of me, watches all my stuff, does my laundry which would not be done otherwise right here and is a big help. Joe said today, 'Can't you see us in a Victory Parade after we win this war? I could go ahead of you with a broom and sweep the street when we parade down Fifth Avenue.'

"Have picked up a few really excellent additional officers. . . . Porter as G-2 and [Kermit] Mason as G-3 couldn't be better." He closed with another valedictory to the division. "They are 1000% better than they were at Indiantown Gap. They are young but are hard and fit. Only hope I have done all that could be done for them."

Robert W. Porter actually became Allen's intelligence chief while the 1st was still assembling at Indiantown Gap. Porter had been on duty in Washington when he suddenly received a call from Allen. The general was in Washington to see his mother and asked Porter to breakfast with him at the Army and Navy Club the next morning. Porter then lived in Alexandria and often encountered traffic delays on the bridges that led into the city. "I was about ten minutes late," recalled Porter. "Terry Allen was pacing up and down Vermont Avenue in front of his mother's house. He really laid me out when I stopped to pick him up. He said, 'You have the reputation of being on time, but here you are ten minutes late.' Terry Allen was a man who was always late. In the 1930s when I worked with him, if he got to a party within an hour of the appointed time that was pretty good. We had great difficulty getting him to class on time. It took his exec and his secretary both, because he was so busy on projects he'd forget all about what he was supposed to be doing.

"During breakfast he said, 'I'd like to have you come to the 1st Division to be my G-2.' He was just taking command. I knew the 1st Division from the reading I'd done over the years on World War I and the reputation of the Big Red One. I said, 'Sir, you can't do that.' He said, 'What do you mean, I can't?' 'You can't bring outside people into the 1st Division. You've got to take what you find there and make it work.' He looked at me as if I'd slapped him in the face. He said, 'Who are you to tell me how to run my division.' I said, 'I'm not telling you how to run your division but I'm telling you it won't do you any good to take me down there. You've probably got a very competent G-2 and you haven't even seen the people yet. You shouldn't begin making promises or asking people to come on board until you look the place over.'

"He was as angry as he could be. Our breakfast finished without anymore conversation. He had to catch a plane and I wanted to go to work. As we got up from the table, he picked up the check. Going over to the cashier, he said, 'If I lost my G-2 would you come?' I said, 'Of course.'

"The next thing I hear was when I got this call from Mark Clark who was then Chief of Staff to General Leslie McNair at Army Field Forces. He said, 'Porter, you're the best G-2 in the United States Army.' I said, 'Sir, I don't know anything about G-2 work.' I didn't know General Clark. I had just been promoted to major. He said, 'Don't tell anybody about it because we took the G-2 that Terry Allen had in the 1st Division. He agreed with the understanding that he could have you as his G-2.'"

When Porter checked in at Indiantown Gap, Allen braced him. "Your job is to keep me abreast of the enemy situation. As long as you give me good advice and good recommendations I'll do anything I can to help you in any way as far as personnel resources, or the use of reconnaissance elements of the division, artillery, anything you want. But the first time you give me bum advice and we lose a battle, I'm going to cut your head off. Is that clear?"

Porter said he answered, "Yes, I'd like to play on that relationship." According to Porter, Allen was unhappy with the state of his G-2 section. He told him that the 1st Division did not know anything about reconnaissance, they didn't know anything about map reading, and they didn't understand intelligence at all. They were, said Allen, gung ho to go in and close with the enemy and get them. They did not understand the need for a base of fire—the need to maneuver and hold back reserve elements until the moment they can come forward and win. Porter interpreted Allen's remarks as using "cavalry tactics, right from the beginning, but translating them into infantry terms." Porter instituted a full program to teach proper reconnaissance.

On 26 October, Pennisi mailed a note to Terry junior, "All we ask of you is a little prayer and we will give that Bum Rommel the works. We are all feeling fine, especially your 'daddy' [who] is in the best of spirits and ready to go, so are we. . . . I never found out about my wife Angie what she bought [sic], a boy or girl, but I hope she is alright.

"We are on our way and just as soon as we dock or invade I will write and tell you of our experiences and you [were] right Sonny when you told me somebody had to start in America, which is the 'Fighting First.' . . ."

9: Desert War

Three separate large convoys bore the Americans toward their assignments for Torch. One, carrying the 9th Infantry Division and assorted support units, sailed directly from the United States. The other two loaded the U.S. 34th Infantry Division, the 1st Armored Division, and the 1st Division, along with a large British contingent. On 27 October, the Big Red One soldiers sailed from Grenoch Harbor, Scotland—the same port where they had landed almost three months earlier. The convoy steamed down the European coast, and on 2 November the troops learned their missions. Until then, according to correspondent Ernie Pyle, some of the men believed they were bound for Russia via Murmansk; others thought the destination was Norway; and a few even speculated they might be going home. Pennisi obviously knew before he boarded his vessel. Pyle reported that the GIs amused themselves with a variety show, but he expressed, "There was the knowledge, deep in everybody's mind, that this was our night of danger. The radio had just brought word that Germany's entire U-boat pack was concentrated in the approaches to Gibraltar."

Pyle mentioned that chaplains conducted religious services aboard the troop ships. Allen himself went to confession, admitting it had been far too long since his last visit. "I know I don't deserve anything from God," he said to the priest, "but maybe He will do something for the division." Allen, although an unabashed Roman Catholic, ordinarily kept his devotions private. He once related an occasion when he was facing a problem with a subordinate: "I went into a latrine tent and got down on my knees and prayed for guidance and God showed me the way to get rid of that guy without holding a court-martial."

Allen later wrote to his son, "My particular headquarters was on one of the big ships which was very comfortable. We had particularly good rations since I made efforts to get rations from the American Navy in addition to the rations already allotted by the British. We had plenty of opportunities for exercise and really enjoyed the trip."

As the Torch troops readied themselves for their introduction to combat, Eisenhower—who occupied a temporary headquarters at Gibraltar—recalled, "Within a matter of hours the Allies would know the initial fate of their first combined offensive gesture of the war." He fretted over aerial reconnaissance that might eliminate the surprise element of Torch, possible bomber attacks, and a decision by Spain (considered friendly to Nazis) to open the gates, which would allow the Germans to pinch off the narrow entry into the Mediterranean.

The strenuous efforts by diplomats and Mark Clark could not pin down the reaction the Americans would meet from the French forces. Some leaders were persuaded they should aid the Allies; others indicated they would oppose any invasion, and yet others straddled the fence. Within a few miles of Oran, the naval base of Mers el-K bir—which defeated the Royal Navy's attempt to destroy it—guarded the city. Because of the threat of these big guns, and on the possibility that the authorities in Oran might still capitulate without a show of force, the idea was to approach the city on the ground, rather than from the sea. However, under the circumstances, the forces had to assume there could be armed resistance.

The strategy envisioned for the Center Task Force with the 1st Infantry Division and Combat Command B of the Armored Division foresaw Terry Allen's troops performing a double envelopment. The infantry division's Y force would come ashore west of Oran while the Z force would drive on the city from the east. Meanwhile the armored units, coming from the southeast, would perform a wide encircling maneuver.

On the ship with the 1st Division's command staff, as the vessel passed through the Straits of Gibraltar, Signal Officer George Pickett brought Porter an astounding message. "It was from II Corps," told Porter, "saying everything was in shape and under no circumstances were we to consider the French as hostile. All we had to do was to say, 'Je suis American' and everything would fall into place. It came in as a secret message, 'Eyes Only for the Division Commander.' I took it up to Terry Allen. He read it and said, 'What do you think?' I said, 'I think you should forget you ever saw this message. I think it would be very dangerous for us at this late hour to begin telling, or trying to brief our troops that the French are going to be with us.'

"He said, 'I guess I better talk to the British liaison people.' I said, 'I wouldn't talk to anybody. That came through Army channels—Fredendall's headquarters.' I said, 'I think the best thing to do is, if you want, put it in my pocket. I'll burn it. I have signed for it. I can go back and tell George Pickett to erase it from the file. But I don't think we need to do that. If we go in with the present instructions . . . we are all right because we are not going to fire until we are fired upon. If we alert our troops, they are leading with their chins, and we could have a terrible morale problem if we gave out the wrong instructions. I think we ought to be prepared for any eventuality.'

"Terry got Col. Cota and tried it on for size with him. He said, 'I agree with Bob. We shouldn't at this late date try to get this message out.' Our troops were on a number of ships, six or eight. It was an impossibility even with 24 hours, considering security. I put the message in my pocket, and after our landing I burned it. It never saw the light of day and it was very wise because we did meet some opposition on the beaches, fighting with French Foreign Legion troops."

Allen had placed Ted Roosevelt in charge of the Y units, the 26th Infantry Regiment, the 33d Field Artillery Battalion, and some support forces. On schedule at 1 A.M. on 8 November, the troops waded ashore in the area of Les Andalouses, fourteen miles west of Oran. Inexperience, darkness, and a lack of knowledge of the coastal conditions caused some landing craft to halt at a sandbar. Vehicles and GIs floundered because the bottom dropped off to a depth of five feet before they reached the shallows. The Americans met only slight opposition on the beach, but the resistance increased as the soldiers marched toward their objective. However, pushing forward aggressively and effectively, the combat novices overcame the French troops—and still adhering to the timetable—held *Djebel* (the Arab word for hill or mountain) Murjado, a steep height four to six miles from Oran. According to the plan, the 26th would attack Oran from the west early on the morning of 10 November.

The Z force, under Allen himself, expected to debark at the port of Arzew and then march some twenty-five miles to Oran. Because the town of Arzew housed a protective battery of coast artillery, the 1st Ranger Battalion led by Lt. Col. William O. Darby and attached to Allen's command, had the initial assignment to neutralize the guns on a high bluff overlooking Arzew. In England, some members of the 1st Division disdained the Rangers as haughty and overly concerned with the polish of their boots. Allen, however, had no reservations about them, and they quickly justified his faith.

Four companies of Rangers led by Darby—about 250 men—scrambled ashore from British assault boats at 1:30 A.M. and clambered up cliffs and a steep road, while carrying mortar ammunition. After setting up heavy mortars, three assault companies climbed the rest of the hill. As they cut through barbed wire, a pair of French machine guns sprayed the area. Darby called on his mortars, which silenced the machine guns; the men tore huge holes in the wire entanglements and stunned the inhabitants, most of whom were still asleep when the attackers struck. Casualties were few on both sides.

Meanwhile, the two other Ranger companies slipped into town, swiftly overcame the inhabitants of a small fort, and—except for a token stand taken by foreign legionnaires at one end of Arzew—secured the town. A delighted Allen declared, "Their initial mission was accomplished with great dash and vigor." He undoubtedly was particularly pleased that their achievements had been made under the cover of darkness, that mode of operations he constantly advocated.

For the most part, the 16th and 18th Regiments came ashore without any opposition. But the usual difficulties of amphibious operations plagued the operation: One landing barge dropped the end too soon, and an officer and driver aboard a jeep plowed into eight feet of water. Other craft smacked into the beaches hard enough for men to jump off without ever getting their feet wet. However, the soft sand mired even tracked vehicles.

Fred Erben, a youthful rifleman of the 16th Regiment, said, "It was easy to land in North Africa. The Vichy French were literally caught with their pants down, asleep. We awakened them [as his unit entered Arzew on the heels of the Rangers] and assembled them in the town square. They were genuinely surprised that the Americans had invaded."

Bill Behlmer, a draftee from South Carolina who had been sent to the 1st Division to become an antitank crewman, remembered, "The English crews dropped some of the trucks and guns in deep water and it was a mess but we made it to the beach. This was the real thing, artillery shells,

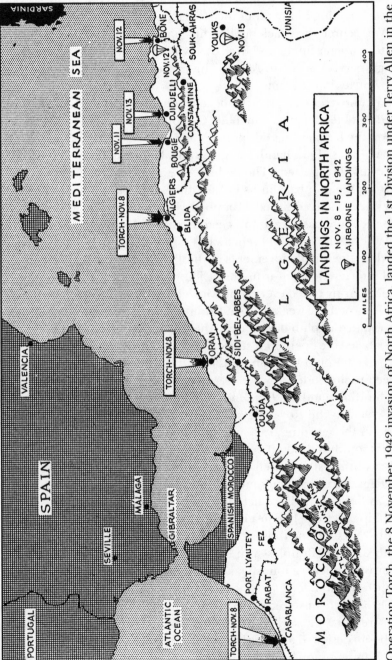

Operation Torch, the 8 November 1942 invasion of North Africa, landed the 1st Division under Terry Allen in the vicinity of Oran, which became the Big Red One's primary objective.

machine guns, mortars, small arms and etc. We had our first taste of the
gnawing feeling in the pit of the stomach. Fear!

"We secured the beach but that first night was terrible. Everybody had
an itchy trigger finger and fired at anything that moved, shot up half of
the grapevines in North Africa. The corporal of the guard shot one of
our sentries in the stomach."

Still, the troops cleared the beaches and headed inland without serious delay. Lieutenant Colonel Ken Campbell bumped into an Arab sleeping on the beach who said some French soldiers were in a nearby building. With his .45 in hand, Campbell sneaked up and opened the door.

Ernie Pyle reported, "The soldiers were all asleep. With quick decision,
he stuck the gun back in its holster, then woke the soldiers. They were
very startled and confused. Campbell who spoke perfect French chatted
with the men, passed around cigarettes, told them they were captured,
and after a bit marched them away."

While the initial movements of the 1st Division proceeded with min-
imal interference, unfortunately a joint venture of the British navy and
the U.S. Army risked everything with a direct approach to the Oran harbor. Almost three weeks earlier, RAdm. Andrew Bennett, commander of
the advance amphibious group of the Atlantic Fleet, wrote to Eisenhower
and labeled the operation "suicidal" because it was timed for 3 A.M., when
the French would know an invasion had started but had not necessarily
agreed to surrender.

The *Walney* and the *Hartland*—a pair of former U.S. Coast Guard cutters given to the Royal Navy—dashed into the Oran Harbor around
three in the morning, carrying an American assault force made up of
almost four hundred officers and men drawn from the 6th Armored Infantry of the 1st Armored Division and flying both British and American flags. Because Allen's men had begun their landings two hours earlier, as Bennett had predicted, surprise was eliminated. However, the
two-ship task force had just been advised that no fire greeted the 1st Division. "No shooting thus far," said headquarters, "landings unopposed.
Don't start a fight unless you have to." As the *Walney* led the *Hartland*
toward the docks, a loudspeaker announced in French that this was a
friendly mission.

The French answered with shellfire and machine guns. As the *Walney*
staggered on, it absorbed more punishment, crashing through a floating boom designed to block just such visitors. Fire blazed on the stricken
vessel, ammunition began to cook off, and explosions rocked its innards.

Those who were not killed or badly injured abandoned ship. Anyone who managed to get to land became a prisoner.

The *Hartland* banged into a jetty and then had the misfortune to swing broadside to a French destroyer. It blasted away at point-blank range. Soldiers and sailors escaped into launches and retreated out to sea to be rescued by Allied ships. The total casualties amounted to more than five hundred British and American army and navy personnel in a pointless venture.

Some coast artillery guns tossed shells at the invasion fleet. In his report to his son, Allen remarked, "My forward group went ahead with me just in the rear of the assault battalions of the 18th Infantry. We used the British assault boats which are bullet-proof and proved to be very effective and landed well upon the beach. At that time the beach was under fire from a seaplane base and various shore batteries that had not yet been knocked out. It happened that our ship was hit twice by enemy artillery just after we left in our assault boat. As a coincidence, it happened that when the ship was struck, one shell fragment went through my cabin, much to the disgust of Joe Pennisi who had been left behind to pack up the remainder of my equipment."

Only a few miles from Oran, French planes based on airfields at La Senia and Tafaraoui also posed a danger to the invaders. To forestall that danger, the 2d Battalion of the 509th Parachute Infantry Regiment loaded on transports in England and flew directly to North Africa for a drop on Tafaraoui, followed by a quick march to La Senia. Unable to locate the targets, some men jumped far from their destination, while a number of C-47s landed in the desert many miles from the drop zone. The first U.S. airborne attack proved to be a total fiasco. Fortunately for some troopers lost in the desert, a column of tanks from the 1st Armored came along and organized a make-shift attack on Tafaraoui. By the time the improvised task force reached the airfield, the destination had already been taken by the infantrymen who had landed on the beaches.

The reaction to the seaborne attack by the Allies portended a difficult time for those committed to the capture of Oran. An intelligence summary said of the local soldiers, "They are rated as second- or third-class fighters, except the French Foreign Legion, which is rated as first-class." The Oran Division had ten thousand French soldiers, augmented by four thousand naval and antiaircraft crewmen.

Porter remembered, "We got held up on the main road between Arzew and Oran. Fredendall came ashore after about 18 hours, just before dark that first day. I had discovered that resistance was coming. Terry was forward and I got in the jeep assigned to me and went charging up the road and ran into him. There was some shelling going on just ahead of us and I was standing there talking to him—getting identification of what I thought might be the enemy unit.

"Fredendall pulled up, coming down the road in an entourage of four jeeps. He came over and started talking to Allen. Within two minutes, the artillery started in on the jeeps sitting there on the road. The II Corps men abandoned their jeeps and got into the ditches right away. Terry was up on a bank behind an almond tree in a grove and so was I. Terry had gone down to the road to meet General Fredendall when he heard the boom of the artillery before it came in on us. He said, 'It sounds as if there is going to be some shelling.' He moved back over the bank up under the almond trees and left Fredendall standing in the road. The II Corps people were all piled on one another in the ditch. It amused Allen a great deal to think that they, including Fredendall whose driver was on top of him, might be afraid."

The 26th Infantry, Allen reported in his summary of the battle for Oran, "met determined resistance from the enemy pillboxes on the Djebel Murjado, hill masses 4–6 miles west of Oran. This resistance was overcome on the night of 9–10 November and by the morning of 10 November, the 26th Infantry was in position to descend on Oran, in full force from the west."

His Z Force had to march a greater distance—about twenty-five miles from Arzew to the target. It began its advance at 1:00 A.M. on 8 November with the arrival of the 16th Infantry on its beach, as the 16th operated on the south, or left, flank, having landed west of Oran. The 18th Infantry coupled with the 1st Ranger Battalion held the right, or northern, flank.

Word reached the division that the French were organizing a strong counterattack from La Macta, a town to the east of Arzew. Rather than deal with an assault from its rear by starting out first for Oran, the 1st Battalion, 16th Regiment, faced the other way and headed toward La Macta. "This threatened counter-attack," said Allen, "was nullified by the aggressive action of the 1st Battalion, 16th Infantry [led by Lt. Col. William A. Cunningham]." Having quickly disabused the French notion of a thrust originating in La Macta, the battalion hastened to join the march toward Oran.

A serious obstacle to the division's advance arose at the town of Saint-Cloud, ten miles southwest of Arzew. The village sat astride the main road from Arzew to Oran; and it was an ideal defensive location, with buildings constructed from stone. A French garrison had organized a strong defense with all approaches swept by fire that included machine guns, mortar, and artillery. By 9 A.M. of 8 November, the 1st Battalion of the 18th Infantry was heavily engaged in a fight for Saint-Cloud. Colonel Frank Greer, the regimental commander, called up his 2d Battalion.

John P. Downing, leader of the weapons platoon in Company F of the 18th, had only hit the beach around nine in the morning of that first day. A first lieutenant by virtue of years in the Michigan National Guard and formerly an overage college senior at twenty-nine—his education delayed by the exigencies of the Depression—Downing deployed his people and sat down for a ham sandwich while awaiting orders. The troops were told to move out, on the road toward Oran.

He told Edwin P. Hoyt, who chronicled his experiences in *The GI's War: American Soldiers in Europe During World War II*, "The molten sun was still glaring down. My pants and shoes had dried but my feet were getting sore from the wet socks. Sweat streamed down my face from the hot and heavy helmet. It trickled down my armpits and the small of my back. The gas mask was heavy and awkward under my left arm. I wanted to throw it away, but abandoning equipment was a court-martial offense. The heavy cartridge belt and the two bandoliers I had slung on my chest pulled on my shoulders. The rifle got heavier with every step."

Ernie Pyle, accompanying the troops, reported, "It was hot in the daytime, so hot that the advancing soldiers kept stripping and abandoning their clothes until some were down to undershirts, but at night it turned sharply chilly and they wished they hadn't." The uniforms issued to the men of Torch were the standard wool ones, rather than the lighter-weight khaki designed for tropical temperatures. The clothing became a contentious issue, particularly when some officers demanded a neat, clean look—almost impossible to maintain as the heat of the day created rivulets of sweat that constantly stained shirts and pants.

Beyond Arzew, Downing saw that despite the rules Americans had started to discard gear, such as gas masks, gas capes, and packs, as well as worse evidence of real war, such as open first-aid kits and empty cartridge cases. Hoyt wrote, "He came upon a dead American soldier. He was lying on his back with a hole through his head, with hands raised toward his head. There was an expression of tension engraved on the dirty face. A staff sergeant. A dead dogface. Lieutenant Downing thought he was going to be sick. So the maneuvers were over. This was war."

Downing and the 2d Battalion soon reached the combat area, and rifle bullets from Saint-Cloud sporadically ripped overhead. Downing heard that the 1st Battalion had lost three company commanders during an unsuccessful assault. Company F crossed a field and warily moved toward the town. The volume of incoming fire increased. Mortars burst out nearby; machine guns chattered. The sun faded, and in the gloom, Downing sprinted forward and then dropped to the ground as he heard shots and the explosions of shells and grenades. The company reached a lone house, surrounded by trees. Orders were to spend the night there.

Bill Wills, a prewar draftee from New York City with the 1st Engineer Combat Battalion, was among the force that was slugging it out for Saint-Cloud. "The first man I saw killed was a good friend, a sergeant shot through his helmet by a French soldier while we were going into St. Cloud."

Despite the added pressure, at midnight of that first day the advance remained bogged down in front of the village. The well-organized defense was mounted by the 2d Zouaves (a unit of Algerians in the French infantry) and a portion of the French Foreign Legion, some six hundred soldiers assisted by French and Arab civilians. Their armament included about a dozen pieces of artillery plus mortars and machine guns. On the morning of 9 November, Greer arranged for a fifteen-minute artillery barrage to soften up the opposition before he threw in all three of his battalions. Downing recalled attacking into Saint-Cloud: His company battled yard by yard into the village, but by afternoon of that second day, they still had not captured it. The defenders stubbornly resisted, inflicting heavy casualties. Later, Allen in analyzing the situation realized that all three battalions had been sucked into a converging attack. They had lost their ability to maneuver and could not budge the enemy.

The general had been temporarily distracted by the potential for a counterattack from La Macta, and he was on his way toward Oran, with elements of the 16th Regiment along a parallel route to the south. Around noon, Lt. Col. Robert W. Porter of the Division G-2 contacted him, requesting he visit the forward command post of the 18th as soon as possible. Allen hastened there, arriving around 1:30 in the afternoon. He learned that the frustrated Greer had now requested a special concentration of all the available artillery in the division—including the 155mm howitzers—upon Saint-Cloud at 2:30. Greer planned that after blasting the village they would resume the assault.

Allen subsequently reported on the situation, "Colonel Greer was then specifically informed by the Division Commander that there would *not* be any *general* [his italics] artillery concentration for the following reasons:

"The town was overcrowded with a great number of civilians, including hundreds of women and children.

"If we bombard the town, and then fail to take it by attack, it would be disastrous.

"We don't need the damned place anyway. We can by-pass St. Cloud, and take Oran by night maneuver."

He directed the regimental commander to "leave one battalion as a containing force to hold the enemy in position at St. Cloud. Disengage two battalions from the present impasse at St. Cloud. Have one battalion by-pass St. Cloud on the south flank, and continue to Oran via Arcole [another hamlet eight miles southwest of Saint-Cloud]. Have the other battalion by-pass St. Cloud on the north flank and close in on Oran via the high ground at Djebel Khar, north of the Arzew–St. Cloud road.

"Initiate reconnaissance and other preparations immediately.

"Make all major *troop movements* under *cover of darkness* [his italics]."

The general also offered Greer the services of the Rangers to strengthen the containment around Saint-Cloud.

In its passage toward Oran, the 16th Infantry also encountered a stronghold in the vicinity of Arcole. Antitank and machine-gun fire stopped other GIs from the Regiment's 3d Battalion. First Lieutenant Victor D. Brosokas of headquarters and 2d Lt. Simon A. Box of the 1st Engineer Combat Battalion volunteered to man a half-track. The pair overran two enemy machine-gun posts that flanked the road, and they destroyed both with hand grenades. They rolled into the hamlet of Arcole, shooting up defenders armed with rifles and machine guns. Their action cleared the way for the column to resume its advance; and, Allen was happy to award Brosokas one of the first Distinguished Service Crosses earned by a member of the division—an honor that Allen felt he himself should have received in France in 1918. During the first three days in Algeria, DSCs went to three other members of the 16th Regiment in recognition of their valor along the road from the Arzew beaches to the heights overlooking Oran.

As the second day in North Africa drew to a close, the 2d Battalion of the 18th Infantry, having detoured around Saint-Cloud on the south, hidden by the night, was about four miles beyond Arcole and approaching Oran. The 3d Battalion of the 18th went around Saint-Cloud on a northerly trek and reached the forward slopes of Djebel Khar, just four miles from Oran. The regiment's 1st Battalion acted as the containment force at Saint-Cloud; and the 16th Regiment forces that were marching on the southern track neared the outskirts of the town. The 26th Regiment, west of Oran, was already poised for its advance upon the city.

At 9:30 on the night of 9 November, Allen held a staff conference at his command post. Apart from his own division staff, a colonel from II Corps and the leader of Combat Command B of the 1st Armored Division attended. The II Corps representative reported that it wanted to speed up the attack on Oran. They agreed that all the infantry units in place would jump off in a coordinated attack at 7:15 the following morning. A few minutes later, Combat Command B's tanks would rumble forward.

Allen's chief of staff, Col. Norman "Dutch" Cota (who would later be on Omaha Beach with the 29th Infantry Division and subsequently command the 28th Infantry Division), suggested to Allen that a written order be prepared for distribution to all 1st Division units that night. Allen then dictated to Cota some specific orders for particular units of the Big Red One, and Cota inquired whether Allen had "any general instructions of all units?"

The division commander responded with the brief directive, "Nothing in Hell must stop the 1st Division." Trite as it sounded, and as Allen would agree, "at best unorthodox, and at worst, commonplace or 'corny,'" it seemed to suit the mood of the times.

Allen reported to his son, "Communications were very difficult owing to the lack of equipment and the lack of transportation, much of which had not yet been unloaded from the ships. It was necessary to personally contact all units and to give them directions verbally for the continuation of each attack. By 10:30 it was apparent that each combat team had overcome their preliminary objectives and would shortly be ready for the final assault. This was ordered to be launched at 12:00 noon on November 10th. By delaying this attack for an hour and a half, it was hoped that we might be able to secure a surrender. . . . About this time, a French General at the French airport reported by radio and in person at my command post that the French forces were ready to cease resistance. By some grapevine or other, it became understood shortly after 12 o'clock that resistance had practically ceased. I was then with the 16th Infantry. We assembled a portion of the 1st Cavalry Reconnaissance Troop (a portion of division headquarters), and took a small group into [for security, Allen had blanked out the names of places, but he was talking about Oran] with the advancing infantry leading elements. This group consisted of two scout cars, my own personal jeep and one or two extra jeeps. We happened to have an American flag available and we fastened this to a stick on the end of a Tommy Gun and carried it in my jeep to indicate to the French who we were.

"On reaching the outskirts of [Oran] it was apparent that resistance had completely broken down and by making a hurried entry we might forestall further resistance. Immediate word was sent to all units to continue their advance but to avoid firing unless absolutely necessary.

"This hastily organized escort of mine then continued to the Hotel de Ville, the town hall of [Oran]. Our passage through the city was most impressive. The entire civilian population turned out en masse and were hysterically enthusiastic at the sight of the American flag. I went into the Hotel de Ville to see the mayor and to get him to contact the military commander and arrange for a surrender at [Saint-Cloud] which was still resisting in our rear. We were held up on the steps going up to the town hall and a tremendous crowd . . . they were quite hysterical and all started to sing La Marseillaise.

". . . The spirit shown by the men could not be beaten. The Division adopted the slogan that 'Nothing in hell would delay or stop the First Division' and they certainly lived up to it. It is true that with training, some of the losses that were incurred might have been obviated, but on the whole, their performance was excellent.

"The men had no sleep since Friday night aboard ship until the capture of the final objective had been completed the following Tuesday night, except for what catnaps individuals were able to pick up now and then. There were no kitchens and no supplies and rations had to be carried by the individual during these three days. The shortage of transportation and even ambulances was most acute. In some cases it was impossible to evacuate the wounded for over 48 hours."

After complimenting several members of his staff, Allen signed off. "All my love old top. Take care of your mother and go after your athletics and also your schoolwork." The order of importance was typical Allen.

The surrender in Oran and, subsequently, Saint-Cloud occurred almost simultaneously with Admiral Darlan—commander of all of the French military in North Africa—directing his subordinates to end their resistance.

For the 1st Division and Terry Allen, the initial phase of Torch was over. But the costs had been significant. The Big Red One counted 418 battle casualties, including 94 killed, 73 seriously wounded, 178 slightly injured, and 73 missing in action. To Allen, the battle that began at Arzew and ended with the occupation of Oran confirmed his faith in nocturnal operations. He noted the "severe setback" suffered by his 18th Regiment during its daylight attacks on Saint-Cloud, and he observed that the impasse resulted from a lack of accurate reconnaissance and the assault units' inability to maneuver. He gave credit to the decision to neutralize Saint-Cloud with a containment force while shifting the other battalions around the town under cover of darkness to the positions where they could attack Oran.

Allen enjoyed this success and the praise of Eisenhower and Corps Commander Fredendall only briefly before he entered into one of the most frustrating periods of his career. All French opposition to the Allies had subsided by 17 November. With Algeria secured, the forces of Torch shifted their eyes east, toward Tunisia. The Axis high command had reacted to the invasion, and British soldiers entering Tunisia clashed with forward German troops, while American paratroopers encountered Italian patrols. A French corps now operated in North Africa under Gen. Henri Giraud, one of the few of his country's military leaders not tarnished by the collapse in 1940. Command of the Allied ground war in Tunisia had been vested in British Lt. Gen. Sir Kenneth Anderson. The achievements of American forces in Oran and at Casablanca made little impression upon the British officers who regarded their ally's soldiers as poorly trained, inexperienced, badly led, and inadequately equipped.

One consequence of Anderson's assumption of overall command and the insertion of Giraud and his XIX Corps was the parceling out of Terry Allen's people to a number of organizations. While Allen and his 1st Division Headquarters stayed in Oran, the 18th Infantry, along with the 32d and 5th Field Artillery Battalions, departed to reinforce the British V Corps—under extreme pressure in the northern sector of the country. The 26th Infantry, less one battalion, flew to outpost approaches for the Atlas Mountains in southern Tunisia, and the 33d Field Artillery moved off to southern Tunisia where it was at the beck and call of the Free French or as attachments to several task forces run by the American II Corps.

That he had been summarily dealt out of the game undoubtedly enraged Allen. Porter said that after the 18th Infantry was ordered to Tunisia, Allen drove in a jeep to Algiers. "He went in and talked to General [Walter Bedell] Smith, who was Eisenhower's Chief of Staff. He was told that [the 18th] was badly needed in Tunisia. General Eisenhower felt that Tunisia would be much easier to deal with if Americans were there with the British [who] were suspect [as] an extension of British colonial power. Terry really wasn't satisfied with that explanation but there was nothing he could do about it except ask to be relieved. This he would not do.

"He came back to Oran, quite upset. We were in reserve. He called up Bedell Smith and got permission to set up an advance detachment in Algiers. He had two aides who spoke fluent French and he took an enlisted man who was a good French speaker, and one of his aides, and made a little liaison group in the Aletti Hotel. We had two rooms in the Aletti. Allen would sort of shuffle back and forth leaving Teddy Roosevelt in command of the division in Oran."

A. J. Liebling theorized that as a former horse cavalryman, Allen thought of his dispersed GIs as dismounted troopers. Liebling reported that, having led the division through the invasion and the capture of Oran, "he felt the same sense of outrage that a football coach might feel if he were to see his squad taken apart just before the big game. 'I blooded them, didn't I' he said to friends."

Time-Life's Will Lang captured some of Allen's frustration as the general reverted to a sports simile. "You can't spread the units around and expect 'em to click. It's like getting stars from the Brooklyn Dodgers and expecting them to work with the New York Yankees."

Allen undoubtedly felt mixed emotions after he received a copy of a message sent from Feriana, Tunisia, on 22 December, by Lt. Col. John Bowen (the CO of the 26th Infantry's 3d Battalion) to Col. Alec Stark. The battalion, along with the 26th's 1st Battalion, had been split off to work under Fredendall's II Corps—which at least placed it under American command.

Bowen advised Stark, "We were certainly glad to see the 'Military Mission to Oran' that I sent return with transport, equipment and supplies that we needed. Chaplain Chase told me that no effort was spared by regiment or division to provide for us. We are deeply appreciative down to the last man—it's good to know that our outfit is looking out for us." Allen must have drawn some satisfaction from the evidence that although the battalion was separated by distance and in the chain of command, it still drew both physical and moral sustenance from the regiment and division.

"On the night of December 16–17," Bowen related, "I took Captain Morrissey with his 1st and 3d platoons, commanded by 2d Lieutenants Falconieri and Megrail with a few other selected men (total 80 men) on a night raid. We raided the town of Maknassy which was occupied by a company of 164 Italians. We swooped into the town from the flank and rear, shot up the place for two and one-half hours, destroyed considerable equipment and transport, took 21 prisoners and made our getaway before daylight to our own lines 52 miles back to Gafsa. We had no casualties except for one man very slightly wounded and a slight wound in the leg on Sergeant Wickam of the 2d Battalion, AT Platoon. He is up and around now. We lost one jeep which was hit by the fire of an AT gun. Captain Morrissey did a superb job of commanding the two platoons and Lieutenants Falconieri and Megrail displayed remarkable qualities of leadership. I estimate we left 20 dead and about 30–40 wounded. Intelligence reports that we have recently received lead me to believe that we have reduced the strength of that garrison by about 50%. The lesson I learned was that night operation was the easy way to do it—and it puts the defender at a tremendous disadvantage. The surprise we effected was of tremendous advantage to us. The Italians were terrified beyond description, particularly when our men shouted, 'Heigh Ho, Silver' and Indian war whoops." (The war cry of the popular radio show *The Lone Ranger* had previously served as the password and countersign among 1st Division troops.)

Allen also must have been pleased by the effectiveness of what he had preached—night operations—and by Bowen's hearty endorsement of the approach. However, surely he was dismayed as Bowen's report continued: "Serving under Raff [Col. Edson Raff had led the contingent of paratroopers on their abortive airborne strike] who actually commanded only 80 paratroopers is a bit awkward as my command is over 900. The paratroopers only guard the airport at Thelepte. The 3d Battalion does all the rest of the work which consists of outposting Gafsa, sending two patrols nightly into the enemy lines, guarding the airport at Youks les Bains, digging and constructing an enormous reinforced concrete bombproof air raid shelter for Raff who is nervous about enemy aircraft, doing all the work of supply and administration, furnishing fatigue details, and occasionally fighting the enemy. Some of the work is menial work for first-class fighting soldiers and some of the results we produce are making Raff and his parachutists famous. The 3d Battalion, 26th Infantry, and the 1st Division have been famous in their own right and it irritates every one of my men to be adding to the fame of this upstart unit which hasn't been in action against the enemy yet! It's an awkward set-up."

That paragraph could only have lit Allen's short fuse. The wholesale separation of his units violated a cardinal tenet of Allen's military bible. As he would iterate and reiterate, "A soldier doesn't fight to save suffering humanity or any other goddam nonsense. He fights to prove that his unit is the best in the Army and that he has as much guts as anybody else in the unit. Break up the unit and incentive is gone."

Others have expressed similar sentiments in different words, but Allen's belief in strength through cohesion governed both his training techniques and the ways in which he interacted with troops under him. Loyalty was a fetish with him. It explains his willingness to leave his bed in the depths of night to rescue a soldier arrested by civilian authorities. And, it is why, when asked how many men he had in the stockades because of courts-martial, he snapped, "None. That's what we have first sergeants for."

10: Setbacks

The Allied forces were thinly stretched and intelligence indicated the Axis was flexing its military muscles in preparation for an attack. A frustrated Allen fumed while he shuttled between Oran and Algiers. He found no horses available, but he sought to maintain peak physical condition by jogging three miles through the hills after breakfast several days a week. He also smoked constantly and downed a certain amount of alcohol. However, Siegmund Spiegel, the intelligence specialist in division headquarters said, "You could smell the liquor on Roosevelt but never on Allen."

Ernie Pyle, who was in Oran at the time, wrote, "Allen not-so-quietly went nuts sitting back in an Oran olive grove watching the war from a distance." Had he been in the field, Allen believed he could have prevented, or at least mitigated, some defeats. As analyzed by Allen, the Faid Pass in the north-central portion of Southern Tunisia opened a route through the south end of the Grand Dorsal Mountain Range, which on some maps is divided into Eastern and Western Dorsal. That gap afforded the most practical avenue for an enemy thrust. Most immediately threatened by an offensive in this sector was the Task Force: composed of the 26th Regiment's 3d Battalion, a handful of airborne from the 2d Battalion of the 503d Parachute Infantry Regiment, a tank destroyer company, and some stray artillerists from the French Constantine Division.

According to Allen, Edson Raff and John Bowen recognized the strategic value of the Faid Pass, and—on their own initiative—in early

December they "decided to take the place, for self-protection." With a makeshift outfit drawn from their assorted units, they led a successful night attack that gave them command of the pass. Raff arranged with the Constantine Division for French soldiers to man the positions in the pass while the Americans withdrew to fulfill other responsibilities.

Allen severely criticized what followed: "Had the Allied High Command seen fit, *at that time* to organize a *strong defending force* for the Faid Pass, with adequate artillery and anti-tank support, a great deal of their later difficulties at the time of the German breakthrough might have been avoided."

His counsel went unheeded, and in all fairness, Eisenhower and his staff may not immediately have had the resources to meet Allen's prescription. But, it is equally true that even with the passage of time and the arrival of replacements and additional ordnance, no effort was made to buttress the thin ranks defending the Faid Pass.

His services still not required at the front, Allen dashed off a 13 December note to his boy. Unlike in his earlier letter, he could not regale Terry junior with any accounts of division action. "I was delighted to find several letters from you and was particularly glad to know that you are doing so much better in school and that you are finally getting an opportunity to ride.

"I have written to Captain Jones and told him that I appreciated his having arranged this for you. I also told him to see Pop Graham, the 7th Cavalry tailor, and if you need any breeches, to see Pop and arrange for you to get them . . . and send me the bill.

"I am particularly glad to know that you are riding my old pony, 'Half Pint.' . . . At this time in your life, your riding will be of more help to you than at any other time, since the skill you get at your age is acquired faster and will last all your life. . . . I am particularly anxious that after every day's ride you do about 15 minutes work without stirrups and continue with your suppling exercises." He enclosed a ten-dollar money order to add to a twenty-dollar one previously sent for Christmas and New Years.

The quick capture of the first three major targets may have given the Allied commanders great satisfaction, but no reason for complacency. They had not been confronted by the enemy's first team; rather, for the most part they were confronted by an inadequately armed and half-hearted foe. As 1942 drew to a close, the strength of the legions under Eisenhower were less than overwhelming. His ground commander, Lt. Gen. Sir Kenneth Anderson, who was working from a scenario that des-

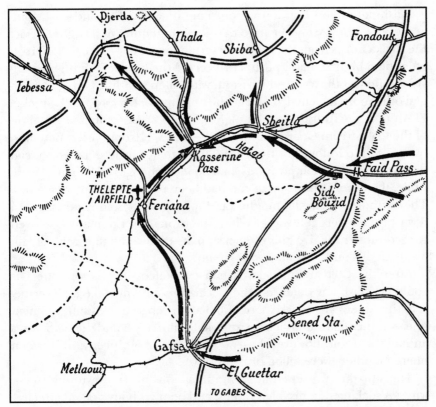

On 13 February 1942, German armored forces swept through Faid Pass in
an offensive that reached its high water mark at Kasserine Pass.

ignated the two Tunisian port cities of Bizerte and Tunis as objectives,
announced, "My forces available for the rush on Tunis are woefully weak
and before committing them I must be sure of a good start and have a
clear understanding of the odds against them." The troops would have
to contend with formidable mountains broken only by easily defensible
passes, dense scrub, and vast desert. The available roads were not designed to serve the heavy traffic of the military. The rickety railroads were
highly vulnerable to aerial attack. Both the Germans and Italian soldiers
were experienced fighters, and the German armor and aircraft were
largely superior to anything the British or Americans could field. It would
require time for the arrival of sufficient planes and effective radar.

Washington and London were urging new victories, and—as Montgomery's Eighth Army began to develop momentum in its fight to evict the Afrika Korps from the Libyan desert to the east of Torch—Anderson attempted his first major push: He directed the British 78th Infantry Division and its 6th Armored Division, with Allen's 18th Infantry and several other units attached, to attack the objective of Backstop Hill, or Jebel El Ahmere, in Tunisia. On the night of 22 to 23 December, a battalion of the Coldstream Guards jumped off—with GIs from the 1st Battalion of the 18th to follow. But the guides from the Guards, detailed to lead the Americans to their positions, had no idea where to take them. Meanwhile, the other Britons up ahead had been rocked by heavy casualties. They withdrew from the heights, and told the U.S. soldiers that only a few Germans were left there. When the captain of Company B arrived to reconnoiter the five hills of Backstop, he discovered that parts of Hill 3 and all of 4 and 5 teemed with enemy.

After the Coldstream Guards had evacuated—but before the GIs could establish any defense—the Germans counterattacked. Nevertheless, the Americans seized all of Hill 3 and prepared to assault the next one. Another counterattack surrounded Company A and the battalion's antitank platoon, however. Lost were all but one officer and thirteen men; the others were killed or captured.

The situation worsened as communications broke down due to cut wires. A soaking rain disabled radios, and poor visibility denied effective artillery support. A coordinated assault on Hill 4, backed by British big guns, failed, and again losses were considerable. The survivors of the 18th reverted to a defensive mode, an appeal by its regimental commander to the British brought a promise to dispatch four companies of Coldstream Guards to assist. Seven Bren-gun carriers arrived—in darkness, however—and they could not locate targets. The Coldstream Guards agreed to pass through the Americans and renew the attack on Hill 4 by daybreak with support from the GIs. The operation was postponed until late afternoon; aided by the 18th's mortars and machine guns, the British regained control of the objective.

A counterattack was anticipated for Christmas Day, and at dawn, the Germans did not disappoint the defenders. They crashed down upon the troops on Hill 4 with a rolling barrage of artillery controlled by rocket signals. A British company withdrew, leaving the mortarmen of the 18th exposed and unprotected. For a few hours, a French unit was hastily inserted, but it too quit the scene. The 1st Battalion now occupied an untenable position: Mortars, machine guns, and tank fire hammered the already-battered troops. The battalion commander issued orders to re-treat. When the survivors reached the regimental area at Teboursouk, they were minus 9 officers and 347 enlisted men—killed, wounded, cap-tured, or missing in action. This was the first of a succession of setbacks.

News of the disastrous losses incurred by the 1st Battalion of the 18th at Backstop grieved Terry Allen, who constantly searched for ways to protect "his boys," as he sometimes referred to them. Will Lang re-ported Allen raging, "I've lost six of my boys, sent to the front without leadership and who did I lose 'em to, to a Swede named Anderson?" Of course, Allen knew very well that Kenneth Anderson was hardly a native of Sweden.

On 24 December, an assassin gunned down Admiral Darlan in his Al-giers office. The circumstances behind the plot that killed the official leader of the French in North Africa were murky. The murderer sum-marily stood before a firing squad. His quick execution prevented dis-closure of whether Darlan's death had been instigated by monarchists, de Gaullists, British intelligence, or even the American Office of Strate-gic Services—all of whom could have been tagged with a plausible mo-tive. In the byzantine ambience of North Africa in 1942, some French-men had killed or imprisoned countrymen who prematurely supported Torch; others defiantly supported the Fascist cause even as segments of the military eagerly joined the battle against the Axis powers. Flags flew at half-staff starting Christmas Day, until after Darlan's funeral.

In this confused atmosphere, Allen alerted all of the men still under his jurisdiction. He directed that they remain in quarters or bivouacs, pre-pared to move on his command at a moment's notice.

The unhappy state in which Allen found himself reflected a chaotic organization. Eisenhower, who was disturbed by the absence of a follow-up to the initial achievements, had departed Gibraltar and installed him-self and his staff in an Algiers hotel. His contacts with the British ground forces' commander Anderson were unsatisfactory. The Briton seemed determined to advance slowly in a piecemeal fashion. The U.S. II Corps chief, Lloyd Fredendall, displayed no aggressive zeal. The leader of the RAF (Royal Air Force) and Gen. James Doolittle, who was in charge of the U.S. air forces, occupied separate quarters. Still, Ike, who now wore a fourth star, made no changes.

Off the leash that restricted him to Oran, Allen was determined to learn the truth about what happened on Backstop Hill because he had received disquieting gossip brought back by a chaplain. Accompanied by Porter, Allen visited his 18th Infantry Regiment, which was still attached to the British 78th Division. An official report sent by the British V Corps commander to American Forces Headquarters following the Backstop battle denigrated the regiment's performance. The two American officers went forward to the headquarters of Lt. Gen. W. C. Allfrey, who commanded the corps to which the 18th was attached. Porter recalled, "Allfrey was very personable but he was handling Terry with kid gloves. He tried to explain what had happened. There had been a fight. The Germans had kicked the 18th off a hill after they had taken over from the British. Terry listened very patiently and when Gen. Allfrey finished, he thought he had snowed Terry Allen completely.

"Allen said, 'Gen. Allfrey, I know nothing about the situation up front. I have heard rumors. We had a chaplain come back. He is a man of God, but he doesn't know anything about tactics. All he can do is tell stories that have come from men who have gone through the receiving station or that he has heard from the men. But I have [Lt.] Col. Porter with me [the G-2 officer had just received his silver leaf]. I brought him along to make an investigation while I am visiting the troops. He will prepare a report and I promise you, I will show you his report when it is finished.'"

Porter said, "I began talking to our people, the battalion commander, staff and company commanders. One company commander had been killed in this fight. Piecing together what had happened, it developed that the Guards Brigade had been up on this big, bald, massif for several days. The Germans had held the top of it. They then made a night attack and drove the Germans off the top and gained the military crest on the far side. As quickly as they got this military crest, a battalion of the 18th Infantry was ordered to relieve them. This was all to happen in one night. You can imagine trying to make a relief in an area you didn't know anything about or what was going on up in the forward position. This was the first time our troops had been in heavy combat and it just didn't work.

"After they took over, the Germans counterattacked at daylight. The U.S. Battalion called for artillery fire. The British artillery didn't respond. There was a battalion of our division artillery that had been sent forward with the 18th Infantry but the British brigadier, a gunner type, didn't feel that the artillery battalions were competent to fire because they were just coming to forward positions when this attack took place. Our U.S. artillery battalion had just been moved by the British Corps down into that area.

"It was just a fiasco all the way and our men came back off the hill. The British were saying 'Oh, the Americans wouldn't fight. They wouldn't stand.' It was a very unsound relief. We should have had our own artillery with our own forward observers. We had FOs [forward observers] coming forward but they couldn't get a response out of the British by radio. I found that the channels didn't even marry up—so no communication. There were British FOs forward too, but in the dark they weren't married up with the American FOs. I put this all down on paper and gave it to Terry Allen.

"We went back to Gen. Allfrey's headquarters late at night. At breakfast the next morning the British were anxious to see what was in this report. Terry had studied it but hadn't said much of anything to me about it. At breakfast he showed the report to Gen. Allfrey whose face was really a study when he read it. Terry, smoking a cigarette, looked at him cooly and said, 'I have complete confidence in Porter. We have been together since before the war. He worked with me in the Cavalry School. He has been on the General Staff in Washington. He is a competent observer, a graduate of our Command and Staff School.'

"Then he said, 'You know I had some experience in World War I. I was wounded in combat in France, was decorated for valor and I had to take part in reliefs that were made under combat conditions. In our American manuals there isn't any case which would correspond as an example of what took place here. It is very difficult to make a relief in the middle of the night. Even if you have had advance reconnaissance, you have the line taped and you know exactly what foxholes or what trenches the men are going into. We normally have our artillery all tied in so there is good fire support [for a night relief].

"'I can't understand the rumors that I hear from Bedell Smith and Gen. Eisenhower on the Americans being incompetent soldiers—particularly the reports from the higher echelons of command in your army when I get a report like this from trusted staff officers on the American side about their preparation for going into combat.' Allfrey—his face was ashen white—said, 'I have no apologies. I haven't heard anything like this from the commander of the Guards Brigade or the division commander.' Allen said, 'I am prepared to accept this report because I know Porter and my people. I don't feel that they were telling me something that wasn't true because Porter verified the facts by at least five or six different people—all officers.'

"Allfrey said, 'What are you going to do with this?' Terry Allen looked him right in the eye. He took the report from Allfrey and he tore it in two, saying, 'I hope this will be a lesson to the British high command as to how to deal with the Americans. I am not going to cause an international incident over this but I expect that if I get any British troops under my command, I'll give them a lot better treatment than you have given my men. It's going to take some time to get the morale of that battalion back in shape and I think the British have the responsibility for their low morale. I would like to see that you put out proper instructions for using American units to relieve British units. Not only that, but you should put out quietly through your people that the Americans are doing a fine job in Tunisia.'

"Terry Allen was ace high with the British from then on. He told Beetle Smith about it and that was the end of the incident. We [the 1st Division] never had any more problems with the British in North Africa. But they had completely misused this outfit."

Although he had restored the honor of his troops, Allen could contain himself no longer. In January, Allen and Porter traveled to the Allied Force General Headquarters in Algiers, Porter recalled, "to pay his respects when he was visiting our so-called advanced detachment. [Allen] had talked briefly with Eisenhower and made the point that he was very anxious to get the division together. He had been completely out of contact, and he didn't know whether the men were having proper supplies or not.

"Eisenhower said, 'I'm very sympathetic and I'll talk to my operations people about this, and then we will be in touch.'

"Terry went back out to the Chief of Staff's office to say goodbye to Beetle Smith and let him know he was leaving headquarters. The American press was talking to Smith [who] introduced them. Terry said, 'I am in a hurry to get away, but before I go, I have just one question that I forgot to ask the Commander in Chief, Is this a private war in Tunisia or can anybody get in on it?'" Other accounts make no mention of the presence of newsmen during this chat; but, if Porter's version is correct (he was not personally on hand), then Allen had certainly placed Smith and Eisenhower on the spot by publicly questioning the management of the campaign. The reaction of Beetle Smith—a choleric sort quite willing to play the "bad guy" to offset his boss's surface congenial nature—is unrecorded. Smith did, however, become a bitter detractor of Allen.

However it is that the actual scene played, Allen's comment brought a small improvement for his command. Those elements of the 1st Division previously stuck in Oran (including division headquarters with Allen) left the port city for the status of reserves in central Tunisia.

First Division units remained scattered over the entire Tunisian landscape; the 18th Regiment was attached to the British V Corps in the north. Along with the division headquarters, the 16th Infantry, the 2d Battalion of the 26th, two artillery battalions, the 1st Combat Engineer Battalion, and some special troops were under the French XIX Corps in central Tunisia. The American II Corps, which had headquarters at Tebessa, held the rights to the 26th Infantry, minus its 2d Battalion and one field artillery battalion. The territory assigned to the II Corps included a stretch of wild desert and a frontage of two hundred miles, with a series of precipitous mountain ridges extending from the northeast to the southwest.

Winter weather and mud—as well as an awareness of their shortcomings—persuaded the Allied high command to busy itself with integrating replacements, adding artillery and armor, storing provisions, and deploying the mounting number of men at its disposal. Unfortunately for the democracies, the enemy was also gearing up with a veteran of the Russian front, Col. Gen. Jurgen von Arnim, brought to Tunisia to meet any offensive. He had been joined by Field Marshal Erwin Rommel, the celebrated "Desert Fox," for a concerted offensive against the North African invaders. The Germans continued to control the skies.

During January, elements of the 26th Regimental Combat Team moved into a reserve position near Sbeïtla, about thirty-two miles west of Faid Pass. Combat Command A of the 1st Armored Division occupied a position in the Sidi-bou-Zid area west of the pass. The 168th Infantry from the 34th Division climbed to the high ground northwest of the defenses held by the French soldiers. Allen, obviously frustrated by his reduced role, fell behind in his correspondence. Joe Pennisi attempted to fill in with a letter to Mary Fran who had obviously expressed her own unhappiness. "We were sorry to hear that you had a lonely, sad Christmas without Gen. Allen. It made him feel very bad because when he read your letter, he paused. The general also missed you and Sunny at Christmas. If Gen. Allen had more time to himself and he could stay around his quarters a little more he would write you more often. . . . The way things are is why I am writing."

Allen himself wrote home apologizing for his infrequent correspondence. "Just returned from a long inspection tour at the front. . . . Was able to decorate several soldiers in the frontline units and arranged for several battlefield promotions.

"It's saddening to know of and to see some of the losses that occur but all that is part of the cost that must be paid. . . . We have a sort of barter system up towards the front. Nobody can buy anything but we trade off what can be had. My division supply officer sent me a new pair of field boots that he rustled gratis from the British. I traded them off to Hazie [an army acquaintance] for several toilet articles, having lost my own, owing to the blowing up of a jeep.

"It is quite cold up in the mountains but I manage to keep very comfortable. Have the best sleeping bag in Africa. It does grieve one to see the hardships that some of our young soldiers undergo all uncomplainingly.

"Tell Sonny I am delighted he is doing so well in school. . . . Please don't think I am impatient about your mentioning your difficulties. I realize it is all very hard for you."

To his son he said that it had been impossible to write letters for two weeks because of the press of his duties. He again urged, "Keep up your suppling exercises without stirrups following every ride. . . . It is an old fashioned method of learning to ride but is more effective than lots of new tricks that they now use. . . . Mims [James, his bodyguard and chauffeur] and I were driving through the mountains in our jeep the other day and ran into a herd of wild monkeys of a larger type, more or less like small baboons." It was one of the few occasions that Allen's letters dealt with anything other than personal matters or the affairs of the division.

He enclosed a copy of a letter from George C. Marshall: "My dear Allen: From all accounts, the 1st Division under your leadership has been living up to the old World War record [Marshall had served with the 1st for part of WW I]. This note carries my congratulations and the Season's Greetings to you and the officers and men of the Division.

"The dash and precision with which the division carried out its landing and envelopment of Oran awakened memories of other days when I was younger and not compelled to make war from a desk.

"I envy you people and expect great things of you."

Whatever Marshall's unhappiness with Allen at Indiantown Gap, the issue seemed to have faded.

Allen also received a cheerful letter from Eleanor Roosevelt (not the president's wife, but the spouse of his assistant division commander). She was with a Red Cross club in London: "I have been getting letters from Ted quite irregularly. . . . I don't know if Ted knows that we have a new grandson, the fifth T.R. in direct line, born the day after Thanksgiving. . . . Ted wrote me that you were a natural born fighter, and that you were superb while the Division was landing. I hear the same from other sources. Everyone seems to agree that the Division Commander is worthy of the Division and I don't think there could be any higher praise.

"I am bitterly disappointed that there is now an Army regulation that will prevent my following the outfit any longer. No wives are to be in the same theatre [sic] of operations as their husbands. . . . There is so much satisfaction in working for the regular army, and I can't get the same joy out of working for the National Guard.

". . . I wrote Mary Fran as you asked me to, ages ago, but have never heard from her and wonder if my letter was lost on the way. . . ."

The pieces of the 1st Division continued to shuffle about. A portion of the 16th Infantry—the regimental headquarters team, the 1st Battalion, and some medics—journeyed by truck from Saint-Louis in Algeria to Maktar in Tunisia and set up a camp there. The bivouac area was on the left flank of the 26th's people at Sbeïtla. A few days later, the rest of the regiment loaded aboard a motley collection of flat cars, the traditional "40 and 8's" (boxcars designed for forty men or eight horses that dated back to World War I) and a couple of ancient passenger cars. Their eventual destination—reached by truck, after the train deposited them in Guelma—was Siliana, another Tunisian town adjacent to the sector occupied by the 1st Battalion and regimental headquarters. A day later, 24 January, the 16th's 2d Battalion left for Robaa, attached to the 39th British Brigade. After some confusion in guiding the Americans to their designated position, a planned attack on the hamlet El Glib was canceled. The 2d Battalion assumed a defensive stance.

The 26th Infantry Combat Team drew orders to move to the vicinity of Ousseltia, north of Faid and northeast of Kasserine in the Western Dorsal. They were to report to headquarters for the 1st Armored Division's Combat Command B. Colonel Alec Stark, the 26th's CO, and staff members from other units personally reconnoitered the area around Djebel Rihana leading to the Ousseltia-Kairouan Pass, which they would need to control to forestall an enemy attack. On 25 January, a combined force of infantrymen and artillery, and detachments of engineers, medics, antiaircraft crews, and tank destroyers, as well as an armored reconnaissance troop, advanced on their objectives. Their coordinated attack, supported by artillery, drove off the defenders—a battalion of Italian soldiers—sixty of whom were taken prisoners.

While the Americans immediately fortified their holdings, setting fields of fire for machine guns, they also received intensive on-the-job instruction on mines and booby traps. The fleeing enemy troops had mined the evacuated ground and placed booby traps by the roadside, in trees, among abandoned supplies of equipment and clothing, and also had set devices under the bodies of the dead.

Interrogation of the prisoners indicated poor morale among the Italians, most of whom were Tunisian born. Some of them volunteered to help remove a minefield that had impeded vehicles using the road to get to the new American position. The success of the venture inspired Stark to work out a plan with his 1st Battalion CO, Lt. Col. Gerald Kelleher, to hit the right flank of the opposition at two in the morning—again an attack in the dark. The Italians offered only modest resistance. The strike brought few GI casualties, bagged another ninety prisoners, and seized considerable stores of equipment, clothing, and ammunition. The captives revealed they had trained in Italy for three months, and after being outfitted, they flew from Sicily to Tunisia.

The American task force now controlled the vital pass; and, engineers laid mines while riflemen, machine gunners, and mortarmen deployed to defend against a counterattack. On 27 January, the Americans sought to extend their territory. The infantrymen, supported by mortars and heavy machine guns, encountered a more resolute foe. Still, the American-held ground increased, and among the prisoners were the first few Germans taken by the 26th since it had arrived in North Africa. Further progress, however, was halted as enemy armor appeared to be assembling.

That evening, patrol activity by both sides probed for information. At the U.S. command post, word arrived of a battalion—backed by batteries of 88mm guns—that threatened the task force. The following morning, while a reconnaissance patrol captured thirty-two Italian soldiers, the regimental intelligence officer, Capt. H. L. Peter, was killed. After the plans and operations officer, Maj. George Juskalian, left the CP (command post) for a tour of the front line, the sergeant who accompanied him part of the way reported him missing. Enemy patrols became increasingly active, and Juskalian as well as two officers from Company H were believed captured.

Combat Command B ordered a reluctant Stark to call off any further assaults and re-form at the original positions, which left the 2d Battalion and an engineer platoon to mine the pass and hold the ground taken. In a summary of the action, the combat team reported that a major difficulty lay in the Germans' air superiority. "Strafing and dive-bombing of the field train, the CP and the front-line areas was accomplished by the Nazi planes almost at will." A group of U.S. bombers and fighters who were summoned to the scene circled overhead and then left without taking any action. Subsequently a trio of American fighter planes roared in to shoot up the enemy positions for about fifteen minutes, which boosted morale and eased the burden upon the antiaircraft batteries.

Late in January 1943, the remnants of the 1st Division—the 16th Regiment, the 2d Battalion of the 26th, the 7th Field Artillery, and the 1st Engineer Combat Battalion, together with some French units—assumed responsibility for the sector in the Ousseltia Valley in central Tunisia. This gave Allen a command of combat units, yet technically he controlled little more than a regimental combat team; overall jurisdiction lay with the French XIX Corps.

His letter to Mary Fran at the time was more cheery: "Please do not worry too much about me, my dear. I feel quite sure that everything will be quite all right with me. It's a nasty sort of job that has to be done and our share is one that must be done.

"Strange to say, I'm in the best of health in spite of the exposure, ration difficulties, etc. . . . I realize you are having a tough time, my dear and I only wish I could make it easier for you. I really love you more than ever, my dear. I cannot tell you how much I miss you and Sonny. . . . Keep your chin up, dearest."

At Robaa, the 16th Infantry, attached to a British brigade, maintained its position but both sides dispatched patrols frequently until the night of 28 to 29 January. One of the scouting parties detected that a strategic hill appeared to be only lightly defended. As soon as the terrain was taken by Company G and platoons from two other units, the enemy opened with artillery; and the British retaliated with their own shells on the hostile gun emplacements. Two days later, a battalion or more of German mountain troops lunged at Company G's defenses. Simultaneously, another charge pounded at the British Buffs who held the left flank. Tanks and several aircraft buttressed the Germans.

Company G staggered back, slowly yielding one hill after another, until it had returned to the main defensive line—where the foe's advance stalled. The company was so badly beaten up that it retired behind the main line of resistance, counting five officers and sixty men killed, wounded, or missing.

Ernie Pyle, covering the front in this sector, reported, "The officers kept talking about three fellow officers who had been killed during the day, and a fourth one who was missing. One of the dead men apparently had been a special favorite. An officer who had been beside him when it happened came up with blood on his clothes. 'We hit the ground together,' he said. 'But when I got up, he couldn't. It took him right in the head. He felt no pain.'

"'Raise up that tent and pack his stuff,' an officer told an enlisted man.

"Another one said, 'The hell of it is his wife's due to have a baby any time now.'"

Allen advised his son in "a hasty note," of the latest achievements of the troops. "The division is going strong. They have learned to 'dish it out' as well as to 'take it' and are doing well.

"We took a bunch of German and Italian prisoners today. You should have seen Joe Pennisi interrogating Italian prisoners. You know he speaks Italian very well and [Lt.] Col. Porter uses him to question prisoners. He said that some of the Italian officers taken were quite surprised to be bumping into Americans. The German prisoners are a surly lot.

"I ordered a 'commando' knife for you. . . . Take care of yourself old boy and above all take real good care of your mother. Study hard and play hard. . . . Pops."

On 3 February, the 16th Infantry's 2d Battalion was relieved by a French Moroccan organization. The Americans enjoyed a week in a reserve area before moving to a defensive position guarding one of the passes in the Ousseltia Valley.

The pause enabled Allen to advise Mary Fran on the problems of their finances: "I want to be guided by your wishes in regard to Sonny going to Roswell next year. Believe I can handle it o.k. if I continue to economize as I have of late. By March 1st, every single bill should have been paid and all notes etc. What a relief. Have really been saving a lot since my increased pay started. For the last three months have lived on very little."

She apparently had asked if it were not possible for him to arrange a leave. He wrote, "I would dearly love to get home to see you. Doing what I am, leaves and detached service from the division are out of the question. When you mentioned it before, I always knew what I was lined up to do, from the day after we left England and could not get away. My future jobs will be equally binding for quite a while.

"We are having a tough time just now and hope to get this North African mess straightened out before too long . . . but it is tough on the men. Am writing this from a blacked-out dugout. We have to be careful of the Boche planes. They give us hell when they come."

Pennisi continued to do his best to placate Mary Fran. "I want you to know, Mrs. Allen, that the general cannot answer them [letters from her] now because he is very busy and spends his time at the *FRONT*. I'm glad to say we are all feeling fine and in good spirits so do not worry about your husband he is doing good work and looks fine. He does not exercise anymore but will soon because it won't be long before we will control Africa.

". . . All your letters you wrote me I showed them to your husband so do not think I am holding out on you. He also knows about Sonny wearing glasses etc. insurance, your coat and shirts you never got from Abercrombie. So you see Mrs. Allen you must wait and have patience until he gets time to answer you. He is working on capturing Rommel etc, that's why he don't write to you.

"That brown suitcase which Sgt. Mims lost in the sedan was never found yet and Gen. Allen's watch was also in it. I made up for his clothes lost and also his toilet articles but that wrist watch I got him a G.I. one. Whatever you do Mrs. Allen, don't send any more articles we got enough for the duration.

"We do get exciting times lately and we get a lot of fun too, but no matter how dangerous it is we still are going strong. You need not worry about him. I'm doing my best to keep him happy and helping him also. . . . Where we are in Africa there is nothing interesting at all. We do not trust the people here. . . ."

Even Ted Roosevelt participated in the campaign to ease Mary Fran's emotional state after she had dropped him a note that indicated worry about her husband. "Terry is in fine shape. There's absolutely nothing wrong with him. He's as fit as a fiddle and now that we're in the line, enjoying himself." Roosevelt told her that the mail Eleanor sent from England took longer to reach him than letters written from Texas. Furthermore, he confirmed his wife's statement that no wives were permitted in North Africa. In what may have been one of the least-reassuring remarks, he wrote, "All we have here are nurses—married to no one."

Allen vaguely brought Terry junior up to date on 9 February. "Cannot tell you where we are but the division is quite busy. You would have been amused to have seen an Italian officer we captured today. When questioned, he said, 'I wish I could shoot both Hitler and Mussolini, who started all this mess.' Said he had no idea the Americans would be so tough. . . ."

The indulgent father surfaced: "I sympathize with you in having to study so hard. Your mid-year exams are bound to be tough for you, especially since you lost so much time because of illness. I know you are doing your best. If you do have hard luck and fail to pass in any of your subjects, *you must not let it worry you.* I will understand perfectly. You have always tried hard and that's all I ask. You have never failed to do your best for me in every way. Am delighted with your efforts. Just keep on trying, old boy."

He spoke of the efforts to gain admission to N.M.M.I. but cautioned that Mary Fran's wishes were paramount. "It will be expensive but if you can go there, I know you will work hard." He finished with another admonition on "suppling exercises without stirrups."

Against the viselike squeeze of the Axis troops between Montgomery's Eighth Army and the Torch troops, as scripted by the Allied high command, Rommel, and Arnim, initially agreed to shift their attention to the west. Said the leader of the Afrika Korps, "With the move into Mareth [a Tunisian town a few miles across the border from Libya], we were once again able to work on different strategic principles. By exploiting our 'interior lines' we were now in a position to concentrate the mass of our motorized forces for an attack on the British and Americans in Western Tunisia, and possibly force them to withdraw. We had no need to expect any effective diversionary attack by Montgomery during this operation, for any such attack, launched without powerful artillery and bomber support, was certain to come to a halt in the Mareth line, with a heavy cost in casualties to the British. We first intended to eliminate the threat of the two armies [Axis forces] being divided by an Anglo-American thrust from Gafsa to the sea, by smashing the enemy assembly areas. This done, our striking force was to double back to Mareth to attack Montgomery."

Colonel Benjamin A. "Monk" Dickson, the hard-drinking head of intelligence for American II Corps (a 1918 West Point graduate), and his staff detected an ominous buildup of Afrika Korps assets in the towns of Gabès, Sousse, and Sfax. Dickson warned, "Rommel can be expected to act offensively in Southern Tunisia as soon as his forces are rested and re-armed and prior to the arrival of [British] Eighth Army before Mareth." Dickson noted the superiority in German infantry over that of the II Corps and predicted an all-out German attack through the Faid Pass, then the Kasserine Pass, and also the important town of Gafsa. The garrison defending the Faid location consisted of the ill-equipped French troops. Fredendall prudently requested reinforcements for his relatively small force and asked for an opportunity to regroup his organizations. The British First Army, under which Fredendall operated, disputed the findings of the American's G-2. Instead, they believed the Nazi onslaught would originate farther north, in the Pichon area near Ousseltia.

The Germans fooled the British with feints in the vicinity of Pichon before launching their panzers in a swift mechanized blow early in February. The French, according to Allen, fought gamely but were no match for the infantry, artillery, tanks, and 88s of the *Wehrmacht*. At least half of the French Constantine Division became casualties. Rommel claimed the attack bagged a thousand prisoners and explained that the object was to use the pass as the starting point for a thrust at Sidi-bou-Zid and Sbeïtla.

On Valentine's Day, 14 February, Rommel and company swung a mighty punch.

Said Allen, "The German panzers came boiling out of the west end of the Pass and with a whiplash of tanks, guns and men, that knocked the American forces reeling back behind the mountain passes at Sbeitla and Kasserine, 40 miles west of the Faid Pass." Combat Command A and Combat Command C from the 1st Armored Division, positioned at Sidi-bou-Zid, only ten miles beyond Faid Pass, caught the brunt of the German onslaught. Armor commander Lt. Col. John K. Waters, Patton's son-in-law, was among those the rampaging panzers snared. According to Carlo D'Este's book *Patton: A Genius for War*, the tankers of the 1st Armored later complained that Patton was the first general they had seen during their twenty-four days under fire. Patton criticized Eisenhower and Clark for not having visited the front. He, however, was clever enough not to openly rebuke senior American officers. While he would have his differences with Terry Allen, he could never make that charge against the 1st Division commander.

Aware that their original light tanks—Lees and Grants—could not stand up to the heavier Nazi armor or the 88s, the Americans hoped their heavier M4 Sherman, medium tanks, could defy and defeat German Mark IVs and the enemy antitank weapons. They were brutally proven wrong. Near the village of Faid, three platoons of Shermans clanked forward only to meet an ambush of German tanks aided by Stuka dive-bombers. Rommel observed, "With the enemy formations pinned down frontally, one armored group advanced round the northern sector deep into the American flank while another went forward to Sidi Bou Zid and attacked them in the rear, thus forcing the enemy into an extremely difficult tactical situation. A violent tank battle developed in which the inexperienced Americans were steadily battered down by my tank men—veterans of hundreds of desert battles—and soon large numbers of

Grants, Lees and Shermans were blazing on the battlefield. The bulk of the American force was destroyed and the remainder fled to the west." Outmaneuvered and outgunned, the two armored commands lost fifty-four tanks. To add to the disaster, the enemy bashed the 168th Infantry north of Sidi-bou-Zid.

Bill Behlmer, an antitank crewman in the 1st Division, recalled, "We moved into a valley called Ousseltia under cover of darkness. We were told we were to stop Rommel and his Afrika Korps from breaking out. We dug in our guns all night long. Other guys dug in machine guns, mortars, etc. At dawn we decided to light up a cigarette. A few minutes later, a mortar shell hit behind us. Then another in front of us. We dove for cover, because we knew where the next would land. All hell broke loose, and we didn't stand a chance. The Germans had gotten there first and were dug in on the slope ahead of us.

"The out-of-action signal came and we took off, leaving everything behind. Gen. Rommel had won round one."

Ernie Pyle who had prowled around that area of the front reported, "That Sunday morning hordes of German tanks and troops came swarming out from behind the mountains around Faid Pass. We didn't know so many tanks were back there and we didn't know so many Germans either, for our patrols had been bringing in mostly Italian prisoners from their raids.

"The attack was so sudden nobody could believe it was in full force. Our forward troops were overrun before they knew what was happening. . . . Command cars, half-tracks and jeeps started west across the fields of semi-cultivated desert, for by then the good road to the north was already cut off. The column had moved about eight miles when German tanks came charging in on the helpless vehicles from both sides. . . . It was a complete melee. Every jeep was on its own. The accompanying tanks fought till knocked out, and their crews then got out and moved along on foot. . . . We were swamped, scattered, consumed by the German surprise."

As the Allied front crumbled, Rommel counseled swift expansion of the gains. "I urged the Fifth Army which was in charge of the operation to push straight on during the night, keep the enemy on the run and take Sbeitla. Tactical successes must be ruthlessly exploited. A routed enemy who, on the day of his flight, can be rounded up without much effort may reappear on the morrow restored to his full fighting power.

"However, the 21st Panzer Division did not follow up the retreating Americans until the night of the 16th. On the morning of the 17th February, that division was in position in front of Sbeitla. But the delay had enabled the Americans to organize some sort of a defense and they now fought back skillfully and bitterly. . . . However, enemy resistance was overcome by evening. In those few days the 1st U.S. Armored Division had lost 150 tanks and 1,600 men captured. The 21st Panzer Division's losses had been very small."

Delaying actions enabled infantry and artillery units, like that of Bill Behlmer's, to withdraw. Yet, the Germans advanced, and having overrun the Faid Pass, they pushed on to take Sened, El Guettar, Gafsa, the vital airbase at Thélepte, and the southeastern half of the Kasserine Pass. Nothing seemed to bar the way for an avalanche of Nazi power to crash through the western end of the Kasserine Pass. This objective was actually a valley with roads, trails, and paths through the surrounding mountains, which at its western end split: with one route opening to the huge supply depot and headquarters for the II Corps at Tebessa; the other pathway led to the town of Thala.

According to Rommel's statement, he was convinced that a combined thrust by his and von Arnim's armies through Tebessa would oblige the Allies to pull back the bulk of their forces in Tunisia to the safety of Algeria, a serious defeat to the ambitions of Torch. Unfortunately for the head of the Afrika Korps, his counterpart von Arnim, with his Fifth Panzer Army, favored a more conservative holding action. Rommel appealed to higher authorities for approval of his strategy. Not only did the debate delay further attacks, but also when the upper echelons finally agreed to Rommel's proposals, they altered the approach. Instead of concentrating directly on Tebessa, the Axis troops followed a three-pronged attack, splitting off people to hit at Sbiba and Thala to the north as well as going for the western end of the Kasserine Pass.

Rommel had perceived that a move on Sbiba and Thala would bring his soldiers into contact with strong enemy reserves. And indeed, the 1st Armored Division's Combat Command B, released from the British V Corps, had tracked south. It provided the resistance around Sbeïtla mentioned by Rommel, and then it backed off to protect the Thala area and avenues leading to Tebessa. Conscious of the threat from an advance through Thala, more tanks and a British armored brigade rushed south to reinforce Combat Command B. As the German forces increased their pressure, the embattled Americans received help in the form of the 9th Infantry Division's artillery—which went into action after a forced march of 750 miles. With its aid, the Allied contingent engaged in a furious battle. Both sides incurred grievous losses, but the Allies were able to add more and more in the way of armor and men and also to hammer the Axis units from the air. Rommel was blocked from any further advance via Thala.

The 18th Infantry, which formerly was assigned to the British V Corps, came down from the north to defend the area of Sbiba. On 19 February, the foot soldiers repulsed enemy armored-infantry attacks and inflicted significant casualties. Rommel reported that his 21st Panzers had run afoul of waterlogged roads and "a dense minefield" in front of the determined Americans. The left flank of the American II Corps remained intact.

According to Porter's memory, there was uncertainty about where the elements of the 1st Division should be inserted. "We went to General Fredendall's headquarters which was way behind his forward elements, in a big mine, completely out of touch with everything. He must have been 30 or 40 miles behind the line. He was so far back that it looked wrong to Terry Allen and to me." Fredendall had actually ordered two hundred army engineers to blast a dugout in a ravine. A dismayed Eisenhower commented, "It was the only time during the war, that I ever saw a divisional or higher headquarters so concerned over its own safety that it dug itself underground shelters."

The problems at Thala and Sbiba, said Rommel, led him to believe that the Allies were weaker at Kasserine. He said, "I decided to focus the weight of our attack in the Kasserine sector." Kasserine Pass became the pivot on which to pin any Axis success. The initial investment of Allied forces in the pass included the 19th Combat Engineer Regiment, an outfit newly formed by the II Corps and who occupied high ground on the right.

On the night of 18 February, Fredendall telephoned Col. Alec Stark, CO of the 26th Infantry Combat Team, and tersely dictated, "Colonel, your Hq Company and Communications Sections are to be alerted. I want you to go to Kasserine right away and pull a Stonewall Jackson. Take over up there."

At 7:30 A.M. on 19 February, elements of the 26th Infantry under Col. Alec Stark began to reach the western end of the Kasserine Valley. The enemy had already begun advancing into the gap. Stark barely had enough time to place two platoons on the slopes to the left. The remainder of his forces were trapped on the low ground, unable to climb to a better vantage point. Due to a deep wadi that split the pass, it was difficult—if not impossible—to transfer men from one side to the other because the entire site lay under fire. The 33d Artillery Battalion (part of the 26th Combat Team) moved as close as possible to the pass in order to concentrate its guns. To guard against an end run to the left rear by the Germans, Stark assigned five tanks from the 1st Armored Division supported by an ersatz platoon composed of members of the 1st Division band. Allen's insistence that everyone in the division qualify with a rifle enabled the musicians to replace their usual instruments. Just before dark, soldiers from the 9th Division's 39th Infantry began moving into the left sector.

During the night, the Americans were almost entirely surrounded; and, while riflemen, machine gunners, and artillerymen zeroed in on the oncoming foe, armored vehicles dueled for the right of way up the valley. After a conference with an English brigadier, Stark agreed to a coordinated counterattack to begin at 11 A.M. on 20 February. Unfortunately, the British started their sixteen tanks and ninety riflemen three hours ahead of schedule. The American 6th Armored Infantry caught up with them—but then those up front moved very cautiously. As the foot soldiers milled about behind the slow-moving armor, the enemy methodically set up observation posts to direct fire "right down our throats," said the 26th's Regimental history. Within a matter of minutes all sixteen tanks had been disabled or destroyed. An order for withdrawal followed.

In a postmortem, Omar Bradley sharply criticized the dispositions by Stark, who subsequently was sent home to become a brigadier general. "Deployed men as though he were halting a cattle stampede instead of getting up on the high ground and stopping them with fire. No trees, no cover, country was flat. We came a week after, got [the] impression it had been badly handled." Allen's memory of the Kasserine defeat indicates his subordinate may not have had time to post his men on the elevated areas.

Allen conceded that after they brought up 88mm guns and mortars, the Germans punched through the combat engineers and the 26th Infantry. They swept clean minefields, and their tanks began rolling along the thirty-mile-long valley through the mountains. The Americans fell back, narrowly escaping from a complete encirclement. Disorder governed, and not only in the defenders' ranks. Lieutenant Colonel Kelleher, of the 1st Battalion, a Colonel Grimmer from the 39th Infantry, and two lieutenants were trapped in the panzer onslaught that surrounded the command post of the 1st Battalion. Kelleher pretended to be a doctor and Grimmer his badly wounded patient. The Germans temporarily

stashed them in a tunnel from where the two officers escaped back to
the American lines. They reported the deaths of two officers and that
three other officers were taken prisoner.

The desperate situation provided Allen his opportunity. The II Corps
directed him to put the pieces of the 1st Division he still controlled into
the line in central Tunisia, the province of the French XIX Corps, rather
than the American command. Allen oversaw the division reserves: the
16th Regiment, a battalion from the 26th, the 7th Field Artillery, and the
1st Engineer Combat Battalion. The area around Ousseltia (eighty miles
northwest of Thala) was ominously deserted, no Allied troops at all were
there when they first arrived. Soon, a combat command from the 1st Armored showed up. Reconnaissance discovered masses of enemy soldiers
a few miles off. Allen, the senior officer, held a conference, and the top
echelons agreed upon an attack that would threaten the German lines
of communication at Kairouan. Allen had established a close working relationship with Gen. Louis Marie Koeltz, who headed the French III
Corps and was responsible for the sector. As the German offensive
gained momentum, Koeltz telegraphed Allen, "This is a warning. General Anderson has just issued a directive to Colonel Fechets; Regiment
[the 16th Infantry] to go to Fredendall as soon as possible."

It appeared that Allen was about to lose a major portion of his already
reduced command. He promptly asked Koeltz, under whom he nomi-
nally served, to arrange that the requested reinforcements be provided
on a divisional basis, instead of merely detaching a component. Koeltz
acquiesced, detailing the transfer without delay of all available combat
units in the 1st Division to support the beleaguered American II Corps
to the southeast.

At dusk on 18 February, Allen, together with several staff people, left
the Ousseltia Valley to confer with II Corps headquarters at Tebessa. En
route they met Fredendall with his aides on the road at Haidra, some
twenty miles northeast of Tebessa. Allen remembered, "Fredendall was
cheerful and optimistic. He outlined the latest development at the
Kasserine Pass and stated that the 1st Division must be prepared to
counter-attack when needed. He directed the 1st Division to make early
contacts with Gen. Welvert [commander of the Constantine Division]
and have him coordinate his efforts with the 1st Division."

Allen quickly arranged for his division artillery commander, Gen. Clift
Andrus, to turn over his responsibilities at the Ousseltia site to French
units and immediately lead all of the combat units of the division to an

assembly area southeast of Tebessa. Allen contacted the command post for the 33d Field Artillery, one of his units already installed in the defense of the Kasserine Pass. "This CP," said Allen, "was operated by Captain Theodore Crocker, S-3 of the 33d FA. Crocker was not particularly worried, now that the remaining 1st Division units were on the way. He was a unique type of combat soldier, and quite a 'rustler.' He even produced Gen. Welvert, at 2 a.m. on the morning of 20 February. Gen. Welvert was a gallant old soldier. But, having had 10–15 years served, as a major general in the French Army, he was very jealous of his prerogatives. But he finally offered to have the French Constantine Division cooperate 'full out' with the 1st Division."

During the night of 19 to 20 February, the weary elements of the forces under Allen in the Ousseltia Valley rolled into an assembly area near Bou-Chebka, west of the Kasserine Pass. They arrived none too soon. The Afrika Korps had rushed into the pass. Devastating fusillades by American artillery and mortar fire from the overlooking hills halted the initial advance. According to Rommel, who on the morning of 21 February had motored up the Kasserine Pass to inspect the damage, "A long column of captured armored troop carriers was moving back through the pass, some of them still filled with American prisoners. Three completely shattered enemy troop carriers lay on the road where they had driven onto their own mines. . . . The enemy's plan now appeared to be to fight delaying actions in new positions and to stay on the defensive."

The German field marshal threw in both his 10th and 21st Panzer Divisions, and although they hurt the Allied defenders badly, the resistance sapped the German strength. Von Arnim, said Rommel, refused to let him have nineteen new Tiger tanks—56-ton behemoths mounting 88s, and thicker armor. The head of the Fifth Panzer Army wanted to keep these for his own initiatives. The U.S. Army Air Force, bolstered by an influx of planes and crews, held a tactical feast on the gridlocked Germans, who were unable to maneuver in the narrow confines of the valley.

As Rommel left the bogged-down 10th Panzers, he saw a heavy artillery duel hovering over his Afrika Korps attack. He remarked, "It looked as though their columns had made little progress and this impression was confirmed by the reports which awaited me at H.Q. After some initial success, the division's advance had steadily slowed down in the face of continually stiffening resistance. Unfortunately, it too had kept to the valley bottom and had not simultaneously advanced over the hills on either side in order to reduce the positions in the pass by an attack around their flank. Here again the right course would have been to put the main weight of the attack on the hills, bearing in mind, however, that the use of tanks would have been impossible in view of the wooded terrain. The American defense had been very skillfully executed. After allowing the attack column to move peacefully on up the valley, they had suddenly poured fire on it from three sides, quickly bringing the column to a halt. Buelowius's [General Karl; Rommel's subordinate] men had been astounded by the flexibility and accuracy of the artillery, which had put a great number of our tanks out. When they were later forced to withdraw, the American infantry followed up closely and turned the withdrawal into a costly retreat."

Rommel further observed, "An attack by Panzer Grenadier Regiment 'Menton' [named for its commander] after achieving some initial success also collapsed. The trouble was that they had gone the wrong way about it. After fighting for so long in the desert, the officers had suddenly found themselves confronted with a terrain not unlike the European Alps. The hills on either side of the pass ran up some 5,000 feet and were held by American troops accompanied by artillery observers. Menton had unfortunately confined his attack to the valley, probably having underestimated the Americans. He should have combined hill and valley tactics and should have taken possession of the hills on either side of the pass in order to eliminate the enemy artillery observers and get through the enemy's rear."

Unfazed by the considerable losses to the grenadier regiment, Rommel had resumed the attack, which he said included "fierce hand-to-hand fighting. Finally, at about 1700 hours the pass was at last in our hands. The Americans had fought extremely well."

As expected, Allen received orders from Fredendall's headquarters for the GIs to be ready at daylight on 21 February to block the north exit of the pass and then to counterattack from positions west of the valley against any German forces trying to advance toward that north end. Allen deployed one battalion, with antitank weapons attached, on the heights of Djebel Hamra to block enemy armor. He set up the two remaining battalions of infantry as counterattackers aimed at the left flank of any trespassing German infantry.

Fredendall relayed to Allen and the 1st Armored Division commander, Orlando Ward, a message from the overall field commander, Briton Kenneth Anderson. "It is absolutely essential that all individuals stand fast to their posts and not withdraw under any excuse. If enemy infantry or armor breaks into a position or around its flank, the garrison will hold firm, fight to the last and do its very utmost to prevent further enemy troops or transport following. . . . The post will not be abandoned."

At 3 A.M. on 21 February, the 2d Battalion of the 16th Infantry sifted into the Kasserine Pass and set up roadblocks. The combat history of the regiment notes, "The roads over which the battalion was directed to go did not exist, and the passes that the battalion was directed to defend were only trails made by camel caravans and were not feasible for use by attacking troops other than mountain troops."

Allen directed the 1st and 2d Battalions to attack at dawn. After considerable close-in and hard fighting, the German infantry struggled to withdraw to the north. But escape in that direction was cut off by British and American tanks bolstered by the 7th Field Artillery. Allied planes flew a series of effective sorties against enemy tanks and guns that "jammed up, bumper to bumper" in their hurry to escape being bottled up in the pass. An unofficial report listed three hundred taken prisoner.

As the day drew to a close, the GIs shifted about, often during the dark, to find advantageous spots before finally settling into positions that guarded the main gateway through the valley. On the morning of the 22nd, a heavy fog and light rain enveloped the scene. The unmistakable sound of bursts from German machine guns pierced the wet gloom. During the night, the enemy had slipped around the flanks of Company G and surfaced behind batteries of the 33d FA. All but one battery managed to extricate itself to the rear, but enemy guns trapped a batch of artillerymen. At the request of Company G, two companies from the 3d Battalion of the 16th counterattacked, assisted by the 6th Armored Infantry. The intense firepower of the Americans routed the enemy. At first, the poor visibility and the loss of an artillery liaison left the 33d FA shelling blindly while the foot soldiers emptied bandolier after bandolier of ammunition. But as the mist cleared, from their high-ground aeries the Americans showered the attackers with deadly effect.

While the 2d and 3d Battalions had been so occupied, the 1st Battalion of the 16th, with the 7th FA as its support, also faced the oncoming Germans. As the infantrymen moved into their positions, they discovered they were operating in a sector assigned to Combat Command B of the 1st Armored. Confusion arose over who commanded whom. The 16th Battalion commander—with an eleven-mile front—chose not to argue, but rather resolved to cooperate with Combat Command B as long as orders concurred with those issued by his regiment.

To the right of the 1st Battalion was the 2d Battalion; there were large gaps, however, between them and the next American outfit, the 9th Division's 39th Infantry. The foot soldiers held themselves along the slopes, while on the floor of the battalion about fifty tanks from the 13th Armored Regiment awaited the enemy. All three passes within the zone held by the 1st Battalion had been heavily mined in anticipation of hostile visitors.

Rommel conceded failure. "Next morning, the 22 February, I drove up to Thala and I was forced to the conclusion that the enemy had grown too strong for our attack to be maintained."

While the 2d Battalion had to fight for its life on 22 February, the 1st had no contact with the enemy; its sole action consisted of patrols. After two days with no confrontation, the battalion received orders to attack on 25 February. After a softening-up barrage by the 7th Artillery, the soldiers left the line of departure shortly before dawn. They reached the first objective in less than three hours; there was no contact. The men warily moved farther; again no resistance. The Germans had abandoned their Kasserine offensive entirely.

11: On the Offensive

The flood tide of the German advance had halted. While the Allies were no longer threatened by the possibility of being thrown back to Algeria, much of the ground seized earlier on the way to the seaports of Bizerte and Tunis had reverted to Axis control. Although the Germans and the Italians had lost substantial numbers of men and a considerable amount of their armor, the British and American commanders understood this could not be called a great victory. American casualties in the nine critical days of 14–23 February added up to 192 dead, 2,624 wounded, and 2,459 either prisoners or missing. Hundreds of tanks, half-tracks, trucks, and other stock had been destroyed.

Eisenhower had urged his II Corps commander, Fredendall, to chase the retreating Germans immediately; but Fredendall begged off, fearful "that the enemy had one more shot in his locker." In an after-the-fact analysis, Allen noted, "Once the German withdrawal to the south had started, their evacuation of the Kasserine Valley was conducted with remarkable celerity. The lack of any pre-planning for an organized direct pursuit had delayed the regrouping of any mobile II Corps troops."

With neither side able to mount an offensive, both paused to regroup and reequip. The Axis troops would depend upon only what they could salvage and scavenge, however, since the severance of their line of supply across the Mediterranean. Allen wrote to Mary Fran, "We are having a brief rest period . . . but there are countless interruptions and constant demands for this and that. Had to spend most of yesterday with General Alexander, the British commander-in-chief.

". . . As a matter of fact most of the division has been at various sectors of the front since early January. I tried to see as much of them as I could and to give them all the help possible. Consequently had to spend a lot of time in the British sector.

"Got a big kick out of the clippings you sent about the café life in Oran and the American movie actresses on the Eastern front. Guess that stuff must be restricted to the rear echelons because there's nothing like that up here.

". . . It's not possible to go into much detail . . . but when things were looking worst about Feb. 22, the good ole Fighting First was hurriedly moved to meet the Boche . . . where the penetration was most critical. It was said that the vigorous defense and aggressive, coordinated counterattacks of the First Division really turned the trick and started a general Boche withdrawal. . . .

"Now that you know what we have been doing, guess you can see how impossible it has been for me even to think of a leave or a trip home." He added that he had asked everyone who was reassigned to the States to telephone her.

"George Patton is our new Corps Commander and is doing awfully well. It seems like old times to see some of the old cavalry faces.

"At several stages during the last operations I was commanding a French division along with the 1st Division. You can imagine my orders being given in French. . . . Believe me, there is nothing exhilarating about this war over here. . . . I try to use every means to get every mission accomplished as quickly as possible and with the least cost to the division. . . . You remember Johnnie Waters (Bea Patton's husband). He has been reported 'missing in action.' He was either killed or captured. It is not known just exactly what happened to him."

In retrospect, Eisenhower admitted the "embarrassment" inflicted by the enemy resulted from a number of causes—most notably the "long-shot gamble to capture Tunis quickly." That risk, taken at his direction, was a major factor in the fragmentation of units. He also charged the intelligence staffs with mistakes such as the conviction that the attack would be at Fondouk rather than through the Faid Pass. Also, the supreme commander faulted the defensive strategy and handling of reserves. His fourth reason for the weaknesses shown was the "greenness, particularly among commanders."

Although he recognized that breaking up divisions and handing the pieces over to other organizations seriously reduced efficiency, Eisenhower briefly bowed to a perceived necessity: Instead of being brought back together following the Kasserine Pass confrontation, bits of the 1st Division were assigned to the British First Army in the north, which was subjected to sporadic attacks by the Axis who were anxious to keep Bizerte and Tunis open.

The battle that culminated with the enemy backing off at Kasserine ended, in Allen's eyes, as a stalemate. While he deplored the outcome, he refused to make Fredendall the sole villain. Under the structure of Torch, the II Corps could never operate as a separate, autonomous command. "It had not been possible for Gen. Fredendall to exercise the proper cohesion and control of his major units."

But a stalemate was not what Washington or London had in mind when they approved Torch. Marshall had shipped to North Africa Eisenhower's West Point classmate, Lt. Gen. Omar Bradley, to act as Ike's "eyes and ears"—a euphemism for a domestic spy, which is exactly what Patton termed Bradley. Part of the job was to ascertain why the Americans had not done better. Someone was to blame, and the most popular candidate for the chopping block was Fredendall who, to Eisenhower and others, was a reluctant warrior. He, as well as some of the intelligence specialists and, subsequently, the 1st Armored Division commander, were the principal victims of the purge. With his bunker mentality, Fredendall had been damned by almost everyone.

As Allen said in a letter to his wife, in the reorganization, Patton—who had been drafting plans for the invasion of Sicily—assumed Fredendall's role. But, unlike Fredendall, Patton was only responsible to Gen. Sir Harold Alexander, the field commander for the entire Allied force. Among Patton's first actions in his new role, he decreed strict observance of spit and polish and military courtesy, which was characteristic more of garrison encampments than frontline combat. The Patton reign refused to take into account the blistering daylight temperatures in which GIs—clad in heavy wool uniforms, short of water, and laboring in an environment of dirt, oil, and grime—sweated until their clothing became stained and unkempt. In his diary, Patton noted, "It is absurd to believe that soldiers who cannot be made to wear the proper uniform can be induced to move forward in battle. Discipline," said Patton, "consists in obeying orders. If men do not obey orders in small things, they are incapable of being [led] in battle."

As Bryce Denno, then a young 1st Division staff officer, observed, "Casual in his own dress during combat, Gen. Allen did not recognize an infallible relationship between the wearing of the uniform and combat performance."

To the British commander, Gen. Sir Harold Alexander, however, the Americans simply lacked the qualities of first-class soldiers. He described them as "soft, green and quite untrained. . . . There is no doubt that they have little hatred for the Germans and Italians and show no eagerness to get in and kill them." On what grounds Alexander based his opinion of American timidity is unknown. Perhaps he relied on the infamous critique issued by the British V Corps that Allen had rebutted. For the most part, men under fire usually are all too eager to retaliate. After the shooting stops, they may accept the opponents as simply players on the other side. However, many U.S. veterans still despise the enemy more than fifty years later.

Like most of his countrymen, Alexander, a typically class-conscious Briton, had no confidence in the U.S. soldiers or their officers. He regarded them as little more than an armed rabble.

Allen hardly seemed to fit Alexander's description. As Ernie Pyle portrayed, "If there was one thing in the world Allen lived and breathed for, it was to fight. He had been all shot up in the last war, and he seemed not the least averse to getting shot up again. This was no intellectual war with him. He hated Germans and Italians like vermin, and his pattern for victory was simple: just wade in and murder the hell out of the lowdown, good-for-nothing so-and-so's." Pyle admitted he could not capture on paper Allen's wonderfully profane speech. While he offered no quotes to support his statement on Allen's attitude, Pyle was an accurate enough reporter not to make it up. Will Lang noted that the general referred to the enemy as "squareheads," "krauts," "boche," or "wops."

Fred Erben, a stripling rifleman with the 16th Infantry, gave the lie to Alexander's caveat about Americans. "The first death I saw was the result of an ambush. A friend named Bob Katz was shot while on a jeep patrol. The men became very angry and wanted to go on a patrol to retaliate. We later caught up with those responsible for his death. We shot them because they would not give up. I never knew I could actually shoot somebody. I was remorseful. I felt taking a life was wrong. But it was kill or be killed. I felt it was my duty and I was here for a reason. Many men felt as I did but we had some who did not care to take prisoners unless ordered. Many of the men had family in Europe who were persecuted by the enemy." The 1st Division included a large number of soldiers from the northeastern United States, home to many refugees from Nazi Germany.

More directly problematic for Allen was his new boss, Omar Bradley, a teetotaler. Allen thoroughly enjoyed hard liquor. And Bradley, when quizzed about Marshall, noted that Marshall was very rigid on the question of drinking—that was the law and he insisted that his officers obey it. "Rightfully so," pronounced Bradley. The new Eisenhower agent was prim—if not prissy—in speech compared to the profane, gregarious Allen. Bradley was a man proud of his good academic record at West Point, as opposed to Allen who flaunted his lack of classroom credentials. And Bradley was offended by the 1st Division commander's personality and his admiring troops.

In a curiously distorted posthumous memoir written with Clay Blair, Bradley said that on taking over II Corps, he visited three infantry divisions. "An old friend, Terry de la Mesa Allen (Class of 1911) [they were never friends and Allen was recognized as 'found' from the 1912 contingent]. . . . The 1st Division had been committed piecemeal but blessedly had been spared heavy casualties. [To the contrary, the division had probably lost about 10 percent of its people, or in Allen's words, 'considerable battle casualties.'] Neither Allen nor Roosevelt had any confidence in Fredendall, but I weighed their comments with a grain of salt. [Actually, Allen had been one of the few to offer at least the faint excuse that the former II Corps head never received sufficient control.] Both men were exceptional leaders revered by their men but both had the same weakness; utter disregard for discipline, everywhere evident in their cocky division. It was clear that the division needed firm discipline and intensive training. I was not certain that Allen or Roosevelt had the inner toughness to impose the discipline and training or the willingness to take orders from and play on the same team with the higher command."

If Bradley truly arrived at these sentiments after two weeks in North Africa, he could not have formed his conclusions on any solid evidence. He had not been present in any of the combat and his brief days on the scene could hardly have been sufficient to determine whether the 1st Division soldiers lacked discipline or understood the concept of teamwork. The charge that Allen had an "utter disregard for discipline" is false. A prime source of information for Bradley was probably Beetle Smith, Eisenhower's chief of staff who had already been offended by Allen's demand to get into the fight. The entire statement in *A General's Life*, published in 1983, smacks of hindsight and justification for what happened after the North African campaign's conclusion.

After Patton issued his clean-and-neat requirements, Bradley chortled, "Each time a soldier knotted his necktie, threaded his leggings, and buckled on his heavy steel helmet, he was forcibly reminded that Patton had come to command the II Corps, that the pre-Kasserine days had ended, and a tough new era had begun." Patton dispatched members of his staff to walk through American-occupied towns and enclaves where they would instantly arrest individuals not properly uniformed. They confiscated the wool or stocking hats designed to be worn under helmets but which many, including Ernie Pyle, used as their only headgear. According to Bradley, Patton filled his staff car with these hats. But there was little they could do about Allen's dress. Allen had ordered a slightly non-regulation uniform while in England, and Bradley was taken aback by his appearance: "Terry sat [at his mess] with his black hair disheveled, a squinty grin on his face. Allen wore a funny old green uniform and his orderly had sewn creases into his trousers but they had long since bagged out. The aluminum stars he wore had been taken from an Italian private, and were stitched to his shirt."

Bradley was put off by other manifestations of what he called "the initiative of the 1st Division." He remarked on Allen's mess, "where his rough table boasted rare roast beef while the other division COs made do with conventional tinned rations." The meat, Terry explained, was "casualty" beef, from cattle accidentally killed by enemy fire. Despite the warnings of veterinarians about sick cattle, these casualties happened with suspicious frequency, making their demise at the hands of the enemy doubtful.

According to Fred Erben, "The ordinary barriers between officers and enlisted men tended to fade in combat where we were all alike. The sirs and salutes were used only while in rear areas. Officers preferred it that way, figuring if you saluted them on the line, the enemy would pick them off. What the enemy did not realize was that any one of the enlisted men could take over because of the training received. Many enlisted men would receive combat commissions.

"The men felt they were good. We were cocky because it was instilled in us we were number one. Each man backed up his partner. We got to know about each other and the problems at home. We became like family."

To anyone who would listen, Allen boasted of his soldiers. "These boys of mine," he said to Lang, "are convinced they can whip the Boche any day. You can pick any of the boys out of this outfit, truck drivers, artillerymen, riflemen, they're all good."

Allen did his best to narrow the usual gap separating officers and enlisted personnel. Pyle said, "As far as I know, Terry Allen was the only general in Tunisia who slept on the ground. All the others carried folding cots [or slept in houses, villas, or hotels]. General Allen wouldn't allow any of his staff to sleep on a cot. He said if everybody in his headquarters did it would take several extra trucks to carry them and he could use the trucks to better purpose."

Allen invited Pyle to share his tent for several nights. "There was one bedroll on the ground. That took up half the tent. The other half was occupied by a five-gallon tin of water sitting on some rocks over a gasoline flame on the ground and by a rough unpainted folding table." An orderly made space for Pyle by removing the water can and shifting the table around.

The correspondent slept in his clothes, while Allen had stripped down to long underwear. Both men awoke in the morning, after a windstorm, covered in sifted dirt. "It took us about thirty seconds to dress and then we just walked out of the tent and went to breakfast, without washing or anything. That's how life was for one general at the front."

Will Lang's notes on a general's life read, "bug-eyed, wears English battle trousers, sucks air while talking and smoking, happy as hell to be back at the front, refused a cot in his tent CP. 'Your junior officers can't take it but I've slept on the ground before. Get that goddamn cot out of here!'"

Patton, until he acceded to II Corps Command, had a friendly rivalry with Allen through association that dated back to the fracases on the Mexican border, polo matches, and the camaraderie of the cavalry. Patton had been a member of the cavalry faculty at Fort Riley at the same time Allen instructed there. As Robert Porter said, they argued over the cavalry manual drafted by Allen but seemed to respect one another. Indeed, shortly after their joint promotions, Patton wrote to another friend (Robert Eichelberger, who would later command the American Eighth Army in the Pacific) that "at last they have had the sense to promote the two best damn officers in the U.S. Army."

However, shortly after being named, during his inspection tour of the infantry divisions, with Omar Bradley accompanying him, Patton committed an egregious act that could have soured Allen's attitude toward him. The visitors arrived at the 1st Division CP, a set of tents by an oasis, early in the morning. It had been a long, and quite possibly bibulous, night for Allen and Roosevelt (who appeared still in his bathrobe). The senior officers came upon a number of nearby slit trenches used for protection from *Luftwaffe* raids. According to Bradley, "Patton strode about eyeing these slit trenches with utter contempt, as though they were cowardly retreats. In his squeaky tenor, he said, 'Terry, which one is yours?' When Allen pointed out his slit trench, Patton strode over, unzipped his fly and urinated into the trench. Imperiously rezipping his fly, Patton sneered at Terry, 'Now try to use it.' With this earthy GI gesture, Patton had virtually labeled Allen a coward in front of his own men. I was no less shocked than Terry and I had to wonder if this was indeed good leadership."

When Carlo D'Este researched this episode, he found that the burly bodyguards for Allen and Roosevelt, armed with stripped-down Thompson submachine guns, unlocked the safeties on their weapons—making a clearly audible noise. "Had either commander given the order, there is little doubt they would gladly have shot Patton where he stood. Patton got the message and left as quickly as he had come. It was an ugly incident, a humiliating experience for Terry Allen and one that did no credit whatsoever to Patton, who always seemed to overact when they came into contact." Peeing on something of presumed value was a hallmark of Patton's calculated histrionics. When he reached the Rhine River in 1945, he emptied his bladder from the bank, in supposed emulation of William the Conqueror.

Ladislas Farago, in his biography, *Patton: Ordeal and Triumph,* wrote off the incident as a bad joke that no one took seriously; but in light of Patton's continuing clashes with Allen in the coming months, the insult at the oasis was only the opening salvo. Patton actually sprayed his disrespect toward all who came within range, sneering behind their backs at Eisenhower, Bradley, and Clark.

Although he would hardly have publicly admitted it, Terry Allen believed his troops could improve: Under the new order of battle, he finally had all of his division under his command. And in the weeks after the end of the Kasserine Pass affair, he instituted a rigorous training program at Morsott. Ostensibly it was a school for incoming replacements, in which newcomers were instructed by a cadre from the veteran officers and enlisted men. Those enrolled not only underwent intensive physical conditioning and practice with infantry weapons and tactics, including night combat, but they also went through orientation on the background and traditions of the 1st Division—in accord with Allen's theory of loyalty to the unit. The work at Morsott inevitably sharpened the skills and discipline of the old-timers as well.

George Zenie, in charge of an antitank gun crew, noted that the veterans of the early days in North Africa had absorbed vital on-the-job instruction. "We learned to dig foxholes in the sides of hills and cover the tops for protection against artillery fire. We learned never to flash a mess kit in the sun because the reflection would bring enemy artillery. When we went on patrols to gather information or capture a prisoner we learned to stay quiet, wear dark clothes and blacken our faces. Sometimes there were assault patrols that used automatic weapons and grenades. Here the purpose was to make a lot of noise and trouble before returning to our units."

With Rommel turned back, Alexander as the Allied ground's new commander-in-chief called for a renewed offensive that would smash von Arnim's Fifth Army in northern Tunisia, while Montgomery would whittle away the Mareth line in the southeastern part of the country. For Patton's II Corps, the immediate objectives were the hill towns of Gafsa, Sened, and Maknassy. Allen and the 1st Division drew the southernmost aspect of the drive, Gafsa—a road center and railroad junction some fifty miles south of Kasserine. The attack on Gafsa bore the unlovely name "Operation Wop."

As it began, Allen wrote Mary Fran a few brief sentences. "Our gang is working again. Sure they will get the job done. All my love sweetheart. I love you very dearly."

Pennisi followed up with letters to mother and son. To Mary Fran he wrote that her husband had been at the front, and he said, "I had not seen him for a couple of weeks. I knew he was well and very busy and when he did return he was in the best of condition and looked good.

"We got him a room in a hotel with a nice warm soft bed, a fireplace and a bath, which he really did enjoy. . . . The things you have read in the newspapers from Ernie Pyle don't believe it. We have yet to see a show, or go to a dance or any other entertainment. Maybe Corps or the other bunch of soldiers have the opportunity to see these shows, not the Fighting First.

"We are always busy and in the field, how can we go to Oran to see those actresses when we are about 500 miles away. Remember this, Mrs. Allen, it's going to be the 1st Division that is going to win this war.

"I asked your husband, how come other officers go back to U.S. Why don't he? He answered, 'Pennisi, I would love to but it can't be done.' He wants to stay with the 1st Division, and if the men can't go back, neither will he. . . . We were very glad to hear Sonny has passed in school and feeling well. Also glad to hear your voice on the Victrola Disc on your birthday and your husband did get a kick out of it. He sure loved it very much, also when he heard Sonny's voice."

To Terry junior he reported, "We certainly did get a laugh from the disc on your mother's birthday, especially your daddy he laughed so much he got tears in his eyes. . . . Right now things are a little quiet but we will be on our way in a few days. Your daddy and Gen. Roosevelt have already left for the front but before they left they said you should be good and take care of your mother. . . ."

The town of Gafsa, previously occupied by Americans who evacuated after the enemy breakthrough at Faid, was now held by a mixture of Germans and Italians. The night of 16 to 17 March, under cover of darkness, the entire division boarded trucks and other vehicles to rattle across the fifty-mile stretch of desert. In the vanguard traveled the 1st Engineer Battalion, removing mines and obstacles. Allen actually wanted to launch the attack in the darkness, but Patton vetoed the idea.

Intelligence specialist Monk Dickson, invited by Patton to accompany him, visited Allen at the 1st Division command post. "We found morale was sky high as the Big Red One was fighting as a unit for the first time since its November landings."

By 6 A.M. on 17 March, all three infantry regiments were in position. A fog delayed the jump-off by four hours, but following an aerial bombardment, the assault troops closed in. Only then did they learn that all of the twelve hundred defenders had departed the town. Reconnaissance informed Allen that Gafsa was not defensible from a counterattack from the east but that the hills around the village of El Guettar, about fifteen miles to the east, would furnish control over the surrounding territory.

Allen initiated an aggressive patrol of the roads leading toward El Guettar by his reconnaissance troop. He also dispatched the 1st Ranger Battalion, attached to his organization, to outpost a screen. A horseshoe-shaped mountainous area dominated the two roads between Gafsa and El Guettar. Intelligence reports indicated the presence of six thousand Italian soldiers manning stalwart defensive positions in the hills.

Three key enemy positions needed to be taken. Djebel El Ank, a knife-like ridge seven miles northeast of the town, anchored the northern flank of the main defenses. Djebel Berda, a horseshoe-shaped hill mass eight miles east of El Guettar, served as the central stronghold for the Italians. Djebel Berda, another mountainous pile infested with troops, lay nine miles southeast of the village. Allen deployed the 26th Infantry against Djebel El Ank while the 18th Infantry was assigned to attack Djebel Berda. The Rangers would protect the 26th Infantry striking along a mountain ridge known as Djebel Orbata to the left of the 26th. The 16th Infantry was to trail in reserve, prepared to jump in quickly.

The initial attack began at midnight 20–21 March, as the 26th Infantry under Col. George Taylor assaulted Djebel El Ank. Vigorous aid was rendered by the Rangers who, led by Col. William O. Darby, stealthily climbed twelve miles up steep hills to the rear of the defenders. The two American forces fell upon the Italians, and by midmorning the defenders of Djebel El Ank were dead, wounded, captured, or in full flight.

Success also attended the assaults on the other objectives, and the 1st Division extended its holdings eight miles east of El Guettar with the capture by the 18th Infantry of another series of escarpments, Djebel Moheltat. But beyond were extensive Axis ground forces. From *Luftwaffe* nests coveys of Me-109s and Junkers 87Bs roared to strafe, bomb, and harass. Resistance stiffened, and probes felt for soft spots in the American lines as von Arnim's soldiers mobilized for furious counterattacks. To forestall a breakthrough, the 39th Infantry of the 9th Division entered Gafsa, allowing the portion of the 16th Infantry in reserve there to advance to El Guettar.

Patton visited the front on 21 March and barely escaped serious damage when several German artillery shells exploded on a hill in front of him. Bryce Denno said that the II Corps chief visited Allen's command post almost daily "to complain about the division's performance, especially its lack of drive during a counterattack."

On 23 March, the foe surged forward. Shortly before 5 A.M., an outpost of the Reconnaissance Company saw a pair of motorcyclists on the road. One soldier was shot, the other captured. The Americans were alerted by radio that sixteen tanks, accompanied by two companies of infantry, were spotted advancing. The GIs opened up with machine guns, 75mm HE and AP (high-explosive and armor-piercing shells). Units of the 16th and 18th Infantries were under fire, and the enemy threatened to envelop the flank of a battalion. At 7:01 A.M. word passed back of "the road lined with enemy vehicles." The Ranger observation post saw tanks on both sides of the road creeping toward them, while spewing out shells. The 10th Panzer Division—battered at Kasserine, but now replenished—was to test the 1st Division again.

Ted Roosevelt made his way to the 18th Infantry observation post and confirmed the bad news. German Infantry units had reinforced the Italian defenders of Djebel Moheltat and those on the Djebel Berda, and these German units were pressing hard against the 18th Infantry battalions that had attained the forward slopes of the two objectives. Also, probing columns of German infantry and tanks infiltrated behind the 3d Battalion of the 18th Infantry and overran some field pieces from the 5th and 32d Field Artillery. A report tallied, "All the guns of Companies B and C, 601st Tank Destroyer Battalion and 7 guns of 899th Tank Destroyer Battalion were lost. 30 and possibly 40 enemy tanks were knocked out."

About fifty Mark IV German tanks joined in the assault. Ten Ju 88s, escorted by Me-109s and Fw-190s, dodged antiaircraft sent up by the 105th Coast Artillery Battalion (anti-aircraft), which claimed four of the Junkers shot down. Company A of the 1st Engineer Battalion put down their tools and picked up rifles to become infantry. Still, an estimated thirty-eight German tanks plowed forward. Dive-bombers now preceded them but did little damage. Jeeps scurried back and forth on ammunition runs. A message from the 18th Infantry Combat Team noted, "Troops started to appear from all directions, mostly from tanks; hit antitank Company and 3d Battalion. Our artillery crucified them with HE shells and they are falling like flies. Tanks seem to be moving to the rear, those that can move. 1st Ranger Battalion is moving to protect the flank of the 3d Battalion which was practically surrounded. The 3d Battalion drove them off and the 1st Battalion crucified them." Strangely, the officer drafting the communiqué saw fit to twice employ the Christian imagery for this savage struggle. Some ground was given, but the Americans still occupied most of their objectives.

At 3:18 P.M. Allen was informed, "We have positive information that the 10th Panzer Division will attack at 1600 hours today." The communiqué listed a formidable number of infantry battalions and artillery that was expected to participate, along with a massive amount of oncoming armor. The combat intelligence and radio experts of higher headquarters had broken the German radio battle code. Later, an intercept revealed the counterattack was postponed until 4:45 P.M. The 1st Division Signal Company was directed to broadcast a message over the German radio battle net at 4:15 P.M.: "What the hell are you guys waiting for? We have been ready ever since 4:00 P.M." It was signed, "First Division."

Porter, as the senior intelligence officer with the division, had been receiving the results of the intercepts. He felt it necessary to advise the troop units with messages sent "in the clear" (i.e., uncoded) of the imminent attacks and the subsequent delays. While that alerted the Americans on the German plans, it also informed the enemy that their code had been broken. "I knew the British were upset over this message going out in the clear," said Porter. "As quickly as Allen came back, I told him what I had done and he said, 'I would have done the same thing.' Terry Allen, when there would be official queries [about disclosure of the code breaking], would state the facts and would add over his signature: 'What would you have done in Porter's place?' There were no further questions [about Porter's actions]."

At the appointed time, the Axis forces indeed renewed their offense, with infantry preceding the tanks. But from their protected positions, the Americans, with the luxury of strong defensive areas, broke up the push by the 10th Panzers. The Germans ended the engagement and retreated past the bodies of their dead and wounded, the burning and broken hulks of their tanks, of which an estimated fifty-five had been knocked out.

Bill Behlmer recalled, "We were getting smarter. [After] Gen. Patton took command of the II Corps we knew he was there to win even if he had us all killed doing it. We got the Africa Korps out of Gafsa, Feriana and El Guettar. But we also found our 37mm antitank guns were peashooters and ineffective against the big Tiger tanks. We played hit and run aiming for the treads and exhaust pipes."

George Zenie agreed: "At El Guettar we discovered how inadequate our antitank guns were against German armor. [Both the 37mm and its successor the 57mm cannon were incapable of penetrating the heavily armored enemy tanks. Yet eighteen months after the fight for North Africa, the campaigns in Sicily, Italy, and in Normandy, U.S. replacements still trained to fight with the 37mm and 57mm weapons]."

The offensive that included El Guettar presented Patton with his first opportunity to demonstrate what he could do with II Corps. According to Bradley, as the 1st Division troops had struck off on the road from Gafsa toward El Guettar, Patton exhorted Allen every inch of the way.

How Allen reacted to these face-to-face confrontations is unrecorded. But the switchboard operators for field telephone communications frequently eavesdropped on conversations. Carlo D'Este noted, "The air would turn blue as the two friends cursed each other in the most obscene terms. Patton may have outranked Allen but in all but their public exchanges, Allen cursed his friend and superior as an equal."

Allen viewed the battle from a hill position, while artillery fired over his head, and his command post—a collection of tents more to the rear—was still only two miles from the lead elements of the German tanks. A nervous aide suggested that perhaps it was time to strike the tents and withdraw. "I will like hell pull out," snapped Allen, "and I'll shoot the first bastard that does." Asked if he had known of the presence of the 10th Panzer Division, Allen had replied, "No, but I knew something was fishy, and we were ready for anything, weren't we? We won this battle yesterday, when we got up on those hills and only the infantry could have done it."

He held a press conference for British and American correspondents at his command post. "The affair," said A. J. Liebling, "resembled a mass interview given by a football coach right after winning a big game. The correspondents gathered around the General under a blossoming almond tree, amid the noises of guns, mostly our own, and of reconnaissance-plane motors, mostly German. He tried to look grave and modest, but the corners of his eyes and mouth occasionally betrayed him. 'I think the division has done fairly well today,' he said, 'and I want to stress the idea that whatever it did was due to teamwork. Everybody in the division deserves credit. The artillery deserves credit, and so do the engineers, the tank destroyers, and the Ranger battalion and don't forget the medics and the birds who drive the trucks. I don't want anybody to think I'm sore about air support. [U.S. planes had not been visible over the battlefield, but coming via a route that kept them away from the eyes of the men around El Guettar, they had been attacking rear assembly areas of the enemy.] I guess the Air Force here has a lot of demands on it. I guess maybe there was some other division on the front that was attacked by two or three Panzer divisions and the Air Force had to help them first.'

"A correspondent interrupted him to say, 'General, may I ask how many tanks you had in battle?'

"'None,' the General said. Another correspondent asked him if the 1st Armored Division in the adjacent sector had progressed enough to take any pressure off his flank.

"The General said, 'I guess they had motor trouble. [The 1st Armored bogged down in a quagmire while seeking to overrun Maknassy on Allen's left flank.] There is one thought I would like to leave with you gentlemen and that is that this teamwork is due to having the division together as a unit. It is a good thing to have teamwork when you're playing Notre Dame. It is good to have a division functioning as a unit when you're on the five-yard line. I would like to quote a couple of lines from the 1st Division song: 'We're a hell of a gang to tangle with; just stick with us and see. The 1st Division will lead the way from hell to victory.'"

Liebling said the press conference broke up ten minutes before German dive-bombers struck at nearby gun positions. Allen's comments fed newsmen filing for the edification of the folks in the States. But he knew his remarks would be heard by his troops, the brass at II Corps, and Allied Headquarters—undoubtedly they were the ones for whom the message was intended.

Outside El Guettar, Allen peppered the correspondents with his sports lingo. "We've got three of four combinations, A, B, C, D, and all we've got to do is wait until they show and then come out of the huddle. If the left end is any good, we'll run off their right end. When two men slug it out in the middle of the ring, one of them has got to give ground. The Germans gave today, pulled back during the night."

He had begun to articulate a maxim for operations: "Find 'em, fix 'em and fight 'em."

The command post regularly received nightly visits from a Junkers 88, remembered Siegmund Spiegel, the intelligence specialist assigned to the division. "We had no night fighters to protect us. The plane would come in very low, drop flares and then bombs on parachutes. These exploded above ground. We dug holes so deep you could call them graves."

Chester B. Hansen, Bradley's aide-de-camp, jotted in his diary, "The CP is in a date palm grove that looked like grounds at a Florida resort. They were however pitted throughout with slit trenches. I remember Terry Allen's CP tent was put down about five feet in the ground. There were very frequent air attacks on the CP." This sort of threat emphasizes the outrageousness of Patton's defilement of Allen's slit trench.

The performance at El Guettar impressed even Bradley. "Allen was very well prepared," wrote Bradley, "and mauled the Germans and Italians, destroying 32 tanks. This victory was doubly sweet. . . . It was the first solid, indisputable defeat we inflicted on the German Army in the war. Kassarine Pass had now been avenged."

As the fight for El Guettar ebbed, the 1st Division soldiers sorted through the debris of the battlefield. Among the piles of spent shell casings, burned-out tanks, and discarded and smashed weapons, they occasionally came across unburied GI dead. Allen took notice of one case in his official account. He reported that a half-finished letter, found beside a body at one of the forward positions (apparently written during a lull), began with, "Well folks, we stopped the best they had."

"That unfinished note, left on the battlefield, summarizes the spirit of the 'Fighting First,' far more than the plaudits of the so-called expert military writers."

After the 1st Division repulsed the Germans on 23 March, the II Corps attempted to score a quick breakthrough along the highway that ran from Gafsa to Gabès, a port city. Two regimental combat teams from the 9th Division relieved the battalions of the 18th Infantry that occupied the hill of Djebel Berda across the valley south of the Gabès Road. While the 9th Infantry Division on the right flank pressed the Axis forces, the 1st Armored dispatched a special tank force to pierce the defenses blocking the Gabès Road. Meanwhile, the 1st Division units slowly wiped out resistance that was hunkered down in the crevasses along the ridge-lines of the El Guettar sector. Not until 6 April did the Germans retreat, And the following day, the armored organizations broke through to tie in with the British Eighth Army, which had penetrated the Mareth line farther to the east.

"On Easter Sunday," said Bill Behlmer, "we were in a command car looking for a gun position. The lieutenant, platoon sergeant and another corporal were in the back seat, the driver, Swede Johnstone and myself in the front. I was on the outside and . . . Lt. told me to find company headquarters and report back. I had gone about fifteen yards when I heard a loud explosion and something hit me in the back. I turned and the command car was smoking. The right front wheel had hit a land mine. A piece of tire had struck me. I ran to the car and started pulling them out as an ambulance showed up to help. Swede was lying next to the wheel, blown open and dead. The Lt. and platoon sergeant were just shook up. The driver had a broken leg and the corporal in the back died on the way to the hospital.

"It was a horrible sight and a narrow escape for me. Swede's wish came true [he had previously said if he were hit, Behlmer should get his position]. I got his corporal stripes and his squad but at a terrible cost."

Allen scribbled a note to Mary Fran: "My CP just now is in an old Arab stable. We attack again at 4:00 a.m. . . . Went to mass on Easter Sunday, strange to say, one of our regimental Catholic chaplains said mass at 4:00 p.m. behind the front lines. Airplanes were flying overhead and our own artillery was firing behind the next hill, 100 yards away. . . . I love you very dearly and miss you terribly. Will only want to be with you and Sonny when this mess is over."

The advances could be labeled only partially successful because the combined Allied efforts had failed to cut off the line of the Axis retreat;

the main enemy forces remained intact in northern Tunisia. Axis troops occupied a quarter-circle enclave that included the cities of Bizerte, Mateur, and Tunis. In his autobiography, Bradley said he proposed shifting the entire II Corps north of the British First Army in a final drive on Bizerte with the 1st Division battling for the city of Tunis. Bradley grumped that others credited the strategy to Patton, and Eisenhower claimed he originated the deployment. The father of the plan might be disputed, but it was accepted and set in motion by Alexander.

In the first phase, Alexander created the IX Corps, which included the U.S. 34th Infantry Division along with British units. The initial attack bogged badly, and the Americans were mauled unmercifully. At the same time, Patton's tour as head of II Corps ended. He left for Morocco where he was to draw up the plans for the invasion of Sicily. Bradley succeeded Patton, and Brig. Gen. Harold Bull replaced Bradley as Eisenhower's "eyes and ears," again the proverbial fly on the wall who would buzz back to the supreme commander with word on his subordinates.

A triumphant Allen wrote to his wife—he rattled off the successes in the Ousseltia Valley, the defense at Kasserine that "stopped the Boche in his tracks," and then "the Gafsa show. George Patton and Gen. Alexander both came up and congratulated the Division for having pulled the first outstanding successful American operation in North Africa since the initial landing operations." Allen remarked on the heavy counterattacks by the 10th Panzer Division that were broken down. "Seven hundred German prisoners were taken and their other losses were heavy. Our losses were saddening but comparatively slight. I attribute this to the really excellent morale and training. . . ."

In a subsequent letter—written by candlelight in a cave—he referred to the tempest that had disturbed him just before the division sailed from New York: "When I stop and think of the prejudiced reports and allegations that were submitted against me regarding drinking, inattention to duty, cruel and harsh treatment of subordinates etc. just at the period when we were accomplishing such effective preparations for the acid test, I cannot help but feel a certain amount of amused tolerance towards the small minded 'muck rakers' who lack the 'guts' to fight in the open."

He devoted a paragraph to Frank Greer, an officer he chose to take command of the 18th Infantry and who had been so outstanding that he was recommended for promotion to brigadier general and a DSC. Then he returned to the Indiantown Gap episode: "For a long time I kept a file of the proceedings of the ridiculous investigation made of me at Indiantown Gap. I also kept General Marshall's letter reiterating ridiculous allegations made against my personal habits and qualifications as a leader.

"But when we started for the front on this last jaunt I burned up all that, not wishing to face this last acid test with any rancor or ill will on my mind or in my heart. The quick completion of this tough and nasty job is too important to let oneself be influenced by the feeble minded efforts of 'muck rakers' to tear down their betters. It has all been just so ridiculous to even worry over, although I admit it did give me many anxious hours. . . . When it's all said and done, the only persons whose good opinions and confidence I really crave are you and Sonny. All others are small change to me. So, 'What the hell.'

"Have been attending mass quite regularly and have received communion several times in the last few weeks. I never commit one of our units to battle without a prayer for their success, for the effectiveness of our plan of action and for the reasonable safety of our men." He closed with several paragraphs of encouragement and of his devotion to her.

Although he professed to be unconcerned about the opinions of others, Allen did not allow anyone to belittle the performance of his organization. He responded rather sharply after Mary Fran reported two returning officers had been saying that his chief of staff, Norman Cota, had sought a transfer, that the 1st Division had not participated in the "big battle" and Allen would soon be assigned to duty in London. "You must not pay too much attention to what these loose-tongued gossips have to say. . . . Dutch Cota was promoted for battlefield *efficiency* and now has an important staff job in London. He left the Division much against his will." Allen added that it was a matter of recorded history that his 1st Division had been in action as a unit since the Kasserine Valley attack and had "knocked the hell out of the Italian Centauro Division and five times met and defeated the best German Division, the 10th Panzer, and elements of the 21st Panzer Division. "Maybe he [an officer he identified as Chick Sheldon] saw this battle in the cafes of Algiers and Constantine, which we have never seen.

"I have always been the victim of the gossip of small-minded people and it worries me very *little*, but I do get worried when such people go out of their way to make such assertions concerning *this* division. . . . Frankly we expect the Division to continue to be very busy until Rommel has definitely been 'Dunkirked' out of North Africa. . . . It is impossible to even consider quitting this particular job until it is well done. . . . It might be well to discount most of what you hear except from people who [you] definitely know to be real friends of mine. . . ."

While his letters constantly told Mary Fran not to worry, she could hardly have been calmed by one communiqué that announced, "Jimmy Curtis was with me in my jeep yesterday and we had a great time dodging air bombs."

After another period of rest and refitting at Morsott, the division traveled a distance of 130 miles through the British lines to work the northern flank of the British First Army. By 16 April, the organization was primed for an advance in the vicinity of Béja, which sat at the juncture of roads from Mateur and Tunis about thirty miles away. The three infantry regiments and the artillery battalions relieved their British counterparts for an attack that would strike northeast from a line west of Tine Creek. They planned to break through the main German defenses, west of the Tine Valley, to open up the approaches to Mateur for a swift thrust by the 1st Armored Division.

Although their situation was hopeless and they could not expect reinforcements, supplies, or air cover, the remnants of von Arnim's army and the Africa Korps survivors—utilizing the natural ramparts of a seven-mile-deep series of hills—doggedly fought on. Because the front was so wide, in the dark of the first hours after midnight, all three of the 1st Division's regiments headed out abreast of one another. In the sector assigned to the 26th Infantry, the enemy offered sparse resistance; the 18th Infantry fell back temporarily, however, due to a counterattack that occurred before U.S. artillery pounded the enemy hard enough for the foot soldiers from Company E, aided by tanks, to take possession of Hill 350. The highest of the slopes in the hill chain, 350 overlooked "windmill farm," believed to be an outpost. When Company G attacked the farm, it uncovered a hive of enemy who organized a counterattack that drove off the Americans with substantial casualties.

The morning light caught the GIs, before they could dig in, on a landscape littered with booby traps. Companies E and G now attracted a sustained counterattack, while German artillery battered the hapless soldiers. Forced to retreat, the two organizations suffered 40 percent casualties from the encounters. Company F of the 2d Battalion, moved through intense mortar, machine-gun, and artillery fire, and managed to oust the foe from Hill 350. Not even a barrage from the artillery could dislodge the Americans.

The 16th Infantry similarly met stubborn defenders from the hills it faced. Not only did the Axis troops hold the high ground, they were also endowed with abundant automatic weapons covered by mortars and artillery. General Leslie McNair, chief of the army ground forces, had flown in from the States for a firsthand look; and, while at the 16th Regiment sector, he earned a Purple Heart after being nicked by a piece of incoming shrapnel. Hill 394 defied the 3d Battalion for hours—when the enemy finally abandoned it to the GIs, cascades of shells showered Hill 394.

Enemy fire pinned down all of Company K in a green wheat field that led up a slope. Shards of shrapnel ripped into the legs of Richard Cole, the CO, as he lay hiding in the wheat with his men. Ernie Pyle reported that the jagged metal shattered one of Cole's legs. With medics unable to venture into the killing field, Cole improvised a tourniquet, using his handkerchief with a fountain pen as the lever. Periodically, he loosened the bandage to prevent gangrene, and as night fell, he crawled toward the American lines. At some point he felt a telephone line, and with his knife he severed it, knowing that eventually communications people would search for the break. For twenty hours, Cole remained on the battlefield until rescued by the linemen.

When Lt. Theodore Antonelli realized Cole had been disabled, he assumed command of Company K. At dusk, the GIs and Antonelli worked around the hill until, with bayonets, they rushed the enemy from the rear. A grenade sprayed fragments into Antonelli's chest, knocking him down. First Sergeant Arthur Godwin now took charge, and the enemy fled in the face of the bayonets. A few hours later, when matters were temporarily secure, one of the battalion officers replaced Godwin at the head of Company K. But Allen, apprised of Godwin's feats, conferred a battlefield commission on the sergeant.

In the struggle west of the Tine, several of the heights changed hands two, or even three, times in the wake of attacks and counterattacks. Some of the fiercest fighting centered on Hill 523, which yielded only after a bayonet assault by the 1st Battalion led by Maj. Charles J. Denholm ("Mother" as he had been known by Behlmer at Fort Devens). Allen visited the 16th's CP: He pronounced himself proud of the unit's achievements and promoted Denholm to lieutenant colonel. Unfortunately, during a subsequent struggle for Hill 523, Denholm, with others, was taken prisoner and transported to Bizerte for shipment to a German POW camp.

One can sense the stress upon Allen from a letter written to Mary Fran on 28 April. After a paragraph dealing with silver bracelets he had sent to her, he remarked, "I spent my birthday during the Battle of El Guettar. Some birthday! . . .

"We have been in the line again for the past six days and, frankly, the Division has been having one hell of a battle. Cannot say exactly what we are doing but we are acting in cooperation with the British and are closing in for the 'kill.' The Division is carrying the brunt of the American effort and has had very hard going. We are fighting the best German soldiers that Rommel has and have made our way inch by inch through very desperate resistance. . . .

"Our losses are mounting and are saddening . . . however am thankful that we are getting the job done with the maximum damage to the enemy and the minimum damage to ourselves.

"Dick Harris is now commanding a machine gun company in the 16th Infantry and Bill Gordon a rifle company in the 26th Infantry. The responsibilities that these kids have had to assume are appalling, but they are doing it like veterans. Many replacements have been received because of the casualties which have been heavy among the officer personnel."

He shifted to family concerns. "Am delighted that Sonny is growing so fast and is maturing so greatly and doing so well at school. I realize what a struggle it must be for him to have to study the way he is and deeply appreciate the efforts that he is making. Please tell him so for me.

". . . I sent Sonny a trench coat by mail. I hope he will have received it by this time. It should make him a very useful garment and I know they cannot be obtained in the United States. The stars on the coat are stars I got from one of the captured Italian officers."

He reiterated his belief that she should make the decision about whether Sonny should attend N.M.M.I. and assured her, "Am feeling fit and am sure that my luck will hold as it has in the past."

The 1st Division effort involved not only its three infantry regiments and the organization's artillery and combat engineers, but also attached units. The 701st Tank Destroyer Battalion, the 6th Armored Infantry, and elements of the 34th Division, working on the flanks, seized a key objective, Hill 609. In his account of the campaign, Allen was careful to give full credit to the brother division. By 30 April, however, the Big Red One declared its three regiments of infantrymen substantially below its normal complement by 60 officers and 2,359 enlisted men.

The relentless American push shrunk the Germans' controlled territory. The pullback by the foe enabled the 1st Armored Division to plunge ahead, entering Mateur, fourteen miles beyond the former front lines. The 9th Infantry Division approached the outskirts of Bizerte. On the night of 1 to 2 May, the Axis soldiers set up defensive positions on the east bank of the Tine River, and in the mountainous area, for a final stand in front of Tébourba and Tunis.

In the account of the Combat Operations of the 1st Division covering North Africa, it says, "The CG [commanding general] of the Division, received instruction from the American II Corps, directing him to 'Impel the advance of the 1st Infantry Division. Insure a quick crossing of the Tine River, in the area opposite the Djebel Douimiss, indicated on the map. And to contain or destroy enemy forces, contacted in that area, immediately *east* of the Tine River.' In preparation for the execution of this mission, the 1st Division occupied the high ground, *west* of the Tine River . . . late on 5 May."

The 16th Infantry, in obedience to the instructions issued under Bradley's command, jumped off from the west side of the river on 6 May at 3 A.M. with the 18th working to the left, or north, flank while the 26th attacked farther south. As the Americans' foot soldiers forded the Tine, which was more of a creek than a river, but still wide enough and deep enough for armor to require a bridge, they were greeted by heavy shelling from the highlands beyond. "I need help," radioed the 18th Infantry. "3d Battalion has gotten lost; one company is in the wadi east of [Hill] 232 and may be cut off if we don't get help. Resistance is strong and we are getting hell. 2d Battalion is making progress toward the hill, but there is something forming in back of the hill."

The ominous foreboding became a terrible reality. As light streaked over the battlefield, two companies from the 18th were trapped in crossfire of machine guns and mortars on a ridge northeast of Hill 232. The GIs were caught in the open and reeled under punishing fire, with many killed, wounded, or captured. Some were able to infiltrate back to the line of departure, while the battalion attempted to reorganize in the riverbed.

Engineers hastily constructed a pontoon bridge for a tank crossing. After four Shermans crept over, the structure collapsed. The remainder of the armor could only contribute long-range fire. The advance across the Tine began to collapse with a number of units in dire straits. Frantic calls for help brought no reinforcements. When the 18th talked of a pullback, the 26th advised such a withdrawal would seriously hurt it. Allen informed the 18th, "Orders from Corps and General A [Alexander] to hold your positions. 26th can hold with our help on left rear flank. . . . This is his [enemy] last chance to maul the 1st Division. We will have complete domination if we hold."

But the foothold across the Tine was too exposed. Allen requested permission to bring his men back, and permission was granted. By evening, the Americans had returned to the west side of the river. Allen explained to II Corps, "We got stuck out too far. All our rifle companies are down to the strength of a reinforced platoon. . . . They will need a chance to get reorganized. We have been in too long." The opposition across the Tine consisted of the elite Barenthin Regiment, the same aggregation of paratrooper and glider-borne volunteers that had so stoutly fought for Hill 609.

The defeat at the Tine River brought criticism of Allen as being too aggressive, that he should have held his ground rather than advancing eastward. Bradley complained, "Terry Allen foolishly ordered his division into a completely unauthorized attack and was thrown back with heavy losses. From that point forward, Terry was a marked man in my book. I would not permit him or his division to operate as a separate force, ignoring specific orders from above. Had we not been on the threshold of our first important U.S. Army victory in Africa, I would have relieved him—and Teddy Roosevelt—on the spot."

As usual, no one casually accepted the discredit for failure. When Allen drafted an account of the northern Tunisia campaign, he quoted a communiqué from II Corps that ordered the division to cross the Tine and then "contain or destroy enemy forces contacted in that area immediately *east* of the Tine River." Either Bradley forgot what he had told Allen to do, or else the 1st Division commander invented the order from II Corps. If the 1st Division soldiers had stopped after they secured a bridgehead on the east banks of the Tine, they would have been sitting ducks for German gunners in the nearby hills. Whoever was responsible, the Big Red One took a pasting for an unnecessary venture.

When Bradley wrote that Allen was "an old friend" he ignored what one intimate described as a "class, visceral personality conflict." During the last stages of the war in Tunisia, the omnipresent telephone operators heard an irate Bradley say, "Allen, let me remind you I am your Corps Commander." Allen hung up, later labeling his superior a phony Abraham Lincoln. On another occasion he called Bradley, "a sanctimonious bastard."

Eisenhower and several of his staff toured the II Corps on 7 May and visited 1st Division headquarters. They were taken aback by Allen's demeanor. Harry Butcher, Ike's aide, told his diary a few days later, "General Terry Allen was roused from a sleep in mid-afternoon to tell his story to the General. Allen had been out most of the night on his duties. Obviously he was very tired. His discussion of the situation was given in monosyllabic monotone. Said some of his companies were reduced to the size of platoons, casualties amongst his combat troops having been high. His men were tired and without saying so explicitly, his story begged for relief. . . . As I heard Allen's story, and knowing of the fine work of the 1st Division, I thought how much better it would have been if Allen had been thoroughly cheerful, buoyant and aggressive, as such an attitude would have been more in keeping with the fine performance of his Division and of himself."

As the 1st Division tried to regroup, Allen said tentative plans were made to retake the high ground east of the Tine. But the Big Red One had shriveled, with twenty-four companies able to field less than 100 from the normal contingent of 185 to 200. Seven companies were below 50. Battle casualties for the past seventeen days amounted to more than 2,000. Then II Corps reported the capture of Bizerte and the British moving in to Tunis. The newly arrived 3d Infantry Division would assemble behind the 1st and then take over its turf. The war in North Africa was over for the 1st Division, and on 13 May came the final surrender of the Axis forces.

"The Afrika Korps," said Behlmer, "was bottled up and surrendered. The Germans marched in, stacked their arms, and sat by the railroad tracks waiting for boxcars to haul them out as POWs. They were very orderly and made no waves. We offered cigarettes and smoked with them. We didn't hate them nor did they hate us. We were soldiers with a job to do and they had lost."

While the exhausted 1st Division soldiers boarded trucks bound for Oran, British and other American units paraded through Bizerte. Allied planes bombed and strafed Axis ships fleeing into the Mediterranean. The crew abandoned a vessel bearing POWs and Lt. Col. Denholm, who was aboard, took charge. The ship limped back to harbor, and Denholm rejoined the division.

12: Operation Husky

Even before the windup in Tunisia, the Allies began to lay plans for an invasion of Sicily. Overall command of the forces on Sicily would reside with Alexander. While Winston Churchill viewed the island as a stepping-stone into Italy, American strategists, who were intent on a main showing in France, argued that intensive aerial bombing raids could knock the Italians out of the war. A series of high-level meetings brought only agreement that a decision regarding land operations in Italy would depend upon the outcome of the campaign in Sicily, Operation Husky.

Just before the ill-fated attack across the Tine, another contretemps generated bad feelings between Allen and Patton. A *Time* piece on Patton contained quotes from him in which the former II Corp commander denigrated the U.S. soldiers. Patton wrote to his wife Beatrice, "That damned article in *Time* has just raised hell. Terry accused me of criticizing our troops and I hear Doc [Charles Ryder, CG of the 34th Division] feels the same way. Of course I never said any of the things against Americans. I am their great advocate, but I can't help it [what the magazine says]."

Allen sent an angry message regarding the *Time* quotes, and Patton answered, "I should be somewhat hurt with you for writing me the letter . . . if I did not realize that you were very tired. . . . After the amount of publicity you have personally received, you should know that any one can be quoted without ever having been seen; and if you were not tired, you would know very well that I have never at any time, nor at any place criticized any American troops for anything. And certainly after the letters [of commendation] I have written you and your division, you must be a fool to think that I have anything but the highest opinion of their value and efficiency."

Writer Martin Blumenson, who published an edited version of *The Patton Papers 1940–1945* (the files had been expurgated by the family), reported that the magazine's North African correspondent protested to his editors that Patton had not disparaged the GIs. Blumenson also sagely commented on Patton's note to Allen, "The term 'very tired' was ominous."

The highly complimentary stories about Allen by both Ernie Pyle and A. J. Liebling sat poorly with people such as Beetle Smith, Eisenhower, Bradley, and Patton, among others. Allen was being praised for his close association with the troops—who were being lionized as the best of the U.S. Army. At higher headquarters people groused about the unruly behavior of the 1st and its commanders. Bradley commented, "Among the division commanders in Tunisia, none excelled the unpredictable Terry Allen in the leadership of troops. He had made himself the champion of the 1st Division GI and they in turn championed him. But in looking out for his own division, Allen tended to belittle the roles of the others and demand for his Big Red One prerogatives we could not fairly accord it."

It is true that Allen had offhandedly remarked on the failure of the 1st Armored Division to support him—"I guess they had motor trouble"—but there were more severe critics of the 1st Armored, which caused its general, Orlando Ward, to be sacked. Patton and Bradley chided Gen. Charles Ryder of the 34th Division for his lack of initiative and nearly relieved him. Fredendall was sent home, and almost everyone on the ground expressed anger about the air corps for either failing to confront the *Luftwaffe* or for dumping ordnance on friendlies.

Bradley admitted that Allen enjoyed intense loyalty from his troops. Despite the disaster at the Tine, the men were convinced he would not jeopardize them without just cause. Liebling quoted a young West Pointer on his staff saying, "There are some generals that if they find the enemy in a strong position, they will go ahead and get you killed. But old Terry will find the way around and kill them all."

Allen's near obsession with the welfare of his people was another sore point in his dealings with Patton. While Patton still was in charge of II Corps and the climate of North Africa turned even hotter and more humid, Allen went to Patton's headquarters. He demanded that the quartermaster issue khaki summer uniforms in place of the woolen ones. An eyewitness remembered Patton yelling in his inimitable high-pitched voice, "The yellow bellies of the 1st Division don't need khakis. Tell you what I'll do, if you get a third of your sons of bitches across the sands, I'll see that those that are left get some khaki uniforms." A furious Allen stalked out of the meeting. Incidentally, Patton's sneer about "yellow bellies" hardly squares with his assertion that he would never denigrate an American soldier.

With the campaign in North Africa concluded, Allen unburdened himself a bit to Mary Fran. "Our losses have been considerable and are saddening. Of course many of our wounded will be back for duty, but there are a great many who will never come back. On the whole our losses have been comparatively minor compared to the accomplishments of the division. Most of our infantry rifle companies are now down to one rifle platoon [about a quarter to a third of the normal complement]. But necessary replacements have been received.

"It has been a terrific responsibility to have had the division during this period. Because very frankly, we had to win and the 1st Division had to set the pace. . . . Have attended mass quite frequently and have received communion quite regularly. I always pray that our plan of operations will work with the least losses to the division." As usual he also spoke of money sent to her and to the bank.

"I know how you feel about my return on leave, dearest. But frankly it does not seem possible just now. I cannot leave the division and they would not even listen to such a request. . . . Am awfully fed up with all the cheap publicity that gets about, such as calling me 'Terrible Terry,' 'Wild Man' etc. As a matter of fact I've never been more seriously attentive to this all-important job."

As the plans for Operation Husky jelled, the organizations that were expected to participate jockeyed for additions to personnel. John A. Heintges, a 1936 graduate of U.S.M.A., spent the North African campaign as a training officer for newcomers to the theater. Allen's chief of staff, an old friend, arranged for Heintges to transfer to the 1st Division. But when Heintges picked up his orders, they specified the 3d Infantry Division.

Heintges recalled boarding an airplane in Oujda that was headed for Algiers and then Bizerte, where he would join the 3d: "We stop off in Oran, and who should get on the airplane but Terry Allen who was on

his way to Algiers. My valpack with my name on it was in the middle of
this bucket seat. Terry Allen comes and sits right next to me and he's got
a terrible hangover. Apparently, they must have had a wild party. It was
after the war and I could smell him a mile away. The minute he sits down
he puts his head in his hand and starts snoring, goes to sleep. About half
an hour before we get to Algiers, he straightens out, takes a couple of
deep breaths, looks around the airplane and sees my name on this valpack. He looks over and says, 'I'll be goddamned. You're coming to my
division.' I said, 'No, sir.' I pulled out my orders, '3d Division.' He said,
'I'll be goddamned. Those people up there don't know what the goddamn hell they're doing.' He said, 'I've been working on getting you into
my division, God knows for how long.'

"I said, 'I know it, Sir.' He said, 'Where are you going?' 'I'm going to
Bizerte.' He said, 'Well, you're going to stop off in Algiers and I'll see
about this.'

"He puts me up at the hotel which is a general officers hotel in Algiers.
He has one room and I have the next one. That night we had dinner together, and he tells me why he's up there. He said, 'During the battles I
promoted people, I decorated them, I gave out some D.S.C.s and Silver
Stars, and do you know that Algiers disapproved them all.'

"I said, 'No, Sir. That's impossible. You, a division commander, rode
out and gave a battlefield promotion and it was disapproved?'

"'Yes, and that's the same goddamn foul up with your assignment to
the 1st Division. They disapproved it up there.'

"The next morning I go to headquarters with him and we go to the
G-1 [personnel officer] of Eisenhower's headquarters. He was a thin
man, very pleasant. Anyway we sat down in front of his desk and Terry
Allen starts lamenting about all these dirty tricks that they pulled on him.
He had case after case, sheets of paper where he had given out Silver
Stars, D.S.C.s which he was not authorized to do, battlefield promotions
which they were reluctant to approve. And here are these poor guys who
were already wearing captains' bars and there were no orders out on
them.

"Finally he gets through all of that, and boy, he's cussing up and down.
Cussing Eisenhower and everybody else, especially the staff. Finally, he
says, 'And another thing, I've been trying to get this young man into my
division for months. Now he tells me he's going to 3d Division. Now what
the goddamn hell kind of thing is that? I want him in my division. He's
going to get a battalion.'

"This general turned to me and said, 'Where did you come from and where are your orders?' I showed him my orders. He said, 'I'll see what I can do. Come back tomorrow morning about that.' When Heintges returned, Allen was gone and the G-1 contacted Fifth Army Headquarters formed under [Lt. Gen.] Mark Clark. The latter got on the telephone and, said Heintges, "just ate my ass out. Get the hell out of there and get on your way to the 3d Division." Although originally ticketed for the 1st, Lieutenant General Clark and Maj. Gen. Lucian Truscott of the 3d Division had changed the assignment.

Allen not only lost an officer, but his performance with the G-1 could not have played well with either Beetle Smith or Eisenhower. His cavalier disdain for the prerogatives of the Algiers desk warriors responsible for certification of medal awards undoubtedly added to the ranks of the anti-Allen forces. His promotions and battlefield commissions caused even more rancor as those in the G-1 warrens tried to assign and transfer officers—only to find that Allen had filled slots.

Allen seemed uninterested in personal glory: His yearning for the Distinguished Service Cross in World War I had been replaced by concern and appreciation of his subordinates. Bryce Denno, as a non–West Point junior officer with Allen, recalled in a 1984 letter to D'Este, "The General assembled small groups of 1st Division officers and men and described the battle they had just won. . . . Speaking quietly and without heroics or even gesticulation, he told us how proud he was of the way we had performed and how privileged he considered himself to command men of our courage and competence. At no time did he so much as mention his own role in the battle. As he concluded his remarks, I glanced around me and I realized that he had captured every man in his audience."

Speaking to another group, Allen said, "I feel unworthy of the position I have the honor to hold. It is the most honorable place in the most honorable army in the world—the commander of the First Division."

He had a capacity to engage people one-on-one. When Robert Porter was promoted to become the division intelligence chief, Allen straightforwardly told him, "You're my G-2 as long as we win; if we lose I will fire you." Siegmund Spiegel noted, "He would put his arm around you, ask how you are doing. He was not a blood and guts type."

At the time of the fight around El Guettar, Allen had tea with a *Time* correspondent and after some small talk about his home, his wife, and Terry junior as a polo player, Allen remarked, "All this talk about division spirit just means the men won't let the other men down." The correspondent then summarized Allen's musings, to the effect that he would be forced to order men in harm's way but accepted the responsibility. For that reason he was determined to see that his soldiers received the best in creature comforts. He credited the morale of the 1st Division to this policy.

Solicitous of the well-being of his people, Allen also functioned like the coach of a team before a big game—rousing the troops with speeches. To officers of a tank-destroyer unit that had just been attached to the Big Red One, Allen said, "When the big day comes, we will have no transportation, no equipment and no ammunition, because it's always that way, but there will be no reclassification of officers in this division from combat to noncombat jobs. You win or die." Liebling said the listeners cheered and Allen, using a line from a Princeton football coach concluded, "The team that won't be beaten can't be beaten."

The respite between the fighting in North Africa and the assault on Sicily provided the setting for further confrontations between Allen and his superiors. Given passes to Oran, some of the 1st Division troops trashed clubs restricted to rear-echelon personnel, celebrated too enthusiastically in wine bars, and ran afoul of military police who were assigned not only to keep order, but also to enforce dress code regulations and other army niceties. The disorders grew large enough to require an infusion of soldiers to restore tranquility and even an order from Eisenhower for Allen to remove all 1st Division men from the city.

Merle Miller, as a staff correspondent for *Yank*, the magazine produced by and for the military, described what happened and the atmosphere: "Passes were not issued until 6: it took an hour to get to town from the bivouac area and the bars closed at 8. In the second place, members of the 1st were almost the only troops in the overcrowded, foul-smelling town wearing ODs [woolen, olive drab]. Everybody else was neatly dressed in suntans. Also, most of the rear-echelon troops were wearing campaign ribbons, which the men of the 1st had never seen before.

"A rifleman of the 1st would go up to a clerk, point menacingly at his ribbon and inquire: 'Were you at El Guettar?'

"'No,' the perturbed clerk would answer.

"'How about Kasserine?'

"'No.'

"'St. Cloud?'

"'No.'

"'Then take off that goddamn ribbon,' the embittered doughboy would say, tearing the decoration from the clerk's clean khakis and pinning it on his own grimy OD shirt.

"By this time a crowd of other 1st Division men, mixed with SOS [Services of Supply] troops, would have gathered and often a minor riot would follow, with anywhere from one to a dozen 1st Division men in jail for the night."

The misbehavior of the men from the 1st Division infuriated Eisenhower, Beetle Smith, and Bradley—all placed the blame on the cavalier attitudes of Allen and Roosevelt. An inflammatory remark attributed to Allen, was, "Once we've licked the Boche, we'll go back to Oran and beat up every MP in town." He was quoted, "We took Oran once and we will take it again." Whether he actually said these things is unknown.

Carlo D'Este contradicts the view Bradley presents of Allen unconcerned about discipline. D'Este's research shows that once apprised of the Oran riot, Allen directed Roosevelt, "in the strongest language . . . to root out and court-martial the culprits. . . . The lax leader depicted in *A Soldier's Story* simply did not exist." When Eisenhower heard that the 1st Division GIs had trampled a vineyard, he sent his deputy, Maj. Gen. Everett S. Hughes, to investigate. Hughes cleared the 1st Division of any wrongdoing and noted that the discipline and military courtesy he saw was the best he had observed in North Africa.

Drawing on the wisdom of some homegrown psychology, Bradley contended, "Despite their prodigal talents as combat leaders, neither Terry Allen nor Brigadier General Theodore Roosevelt . . . possessed the instincts of a good disciplinarian. They looked upon discipline as an unwelcome crutch to be used by less able and personable commanders. Terry's own career as an army rebel had long ago disproved the maxim that discipline makes the soldier. Having broken the mold himself, he saw no need to apply it to his troops. Had he been assigned a rock-jawed disciplinarian as assistant division commander, Terry could probably have gotten away forever on the personal leadership he showed his troops. But Roosevelt was too much like Terry Allen. A brave, gamy, undersized man who trudged about the front with a walking stick, Roosevelt helped hold the division together by personal charm. His cheery bullfrog voice had echoed reassuringly among the troops in every Tunisian wadi in which his riflemen fought the German."

The uproar in Oran was the product of several factors. Those who had been shot at and shelled had a natural distaste for noncombatant service troops. As Miller noted, the men from the 1st Division came to town in the same dirty, torn, heavy woolen uniforms worn in combat: They had no other clothing. Military police considered their dishabille a sufficient breach of regulations to harass them. Furthermore, it was rumored that they would return to the States, and when they learned that instead they were ticketed for further battles, many—not only in the 1st but also the 34th Division—were angered.

Miller quoted TSgt. Lawrence Zieckler of the 16th Infantry saying, "We were bitter then. . . . Actually what really peed us off was that we thought we were going home after Tunisia." One of the culprits for the tale of a stateside assignment was Ernie Pyle who had written some columns that raised the expectations.

Regarding the fuss over uniforms, in his two autobiographies, Bradley argued that khakis were impractical for field wear and that the changeover from woolens would have added an unnecessary burden to the supply system. Furthermore, he argued that a shift back to woolens for the invasion of Sicily would have tipped the timetable to the enemy. While shipping and issuing an adequate set of new uniforms might have been a problem, there were plenty available for rear-echelon people. Bradley's other concerns seem disingenuous: Soldiers in the Pacific, dressed in khaki, seemed to have no problem in the field as they fought the Japanese. Husky was to be a summer operation. In light of the semitropical climate of Sicily during these months, khaki would seem to have been appropriate.

The most significant result of the Second Battle of Oran, as some referred to it, was Bradley's reaction: "This incident (and others too numerous and trivial to mention) convinced me that Terry Allen was not fit to command and I was determined to remove him and Teddy Roosevelt from the division as soon as circumstances on Sicily permitted."

If it had been up to Eisenhower and Bradley, Allen and Roosevelt would both have been shipped home before Husky. Eisenhower could have had reservations about Allen after the 7 May visit in which Allen was visibly worn down. Bradley was quite vocal on Allen's problems. He said, "I was not happy with Terry Allen. I had already expressed my misgivings about Allen several times with Ike, and he had decided the best solution would be to return Allen to the States, without prejudice, recommended as a corps commander. [A similar arrangement had been made in the relief of Fredendall as II Corps leader.] But Patton valued Allen's battlefield swagger and insisted on keeping him 'at least until the initial phase of the operation is consummated.' I agreed—reluctantly—meanwhile persuading Patton to tone down a commendation he was writing for Allen's service in Tunisia with a warning: 'He's a very poor disciplinarian.'"

As the strategists worked out the details for Husky, Allen offered his own analysis of the North African campaign. He filed a report that covered "Combat Experiences and Battle Lessons for Training Purposes." He reiterated the importance of terrain and pointed out that the seizure of a dominant hill by his 18th Infantry had enabled the capture of El Guettar. He argued that the achievements of his units had demonstrated the value of night operations. Simple plans and limited objectives had proven best for after-dark ventures, and assault grenades had served better than fragmentation ones. He praised the Rangers for their prowess in this field.

Allen endorsed the partnership of tanks and infantrymen—as he put it, it paid "dividends." But unlike Patton, who promoted the theory that foot soldiers should support armor, Allen reversed the roles, conceiving of tanks as a "specialized" form of support for the infantry, like artillery. The dichotomy between the adherents of armor as primary and tacticians who placed the infantry's mission as foremost during World War II generally resulted in poor coordination between the two branches.

The old cavalryman remarked that in the Tunisian campaign—where no roads existed—horse cavalry could have been used to good advantage. Mounted troopers could have done reconnaissance where distances were too great for foot patrolling. In the arena of intelligence, Allen said some offensive plans did not allow enough time for any kind of reconnaissance. Orders to move out came when it was already dark. He pointed out the troops' deficiency when called on for patrols; performance could be improved through emphasis upon definite objectives and a stress on aggressive pursuit of these.

He praised the location of a clearing platoon from the 1st Medical Battalion only five hundred yards behind the aid station. Immediate surgery was "very worthwhile." Allen noted that at El Guettar 5 percent of the casualties were diagnosed as "war neurosis" or exhaustion.

He argued for prompt promotion and battlefield recognition of deeds. Perhaps the scene witnessed by Heintges flitted across his mind. He quoted another military maverick: "Napoleon's theories on the value of a ribbon is [*sic*] as true today as it was in the 19th Century." He added an aggrieved comment that at the close of the North African campaign he had recommended twenty-three men for a Distinguished Service Cross. None had been approved, nine were disallowed, and fourteen remained pending.

Allen admitted that the presence of combat troops in rest areas is "a delicate matter." He commented that most service and supply soldiers were held in contempt by those who had been under fire while the rear-echelon people resented the superior attitude of the latter. He suggested special consideration for the men who had been in battle, urging that service and supply troops temporarily yield some of their recreational facilities. "After a few days break from combat, the soldiers are more interested in rest, bathing, a little beer and sightseeing. Then tighten discipline."

A new face appeared on the scene, that of Maj. Gen. John Lucas, a graduate of Allen's first class at West Point (1911). Marshall shipped him to Eisenhower with the understanding that the American theater chief could use him in any fashion he chose. Eisenhower named Lucas his deputy commander—with the responsibility to report directly on general conditions and the functioning of the combat elements. He was, in short, another source of information to Ike. Lucas had long been a friend of Patton, having served with him in Mexico. And he would become one more critic of Allen.

Eisenhower confided his doubts about the 1st Division to Lucas. In his diary, Lucas reported, "He [Ike] is not satisfied with the 1st but neither am I. The division has been babied too much. They have been told so often that they are the best in the world that as far as real discipline is concerned they have become one of the poorest. They look dirty and they never salute an officer if they can help it. They should be worked over by II Corps."

A subsequent entry said, "Drove out and told Terry to get after the saluting in the division. The military salute is the sign of the fraternity and is important because it induces the pride the individual takes in being a soldier and wearing the uniform of the Great Republic. It has always seemed significant to me and I know this from my own experience [he picked up a Purple Heart during World War I while with the 33d Division] that military courtesy—saluting, proper reporting, etc.—improves as one approaches the front." That comment suggests either that World War I troops behaved differently than those of World War II or else that Lucas was incredibly naive. Officers within range of enemy fire regarded salutes as an invitation to enemy snipers to single them out.

Lucas remarked, "Terry was rather on a spot because of the discourtesy of his men when the commander-in-chief drove through the area it was hard to understand how a car with four stars on it could fail to be noticed. . . . It was reasonable to suppose that if Gen. Eisenhower were treated in that fashion, one of lower rank would hardly be treated any better."

Little more than a week before Husky kicked off, Lucas inspected the 1st and thought the division "has bucked up considerably. Roosevelt has a tendency to spoil the men. They need a firm and stern disciplinarian. Theodore is not that and neither is Terry."

It had been suggested to Patton, the architect and commander of the U.S. Seventh Army for the invasion of Sicily, that the initial force include the 3d, 45th, and 36th Divisions. The latter two were unblooded National Guard organizations. Patton protested he did not want to depend so heavily on untested outfits. Regardless of his spats with Allen, Patton told Eisenhower, "I want those [1st Division] sons of bitches. I won't go on without them."

Robert Porter remembered that Patton had called Allen and asked him to lunch. "Bring one staff officer, preferably Porter, with you," instructed Patton. "At lunch, General Patton told Allen that he had gotten the 1st Division added to the troop base for the attack on Sicily. General Allen was very much surprised. He had thought that we probably would have a longer rest period out of the line than we would if we went to Sicily to help with the initial landing. . . . Patton had looked over the new divisions that were coming and he decided that he needed at least one division that had made an amphibious landing in the Mediterranean. He asked General Eisenhower if he could substitute the 1st Division for the 36th Division which was originally scheduled to go in on the beaches in Sicily. Eisenhower said he didn't have the authority because some of the troops were coming from the United States. He went back to General Marshall. . . . The Joint Chiefs of Staff agreed that the 1st Division should go into Sicily."

About this time, Allen wrote home explaining that his organization was now training vigorously. "The division has been visited and inspected lately by a great many of the higher-ups. All have been [lavish] in their praise of the division and acknowledge very frankly that the division was always assigned the hardest missions and against the toughest opposition.

"Our friend George (whom you may remember as having sent me a letter which I received just a few hours before sailing from N.Y.) saw me the other day. He was most cordial and could not have been more enthusiastic in his praise of . . . the division. To me personally he has never been more cordial or more appreciative. . . . I long felt rather badly about such incidents in the past but nowadays is no time for harboring worries and grievances. Too many of our fine young soldiers are making the Supreme Sacrifice, for us to worry about our individual troubles. Have burned up the complete file on all that trouble."

He repeated that under the circumstances there was no possible way for him to come home. "The higher command put it to me that the needs of the division are paramount and that my services cannot be spared at present. . . . I love you sweetheart more than anyone in the world. . . ."

Not only did Patton insist on the 1st Division, but he also assigned it the most difficult of the landings, that at Gela. While the Rangers under Darby, now expanded to three battalions, would actually attack the town to create a diversion, the main 1st Division forces would come ashore on the beaches to the east of the town. Once Allen and his division became part of the equation, he and Patton began to bicker over strategy and tactics. In his diary, Patton said, "Bradley, Terry Allen [and others] came over for me to settle some arguments. Terry wanted the paratroopers [the 505th Parachute Infantry Regiment led by then-Col. James M. Gavin were to drop behind the defenders] to land on his left instead of his right. They can't due to terrain. Next he wanted to open fire at 2300, D minus 1 [the evening before the assault]. No. Then he wants some self-propelled guns. He thinks that the 1st Division is the only unit in the show."

Gavin recalled his meeting with Allen for a final briefing on the invasion strategy: "Having spent years learning how to issue an appropriate battle order [he was a "mustang"—an enlisted man who had won entry to West Point (graduating in 1929)], I was looking forward to hearing the seasoned and legendary Terry Allen tell us what to do. When his staff got through explaining what was expected of us, he concluded by saying, 'I don't want any Goddamned bellyaching. I want you to do your job and let me know what you are doing.' So much for the five-paragraph field order." Allen had apparently scaled back even further on his outline for field orders while he attended the Army War College. He habitually delegated responsibility to subordinates and, unlike Bradley for example, never attempted to micromanage.

Patton earlier had been enthusiastic about Ted Roosevelt, but now voiced second thoughts about Allen's deputy. He notified his diary, "The 1st Division is back on its feet and so is Terry. Teddy . . . is a problem but I think should have the 1st Division when Allen goes. He will need a strong No. 2 as he is weak on discipline but a brave and fairly good fighter. He bootlicks me to beat Hell."

Although he had demanded those "sons of bitches," Patton spared them none of his fury when they did not perform to his standards. During a practice assault landing, as his bosses—Gen. George C. Marshall, Eisenhower, and Bradley—looked on, Patton exploded at one infantry squad. "George blistered them with oaths," said Bradley. "Just where in hell are your goddamned bayonets?"

Allen himself continued to vex Bradley, and presumably his closest associates, Beetle Smith and Eisenhower. As the various organizations prepared themselves for the opening phases, Bradley noted, "While unit quartermasters trucked from depot to depot, requisitioning and laying in supply, Terry Allen's 1st Division reverted to its old freebooting procurement habits. Allen had learned his tricks in Tunisia where chicanery helped him secure extra supplies when necessary. This time Allen sent an aide to Eisenhower's headquarters in Algiers to seek help in circumventing the depots on critical items of supply.

"When I learned of this I went to Terry Allen. He grinned like a boy caught in a pot of jam. The 1st Division was piratical at heart; regulations were not likely to change it." Throughout the war, savvy commanders and supply officers frequently transgressed when it came to giving their GIs what they believed was vital to continued operations. The ultimate freebooters would turn out to be Patton's Third Army in France and Germany as it raided supply dumps to appropriate fuel and materials consigned to other units. Bradley offered no criticism of Patton for the sins committed in his name.

The island target, about 140 miles by 110 miles, had great strategic and tactical importance. It was separated from the Italian mainland at the northeastern tip by only the narrow Strait of Messina, named for the Sicilian seaside town. Stretches of rugged mountainous terrain wrinkled the surface of the island, affording excellent natural defensive positions. The basic scenario for Husky allotted the southeastern beaches to the British Eighth Army under Montgomery, while the three American assault forces would strike along the southern coast, which faced Tunisia and Libya. While the 1st Division busied itself at Gela, the 45th Division would strike

Operation Husky, the invasion of Sicily, began with airborne drops on 9 July 1942. During the Sicilian campaign, the Big Red One drove up the center of the island before turning right for their ultimate battle near Mt. Etna.

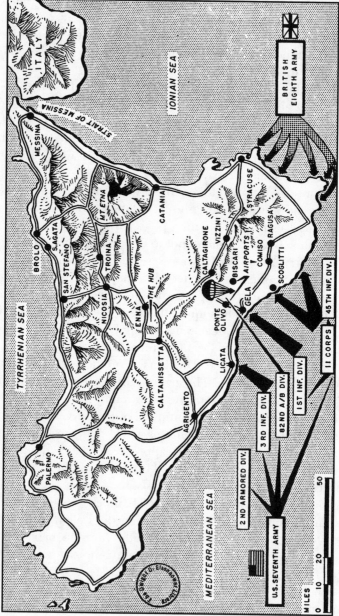

around Scoglitti to the east of Gela, and the 3d Division would attack Licata to the west. The experts believed the Gela sector would be the toughest to crack; and to strengthen the Big Red One, they attached Combat Command B of the 2d Armored Division with its tanks. Unlike North Africa—where an inferior, low-morale French army defended the shores—the Axis garrison included three German divisions and ten Italian ones. Because the fighting would occur on their home turf, the Italians were expected to battle much harder than before.

As D day for the invasion approached on 5 July, Patton met with Eisenhower. Rather than offer his best wishes for Husky, Eisenhower launched into a diatribe on the absence of discipline in Allen's 1st Division troops. Patton later said of this conversation, "I told him he was mistaken and that, anyhow, no one whips a dog just before putting him in a fight."

A mighty armada sailed on behalf of Husky, with nearly 2,000 ships listed for the initial assault. Another 1,200 vessels would assist in the operation. The 45th Division soldiers embarked in Oran; Allen and company departed from Algiers; while the shortest voyage involved the beefed-up 3d Division (27,000 compared to the standard 15,000), which left from Bizerte.

At 2:30 A.M. on 10 July, after a sudden storm whipped the seas so violently that the operation was nearly scrubbed, the first wave of assault units—the 1st and 4th Ranger Battalion forces—loaded into small boats and headed for the shore six miles off. The Rangers could see large fires caused by intense aerial attacks upon the big concrete pillboxes, barbed-wire entanglements, minefields, and coastal batteries looking to the sea.

Porter described, "The wind was very bad the night before our attack, and we had three lines of surf to go through the morning we landed. That meant the men would really get wet going ashore."

In the distance, the troops could hear enemy antiaircraft aimed at the paratrooper planes. Searchlights from Gela stabbed the sea to pick out targets for the coastal guns. The Navy slipped closer to land and began lashing the flanks where the foe's artillery bombarded the oncoming invaders. The Rangers methodically cleared the pillboxes of Italian troops, fanned out to silence the western coastal guns, fought their way into the center of Gela—and by 8 A.M. eliminated all but sporadic resistance. Quickly, Darby created a perimeter defense facing the Gela Plain, from where a counterattack most certainly would be mounted.

Meanwhile, to the immediate east, GIs from the 26th Infantry waded onto the sand, and on their right flank (four miles from Gela) sloshed the 16th Infantry. The 18th Infantry was initially held out as the reserve. The Big Red One met rather weak resistance; the first Italian troops that were encountered showed little appetite for fight even if it was their homeland being invaded. By 9 A.M., the 26th Infantry had met the Rangers in Gela; Allen now pushed his troops forward expecting to link up with Gavin and his paratroopers to seize the Ponte Olivo airdrome. The invaders had not gone far before they encountered stiff opposition—so much so that the Americans were obliged to switch from offense to defense.

Unfortunately, the airborne operations, fifteen hundred Britons in gliders and thirty-four hundred Americans in parachutes, unfolded with calamitous results. The pilots of the tow planes and transports, mostly from the Air Corps, were inadequately schooled in airborne exercises, short on navigational skills over water and at night, and green to combat missions. During the long flight from Tunisia over a complicated route designed to avoid prowling enemy planes, the high winds of the storm had blown the planes far off course. About fifty of the gliders had crashed into the sea; only fifty-four actually reached Sicily—and of these a mere twelve touched down near the objective. Gavin and his paratroopers, although not coming down in the water, dropped far from their designated zones and were strewn over a sixty-mile stretch of southeastern Sicily, well away from where they expected to converge with the 1st Division.

The most endangered beachhead belonged to the 1st Division. Allen and his staff had stepped ashore in the morning and located the CP northeast of Gela on the road to Niscemi. That was all according to plan; however, sandbars grounded the landing craft short of the beaches and delayed the arrival of artillery and armor attached to the Big Red One. Although the Allies held air superiority, German planes conducted sporadic raids the first day, doing some damage to vehicles, crews, and guns. Division artillery finally reached the beaches by six o'clock in the evening. Throughout the Sicilian campaign, the ground forces complained that the air arm, under overall control of a Briton, ran its own war and failed to supply coordinated tactical support.

The absence of Gavin and his people meant that Allen no longer had the luxury of keeping a regiment in reserve. The 18th Infantry would have to be committed as the enemy resistance stiffened. Predictably, after a night of reconnaissance and probing by both sides, the Axis rushed to counterattack, aiming to knock the trespassers off the island.

John Lucas, as Eisenhower's personal observer, noted in his dairy that he had arrived on the beachhead at Gela at 7:30 A.M. He was disturbed to see officers and enlisted men digging slit trenches while two-and-a-half-ton amphibious trucks parked close together. "If I ever command troops again, I will teach them nothing about digging. The slogan 'a soldier's best weapon is his shovel' has taken a lot of fight out of our army." Lucas was a friend and confidante of Patton and obviously shared his low opinion of digging in.

According to Porter, "Our G-2 section had told the commanders that if they met tanks the first day, they would be able to stay on the beaches because there would be no infantry with [the panzers]. If they met tanks the second day, there would really be a bad fight unless they got in tank-proof terrain the first night ashore. It would be very difficult for us since our antitank weapons were not due to land until the middle of the second day due to the shipping schedules. We estimated that by daylight on the second day, the German artillery, tanks, infantry could mount a coordinated attack. If the tanks came on the first day, that meant they were throwing things in piecemeal and we could deal with them.

"I was surprised to find the tanks appeared in the afternoon on the first day. They almost overran our positions. The artillery had just gotten their pieces ashore. Fortunately, they were behind an Italian minefield that the artillery didn't know was in front of them. They did have some protection from the tanks, but they cut their fuses for time fire set to burst about one second from the muzzle. There were a number of tanks left on the battlefield and the German attack was stopped short of the beaches."

Porter added, "Our units, after having taken on the 10th Panzer Division at El Guettar, were not too upset by the appearance of German tanks. The stream which they were using as their boundary between two combat teams was heavily eroded. Infantry units moved through the wadies and the tanks had no way of depressing their guns enough to get at them. The wadies were so deep that tankers without infantry would have had to get out of their tanks and fight on foot. This a tanker won't do. That was one reason the German tank attack was a failure. The [U.S.] infantry got into tank-proof terrain."

By dawn of 11 July, D-plus-1, the Hermann Goering Panzer Division, spearheaded by Mark II and Mark IV tanks, struck again along the entire division front. Ted Roosevelt stationed himself at the communications center of the 26th Infantry CP, which was located on the Gela–Ponte

Olivo Road. The site also placed him in close contact with Darby and his Rangers. At 6:40 A.M. Roosevelt advised Allen via field telephone, "Terry, look. The situation is not very comfortable out here. The 3d Battalion has been attacked by tanks, and has been penetrated. The 2d Battalion is in support but that is not enough. If we could get a company of medium tanks, it sure would help. If we are to take the Ponte Olivo airport, we must have those medium tanks."

The condition of the 16th Infantry grew equally precarious. Holding the division front's right flank, or eastern portion, the fighting intensified. Lieutenant Colonel Denholm, in command of the 1st Battalion and a POW two months earlier, was seriously wounded while personally manning an antitank gun, and he evacuated. Lieutenant Colonel Joseph Crawford, the 2d Battalion CO, suffered the same fate. Colonel George Taylor, the CO, issued these orders: "Everybody stays put just where he is. Under no circumstances will anyone be pulled back. Take cover from tanks. Don't let anything else get through. The Cannon Company is on the way. Everyone hold to present positions." Some thirty tanks menaced the regiment. Not until 10 A.M. could the 16th welcome the arrival of the Regimental Cannon Company, which finally had been able to debark.

The *Luftwaffe* and the Italian air force committed more than 450 planes to attacks upon the Allied beaches on 11 July. According to Bradley, "Axis air hit us with full fury, causing chaos in our landing zone. The enemy air was incessant and unrelenting. It blew up an ammunition ship off the beach and forced other ships to up-anchor and scatter. . . . In vain we searched the skies for close air support from our airmen." During the first desperate days on the Sicilian shore, the air command, under the British, pursued its own agenda—interdiction of roads and supply depots. No tactical air support arrived to rip into the German armor that threatened the 1st Division.

Monk Dickson's diary entry says, "The 1st Division suffered more shipwrecks than Sinbad the Sailor. It had its infantry but no artillery ashore when the counterattacks started with Italian armor and the Hermann Goering Panzer Division. The Big Red One called for naval support. We could see the destroyers in pairs run in, turn just short of the breakers and bring broadsides to bear on the hostile tanks."

As the Hermann Goering armor infiltrated beyond the outposts of the right flank, they approached division headquarters. Bullets ripped through the air and tank shells exploded near the CP. The Division Headquarters Defense Platoon combined with men from the 531st Engineer Shore Regiment in a last-ditch effort to repel the Germans.

In the midst of the battle, the Italian Sixth Army said it intercepted a message from Patton to Allen saying, "Bury the equipment on the beach and be ready to re-embark." Historians have been unable to find the original document with this order, but it was mentioned in the army war diary. Carlo D'Este in *Bitter Victory* calls preposterous the notion that Patton or any member of his staff issued such a message. A British researcher has suggested that a senior officer in the Gela bridgehead might have been responsible. But according to D'Este, the three most-senior U.S. commanders on the scene—Darby, Allen, and the 2d Armored's Col. Isaac D. White—"were strong-minded leaders who had no intention of surrendering their foothold in Sicily." White denied he ever authorized such a message. And Allen's G-2, Robert Porter, said, "There was no, repeat no, thought on the part of General Allen of leaving our beachhead at Gela. Darby did not survive the war but it would have been totally out of character and certainly not his prerogative to have called for a retreat."

Patton reached the Gela area on the morning of 11 July and stayed until around seven at night. Rather than authorize a re-embarkation he directed the navy men ashore, "Get all hands up here to fight." Bradley, agonizing over a severe attack of hemorrhoids, inspected the Gela sector to see the situation for himself.

George Zenie, who led a tank crew with the 18th Infantry, recalled, "Everyone in our LCI [Landing Craft Infantry] was seasick and miserable. We were constantly under enemy air strafing and bombing attacks. They sank the cargo ship containing all of the heavy weapons for our company. We had only the weapons we carried ashore, rifles and hand grenades, to fight off an attack by forty to fifty enemy tanks. We helped the artillery move their pieces to positions where the armor would be under direct fire. Many [enemy] tanks were destroyed and the rest retreated."

Bill Behlmer, as an antitank crewman, endured another ordeal: "The Hermann Goering Panzer Division encircled us. Tanks everywhere. We thought we could outlast them. The 57s which had replaced our 37 mm cannons performed beautifully. Finally, their big guns had us zeroed in and the German armored infantry was advancing. We knew we had to change our position, but we couldn't get the trucks up the hill to move our guns. I could see we were surrounded and got going. The Germans captured our guns and spiked them. The heavy cruiser *Savannah* and our own artillery saved the day. The *Savannah* steaming back and forth off the beach knocked out the tanks."

The combat journal for the 16th Infantry reported knocking out a trio of enemy tanks shortly after nine in the morning, but dozens more relentlessly clanked toward the infantrymen—who had only a few 57mm guns to add to their small arms and mortars. Cannon Company with 105mm howitzers was not immediately available; division headquarters had needed it elsewhere. An urgent plea for its return went out. The 26th Infantry advised, "Enemy tanks headed southeast along highway, just back of Yellow and Blue Beaches. Beach dumps being attacked." The enemy threatened not only the vital supplies, but also endangered possibilities for retreat.

The only impediment to the German advance had been the absence of its infantry. As the day wore on into the early evening, however, American observers saw twenty trucks unload foot soldiers and a quarter-hour later another thirty-five vehicles brought more infantrymen. All appeared lost as the German tanks now started to roll down the hills with the Mediterranean in sight. But just about this time, Cannon Company arrived. The guns were unlimbered, and they methodically hit tank after tank—destroying more than a dozen within a few minutes. Stunned by the sudden reversal of momentum, the Germans retreated.

Patton, garbed impeccably in his gabardine shirt, with necktie tucked in according to regulations, knee-high leather boots, and his ivory-handled pistols hanging at his waist, had marched into town to the headquarters of Darby's Rangers. Darby himself had been firing some captured Italian guns against the oncoming enemy tanks. The Airborne's Jim Gavin and a small group of paratroopers had been fighting off Axis armor with bazookas. Patton spotted a naval officer equipped with a radio and bawled to him, "Hey, you with the radio. If you can connect with your Goddamn Navy, tell them for God's sake to drop some shell fire on the road." The cruiser *Boise* soon started to hammer the tanks with five- and eight-inch shells.

The first elements of Combat Command B, under Col. Isaac D. White, finally crunched up the beaches where they could add their guns to the chorus of howitzers. With tubes depressed, the 57mm and 75mm cannons, 4.2-inch mortars, and bazookas, all sounded off at the enemy. The combination of firepower stifled the counterattack, and the badly mauled 1st Division savored a temporary respite.

Patton had paused at Allen's CP but found him away directing his forces. When a near-exhausted Allen returned, a cheerful Patton sat behind his field desk; with cigar in mouth, Patton casually inquired on the progress of the battle. Allen answered that it had been difficult but the division was holding its own and needed additional artillery support. According to D'Este, Patton responded, "I'm now an Army commander. Take that up with Bradley."

Patton then chided Allen for the failure of his soldiers to capture the Ponte Olivo airport. That hardly sat well with Allen who, as Patton's biographer noted, "was one of the most attack-minded officers ever to command a U.S. division but at that moment his one and only concern was to ensure that his battered division somehow survived the fury of the German counterattack." Allen recalled that while he had traveled about his tiny enclave in nothing more than a jeep, Patton toured with an escort of tanks and armored cars. He described the Seventh Army commander as "very wrought up" because the 1st Division had not yet taken the Ponte Olivo airport, scheduled for capture on D-plus-1. "Gen. Patton was told very positively that D plus 1 was not over until midnight that same day and the 1st Division would launch a coordinated attack at midnight that same night with Ponte Olive Airport as its primary objective. He was assured that the attack would go through 'Come hell or high water.' Gen. Patton finally left, somewhat mollified, but still dubious as to any assurance of any early capture of the Ponte Olivo Airport."

Allen drew a much more flattering review from his usual critic, Omar Bradley, who saw dust and smoke rising near Gela and surmised a tank attack. "A dog-tired Terry Allen waited for me in a makeshift CP near the beach. His eyes were red from loss of sleep and his hair was disheveled. His division was still under serious attack.

"'Do you have it in hand, Terry?' I asked.

"'Yes, I think so,' he answered, 'but they've given us a helluva rough time.' He briefed me on the start of the attack.

"'We're going to have a helluva time stopping them,' he said, 'Until we get some antitank stuff ashore.'"

Bradley noted that while Allen's artillery and antitank weapons were still being dragged ashore from the landing craft, two columns of Axis tanks were trying to converge and cut off the infantry from the beachhead. Allen had met the challenge by ordering every gun in the outfit to shoot at the armor from point-blank range. While trucks lumbered over the sand seeking to pull additional artillery into position, forward observers clamored for navy guns to shell the Gela Plain. Said Bradley, "Roosevelt hurried down to the beach, got an AT company being unloaded and rushed them up into position. Though overrun, Allen's infantry did not fall back. Instead they burrowed into their foxholes to let the panzer wave wash through while they waited to repel the grenadiers advancing behind it." The tactics and the additional artillery helped stop the foe, although the enemy tanks advanced to within two thousand yards of the beach—little more than a mile—before they were forced to retreat.

The battle around Gela ranged for nearly two days with the 1st Division using bazookas, mortars, antitank guns, and the division artillery to fight off the enemy tanks. But, as Behlmer noted, a key element was the naval gunfire support. Allen judged it particularly effective in its accurate engagement of enemy tanks and infantry reserves at this critical stage.

"Admiral John L. Hall, who commanded the U.S. Navy fleet that took the 1st Division into Sicily, will always be remembered by the 1st Division for his courageous support of the division in their landing at Gela. He not only landed the Division there with maximum efficiency and seamanship but he kept his ships close-in off-shore and gave the division highly effective naval gunfire support.

"One of his destroyers, the *USS Edson* thereafter sported 13 miniature German tanks painted on the forward smokestack. The skipper of this gallant little ship claimed that this was an authentic score of verified German tank casualties, accounted for by his gun crews while supporting the landing of the 1st Division in Sicily.

"This effective naval gunfire support had not been accomplished without heavy losses in the naval spotter aircraft in Admiral Hall's fleet." The achievements of the warships also owed much to a handful of forward observers from the navy. Allen's comments indicate that despite the sneers of his critics, he was quite willing to praise others.

Bradley commented, "I question whether any other U.S. division could have repelled that charge in time to save the beach from tank penetration. Only the perverse Big Red One with its no less perverse commander was both hard and experienced enough to take that assault in stride. A greener division might easily have panicked and seriously embarrassed the landing."

When John Lucas met with Eisenhower and Beetle Smith, he said they praised Bradley and Maj. Gen. Lucian Truscott, CO of the 3d Division. Lucas remarked that he saw no evidence of their efforts. Although no fan of Allen, he added, "Terry Allen's 1st Division had done most of the fighting."

The 1st Division was also fortunate that the Hermann Goering Division—believed to be a crack outfit—was more reputation than substance.

The organization had absorbed severe punishment in Tunisia, and the ranks had been filled with raw replacements. With leadership that was at best mediocre, the tanks and infantry were not trained to coordinate. And the huge sixty-ton Tiger tanks, which outgunned the more lightly armed and armored U.S. forces, were not well suited to the rugged hills and the narrow streets of Sicilian villages.

When the counterattack at Gela broke down and his men abandoned the field, the division's commander, *Generalleutnant* Paul Conrath issued a wrathful statement: "I have the bitter experience to watch scenes during these last days which are not worthy of a German soldier, particularly not of a soldier of Panzerdivision Hermann Goering. Persons came running to the rear hysterically crying because they had heard the detonation of a single shot fired somewhere in the landscape. Others, believing in false rumors, moved whole columns to the rear. . . . I want to state in these instances that these acts were committed not only by the youngest soldiers but also by NCOs and warrant officers. Panic, 'panzer fear' and the spreading of rumors is to be eliminated by the severest measures. Withdrawal without orders and cowardice are to be punished on the spot, and, if necessary by the use of weapons. . . ." He added he would not hesitate to impose death sentences upon any who persisted in such acts.

That same day witnessed a serious confrontation between Bradley and Patton: German soldiers filled a gap between the 1st Division and its neighboring organization, making the Big Red One vulnerable. As head of the II Corps, Bradley had issued instructions for Allen to plug the hole, but Patton had blithely countermanded the order, directing Allen to bypass the German pocket. Under the protocol, Bradley held the right to instigate tactical operations—clearly Patton had usurped his privilege. When the outraged Bradley confronted Patton about his breach, Patton apologized for stepping out of line. Unwilling to let it go, however, Patton later told Eisenhower that the II Corps commander was "not aggressive enough." Eisenhower passed the remark along to Bradley, who regarded the comment as an unforgivable slur. As much as Eisenhower favored Bradley, he also had a long and close relationship with Patton. Bradley could only swallow his pride and remember.

For the moment, such friction in command was the least of Husky's travail. In an effort to reinforce the American positions, a flotilla of transports flew the 2,300 paratroopers of the 504th Regimental Combat Team from North Africa toward a drop zone on the Gela plain. Shortly before the planes neared Sicily, a large number of Axis aircraft had raided the Allied fleet offshore. When the C-47s appeared some fifty minutes later, anxious naval gunners assumed they were being attacked again. The sky lit up with antiaircraft fire; flaming American planes fell out of the sky, some crashing into the sea or land, while paratroopers spilled out of others. The airborne forces lost 318 troopers to the friendly fire.

The 504th's arrival was part of a master plan to widen the territory held by the Americans. The strategists of the II Corps and those at 1st Division reasoned that the attack of the panzers during the daylight hours of 11 July had been a preemptive strike that aimed to evict the invaders from the beach before they could build up reinforcements and supplies. It had been a gamble by the Axis generals, who dispatched their armor without waiting for foot soldiers to accompany it. Having seen the tanks turned back, the Germans were now believed rushing infantry to assembly areas in preparation for a full-scale assault.

As Allen had indicated to Patton at their somewhat testy encounter, "This situation necessitated *immediate positive action* by the 1st Division." In the operations report that Terry Allen later prepared, he said, "That evening when all elements of the 1st Division were holding on by tooth and nail, the Division Commander directed that a *coordinated attack* be launched that night, *at midnight, July 11th*. Word went out to the Division, to 'Sock the hell out of those damned Heinies, before they can get set to hit us again.'"

In the words of Gavin, "Terry Allen . . . with characteristic courage ordered an attack."

The 18th Infantry, previously in reserve, was released to the division, and parts of it were committed to the midnight venture. A concentrated artillery and naval-gun barrage supported the attack—which jumped off on schedule. "The surprise effect was instantaneous," said Allen. "By 3 a.m. July 12th, the 1st Division attack was rolling along in high gear, with an upsurge of combat morale throughout the entire Division.

"The 26th Infantry on the left maintained its advance. Before noon, the Ponte Olivo Airport had been seized, and a local enemy counterattack repulsed. Through the prompt efforts of Major William Gara and the 1st Engineer Battalion, all enemy explosive and time bombs were removed from the Airport, to assure its *immediate use* by our own fighter planes. The quick capture of the Ponte Olivo Airport resulted in nullifying the overwhelming air superiority which the Germans had previously maintained, in the II Corps beachhead area.

"Intelligence reports, from German prisoners, indicated that the Germans had been caught completely by surprise, while preparing to make their own renewed, coordinated attack at dawn; and that they had suffered heavy losses and considerable disorganization. Before the enemy could 'get set.' the 'Fighting First' had beaten them to the punch. The Germans had concentrated their principal counterattacking effort against the 1st Infantry Division, in the critical Gela area and they never recovered from the mauling they received by so doing."

Allen may be forgiven some of his boastful pride, but the battle for Sicily was hardly over with that successful invasion—and the 1st Division was neither out of the woods nor through the hills that stippled the island.

Gussied up for a formal photograph, Terry Allen much preferred rough and tumble play with other children on army posts. He later claimed that through his association with the youngsters of the enlisted men he learned to smoke, cuss, chew, and drink.

Allen matriculated at West Point as a member of the Class of 1911. His mother had persuaded President Theodore Roosevelt to obtain an appointment at large to the academy for her son in spite of his weak academic credentials.

After service on the Mexican border from 1912-1917, Allen fought in World War I and was twice wounded. He rose to the rank of Lt. Colonel with the 90th Infantry Division and did occupation duty in Germany until 1920.

With the permanent rank of major, Allen spent most the years between world wars as an officer in cavalry regiments. He captained army polo teams and also participated in horse shows, like this one held in 1925 at Fort Riley, Kansas.

Mary Frances Robinson, who would marry Allen, was the handsome, vivacious daughter of a prominent family in El Paso. The marriage was celebrated at St. Patrick's cathedral in El Paso and featured an honor guard of Allen's fellow officers.

When Terry Allen wed Mary Frances Robinson in 1928, he was 39 and she only 20. But they remained devoted to one another in spite of long separations caused by his assignments and World War II.

Terry de la Mesa Allen Jr., born in 1929 learned to ride at an early age under the proud eyes of his devoted father who called him "Sonny."

As a cavalry officer, never more comfortable than when he wore a horseman's boots, Allen caught the eye of future Chief of Staff Gen. George C. Marshall, during a stint as an instructor at the Fort Benning Infantry School.

Lord Louis Mountbatten, who had organized the British Commando units, towered over Allen when they met in 1942 while the 1st Division trained in England.

Allen rode a jeep during a triumphant tour of Oran in November, 1942, after the French garrison surrendered.

Clarence Huebner (left), a veteran of World War I, like Allen, replaced him in 1943 as commander of the 1st Division at the close of the campaign in Sicily.

Allen enjoyed a laugh with Omar Bradley, (left) his superior in North Africa and Sicily, and others from the Allied forces. However, Bradley became a bitter critic of Allen and eventually arranged for him to be relieved. (U.S. Army Fort Bliss Museum)

Allen, flanked by Brig. Gen. Theodore Roosevelt Jr., his deputy commander and drinking companion, received a Croix de Guerre from Free French commander in Gen. Louis Koeltz. Said Allen, "I dodged when he tried to kiss me on the cheek."

Allen drilled his 104th soldiers in after dark operations, leading his severest critic, Omar Bradley, to remark that the division were the only one in Europe skilled in night combat.

Dwight D. Eisenhower, (center) flanked by Patton and Bradley, privately expressed dismay at Allen's failure to enforce discipline. Ike wanted to strip Allen of his command after the completion of Operation Torch but Patton insisted he needed Allen for the invasion of Sicily. (National Archives)

A rifleman from the 104th anxiously scanned the windows in Cologne where the Timberwolves fought house to house before they ousted the Germans. (National Archives)

The always nattily uniformed Lt. Gen. George S. Patton Jr. met Allen while both men served on the Mexican border. The pair enjoyed a friendly, sometimes contentious rivalry that continued when Patton assumed command over Allen in North Africa and Sicily. (National Archives)

Soviet Field Marshal Ivan Konev pinned the Order of Suvorov II on Allen after the 104th met Red Army troops across the Elbe River. A boozy party followed the ceremonies.

With World War II over, Allen and the 104th Division were at Camp San Luis Obispo, California, when Bob Hope and his second banana, Jerry Colonna, came to entertain. (Courtesy U.S. Army Fort Bliss Museum)

Retired from the army in 1946, Allen, living in El Paso and seemingly shrunken in a rumpled suit, sold insurance. He frequently visited Fort Bliss commanded by Maj. Gen. Charles E. Hart.

As a schoolboy growing up in El Paso, Terry junior attended Coldwell Elementary School and then Austin High School. Like his father, he struggled with his studies.

Terry Allen, Jr. was a member of the Class of 1952 at West Point. He graduated as the "goat", last in his class of 527.

As the CO of the 2d Battalion, 28th Infantry, attached to his father's old command, the 1st Division in Vietnam, Terry junior (left) conferred with other officers before a mission. (Courtesy Consuelo Allen)

At Long Binh, Vietnam, in September 1967, Terry junior, now a lieutenant colonel, worked with his executive officer, Maj. Jim Shelton (left) and Cmd. Sgt. Maj. Francis Dowling (right). Allen, who had briefly gone home to try to restore his shattered marriage, and Dowling were both killed in action a month later. (Courtesy Jim Shelton)

13: Victory and Defeat

Firmly seated on the island, the Allied armies picked up momentum as they swept forward. The British bagged Syracuse and Augusta on the east coast, and Montgomery's Eighth Army advanced toward the ultimate objective, Messina. The Americans—including Allen's 1st Division—drove up the middle of Sicily. Unfortunately, a woeful lack of planning invited chaos and doomed any hopes for swiftly overwhelming the defenders.

Allied army group commander Harold Alexander continued to regard American soldiers as inferior in battle. In the words of D'Este, "What passed for strategy was Alexander's notion that Patton would act as the shield in his left [western] hand while the Eighth Army served as the sword in his right." Beyond that, he issued no specific assignments to the U.S. Seventh Army. Bradley later recollected that the Americans were to get off the beaches, seize some airfields, and then cut Sicily in half to trap the defenders between the two Allies. But it was all in general terms, with no detailed division of responsibilities nor allocation of objectives, particularly where the two Allied armies abutted one another. When the British Eighth Army trudged forward from its first footholds, the route lay directly across the front of the U.S. 45th Division. Although that organization was in the best position to assault the key town of Vizzini, Alexander solved the dilemma by ordering Patton to shift the 45th west. At one point, when a Canadian segment of Montgomery's Eighth Army encountered stalwart defenders, the 45th Division artillery, which was only one mile from the objective, remained mute while the Canadians incurred heavy casualties. The American 45th dutifully complied with its orders, and the maneuver required the entire division to go back to the Gela beaches and then strike out on the left flank of the 1st Division.

The meek acceptance by Patton of a foolish deployment that proved costly in lives and time puzzled Bradley as well as historians. Some have suggested that Patton held his tongue for fear Eisenhower would cashier him, because he had already been blamed by Eisenhower for the mishap with the 504th Parachute Regiment; he was chewed out for failing to inform the supreme commander promptly; and then he was in more trouble because of some atrocities committed by GIs who claimed a speech by Patton incited them to murder prisoners.

According to Lucas, Eisenhower defended his hands-off policy on the overall strategy. "He [Ike] had never seen a case where the British tried to put anything over on us. He said put myself in Alexander's place. He first came in contact with American troops when the fighting at Kasserine and Gafsa was going on; that they did so poorly that the British lost confidence in us as offensive troops. . . . Later the same divisions did well in Tunisia but in Sicily there were two new divisions . . . the 45th had no combat experience and the 3d with only a little." Lucas claimed he disagreed with his boss.

Eisenhower placed any blame for faulty strategy upon his Seventh Army commander. Lucas wrote, "Ike said Patton should stand up to Alexander. He would not hesitate to relieve him from command if he did not do so." But as the man in charge of all theater operations, Eisenhower of course had approved the plans. If the blueprints were flawed, he too had a responsibility to speak up.

Lucas commented on a rising tide of "sniping and bitching about [the] British from junior staff members." In his own view, "The British are rather surprisingly slow. Two reasons . . . 1. Strong opposition. 2. Montgomery is notorious for the meticulous care with which he prepares for his operations. This virtue like any other can become an obsession that finally defeats its object. He will not move until everything, every last ration and round of ammunition is ashore and in its proper place. This was what was needed in the desert against Rommel. Here [Sicily] speed would seem to be the better part of wisdom. Destroy the enemy before he can be reinforced from the mainland." While Field Marshal Bernard Montgomery was indeed known for waiting until he allocated every last man and bullet, what delayed the Eighth Army was not caution but a buzz-saw defense by the Germans.

While the British Eighth Army slowly tried to pick its way forward, the Americans accelerated their advance. Along the way, Patton bought himself an additional big dose of ill will with the 1st Division troops, many of whom already resented him for his strict enforcement of the dress code and the way he interpreted and enforced military discipline. Monk Dickson reported that during the Sicily campaign the head of the U.S. Seventh Army happened upon a sweaty Big Red One GI as he labored to load 105mm ammunition. The general immediately fined the soldier fifty dollars for failing to wear the prescribed leggings. He refused to rescind the penalty even after it was explained that the man's ankles were so badly swollen that he could not fasten on the leggings. Rather than reporting to sick call, the soldier had insisted on doing his part, albeit out of uniform. Dickson commented, "By sundown, the whole 1st Division resented the affair."

Having secured the Ponte Olivo airstrip, the orders to the 1st Division directed Allen to advance due north toward Cefalù, on the north coast. Along the way, the division would need to capture Enna, which previously belonged in the Canadian zone. The Big Red One welcomed reinforcements in the form of another battalion of medium howitzers and a battery of 155mm guns called Long Toms. The 91st Reconnaissance Squadron, with light tanks and armored cars, and the 70th Light Tank Battalion were added to the mix, creating more mobility in the rugged countryside.

Intelligence named the opposition: the I and II Grenadier Regiments from the 15th Panzer Division, a separate infantry regiment, a *Nebelwerfer* (heavy mortar) Battalion, tank units from the Hermann Goering Division, and the Italian Aosta Division. The retreating foe exploited the mountainous terrain with its gorges and canyons; roadblocks hampered passage along trails; sappers blew bridges.

The 1st Division plan envisioned the drive north occurring in two columns. Comprised of the 26th and 18th Infantries, the left or western flank would start from Ponte Olivo and head for Petralia. The 16th Infantry drew the right flank, and its column advanced out of Niscemi. Initially its objective was to cross the Salso River with an ultimate target of Caltanisetta, a site of a ridge. Possession of the high ground would deny the enemy movement west.

Allen issued a verbal order for the regiment to seize the high ground, and after reconnaissance, under the cover of night, they would get soldiers across the Salso where they could protect engineers constructing a bridge. The reconnaissance party discovered a company of Germans eating a meal. An artillery barrage dispersed the enemy. The GI patrol detected antitank guns and armor lurking in the brush. The 7th Field Artillery zeroed in, and the tanks retreated with some losses. Allen assigned a full battalion of engineers to the regiment.

At 10 P.M. the infantrymen started to ford the stream. They encountered surprisingly light resistance. Enemy bombers and artillery struck at the Americans, but on the ground the Italian foot soldiers surrendered in increasing numbers.

The left, or west, column seized Mazzarino, twelve miles northwest of Ponte Olivo; and after a two-day battle against artillery, mortars, and a company of Mark IV tanks, they captured Barragranca, seven miles farther north. Within a week, the 26th and 18th Infantries had traveled within fifteen miles of the north coast of Sicily. The objective of Petralia fell after several hours of night fighting. Said Allen, "The night maneuver caught the enemy completely off base and was an outstanding example of bold night fighting tactics."

During a tense session at Allied Headquarters in Tunis on 17 July, Patton appealed for the right to an all-out charge to the northern coast with the goal of splitting the island in half. Alexander acquiesced. The entire U.S. Seventh Army was in full gallop toward its objectives as the Italian army, delegated to defend the western half of the island, collapsed. In ten days since the first desperate moments on the Gela beaches, the Big Red One advanced some seventy miles and the objective of bisecting Sicily was accomplished.

The only stiff resistance to complete subjugation of Sicily lay in the Plain of Catania, a flat, swampy lowland just south of the historic rugged volcano, Mount Etna. Fierce, steep-sloped Etna, just shy of eleven-thousand-feet high, with a twenty-five-mile diameter cone, stood as an impassable barrier. Access to Messina could be achieved only through a narrow coastal shelf that began at Catania in the British zone. The bulk of the Germans on Sicily, concentrated against this naturally defensive terrain, stubbornly held off Montgomery. Although the allied airmen vigorously raided the docks at Messina and on the Italian mainland, they could not halt the flow of military supplies and equipment from the mainland to the forces on Sicily.

Both sides hurled airborne forces into the fray, which centered around Ponte Primosole, a four-hundred-foot-long bridge over the Simeto River seven miles from the city of Catania. Furious battles only piled up hideous numbers of dead and wounded in exchange for a few yards of territory. Even though the British managed to get across the Simeto span, a torrent of antitank fire turned the area into a junkyard for their Sherman tanks. When the British 151st Armored Brigade finally forced its way beyond the Primosole, the two opposing forces lay exhausted, unable to continue for the moment. A historian for the 151st later wrote, "The area around the bridge was a regular hell's kitchen; it was littered with smashed rifles and automatics, torn pieces of equipment, bloodstained clothing, overturned ammunition boxes and bodies of British and German dead. It was a scene of terrible destruction and telling evidence of a bitter struggle in which neither side had asked or given any quarter." The outfit that relieved the 151st bumped into a wall of German soldiers, no more willing to relinquish their turf than those who had bled out in front of them. For the moment, the battle for the Plain of Catania was a stalemate.

Patton now elected to make a seemingly dramatic stroke that would demonstrate to the British the power of the American forces. His gambit, in fact, was of small strategic value. With Montgomery stalled, instead of simply guarding Montgomery's left flank against what was rapidly becoming a nonexistent, or at least noncombatant, Italian army, Patton focused on capturing Palermo, the capital of the island on the northwestern coast. He created the Provisional Corps for an operation that would send the 3d Division, elements of the 82d Airborne, the 2d Armored Division, and Ranger Battalions on a one-hundred-mile march through rugged country. While Palermo had once been a primary objective along with Messina, the deployment of the surviving Italian units and the German organizations to the east dropped the value of the city considerably.

Bradley contributed greatly to the evaporation of resistance by Italian forces. On his own, he directed his II Corps staff to pass the word that any captured Sicilian citizens would be allowed to leave the POW pens and return home. The amnesty offer traveled swiftly through the vineyards and villages. Although Seventh Army headquarters initially disapproved, it soon realized the benefits of the gesture, and leaflets with an official imprimatur convinced thousands of Sicilian soldiers—would-be foes—to desert. That in turn depressed morale among other Italian troops, and they too quit the fight.

Under the circumstances, a far better strategic move than Patton's would have been to launch an attack toward the Plain of Catania, squeezing the Germans in the pincers of the U.S. Seventh Army and the British Eighth. Indeed, Bradley regarded Patton's strike at Palermo as rather a publicity stunt, one that would confer prestige upon the troops and of course their commander, than a bona fide contribution to the Sicilian campaign.

However, the scenario for the Palermo push required a shift of the 1st Division eastward toward Nicosia and an eventual rendezvous with disaster at the mountain town of Troina, west of Mount Etna. In so doing, Patton satisfied the demand of Alexander that Montgomery's left flank would be protected, as the Eighth Army—stymied on the Catania Plain— now swung left on a detour west of Mount Etna.

According to Bradley, "Monty—without informing us—constricted [Lt. Gen. Oliver] Leese's [leader of British 30th Corps] encirclement of Mount Etna and left it to us to take Enna. We were not informed of this abrupt change in plan, and, as a result, our whole right flank was left exposed to enemy counterattack." Leese subsequently apologized for the error.

The poor communication between the Allies notwithstanding, Allen's 16th Infantry homed in on Enna. As hub of a network of roads, and located on a steep hill mass, the city was expected to be strongly defended. But after a motorized reconnaissance observed civilians working their farms, intelligence realized that the bulk of the garrison had departed. On 20 July, in company with the 70th Light Tank Brigade, the foot soldiers mopped up Enna; and the following day, the 18th Infantry secured Calscibetta, eight miles northwest.

During this period, Allen does not seem to have paused to write Mary Fran other than a single-page note that advised her the 1st was "in the midst of a hard drive . . . that was all right. . . . There are a great many worries to overcome but I guess that [is] to be expected."

The next objective, the city of Nicosia, loomed as a much more difficult task than Enna. Although Allied planes now dominated the skies, an increasing number of enemy tanks showed up in the vicinity of Nicosia. Civilians who were fleeing trouble toward the embattled east reported heavy military traffic coming from Troina into Nicosia.

The GIs of the 1st Division advanced doggedly over a series of hill masses, pelted by artillery, and hammered in counterattacks. As everywhere in Italy, mines—planted as thickly as olive groves—extracted a toll and slowed the pace. Allen resorted to a change of tactics. Correspondent Richard Tregaskis in his *Invasion Diary* quoted Allen: "Had we kept up just a frontal attack, it would have meant just a bloody nose for us at every hill. . . . This was about as stubborn as any resistance we've encountered so far."

The 16th and 18th Infantries aggressively outflanked the Axis troops hunkered down within Nicosia. In what was becoming the standard mode under Allen, the moves into mountainous terrain occurred at night. Allen commented, "It was expensive on shoe leather but it did assure quick tactical success, with a minimum of battle casualties." During these operations, acting at the center as a "pivot of maneuver," the 26th Infantry occupied, backed off, and then reoccupied a series of hills in front of Nicosia because of strong counterattacks.

As darkness descended on 26 July, the 18th Infantry swung wide north along the high ground and by midafternoon controlled the road that exited in that direction. Further advances shut down escape to the northeast. Simultaneously, the 16th Infantry grabbed the territory south and southeast of Nicosia. The 70th Light Tank Brigade plus a company of mediums, assembled under cover on 27 July; and again, at 8:30 P.M., hidden by night, they battered the enemy for an hour, inflicting heavy losses west of the town. The armor withdrew, having accomplished a dual mission by distracting the defenders while the two infantry regiments outflanked the town and administering a morale-sapping attack.

On the following day, an artillery barrage further discomfited the Germans, whom Allen claimed had intended to make an "all-out" defense. The Panzer grenadier regiment and the *Nebelwerfer* battalion abandoned the city and retreated toward Troina. More than seven hundred Italians surrendered along with a handful of Germans. Having consistently disparaged the efforts of Americans, the BBC in London outraged Eisenhower and his staff with an announcement that the British had captured Enna. He dashed off an angry letter to Churchill protesting the snide comments of the BBC. It was one more mote of grit to increase friction between the Allies.

In central Sicily, the 45th Division led the one-hundred-mile sprint to Palermo, traveling over rugged hills in little more than seventy-two hours—much of it on foot. The GIs under Lucian Truscott had been trained to march five miles per hour (the Truscott Trot) rather than the standard three. Elements of the 2d Armored arrived a few hours later. While crediting Maj. Gen. Geoffrey Keyes, the nominal commander of the Provisional Corps, Patton played up the victory with as much pomp and circumstance as he could muster. However, he fixed his eyes on a more glittering prize. Looking due east along the north coast, he lusted for Messina, the most valuable objective on the island and the one that his rival, Montgomery, had been unable to bag.

As the struggle for Sicily continued, Patton, like Allen, had become an anathema to Bradley. Again personalities clashed significantly. Bradley was offended that Patton, a man who conversed with impeccable language and about matters of culture and history in certain company, descended to the crassest vulgarity when he addressed common soldiers. Patton's natural flamboyance annoyed Bradley. "He steamed about with great convoys of cars and great squads of cameramen." The publicity generated by Patton's grandiose challenges of going one-on-one in a tank duel with Rommel, seemingly mesmerized the correspondents, as did the flashy pistols dangling at his sides. Then, too, the off-the-cuff remarks picked up by reporters disturbed Bradley. He could not forget Patton's sneer that he lacked aggressiveness.

The II Corps commander may have been most angry at the recklessness of his superior. He had been highly critical of Patton meddling in the beach landings at Gela where he committed an almost unpardonable sin, countermanding an order from Bradley. Patton—who charged him with being timid—had himself shrunk from a confrontation with Alexander over the missions of the two Allied armies in Sicily. Now, as they hatched the plans to snatch Messina from under Montgomery's nose, Bradley concluded Patton displayed no talent for the nitty-gritty of strategy. "To George, tactics was simply a process of bulling ahead. He never seemed to think out a campaign. Seldom made a careful estimate of the situation. I thought him a shallow commander."

If Bradley had any doubts about Patton's judgment, it was confirmed by an appallingly callous statement: Patton informed Bradley, "I want you go get into Messina just as fast as you can. I don't want you to waste time on these maneuvers [Bradley had suggested some ideas for evicting the Germans from their positions], even if you've got to spend men to do it. I want to beat Monty into Messina." Bradley described himself as "very much shocked" by Patton's words. And as casualties piled up because of deadly resistance, Patton ignored the losses and instead hectored Bradley, Truscott, and others to go faster. He even slurred Truscott as "afraid to fight."

To Patton's surprise and suspicion, Montgomery suddenly ceded Messina to the Seventh Army. In D'Este's analysis, the British field marshal had realized his route to the city was inordinately tough. Montgomery, as glory-minded as Patton, in this instance recognized that the cost to his Eighth Army would be excessive. When apprised of the agreement between the two army commanders, Alexander accepted it with sour grace.

The formidable German defensive line stretched from Catania, on the eastern coast, through Adrano and Troina, west of Mount Etna, up to the coast at Santa Agata. The mountain roads from Adrano and Troina were the only highways to Messina. The 1st Division's target, Troina—Sicily's most elevated city—perched in the craggy Caronie Mountains. Ridgelines overlooked Highway 120, the vital avenue from Nicosia that ran along the front of Troina. Highway 120 turned left as it passed by Troina and then circled Mount Etna en route to Messina via Randazzo. From the heights, artillery and mortars imperiled any movement along 120.

Extrapolating from Allen's letters, it seemed Mary Fran was unable to grasp his situation. In a letter Allen wrote to his wife on 29 July, he said, "Please don't feel as you apparently do, that I am neglectful and that I've tried *not* to get home on leave or otherwise, when I might have done so. It is not too much fun to know that you may feel that way, when we are working as we are now and the division is fighting as it is. This war is really a very disagreeable job, with long periods of tough going and then relaxation periods for the 1st Division are few and far between.

". . . I've known what we were going to do and that I was slated to take them on this mission ever since May 10th. From that time until July 5th was a period of intensive preparation and for part of that time I was with the Navy."

He allowed that by this date she probably was aware that the division had spearheaded the American invasion of Sicily. He repeated a favorite theme, "Have tried desperately to accomplish every mission assigned with the maximum damage to the enemy and the minimum to our own soldiers."

Allen penned a few words about the admission of their son to N.M.M.I. and the payments for tuition and board but broke off with "Intended to write you a longer letter but have just had word I must go forward and straighten out a situation that is a bit awkward."

The problems of coordinating with the Canadians on the 1st Division's right flank increased Bradley's unhappiness with Allen, although it was not his fault. While Allen was off at corps headquarters for a meeting with Bradley, Roosevelt and the 1st Division's G-3 (plans and operations officer) were busy elsewhere. Porter became the senior staff man at the Big Red One command post. After consultation with Monk Dickson and the plans and operations officer at Corps, Porter nominated a particular battalion to actually enter Nicosia. Unfortunately, Patton and Bradley had other plans for that unit. Porter said, "General Bradley was very unhappy, [as was Patton] and let General Allen know, that they had been moved without his permission." Nothing untoward occurred because of the decision but to Bradley it only confirmed his opinion of Allen as unmanageable. It would have been out of character for Allen to have excused himself on the grounds that the choice of the battalion had been made by subordinates without his knowledge.

The division spent three days regrouping and recovering from the labors at Nicosia before tackling Troina. Intelligence from II Corps indicated that the retreating Germans would only pass through the town to make their stand at Cesarò, five miles farther east. Aerial reconnaissance showed a large bivouac area near Cesarò. The division's own specialist, Lt. Col. Robert Porter, concurred. Both sources deemed the most clearly identified opposition unit, the 15th Panzer Grenadier Division, in wretched shape. In Porter's words, they were "very tired, little ammo, many casualties, morale low." He drew his conclusions mainly from POWs and civilians. The outfit was expected to provide only a token fight before pulling back. The air force provided little information on the state of Troina's defenses because fog prevented aerial photography.

The battle for Troina began satisfactorily on 31 July. Cerami, a hamlet eight miles by road from Troina, fell. Because the 9th Infantry Division was expected to relieve the 1st Division, one of its units, the 39th Infantry—commanded by an old Patton pal, Col. Paddy Flint—had been attached to the Big Red One. Flint was a legendary figure from Allen's West Point Class of 1912. When he took command of the regiment, to instill high morale he ordered that all vehicles and helmets be marked with an inscription that stood for "Anything, Anytime, Anywhere—Bar Nothing"—distinctly nonregulation. Furthermore, during the battle for Troina, Flint frequently strode about the front lines, bare-chested except for a black silk scarf, wearing a helmet and carrying a rifle. He jeered, "See, there's nothing to be afraid of. The damn Krauts couldn't hit anything in the last war; they can't even hit an old buck like me." Later in Normandy, the Germans proved him fatally wrong.

Flint's people passed through the areas occupied by the 16th and 26th Infantries. They captured Cerami and advanced another two miles, backed by fierce barrages from the division's enhanced artillery. Allen had alerted his 26th Regiment to support the 39th if necessary, but they stood down upon the initial success of the 39th.

The easy progress of Flint's regiment convinced Allen that the 39th could continue forward and enter Troina. Both Allen and Bradley visited Flint's command post early in the afternoon of 31 July where optimism overflowed. Civilians still claimed the town held only a few soldiers, a handful of antitank guns, an antiaircraft battery, and one big gun. Again the 1st Division's guns blasted the slopes from where hostile fire might erupt. The 1st Battalion of the 39th Infantry clambered up a key hill less than one mile west of the city, where the Americans could view not only the streets in town but also the German artillery positions guarding the approaches. Although several new prisoners insisted that Troina was abandoned except for "a couple of guns," the 39th ran into heavy concentrations of mortar and artillery fire as it approached the town.

The illusion of victory tainted the command decisions. Flint insisted his forces were adequate for what Troina would require. Allen gave his permission for the 39th to go for the town. The men of the 39th, reinforced by Moroccans, plugged away with an attack begun at five o'clock in the morning on 1 August, but by midnight it was clear to Allen that the attack had been "stopped cold."

Quentin Reynolds was one of the reporters on the scene, and in his broadcast almost a year later he said, "General Allen sat there in an olive grove, giving his officers their orders. Dusk was just beginning to settle a soft blanket of darkness over the Sicilian hills. Terry Allen, in the midst of giving orders, asked to be excused. He walked away in the thin, gray dusk, and his officers waited. After a while, two correspondents followed Terry Allen. They found him about a hundred yards away, kneeling in prayer. The correspondents asked General Allen if he was praying for the success of the operation. 'No,' Terry Allen said, 'I'm praying that tonight there will be no unnecessary casualties; I'm praying that tonight no man's life will be wasted.'"

On 2 August, between the Moroccan goumiers and the 39th, Allen's 26th Infantry awakened around three o'clock under a starlit sky. They progressed perhaps two thousand yards, but at six o'clock the fire from enemy artillery scorched the turf, limiting any advance that would also have exposed the regiment's flanks, because those on either side of it had been pinned down. At one point, some goumiers began looting a small village, but Allen quickly put a halt to the disorder.

Although II Corps still said the 9th Division would relieve the Big Red One, Allen advised his people it was "the moral obligation of the Division to button up the capture of Troina." Toward that end he now ordered an all-out coordinated attack to jump off at 3 A.M. on 3 August. The plans dictated that the 26th Infantry would attack on the north flank; Paddy Flint's regiment would hit in the left center; while the 16th and 18th were to strike on the south flank.

Leading off at 3 A.M., the 2d Battalion of the 16th, with the 3d following on its flank, moved out. The latter element was the first to encounter trouble. First came snipers, then some machine-gun fire, and finally an all-out firefight. At dawn they had climbed halfway up the slopes of the ridgeline as it swept east, only to reel from an avalanche of small arms and machine-gun bullets. The infantrymen could advance no farther. The 2d Battalion drew less attention until it too faltered because of heavy shelling. In the fog of battle, Company E lost its bearings and headed down the wrong road. As many as sixty soldiers, visible on the skyline, walked straight into an ambush. A staggering amount of fire all but destroyed Company E. A message from the neighboring battalion reported, "E has two platoons missing. F had only one-and-a-half platoons fighting strength. One squad of L went out and we have no word of the squad." More than two hours later, another glum message said, "We have what is left of F Company—35 men and 1 officer. G has about 40 men left." By noon, Allen directed a battalion of the 18th to attack from the left of the trapped GIs to divert the pressure upon them. Even before they reached the scene, a German counterattack to drive the two battalions off the slopes was repelled only by the massive firepower of six battalions of division artillery and the obstinacy of the foot soldiers on the hill.

As Allen's intelligence later discovered, rather than having deserted Troina, a reinforced battle group—consisting of elements from the 15th Grenadiers, 29th Motorized Infantry Division, and the Hermann Goering Panzers, plus assorted foot soldiers, artillery, and mortar units—was dug in with instructions to hold Troina at all costs.

The Big Red One's leader sought to avoid the stalemate by proposing to have his 16th Infantry execute a wider swing to the east to outflank the defenders. But Ted Roosevelt, surveying the terrain, advised Allen against the move. He pointed out that the ground consisted of sheer rock. Furthermore, the troops designated for the maneuver were badly scattered and unlikely to achieve success.

Battalions from the 26th Infantry and the 39th, operating north of Highway 120, achieved their objectives, Monte Basilio and Monte San Silvestro, rather easily. Before the infantrymen could settle in, however, sudden squalls of enemy artillery bombarded them. Because the shelling came from a reverse slope, difficult—if not impossible—for the 1st Division artillery to reach, the 26th's Regimental CO, Col. John Bowen, arranged for an air strike. Half a dozen Spitfires, manned by British pilots and shielded by smoke shells from the artillery, answered the call. They swept over the enemy emplacements, strafing and bombing, which reduced the spasms of ordnance from that sector.

The siege of Troina raged on, exposing both the attackers and defenders to dire conditions. Food, water, and ammunition for the Americans could only be brought up during the night by mules. During the day, a summer sun scorched the men—who burrowed into whatever protection they could find while the near incessant shelling exploded about them. Night brought temporary relief with cooling breezes, after days of searing heat. Mines bedeviled movement. The onslaughts of the 1st Division and the air raids staggered Germans as well. The 15th Panzer Grenadiers had lost an estimated sixteen hundred men, and the last of the reserves had been committed.

On Monte Basilio, GIs from the 26th withstood a scythe of artillery fire and an attack by Germans who sought to regain the turf. Private James Reese received a posthumous Medal of Honor for directing his mortar squad into an effective position against the oncoming enemy. When the foe threatened to overrun the squad, Reese sent his crew to the rear while he fired the last three remaining rounds of ammunition, knocking out a machine gun. He then used a rifle until he was killed. While they held their ground, the Americans continued to be pounded from the heights of Monte Acuto and Troina itself. From Monte Basilio, Big Red One observers could direct accurate division artillery fire to interdict any attempt to bring supplies to the Germans along Highway 120.

Elements of the 18th Infantry that were working south of 120 occupied high ground overlooking the left flank of the defenders and moved out at night. At daylight, the Germans discovered the threat and immediately launched a series of combat patrols to keep the regiment off balance. Initially, the contingent hesitated to employ division artillery because of great confusion about the precise location of friendly troops. Only after Allen and the regimental commander came forward for a personal reconnaissance was permission given for a combined aerial and ground-based bombardment on Troina targets. However, the concentration failed to shake the entrenched Germans sufficiently for the 18th to gain any appreciable real estate.

Operating from Mount Pellegrino, which overlooked Troina from the south, enemy patrols poked their way into the 18th Infantry's turf. Having repulsed the intruders, the 1st Battalion sought to erase their base on Pellegrino. Two companies strove toward Troina itself. Along the way, they engaged in brutal hand-to-hand combat. When the Americans formed their perimeter, they were a scant fifty yards from the entrenched Germans.

On the surface, the situation around Troina seemed like the same sort of stalemate that afflicted the British Eighth Army in front of Catania. But the German lease had become increasingly untenable. The Americans could not be budged from heights that enabled them to punish the defenders and that provided observation posts exploited by the division batteries. Artillery and air force actions exacted a steady toll. The Germans also worried that the long-stalled Canadian troops in the south might break through and cut the escape route to the east. The *Wehrmacht* high command had already made plans to evacuate as many of their men as possible to the mainland of Italy. Troina needed to be held only until the execution of the plan.

Late in the evening of 5 August, the Germans began to slip away from the hilltop city. Signs of a withdrawal were detected by intelligence. But a cautious Allen refused to simply plunge ahead. He made detailed preparations for a renewed attack on the following day. The air force was asked to bring in a minimum of seventy-two fighter-bombers, which would be followed by a massive barrage from the artillery.

When the wary Americans approached the town on 6 August, no one barred the way. The enemy had all decamped. It had taken a week for the 1st Division to capture the objective, substantially more time than had been expected. Much of the problem lay in poor intelligence that said the GIs would have an easy time and that a single regiment could occupy Troina. Also, the maps were inaccurate, omitting a critical road and miscalculating heights in certain areas. Some revisionists argue that Allen should have been more aggressive, but others disagree.

A stunning blow to Allen muted the triumphal entry into Troina. Even as he directed the 1st Division's campaigns from Gela to Troina, his superiors had decided to relieve him. At that, he had been part of Husky only because of Patton's demand that he and his battle-tested division remain part of the operation. Eisenhower, his staff, and Bradley—while forced by Patton to accept Allen—had looked for an opportunity to get rid of him.

In a letter to Mary Fran on 5 August, Allen summarized the travails of the 1st Division as it fought to "overcome the stiffest part of the German resistance, has fought 7 or 8 pitched battles, has destroyed 71 German tanks, has taken about 7,000 Italians and about 800 German prisoners.

"Frankly, Mary Fran, it has been quite a strain both day and night for the past six months it has been terribly difficult to write. . . . Just at present, the Division staff is cooped up in the basement of an Italian church where it is a bit cramped but is quite safe from the usual nightly bombing. I am waiting for the staff to prepare plans for a daylight attack and am taking advantage of the interval and this first breathing spell to try and get off a long letter. You would be amused to see Stan Mason, Bob Porter, Jimmie Curtis, Verdi Barnes, [Clift] Andrus and I all huddled over a few candles. . . ."

Astonishingly, on the third page of this letter he casually announced, "I just received orders today which were a great surprise and the actual meaning of which I do not *exactly* know. Ted R. and I have both been relieved from the division and have been directed to report to the American commander in chief (Eisenhower) at Algiers for future assignment.

"George Patton came around to see me today and said that he understood I was being relieved from the 1st Division for reassignment to command a corps at home. He also said that before doing so, I would be temporarily attached to American Headquarters at Algiers and then would be at . . . British Headquarters . . . in order to confer with them regarding the combat methods and operations of the 1st Division throughout the last eight months of campaigning and particularly its combined operations with the Navy, during the Sicilian invasion. All of this, of course, was merely Patton's supposition, and I really do not know what my exact status will be until I have reported to Eisenhower.

"Ted R. does not know what his next assignment will be.

"Personally I did not expect to be promoted to be a corps commander. The accomplishments of the 1st Division would have been equally as good under almost anyone else.

"Needless to say I will be overjoyed at the prospect of any assignment which means a return home and the opportunity to be with you again, my dear, even though my actual start may be a bit delayed and the distant future may involve another combat assignment.

"... It will be a wrench to leave the 'Fighting First.' We have survived hard times together and the whole gang have loyally stood by me through thick and thin. . . . Our doughboys have been marching and fighting steadily now for 27 days and for at least 14 nights. Their tenacity and loyalty in the face of terrific hardships are really pathetic [*sic*]."

In a letter dated nine days later, Allen wrote, "Have written you and called several times in the past ten days. My change of assignment orders were a great surprise. It seems that in accordance with the War Dept. policy of rotating general officers with division combat experience, Ted and I are relieved from the 1st Division for reassignment." This policy was only applied to Allen and Roosevelt. No one else from the North African and Sicily campaigns was removed.

"I was directed to remain with the division until it had completed a very important battle [Troina] which seemed to be the deciding point of the drive in Sicily." Actually it was a necessary part of the overall drive to Messina, the main objective. "I started back . . . stopping at Patton's headquarters en route.

"Patton was most kind and cordial and thoroughly appreciative of the division. . . . He put us up overnight at the Royal Palace in Paduano and sent us back here in his private plane. It was some contrast to the battlefield bivouac that we had been living in for the past 30 days. . . .

"I saw Ike Eisenhower soon after my arrival. Was kept over until today to be decorated and to receive formal orders. They made quite a fuss over giving me the DSM. Enclosed is a copy of the citation. . . . It is most exaggerated as the division really put it over.

"Ike then sent for me and told me I was ordered home to report to Commanding General Army Ground Forces for reassignment. Said I might be returning for a divisional command or might be returning for a corps command. It is all completely a matter of conjecture.

" . . . He did say I had the longest, most arduous and most successful combat record of any general officer in this war and could carry a great deal of prestige." Allen then advised her he would travel to England for a two-week tour at the British Battle School and the Combined Allied Force Headquarters in London to share his experiences and combat experiences.

"Ted Roosevelt is being assigned for some special mission at Fifth Army Headquarters under Mark Clark. . . . He is very sad over leaving the 1st Division but realizes it is simply a result of the War Dept. policy for the rotation of commanders.

"Am taking Bill Gordon and Dick Harris, both, back with me as aides. Having each received a battlefield promotion and having both been decorated for gallantry in action, I feel they deserve to return home if only for an interval. . . . Am bringing Joe Pennisi back with me. He is the best orderly I have ever had. He is a sergeant now."

Allen remarked that someone had just brought him a copy of *Time;* the issue had him on the cover. "Frankly Mary Fran, I am simply fed up with all this lousy pernicious publicity. Have never given any single newspaper man the least bit of information other than a brief summary of the operations of the division when required to do so. They make *alleged* incidents from my past and make up the damndest stories."

On the surface, he appears to have accepted the explanation for his relief and obviously Patton and Eisenhower had vigorously stroked him. His unhappiness with the reporters is hard to explain. While he protested he never provided anything more than a "summary" of information, Pyle and Liebling were both reputable journalists. Allen may not have realized that they might be in his vicinity and able to observe and hear him while he spoke with his people. Furthermore, it is highly likely that after those occasions when he shared drinks he may have been much more open than he admitted.

What is significantly missing from the letters that have been preserved is any derogatory mention of those military figures with whom he may have had sharp differences or exchanges. With the exception of the references of Marshall—"our friend George"—and the events at Indiantown Gap, Allen never cites those with whom he had disputes.

Even after the war, Allen did not respond to the charges thrown at him by Bradley in his first autobiography. Allen was already deceased when Bradley's second autobiography, *A General's Life* (1983), muddied the affair. Bradley contended, "In the initial assault on Troina, Allen flubbed badly. He miscalculated the enemy's strength and verve and was thrown back with heavy losses." Bradley, although writing with hindsight, ignored the fact that it was his own II Corps G-2 who said the German main defensive line would be farther east. Allen's expert, Lt. Col. Robert Porter, had more or less confirmed the estimate of Bradley's people. Allied Forces Headquarters had distributed a more accurate prediction, noting an "intention to halt approximately on the line San Fratello–Regalbuto–Catenanuova and thence to the sea south of Catania."

Furthermore, when Allen and Bradley visited the command post of the 39th Regiment on 31 July, they had agreed that Troina would fall to the 39th without assistance. Bradley went beyond the charge that Allen miscalculated the strength of the enemy: "Throughout the seven days of heavy fighting that ensued he attempted to operate much as he had in the past, as an undisciplined, independent army, unresponsive to my wishes—or in some cases, orders. Without meaning any disrespect to the individual soldiers—who fought with great valor—the whole division had assumed Allen's cavalier attitude. I personally took over the tactical planning, and at the end of the Troina battle . . . when Eddy [Manton]'s 9th Division replaced the 1st, I relieved both Allen and Roosevelt, one of my most unpleasant duties of the war."

This criticism of Allen's performance contradicts the statement made in Bradley's earlier autobiography, *A Soldier's Story*. At that time he said, "Early in the Sicily campaign I had made up my mind to relieve Terry Allen at its conclusion. This relief was not to be a *reprimand for ineptness or for ineffective command. For in Sicily as in Tunisia, the 1st division had set the pace for the ground campaign* [my italics]."

Bradley's timetable simply does not fit the facts. In his 1951 memoirs, he said that while in Tunisia after the 1st Division tore up Oran, he decided to get rid of Allen, but Patton forestalled him. According to Patton, it was he who in July in Sicily sent John Lucas to Algiers with a letter to Eisenhower. That letter recommended Allen and Roosevelt be replaced by Maj. Gen. Clarence Huebner, a combat veteran of World War I with the 1st Division, and Col. Willard Wyman. In his diary, Lucas said he presented the message on 28 July. That is clearly before the battle of Troina even began.

Patton's message insisted that Terry's relief be "without prejudice." Eisenhower instantly agreed to the stipulation that Allen upon return to the States would receive an equivalent command. In Patton's diary he wrote, "I got Ike's permission to relieve both Allen and Roosevelt . . . on the theory of rotation of command." Because Eisenhower had not committed himself to similar conditions for Roosevelt, Patton followed up with a telegram, "I specifically said that unless they could both be relieved without prejudice I would not ask for their relief."

Although Patton and Allen had clashed on numerous occasions, it was obvious that Patton respected his former cavalry comrade and polo adversary as qualified to lead a division in combat. They differed in their combat philosophy: Patton seemed to think in purely military terms, a "see the hill, take the hill, damn the torpedoes" mentality. Allen, no less aggressively minded, also considered the costs to soldiers. In a combat journal of the 26th Infantry, the author noted that Allen, "Once upon hearing that artillery need not be employed against an enemy strong-point . . . he had succinctly stated, 'Ammunition is cheaper than soldiers' lives. Fire away!'" With the 1st Division, Allen would talk of his soldiers as if they were sons, as he would later do with the 104th.

In giving the reasons for replacing Allen, Patton explained to his diary that "the boy is tired." And when Eisenhower advised Marshall in an "eyes only" cable of the changeover, he explained it was "due to nothing else but weariness, occasioned by long and intensive efforts on the various battlefields of this theater." One would think that if Eisenhower had any serious doubts about Allen's abilities, he would have expressed them in a confidential message to the chief of staff.

The words "weariness" and "tired" may have been euphemisms for excessive drinking. Allen never made a secret of his fondness for bourbon and the stress of the campaigns could well have driven him to the bottle. Unfortunately, the tale concocted by Bradley has been accepted as the truth. Sketches of Allen's career, such as one compiled at the University of Texas at El Paso (which houses many of his papers and a documentary on the Big Red One), claim he was relieved because of the difficulties at Troina.

Equally detrimental to his reputation has been the charge that he was not a "team player." Many of those who pasted this opprobrium upon Allen ignored the intense rivalries, animosities, and backbiting that permeated the Allied command and percolated within the American forces—behavior hardly consonant with team spirit. Clarence Huebner, who took Allen's place, became available only because, as an outspoken Anglophobe, he was fired by Harold Alexander, for whom he had served as the American deputy to the Briton's chief of staff. Indeed, Eisenhower grappled with wall-to-wall complaints from most of his countrymen about the lack of cooperation, respect, and coordination from the British. Americans savaged other Americans. Beetle Smith, anti-Allen from the moment the 1st Division commander upbraided him in Algiers in order to get his organization into combat, said Eisenhower biographer Stephen Ambrose, "blistered anyone who came with [in] range." Patton privately denigrated Eisenhower as a staff officer without field experience. Bradley obviously regarded Patton as a menace to carefully laid plans. The air force, particularly in the early years of World War II, seemed to be at war with a different enemy.

The meaning of "team player" itself is subject to interpretation. Quite apart from his rambunctious personality and habits, Allen undoubtedly discomfited his superiors by refusing to always meekly say, "Yes, sir," and carry out the orders. In an organization based on a rather rigid hierarchy, he tested its limits. He committed the heresy of questioning strategy, plans, and missions for his people. Certainly, the American armies might have been better served had some division commanders strongly questioned the strategy that so extravagantly spilled GI blood in the futile Hürtgen Forest campaign, along the Rapido River in Italy, or in the Ardennes.

In the notes his aide Chester Hansen collected for his autobiography, Bradley commented on Allen, "Stubborn, hard to get him to do what one wanted him to. I had to suggest that our plans were his. He was a very difficult commander to handle. Would agree to a plan and then go his own way. Administratively, 1st Division was always trouble. . . . Hard to get Terry to put his pressure where I thought it should go. He would halfway agree and then it would never turn out that way. Possibly the most difficult commander I had to handle throughout the war. Inclined not to follow the letter of the order, had ideas of his own. In Sicily I had a terrible time getting him to use tanks as I thought he should. He lost too many. Maybe I was wrong, maybe he was—the answer probably lay midway."

In these ramblings recorded by Hansen, Bradley said Patton showed him a letter "commending Terry Allen, went all out. Asked me for concurrence. I agreed with his estimate of Terry's tactical skill but discipline in div was bad, drinking, and his health was bad. In Sicily, Patton said I was right about Terry—mentioned it several times. Thereafter asked Ike to relieve him. Particular reason was poor discipline in the 1st Div. 26th Infantry was the worst. Why were these things important during the time we were fighting a war? First div was not a great div because of these things; they were great in spite of them. 1st Div probably had more good regular officers than any other div at the start of the campaign. These officers got out of U.S. before they were cadred. More old-time sgts than any others. Tremendous advantage of professional people. Long period of training together—they should have been good."

The notes compiled by Chester Hansen with Bradley say, "Was Terry Allen a good commander? Yes—the 1st Division did good work. The 1st Div had much better offensive spirit than the 1st Armored at that time. 1st Armored had been beaten up at Kasserine and had grown timid. Were looking over their shoulder. Couldn't blame them for it. Who was the best div commander? Allen. Good sense of terrain. Darn poor disciplinarian. Between him and Ted Roosevelt, there was not much discipline in the div.

"1st Div. had more combat than any others. Had more esprit than others. That counted for a lot. Very few divs were kept together before the war. Good despite poor discipline. Did that discipline affect their fighting ability? Not too much. But it was hard to get first div to follow an order, to play on the team. When you issue order on traffic regulations and one unit disregards them, affects total combat efficiency. Uniform—well—men get killed when they are not wearing their uniforms. [Most likely that referred to helmets.] These things are indications of just how efficient div may be in all lines. Indicates alertness of the outfit. I was occasionally put out with the 1st div because they wouldn't do things the way they should have. Recall once when 1st Div was knocked off a hill—carelessness, I was mad. Terry Allen knew it (just before Nicosia) and said, 'You just stay down here until I can get up to the lines and get them back on that hill.'" Although Bradley claimed that Allen disobeyed orders, he never cited a specific instance.

The question is how large is the team? Harold Alexander, the overall commander for both North Africa and Sicily, and never a fan of the American soldiers or their officers, said of Allen, "Good combat soldier, energetic, vigorous, sick in Sicily campaign." There is no suggestion that the American functioned on his own. The notion that Allen was indisposed more than likely was due to gossip rather than any firsthand observations. To Eisenhower, as Allied Forces supreme commander, and Bradley, as II Corps commander, the team included multiple organizations. While Allen often resorted to the sports metaphor of the team when he talked about his troops, his vision usually extended only down to the last private who wore the Big Red One. But his responsibility was the 1st Division, not the armored or infantry or artillery units under someone else's command. Summing up his association with the 1st Division and its "skillful use of bold night attacks," Allen remarked, "This was made possible largely because of the sense of 'TEAM WORK' [sic] that had been developed in all units and in all staff and command echelons of the Division." When other organizations were attached to the division, he worked with them—notably the Rangers and the 39th Infantry under Paddy Flint, to whom he granted approval to garner the glory from capturing Troina. Robert W. Black, in *Rangers in World War II*, wrote, "The association with Terry Allen's 1st Infantry Division was one of the high points of the Ranger experience. Terry Allen was a strong supporter of the Ranger philosophy."

No one could dispute Allen's white-hot loyalty to his unit, but in his mind that quality ensured that the troops would do his bidding. Whatever his detractors might say, the 1st Division GIs under Allen were hugely responsible for the successes of which Bradley and Patton boasted in North Africa and Sicily. Lucas, who was no fan of Allen and who agreed with Bradley on the discipline problem, nevertheless said he had advised Eisenhower that it would be a mistake to award Distinguished Service Medals to division commanders without one to Allen, who had done more fighting than anyone else.

Officially relieved because of "weariness," and unofficially due to his unwillingness to subordinate his ways and his organization—Allen a few years later told Albert Schwartz (a family friend, who as a lieutenant served under Allen in the 104th Division) he believed he had lost his command because he was not a member of the club (not an academy graduate) and because of prejudice against Roman Catholics. Within the upper echelons, undoubtedly the West Point class ring marked a fellowship. However, a number of other soldiers such as Beetle Smith, Clarence Huebner, and Courtney Hodges also were "found" while attending the academy and were non-alums—yet they were accepted by their peers and superiors. One special circumstance about Allen could have influenced attitudes about him: Many officers must have resented Marshall's promotion of Allen from lieutenant colonel to brigadier. He jumped over hundreds of men senior to him and with West Point diplomas; they well may have formed a cadre of detractors.

In the matter of religion, during the nineteenth and early twentieth centuries, anti-Catholic prejudice raged through the United States. The Masons, a strongly anti-Catholic organization in its beginnings, were well entrenched at the U.S.M.A., but no evidence shows that this affected what happened to Allen.

A certain amount of apocrypha has also sprouted around the matter. A persistent story cited by Schwartz and others claimed that Allen and Patton fell out after the latter ordered 1st Division infantrymen to ride tanks into the Kasserine Pass while the enemy held the surrounding high ground. The Germans supposedly inflicted severe casualties. But such an incident never occurred. Although they had their differences, Allen did not blame Patton for his fate. He corresponded occasionally with Beatrice, Patton's wife, well after Sicily and asked her "Please give George my best and tell the old buzzard that it was a pleasure to have been with him." He also wrote to Patton himself, once saying, "I guess I must have been a pain in the neck at times but frankly it was a real pleasure to serve under your command."

Allen's son, Terry junior, obviously drawing from what his father told him, remarked that Bradley and Smith were the ones chiefly responsible. D'Este found no evidence that Smith was the hatchet man, although he had uttered some very uncomplimentary remarks about Allen.

Although it is unfair to make the "team player" charge against Allen in his relationship to the 1st Division's performance, in another respect there is some truth to the accusation. In his manner, his language, his relations to those above and beneath him, he did not fit the standard mold. Instead of the military's traditional reserve, the careful weighing of words and decisions, Allen tended to react with spontaneity. Patton sometimes manifested that character, but he was also a master of politicking. Allen was a maverick, insisting on night attacks when almost everyone else in the U.S. Army—with the exception of the Rangers, for whom he had such affection—preferred to fight in the daylight hours. He had his own ideas of what constituted discipline. He either would not or could not feign for the benefit of his audience the way Patton could. He exemplified the cliché, What you see is what you get. His military history and his religion may have been factors in his dismissal. But Patton, for one, genuinely believed Allen was showing the signs of stress that Eisenhower observed in Tunisia and perhaps drinking to excess.

Not much has been researched on the role of alcoholic beverages among the military, but historians such as John Keegan have observed that spirits were generally as much a part of military life as weapons. Keegan reports that, until the twentieth century, in the hours before battle men usually received drink—perhaps in the belief that it would help them cope with their fears. Certainly in World War II, every effort was made to get beer to the enlisted men (for use when out of the line), and officers were issued a regular liquor ration throughout the war.

On the other hand, the American attitude has long been ambivalent. The authorities at the U.S.M.A., dating back to its infant years in the nineteenth century, constantly sought to keep the cadets dry; but entrepreneurs just off post catered to the thirst of young men living at West Point. As early as the 1820s, the enterprising tavern owner Benny Havens offered savory victuals to supplement the West Point menu along with home brews, which drew the patronage of young Jefferson Davis and Edgar Allan Poe.

Soldiers on a pass often seem to have only two activities in mind, female companionship and a drink, and Terry Allen grew up in that atmosphere where imbibing is regarded as a sign of masculinity. He was hardly the only general or admiral with a fondness for alcoholic beverages. As a depressant, alcohol can soften stress, and it is not surprising that Allen resorted to it. The high rate of substance abuse in Vietnam is further evidence of resort to liquor and drugs as a way to deal with pressure.

The relief of Allen and Roosevelt may have been justified; but the circumstances of the switch in command was a dismal affair, and in Bradley's autobiography, *A Soldier's Story,* he spun an outrageous fabrication: "To break the news as gently as I could—for I knew it would shock them both—I called Allen and Roosevelt to my CP in Nicosia. En route they were ticketed by a corps MP for violation of the uniform regulations.

"Terry had been riding in the front seat of his jeep, holding his helmet between his knees while his unruly black hair blew in the wind. An MP flagged him down. He reddened when he saw Allen's two stars. 'I'm sorry, General,' the MP said, 'but my orders are to ticket *anyone* without a helmet. My captain would give me hell if he saw you going by.'

"Allen grinned but Roosevelt objected. 'See here, my boy, don't you know that's General Allen of the 1st Division?'

"'Yes sir,' the MP replied, 'and you're General Roosevelt, sir, but I'm going to have to give you a ticket too, sir, for wearing that stocking cap.' Ted shrugged in despair and peeled off the cap.

"'Brad,' he said on his arrival at corps, 'we get along a helluva lot better with the Krauts up front than we do with your people here in the rear.'"

Roosevelt's final comment is the only part of this tale that Bradley might have actually heard and remembered. Everything else, from the MP's blush to Roosevelt's shrug as well as all of the dialogue is at best "recreated." He did not inform the two officers, to their faces in his CP in Nicosia, of their fate. Worse than his attempt to spice up his story, Bradley lied about the sequence of events. On the other hand, Allen must have been aware that he was on the cusp of trouble, and if he were traveling out of uniform, suggests either a careless regard for his situation, or worse, deliberately provocative behavior.

In *Bitter Victory,* Carlo D'Este bases his account largely on an interview he had with Allen's G-2, Robert Porter. D'Este writes, "It is fair to assume that both Bradley and Patton considered the capture of Troina as a suit-

able moment [for the changeover]. At this point, the undertaking became badly bungled. Apparently the order was erroneously placed into
administrative channels and routinely sent to the 1st Division in the daily
pouch from II Corps, arriving at the CP at the apex of the Troina battle.
Porter said the adjutant general of the division came to him with the order for Allen's relief. They agreed it should be shown immediately to
Chief of Staff, Colonel Stanhope B. Mason, who immediately sought the
counsel of Porter. The problem the two officers pondered was whether
or not to inform Allen at once when his full attention was required for
the capture of Troina or wait until the battle was over. In spite of the appalling timing it was decided Allen must be told at once, for the routine
nature of the order's transmission meant that many others who should
not have seen it knew of its existence. For Allen to have learned of it from
such a source was unthinkable."

Porter was not present when Mason showed Allen the order, but he
reported, "Mason said that Allen was really in a state of shock for a couple of minutes. Then he got hold of himself and said, 'Let me go out and
smoke a cigarette and think this one over.' [He] came in and asked me
if I knew about it. Then he went back to the meeting after he'd talked
to General Bradley and said, 'This is a premature message. I'm in command and the attack for Troina is on tonight.'"

"When he telephoned Bradley," says D'Este, "the II Corps commander lamely replied that he had the orders for some time and was awaiting a time when the 1st Division was out of the line. . . . Years later, Allen
recalled that Patton had called him and asked if the order had arrived
for his relief. When Allen replied, 'Yes,' Patton said, 'Well, you're not relieved. . . . I say you're not relieved until you've taken Troina and the 1st
Division has completed its job in Sicily.'"

Troina fell and the 1st Division was destined for reserve. On 7 August,
Allen took leave of his soldiers with a one-page statement that summarized the organization's achievements. In it he said, "I feel most fortunate to have been your commander during the preceding year. You
should all be proud of your combat record. . . . You have lived up to your
battle slogan, 'NOTHING IN HELL MUST STOP THE FIRST DIVI-
SION.'"

14: Fresh Starts

As Bryce Denno (U.S.M.A. 1940), executive officer for the 16th Infantry in North Africa, who was then wounded in Sicily, recalled, "Officers and men in the division were shocked when they received the news that Gens. Allen and Roosevelt were relieved." Most were even more discomfited by the regimen installed by the new commander Clarence Huebner. In Hansen's notes, Bradley smugly remarked, "When Huebner came into the 1st Div. first thing he did was to restore some discipline and order . . . Troops were doing close order drill on battleground where they had fought for Troina. Never was a man more unpopular than Huebner [at] the start. . . . 'Krisake, who is this guy who comes from the states to show us how to march when we been fighting on these damned hills for almost a year?'" Of course, Huebner had not freshly arrived from the States, but had been with Alexander's staff during the North African and Sicily campaigns; either Bradley or his amanuensis sharpened up the generic "quote."

Intelligence specialist Siegmund Spiegel recalled the mandate for the garrison type of exercises. In his words, "Huebner was much more of a disciplinarian. You couldn't get close to him. In personality we identified much more closely to Terry Allen."

The combat journal for the 26th Infantry at that time noted, "There wasn't a man in the 1st Division that didn't know General Terry Allen. He had taken over the division . . . while we were still in Camp Blanding and he [did] the major share of whipping together the 1st Division team, both in the training schedules in the States and the British Isles. He had followed the 16th and 18th Infantry Combat Teams in the fighting around St. Cloud and been among the first to enter Oran."

The journal, produced in August 1943, went on to summarize the North African campaign after Allen gained control of the entire division. "He was as familiar with front lines as with division headquarters, spending most of his time up forward to see for himself how things were faring with his regiments.

"He had landed with the leading waves of troops in Sicily and in the fighting of the first few hours had not paused for rest until he knew beyond any cavil that the invasion bridgehead had been secured. Visiting the bullet-swept areas . . . he had encouraged and inspired the troops by his personal example and his cool behavior under the hottest enemy fire. It meant something to sweating, tired, battle-weary men to see the general walking around when the action got hot and heavy. General Allen was living proof that generals do not stay well back in the rear areas in this war. To as colorful and as capable a personality as Gen. Terry Allen, legends were apt to stick. A young staff officer who hadn't seen any hot fighting was initiated personally by having Gen. Allen escort him to a stretch under heavy fire, and after having spent a suitable interval, with shell bursts landing perilously close, the staff officer was considered baptized. . . . It was not only the fighters at the battlefield that saw the general. To the boys who had been wounded, he was a familiar figure at the hospitals, talking to the boys of his Division, presenting awards and citations, and in general looking after his team.

"Visiting our OP, just after the news came that the 16th had cleaned the town of snipers, Gen. Allen spoke to the men and officers of the OP, thanked them for their loyal and close support in all the action they had been through together. He expressed the hope that the same ability and loyalty would be accorded Gen. Huebner. . . ."

Upon the turnover, Allen and Roosevelt toured units to introduce Huebner before taking their leave of the division. Roosevelt became the Fifth Army liaison officer to the French Expeditionary Forces in Italy and then received the post of assistant division commander for the 4th Infantry Division, which would make the 6 June D-day landings on Utah Beach. He seemed to blame his downfall upon Patton. In a letter he wrote to his wife some months later, he said, "At El Guettar, I was in a slit trench with Terry Allen, only large enough to hold two. Patton came up.

A dive-bombing raid started. I got out & gave Patton my place. He took it. I never thought about it again, but a friend of mine told me two months later the story was being told." Patton at that moment apparently suppressed his aversion to slit trenches.

To the members of the 1st Division, Roosevelt—who was Allen's representative at command posts—was perhaps even more of a father figure than Allen. He constantly looked after their welfare, from the flour issued the mess sergeants to their safety under fire. Bradley related an incident demonstrating how familiar he was with the soldiers: Bradley and Roosevelt had been observing a truck convoy slowly rolling by in the dark. Roosevelt "shouted hoarsely through the night to a passing truck. 'Hey, what outfit is that?'

"'Company C of the 18th Infantry, General Roosevelt,' a hearty voice called back."

In its farewell to the deputy division commander, the combat journal of the 26th commented, "Gen Roosevelt . . . who had been on the go the minute the gunpowder began to burn, sometimes in the thick of the fight, and sometimes even in advance of the most advanced reconnaissance elements. The Gen. Roosevelt who was as apt to turn up at two in the morning as two in the afternoon, but seemingly prowled everywhere; the General with the slight strut and the unmistakable voice, who greeted old-timers by name, and knew every mess sergeant in the regiment. The same General who had rallied the wavering ranks of men at the beaches of Gela when Nazi tanks stormed to within a few hundred yards of the shore, and personally led anti-tank fire against the armored monsters until the iron ranks of the enemy broke. Where the fighting was fiercest, the struggle in the balance, the men could see the General jaunting along, cooler than the traditional cucumber, encouraging, joking, grinning that gold-toothed grin of his. They would always remember that sudden way of his appearance there when the fighting was heavy and the going rough."

Although Patton now declared Roosevelt "no soldier," he had also called him "the bravest man I knew."

Whether Patton's suppositions that Allen would be given temporary posts in the Mediterranean theater were genuine possibilities or attempts to ease Allen's distress, that did not happen. There certainly was no corps command for him. Allen, instead, returned to the United States for a leave and to await assignment. In a letter to E. C. Heid, an old friend and El Paso businessman, Allen wrote some months later, "It was a wrench to leave the old 1st Division, in view of what we had gone through to-gether. However, there was some consolation in knowing that the division had been successful and that in spite of minor reverses, it had won every 'round,' after ten months of hard combat. Also the fact that my successor in command is an officer of outstanding ability was a source of great satisfaction."

Allen then recapitulated the operations in which his division participated before he returned to writing more personal matters. "The exploits of the 1st Division seem to have put me in the decoration groove; I was recently awarded the Distinguished Service Medal by our War Department, the Croix de Guerre and the Legion of Honor by the French and just lately the C.B. (known I believe as the Order for the Commander of the Bath) by the British War Office.

"My relief from the 1st Division was effected immediately after the battle of Troina. I was then told that this was in compliance with a War Department policy for the rotation of commanders of combat experience. However, on my return to the United States, I distinctly received the impression that my relief had been initiated because of the need for rest and recuperation on my part. I base this on having received constant inquiries regarding my health. In fact, it was persistently rumored that I had suffered a physical breakdown. *All of this was utterly ridiculous* [his italics], since I have always been completely 'fit' and in good physical condition.

"I have studiously avoided any sort of newspaper publicity. But there have been numerous recurring requests from the press for information regarding my experiences overseas, and the reasons for my reassignment in the United States. The fact that rigid censorship necessarily restricted publicity regarding the activities of commanders returning from overseas seems to have made some press representatives all the more insistent for detailed information. This has been most embarrassing, but to all such requests I merely repeated that I was acting in accordance with War Department instructions."

Correspondent Quentin Reynolds said, "We were all sick when he was sent home." But attempts by news organizations to find the reasons for the return of the most celebrated division commander to the United States petered out. The Pentagon offered no explanation, but a bigger story quickly attracted the attention of correspondents: Word trickled out that Patton had cursed and slapped several soldiers, including one from the 1st Division, hospitalized for combat fatigue at the time. Lucas, who actually witnessed the incidents, and also Bradley and Eisenhower all attempted to keep the matter quiet. Once the incidents became public knowledge, Eisenhower ordered Patton to personally apologize to the GIs whom he struck and their units.

Siegmund Spiegel was among the 1st Division soldiers who listened to Patton. "We were all in a big field. Before he spoke we were told, 'There'll be no booing.' He rode up, with those pearl-handled pistols. He really talked down to the men, trying to show how macho he was. Back at G-2, I heard a major talking to a colonel who asked, 'What did you think of the general's speech?' He answered, 'It was like hearing my mother use the word *shit*.'"

Monk Dickson, the II Corps intelligence chief, had a different take on the address. "When Patton spoke before the 1st Division in Sicily to apologize for his conduct during the campaign, he ended on a great inspirational note. The massed division, however, remained stonily silent. Not a man applauded and the Division was dismissed. It faded away in silence to the great embarrassment of its commander and the total chagrin of Patton."

Another tale bruited about by Allen devotees says that the 1st Division commander punched Patton after he learned about the slapping incident. That too never happened. While Allen probably had heard about the affair that occurred 3 August, he was busy with Troina at the time and had left the country before it became public.

The actual end of the Sicily campaign came 17 August, when the Americans and the British entered Messina. Unfortunately for the Allies, they failed to shut off the evacuation of German soldiers to the mainland. In a mini-Dunkirk, tens of thousands escaped, taking with them equipment and vehicles.

When Terry Allen returned to the States on a thirty-day furlough, he hastened to El Paso and a joyous reunion with his beloved Mary Fran and his adored son. While savoring his family and making the rounds of parties, he patiently awaited a new post from the army.

On 15 September 1942, the 104th Infantry Division—a reserve organization created in 1921 under provisions of the National Defense Act—was officially activated and opened for business at Camp Adair in Oregon. The 104th was designated the Timberwolf Division, with a shoulder patch of a gray timber wolf against a background of green, and the unit quickly filled its ranks with enlistees, draftees, and junior officers straight out of the Fort Benning Officers Candidate School (OCS). Unlike the

1st Division, which was packed with career soldiers augmented by trained reservists, the Timberwolf was as green as any of the many newly activated or created outfits.

Under Maj. Gen. Gilbert Cook, at the heart of the 104th stood a trio of infantry regiments—413, 414, and 415—backed up by four field artillery battalions and several other units. Camp Adair's activation site consisted of a few uncompleted buildings, lumber piles, and dust-choked streets. Private contractors supplemented their labor force with men in army fatigues. When the fall rains came, the soldiers trained and maneuvered in mud.

Thirteen months after Camp Adair admitted the first officers and men assigned to the 104th, a new commander succeeded Major General Cook: Terry Allen, as promised, relieved without prejudice, had received his new command. He greeted the troops with the statement, "This is as completely fine a potential combat unit as I have ever seen. I have not seen better spirit or a more thorough response to training. . . . Someday, the 104th must follow in the footsteps of the Fighting 1st, and the Timberwolves may be the division to score the winning play in Europe."

Allen advised E. C. Heid, "Am delighted with my present assignment with the 104th Infantry Division . . . and my interests are now completely wrapped up in this outfit. I am sure this division will be *second to none* [his italics] in combat effectiveness. It must make and establish its own traditions, but it will have the benefit of the battle wisdom that we learned in the old 'Fighting First.'"

Jim Williamson, born in the hills of Kentucky, had attended a state university where under ROTC he obtained a commission as a second lieutenant. By attending the monthly sessions, summer camps, and training courses for officers, he was a captain when ordered into active duty in 1941. "I was sent to school right after Pearl Harbor, then a course at the Ft. Leavenworth Command and General Staff College. When I finished I was assigned in August 1942 to join the new 104th Division in Oregon.

"[Maj.] Gen. Cook was full of book learning. He had gone to the Command and General Staff School and he had all kinds of classroom work on the theory of training men for combat and teaching leadership. After the war, while I was at the Pentagon I met a four-star general, very famous. I mentioned to him how fortunate the 104th was to have been first trained by [Maj.] Gen. Cook because he was a theoretical man and then fought under Gen. Allen who was so good at [combat]. I said the Lord help us if they had reversed that. The general said, 'Williamson, you never made a truer statement in your life.'"

Another officer who began with the 104th shortly after its activation put it, "Cook was theory; Allen was nuts and bolts."

Having paid the pro forma tribute to his new command, Allen soon set a furious pace for his new charges. As Kenneth Downs, an aide to Allen, remembered: "The day he arrived, General Allen raised hell with the officers because he had seen some sloppy, unshaven soldiers on the way to headquarters. The division learned early that saluting and discipline were a fetish with him. When the controversy popped later over the Mauldin cartoons in *Stars and Stripes* [the newspaper for servicemen] the general proclaimed, 'There are no Mauldins in the Timberwolf Division, and there won't be any.' He was fiercely against 'Mauldinism.' He felt that Mauldin, good intentions notwithstanding, tended to encourage slovenliness, self-pity and surliness, none of which qualities ever hastened the end of a war."

Bill Mauldin, a sergeant in *Stars and Stripes,* had a huge following for his beat-up GIs, Willie and Joe. Their appearances and punch lines so offended Patton that he banned Mauldin from his command area. Clearly, Allen was determined to afford no opportunity for others to criticize him for alleged lack of discipline among troops under his command.

The 104th entrained from Oregon to Camp Hyder and then Camp Horn, Arizona, where Allen, during a 13-week desert training program, began stamping his imprimatur upon the GIs. While at Horn, Maj. Gen. Alexander Patch presented a Legion of Merit award to Allen for "exceptionally meritorious conduct in the performance of outstanding services" during the landings and subsequent operations in Sicily. Only a handful of officers witnessed the ceremony; training for the troops continued without interruption.

Shortly before Allen assumed command of the 104th, Albert Schwartz (an El Paso native and 1940 graduate of the University of Texas in Austin) was newly minted as a second lieutenant and met the general during his post-Sicily leave. Allen already had his orders to take over the 104th. Schwartz's father, Maurice, owned a local store and knew Allen through chamber of commerce affairs when the general had been stationed at Fort Bliss. Albert Schwartz stated, "I was in the horse cavalry at Bracketville, Texas, when I ran into Gen. Allen at some event. He saw me in uniform and asked me how I liked it down in Bracketville and I told him I didn't like it too much.

"He laughed and told that when he had been a 2d lieutenant cavalry officer he had ridden a horse into the officers quarters and gone up the steps to the second floor on his horse. Then he took these playful shots at my chin—remember he used to be a boxer—just as tough as nails, and he popped me on the chin, damned near knocked my head off. He was just funning. After I told him I wanted to go overseas, he said, 'How would you like to go in the best goddamn infantry division in the U.S. Army, with me?'"

"I said 'I think I'd like that very much, sir.' I didn't know him well, but my folks did. He had two stars on his shoulder and I had one little old bar, brand new. He told me he was going out to this new division and would ask for me. I said, 'thank you very much. I appreciate it.' But I forgot about it after I didn't hear anything from him for weeks. Then they called me to headquarters and there was a telegram that said I was to report for duty as aide-de-camp to Major General Terry Allen in Horn, Arizona.

"I called him and reached him on a field phone. I said, 'General, there must be a mistake in my orders' I didn't know anything about being an aide-de-camp. He used a few choice words explaining to me that the division was over-staffed, way too many people. He couldn't get me in the damned division because they had too many folks and this was the only way he could get me. I should get on my horse and come. I asked if there was a chance of my stopping off in El Paso. He said, 'Oh, hell yes, you can take a week.' I did and dropped my wife Adele off in El Paso where she stayed with my parents.

"I went to Horne, Arizona, a desolate spot. It was a tent camp and the 104th had just moved in. Gen. Allen was very anxious to get back into the fray, using the term 'shanghaied' for what happened to him. He told me this division was green and needed a lot of work. We had our jobs cut out for us. He said, 'Let's go for a little run.' I don't know exactly how old Gen. Allen was then [about 54]. I thought he's old and here I am in my 20s and in good shape. We started out. Several miles later I thought I was going to die. I couldn't admit it. He was in so much better shape than I. He knew exactly what he was doing. He almost killed me. I learned in a hurry that was one of the things he was very strong on, good physical conditioning.

"He insisted on this. There weren't many fat guys in our outfit. He set the pace. He believed in this and he practiced what he preached. He was that way about everything. He was a soldier's general. He was the kind of man who would say, 'Don't give the credit to the officers but to the sergeants and the doughboys.' He never forgot the men. He explained to me during one [of] our long talks in the evenings about how in the cavalry, you took care of your horse first. Then you took care of yourself. When you came in, you saw to it that your horse was properly groomed and watered, stabled, taken care of in every way. Then if you were hungry you got some food or you bathed, but not until your horse had been taken care of. That was the way you had to deal with the troops."

In the desert, Allen not only pushed his young soldiers to strengthen their bodies, he also inculcated his ideas on night actions. Staff Sergeant John Ferraro of Company M, 413th Infantry, articulated his anger at the training regimen: "What seemed really crazy was learning to fight at night. Who ever heard of fighting at night? How the hell could we tell where we were going, where the enemy was, or what we were walking into? I figured the man that was sitting and waiting for you could see you, but you wouldn't see him. . . . These crazy officers; any sensible man could see it wouldn't work. But all the bitching I did was futile. We were to learn how to fight at night."

George O'Connor had commenced his military career as an enlisted man in a cavalry unit stationed in Massachusetts. After graduating from OCS, he came to the 104th while it was still under Major General Cook and O'Connor became Company M commander. In his words, "When Allen took over, he wanted to visit with every company commander. My battalion was out on an exercise and we were the last ones he saw. And with M Company I was the last one he was introduced to. He would ask your name, what your military experience was and a few questions of that nature. When he got to me, he asked, 'How good are you?'

"I answered him, 'I'm as good as anybody in your command, sir.' He looked at me and asked, 'Where do you come from?'

"I answered, 'Brooklyn.'

"'Brooklyn!' He went ballistic. 'You ask somebody from Waco where he's from and he'll say Texas. You ask somebody from Abilene where he's from, he'll say Kansas. But you ask a son of a bitch from New York where he's from and he answers 'Brooklyn!'

"From then on he always addressed me as Brooklyn. We were putting on a demonstration rifle company attack, using live fire. The assembly area for the troops which had been picked before Allen took over was in an arroyo. An enemy would have had the place zeroed in for artillery. I was sitting there watching with a couple of friends and Allen yelled out, 'Brooklyn!'

"I reported to him and he asked me what I thought about the exercise. I said, 'General, you'd get your ass shot off if you had an assembly there.' My regimental commander almost went nuts. Allen said, 'You know how to do it better?'

"I said, 'The only way would be to attack at night.' He agreed with me."

When the 104th completed its term in the desert, it engaged in maneuvers near Yuma, California, where the soldiers had an opportunity to practice their nocturnal skills against another division.

Schwartz remembered, "We stumbled over terrain. While we had maps, we did better when the moon was up and we could see. When it wasn't we went with our blackout drill on how to maneuver when you can't see. I don't remember what division was opposing us but they got tired of being whipped. They had some commando types trained for this particular exercise. They swept through the fairly inadequate command post guards we had set up—nobody thought about this possibility in a war game. They swarmed down upon us and captured the whole headquarters. Rousted Terry Allen out of his sack and that was something else. I can hear him bellowing and hollering to this day."

From the desert, the division moved to Camp Carson at Colorado Springs. Allen brought his wife to the town, and she lived at the Broadmoor Hotel. Terry junior was enrolled at N.M.M.I. in Roswell, New Mexico—where he became a fine player on the polo team and, like his father, struggled with his studies. With the 104th in Camp Carson, Allen codified many of the principles enumerated during and after the Mediterranean theater campaigns into three small, red booklets. He later explained, "During this training period . . . it developed there was a grave shortage of training manuals for use in the infantry units. To offset this shortage, the Assistant Division Commander [Brig. Gen. Bryant Moore] and I got together and prepared three separate Infantry Training Manuals. Later, an inspector came around and wanted to know 'who paid for these special manuals?' He was informed that they were paid for through the proceeds of two nickel slot machines, at the Division Officers Club."

In Allen's typical style, the language employed in the manuals frequently resorted to that associated with sports, but the manuals still stand as sturdy primers for the topics covered. "Night Attacks" spelled out his ideas for ". . . operations [that] are used to effect secret troop movements, for crossing open terrain with minimum exposure, and for executing surprise attacks." He elaborated the virtues of such actions to surprise an enemy, exploit a successful daylight attack's achievements, gain terrain important for future operations, and avoid the higher casualties that might be incurred during the day.

Allen stressed that success in such ventures required well-disciplined troops, map-reading proficiency, orientation to night movement, and patrolling and training that taught how to maneuver in the dark without noise or confusion. Control, secrecy, and vigor in the execution were essentials.

In preparation for a night attack, detailed day and night reconnaissance was necessary. "The plan must be SIMPLE, and prescribed in minute detail. . . . Determination of the objective and the direction of attack are the basic elements of the plan. . . . The objective should be a definite terrain feature, of immediate tactical importance and of limited depth (a penetration in great depth is not practicable at night since surprise is lost after initial contact). The objective should be easily recognizable at night."

The little red booklet covered tactical substance and use of supportive units—including artillery, security, lines of departure, and formation of the soldiers (one or two columns). The booklet also discussed deployment of rifle companies, rifle platoons, battalions, and rarely, entire regiments, for such operations. He noted that the difficulties of maintaining control, direction, and contact increase with the size of command. In addition, the material covered matters of identification, communication, and alternative plans when things went awry.

The twenty-four-page manual ended with a final plug. "The skillful use of night attacks indicates smart, aggressive leadership. Night attacks will frequently attain difficult limited objectives with comparatively few casualties. Attacking troops must be highly trained and imbued with a determination to close with the enemy and destroy him with the bayonet."

On another occasion he argued, "The aggressive use of bold night attacks may be considered, 'the forward pass of the infantry units.' Do it properly and you can score *quickly* with a *minimum* of battle casualties. 'Slop' through it carelessly without proper preparation and your attacking unit will get 'one helluva bloody nose.' To make an 'all-out night attack' work, your infantry leader and your 'fighting GIs' must have 'the will to fight.' This will get the job done, come hell or high water."

It is a measure of how well Allen schooled the Timberwolves in this type of warfare that his frequent detractor, Omar Bradley, who led the American ground forces in Europe said, "He [Allen] brought the only division I know of that was prepared for night combat."

In a second text distributed to the 104th, Allen and his coauthor discussed "Combat Leadership." He allowed that actual methods of exercising command and leadership "will vary in accordance with the personality and characteristics of each commander." He insisted, however, that "all successful commanders must instill a will to fight in their soldiers and must know his job and *the needs and capabilities of his men*" (my italics). When Bradley was asked to rate division commanders after World War II, he remarked, "Terry Allen had [a] great deal of leadership, men loved him, he was colorful, understood [the] common soldier's viewpoint. He looked after his men, took care of them. Principal asset was understanding of his men's problems."

In his essay on combat leadership, Allen expounded on the issue of why GIs fought. "The average American soldier is a self-thinking individual with basic motives of patriotism and love of country." It contradicts the paper he and his team wrote at the Command and General Staff School in the 1930s. Allen in his most recent comments on the theme reverted to the explanation he gave Liebling in North Africa. "Once his own unit is committed to battle, his most urgent incentive is the fact that he is fighting for his unit. Therefore every American combat leader must by training and by his personal example instill the highest degree of combat efficiency and self-confidence into the soldiers of his command so that: HIS UNIT IS WORTH FIGHTING FOR."

He addressed the topic that bedeviled him throughout his career, discipline. He described it as "the foundation of teamwork and efficiency in any organization." But he declared it a common misconception to couple discipline "solely with military punishment." Rather it was what "the American youth learns . . . on school athletic teams, where he must 'play ball, for the good of the team,' or 'turn in his suit.'" (Not really an option for those who wore a military "suit").

Allen went on, "Discipline cannot be attained by fear of punishment. It can only be attained by the precept and example of the leaders. For that reason any military leader must make sure that his orders and instructions are sound and explicit and that they are issued with firmness and impartiality toward all concerned."

He avowed that with good leadership troops realize that the demands upon them are in their own interest. Allen continued, "The American soldier is often a rugged individualist; but, deep down in his own heart, he takes pride in serving in a tough well-disciplined outfit where duty and training requirements are sound and exacting and where his own needs are skillfully attended to.

"Discipline enables green troops to withstand the first shock of battle, to react under fire like veterans and to win when the odds are against them. Excessive casualties are the exception in a well-disciplined unit that has been trained to react instinctively under any emergency." Allen approached the crux of complaints about him. "A well-disciplined combat unit can be recognized by its alert, confident bearing and by its efficient functioning in the field. One cannot expect officers or soldiers to maintain a parade ground appearance during the stress of frontline combat conditions. But, an alert soldierly bearing should be instinctive, even under the most trying conditions. Some individuals are inclined to become slovenly in their performance of routine duties when the going gets tough. But this slipshod attitude is never condoned in any outfit that has a deep pride in itself."

On paper Allen seemed to strike a middle ground between the strict notions of dress and deportment demanded by Patton, Bradley, and others and the rather lax attitude that governed the 1st Division at times during the North African campaign.

Having made his obeisance to the concepts of discipline, Allen's treatise on combat leadership then emphasized the need for realistic training, top physical fitness, team spirit, and belief in the unit. When he spoke of leadership requirements, he voiced the very ingredient that Bradley grudgingly admitted Allen showed—knowledge of the men of his command. That covered taking active responsibility for their food, clothing, health, recreation, equipment, training, and discipline.

Allen spoke of character: "A leader must have determination and sincerity of purpose. If he is guided by selfish ulterior motives, he will soon lose the confidence of the men under his command. He is not expected to be a pantywaist, but must be a 'square shooter' and have high personal standards. A sense of humor that enables him to laugh off petty annoyances is helpful to any leader." Another aspect of character he deemed important was setting "an example of cheerfulness and fortitude even after prolonged exposure to hardship, danger and fatigue."

Allen did not neglect a primary feature—military skills. His ideal commander had to lead and direct his troops decisively in battle, marrying common sense with a practical working knowledge of the job. He had to know weapons as well as how combat units function. In Allen's mind, along with sound judgment, a leader should show "imagination, bold initiative, and the faculty of being able to 'beat the enemy to the punch.'

"It is the leader's responsibility to prepare his men for combat and to make sure that none . . . die in battle because of stupid leadership. He should strive to attain his combat objectives by smart quick maneuver with maximum damage to the enemy and with minimum damage to his own troops. To get the job done quickly with a minimum of battle casualties and other losses is the true test of battle leadership."

He pronounced one more axiom often ignored by his peers—"All commanders, regardless of grade, should frequently visit their forward elements on the battlefield to inspire confidence and to get firsthand combat information."

The third volume bore the title, *Directive for Offensive Combat.* The material was based upon his oft-uttered principle, "Find 'em, fix 'em and fight 'em." To satisfy the first of the triumvirate, Allen advocated intensive reconnaissance from the divisional G-2 section through regimental, battalion, and company intelligence. He included reconnaissance by artillery units, engineers, motorized operations, and active, aggressive foot patrols. He offered details on how scouts should be organized. Curiously, while he spoke of the specific patrol directives that must include "definite objectives, definite routes and must be clearly defined," he omitted a perhaps vital aspect, the value of prisoners and how to obtain them.

Fixing the enemy was through the use of fire from field artillery and infantry working on a coordinated plan. Demonstrating his knowledge of weapons, he offered specifics on where to deploy infantry support, ranging from 60mm and 81mm mortars to 37mm and 57mm cannons and also light and heavy machine guns, as well as the 105mm howitzers, ordinarily part of a cannon company. Allen, the alleged West Point dunce in ordnance and gunnery, rendered a crisp analysis of the most effective means to provide artillery backing to operations.

To "Fight 'Em" Allen spoke of "fire and maneuver. . . . The scheme of attack must be simple. It usually includes some combination of a semi-frontal secondary attack and a maneuvering main attack executed by envelopment of a critical enemy flank. It should be based on an accurate knowledge of the terrain and on the best available knowledge of the enemy's strength and weaknesses."

In a quick, easy fashion, he outlined primary operational factors, salient features of terrain to be considered, the value of surprise, and the basic plan of attack. "Envelopments must be directed so as to pass well beyond the enemy's flank and strike the enemy in the rear of that flank. This is done to maintain freedom of maneuver and to avoid being pinned down by concentrated fire of enemy weapons."

Commenting on the essential need for "sharp, quick maneuver, in order to accelerate the seizure of tactical objectives and to avoid undue exposure to enemy fires," Allen noted, "To quote football terms, 'the cut-back end run' is usually far more effective than the more commonly employed 'off tackle mass play.'"

One section of the booklet dealt with actual combat. "The firefight is conducted by FIRE and MANEUVER, which is based on prompt, intensive application of supporting fires and the *rapid* maneuvering of rifle units. *Maneuver must be conducted with a view to the quick seizure of command ground.*" Artillery and infantry support weapons were to provide a "base of fire" covering the advance of the rifle units closing with the foe.

Allen commented on what he had learned from experience. "German infantry invariably counterattacks very promptly. By anticipating and preparing for such counterattacks, heavy losses may be inflicted on the enemy. American artillery has been particularly effective in this respect. During the Tunisian campaign in North Africa, field artillery units of the 1st Infantry Division killed more Germans in repelling enemy counterattacks than in all other types of fire combined."

In Arizona and California and at Camp Carson, Allen drilled the 104th according to the precepts enunciated in his own little red books. Albert Schwartz remembered, "He preached and preached and preached to us the need to inflict the greatest damage on the enemy with the fewest casualties possible to ourselves. He believed in night attacks. We night attacked all over the damned desert. We didn't spend a lot of time sleeping."

After Quentin Reynolds broadcast his tribute to both the 1st Division and Allen shortly after D day, Allen sent a letter of appreciation. Mentioning his new command, he noted, "It happens that I now have several officers in the division who have been sent home because of wounds received in combat and managed to wangle their way under my command again in this new division. . . . I have heard from numerous old non-commissioned officers and officers in the division who have been rotated and sent back in according with the War Department policy of rotating officers to a new division who had considerable combat experience. I appreciate the fact that nearly all of them have tried to be reassigned to this particular division.

"While I feel that no one can say too much in favor of the old division, I do feel that you laid it on too thick in referring to me as the division commander. After all, I was merely an average quarterback on a hell of a good team. The old division had become imbued with the idea that they had to win, and actually there is very little credit due to me as an individual as the commander."

In the spring of 1944, the Army Specialized Training Program (ASTP) shut down. Established in 1942, it had enrolled tens of thousands of enlisted men, who were academically talented, at colleges around the country—studying languages, engineering, and other subjects that might have some military use. At inception of the program, they were viewed as candidates for a specialized cadre of officers during World War II. Now, the soldier-students were assigned en masse to organizations still in the States; the bulk of the young men were dispatched to infantry divisions such as the 104th.

Marion E. McCreight, who had been in an ASTP unit at New York University, reached Camp Carson in April. "I went to an infantry squad of B Company, 413th Infantry for advanced infantry training. As far as I know, all of us NYU ASTPers had basic infantry training at Camp Hood, Texas, during the summer of 1943.

"I felt that I was welcomed into B Company and made to feel like a fellow Timberwolf very quickly. That boosted my ex-ASTP morale and helped me fit into a tightly knit unit—B Company—with little friction. Whether my virtually seamless integration into a rifle company of a soon-to-be-deployed infantry division was a result of command policy or merely common sense is still unknown to me. However, it did bode well for future replacements of combat casualties.

"At Camp Carson we trained hard, especially in night exercises. And our daylight training, in my opinion, was very realistic and effective. We did a live-ammunition exercise involving an individual advance up a moderately steep trail with our rifle at the hip and pop-up silhouette targets along the trail appearing suddenly at ranges of five to ten yards. The exercise consisted of firing immediately from the hip, using only instinctive aiming. I was happily surprised at the accuracy I achieved and became very proficient at firing from the hip.

"Another practical training exercise involved a squad-sized, live-ammunition 'battle' with enemy silhouettes across a wooded ravine at a range of about 30 yards. The 'enemy' occupied fighting holes while we used trees and terrain for cover. Not only did the exercise provide training in using cover and concealment on an ad hoc basis but just as importantly gave me the feel for firing my new M-1 rifle accurately and quickly from cover. As confidence builders, the exercises were far more important than close-order drill."

Frank Van Valkenburg, another former student under the ASTP, also recalls the emphasis upon Allen's preferred mode of warfare. "We trained a lot in Camp Carson, learning to operate in darkness. We were told often that Gen. Allen wanted us to be known as the 'night-fighting division.'"

Bill McIlvaine, a "student soldier" at Fordham, said that as Allen greeted his group, they listened with the skepticism of college-educated youth. "I am quite sure we were underwhelmed when he informed us of his ideas concerning night training, running up and down the Rockies and preparations for going overseas. I can't recall any cheers from the group when he closed his welcome address with 'Nothing in hell can stop the Timberwolves.' We were aware that Gen. Allen had been the Commanding Officer of the 1st Infantry Division when they invaded Sicily. We heard that they suffered 80 percent casualties [losses were considerably less]. We joked that he was shooting for 100 percent with the 104th."

In his manual on combat leadership, Allen had mentioned the need for a commander to take good care of his troops. Schwartz said, "As an aide at Camp Carson, I spent a lot of time getting guys out of the civilian pokey. Allen told me, 'No Timberwolf is going to spend time in jail.'"

Warren G. Colglazier, who had enlisted in Indianapolis, went through basic training with a rifle company in the 104th before a transfer to the transportation platoon at division headquarters. "I was the relief driver for Maj. Gen. Allen from October 1943 until 1945. I first met him in Phoenix where Mrs. Allen was living. Several times I drove the Packard, taking Gen. and Mrs. Allen and Father Paul Mussell and other friends to parties and clubs in Phoenix. [Lieutenant Colonel Mussell, the division chaplain, was a frequent drinking companion of Allen.] The general did have a drinking problem and most of the time he was able to handle himself. His aides and myself were always able to handle the situation otherwise.

"When we were ordered to Camp Carson I was one of six drivers to drive three-quarter-ton trucks [two drivers per vehicle] to move the general and Mrs. Allen's household and personal belongings to Colorado Springs. While we were there I drove the Packard and a jeep. This was mostly at night, except during the day when I drove Mrs. Allen to beauty parlors and on shopping trips and since Gen. Allen had some troubles with math, I drove T.A. jr. to a private math tutor in Colorado Springs for three weeks. The General kept telling his son to get more math.

"Gen. Allen spent most of his nights at the Broadmoor Hotel. Some nights he would ask me to wait as he knew my wife lived in Colorado Springs.

He would tell me to go home and pick him up at a certain time. He always made sure that I had eaten breakfast, lunch or dinner. If I hadn't he would tell the orderly at the officers' mess, 'Feed my driver,' or at a hotel or other public eating place, he would give me a buck and tell me, 'Go get yourself a hamburger.' The General was always asking his commanding officers, 'Have the troops been fed?'

"One Sunday night, we were on our way back to Camp Carson when he saw a drunken soldier trying to get back to camp. He ordered me to stop and pick him up. After some argument with the soldier, he ordered him into the car. He asked the man what he had been drinking and the soldier answered the name of a very cheap whiskey. The General replied, 'Try Old Granddad.' We drove past the guardhouse and I was instructed to take the soldier to his barracks, and get his name and outfit. The General then told him, 'If your sergeant gives you a hard time or trouble, tell him to call me.' Gen. Allen then told me, 'He would have been in the guardhouse and would have been of no use there.'"

Marion McCreight said, "I sensed that Gen. Allen actually saw us rather than merely looked at us. Usually, he acknowledged us with a slight twinkle in his eye and often a slight nod in addition to the more formal returned salute. It seemed obvious to me that he respected his Timberwolves and that Timberwolves certainly respected him. Indeed that mutual respect was the core ingredient of our discipline and morale. He obviously believed deeply that our morale and, consequently, the discipline it engendered was crucial to battle success. He was [a Timberwolf], and he made me proud to be a Timberwolf.

"I was unaware of any discipline problems. If there were any, they must have been handled fairly, firmly and quietly. I know of one prank at Camp Carson and I understand that Gen. Allen laughed it off. The story was that a mess sergeant, with an excess of vanilla extract in him, had somehow staggered up to the General's quarters at the Broadmoor and invited Gen. Allen to have a drink with him. Possibly the prank was hushed up to protect Gen. Allen from too many such invitations."

Colglazier confirmed Kenneth Downs's testimony that Allen did not condone slovenliness, certainly when in garrison. "He was very strong on military discipline and dress. Uniforms were to be clean, neat and well kept. He hated sloppiness. I had trained with a tough infantry outfit and this was not a problem with me but I was told, 'Your shoes need a little more shine.' When he needed to correct me, it was always a fatherly command, as he would his son, as in fact I was not much older than Terry

Allen, Jr. The sedan had a two-stars license plate that was uncovered when the General was in the car. The car was to be saluted when it passed and we were always stopping soldiers for not saluting." Failure of 1st Division soldiers to show the proper military respect for Eisenhower's car in North Africa of course had been a major complaint about Allen.

For all of Allen's vigor and programs, inspectors from the army found the division inadequately prepared for overseas service mainly because the quartermaster company did not have its vehicles in the kind of condition required. Albert Schwartz said he heard Allen holler his unhappiness, and then the general snapped, "Get your ass down there! You're now the CO of the 104th quartermaster company." A subsequent evaluation by examiners qualified the Timberwolves for combat duty. Terry Allen was returning to the war.

15: Once More Into the Breach

The Allies' invasion of France on 6 June 1944—in which Allen's former command, the 1st Division, struck at Omaha Beach—created a foothold that could not be denied. Patton, restored to military operations as head of the Third Army, exploited a breakthrough at Saint-Lô toward the end of July and beginning of August. American armor raced through the countryside. On the night of 14 to 15 August, airborne forces from Italy began to drop in southern France as part of Operation Dragoon, while a vast fleet brought a second invasion force to the shores. As dead and wounded piled up, only a heavy investment of fresh ground forces could maintain the pace.

In the midst of maneuvers at Camp Carson, on 16 July 1944, the 104th Division received its orders to proceed to Camp Kilmer, New Jersey, from where it would leave to sail for the European theater of operations. As they moved out, a Colorado merchant informed Allen that two junior officers had issued rubber checks, one for fifteen dollars and another for twenty. Incensed at this affront to honor, he sharply reprimanded the pair and obliged them to make good.

During the final week of August, the entire organization loaded aboard four ships to sail in a convoy that included troop transports, freighters, tankers, and navy escort vessels. Allen and his division officers traveled on the *George Washington,* a onetime ocean liner.

Jim Williamson, the boy who earned his commission through the ROTC and became the 104th's ordnance officer, said, "We were on the

George Washington for 12 days en route to Cherbourg. Gen. Allen called his staff to his cabin, one by one and talked to them about various things. We chewed the fat for quite a while. Finally, he said to me, 'Williamson, you know what your job is. When I want my ammunition, I want it at the right place, at the right time and in the right quantity. I want the weapons repaired to the best extent of the ordnance company to do so. I want supplies maintained, weapons and vehicles also. If you do these things, I'll never ask questions.'" Williamson understood perfectly the instructions: Satisfying the division's needs rated ahead of the protocols and restrictions on supply under army regulations.

The 104th became the first American division to sail from New York directly to France, landing at the newly liberated port of Cherbourg. Previously, men and equipment destined for the continent debarked in England and then crossed the English Channel. But although the Timberwolf organization had reached France, their supplies were cached in the British Isles, and the troops could not move out until the gear joined them.

While they awaited orders to the front from the First Army, Allen's men guarded prisoners, military installations, and fuel dumps. They also performed drills in weapons, detection and removal of mines, and more night-fighting routines.

Shortly after the arrival at Cherbourg, Allen—accompanied by Lt. Col. Gerald Kelleher (who had come from the 1st Division to lead the 415th Regiment's 3d Battalion) and several other alumni from the Big Red One—went to the cemetery at Saint-Mère-Eglise to pay tribute and lay flowers upon the grave of his old comrade, Ted Roosevelt. After the pair were relieved at Troina, Allen's former deputy commander had spent several months as a staff officer with the II Corps in Italy before he wangled a second chance as an assistant division commander, with the 4th Infantry Division. As part of the D-day venture, that organization landed on Utah Beach. Because of navigational mistakes, the soldiers from the 4th waded ashore more than a mile off target; but Roosevelt, who had accompanied the first waves, moved the men out promptly, avoiding serious opposition in the first hours.

Roosevelt's meritorious service at Utah Beach and in the first weeks of the Normandy campaign convinced Eisenhower that he deserved his own division. But about six weeks after D day, the 57-year-old Roosevelt's heart gave out while he slept in a tent. He received the Medal of Honor posthumously.

Meanwhile, Patton's Third Army—in its sprint across France—threatened to outrun its stores of fuel, food, and ammunition. As Williamson explained, "We were sitting there, doing nothing, waiting for our equipment. First Army decided to help Patton out. They made arrangements for the French to take two big highways that ran parallel from the coast to Paris and designate them as one-way routes, east to Paris, and west to the coast. First Army assembled several hundred trucks and drivers and these hauled gasoline, food, ammunition, everything Patton needed. They ran these trucks 24 hours a day." The operation became known as the Red Ball Express. Under Col. William P. Evans, the executive officer for the 104th's artillery, twelve truck companies were organized, with qualified soldiers from all units enlisted as drivers.

Williamson noted, "Somebody had to change the oil, do the greasing and keep the trucks running as much as possible. The Army designated different ordnance companies in the area to do the job. I commanded an ordnance company and was given 150 trucks to look after. We took care of the lubrication and as much maintenance as possible—not much—to keep them running. We had two ordnance spots, one at Cherbourg and the other near Paris at Chartres, where the famous cathedral was."

Allen, as he had in the early days of North Africa, fretted about the delay in getting his division into combat. He drafted letters to both Patton and Bradley, to be delivered by hand to Patton's assistant, Gen. Hobart Hapgood. In a cover message, Allen explained, "My dear Hap . . . I thought it might be quicker for the letter to General Bradley to be delivered from General Patton's headquarters. . . . I wish you would extend to [Patton] my heartiest congratulations for his outstanding success with the Third Army.

"I trust it is not inappropriate for me to thus be writing to both General Bradley and to General Patton. One cannot be condemned for *not* [his italics] wanting to sit on the sidelines while a fight is going on. Is this a free fight or a private fight? I know I ain't no military genius or expert on all the angles of military administration, *but frankly I have the utmost confidence in this division* [his italics] and believe they will be highly effective in combat." The letter echoes his words to Beetle Smith in North Africa.

The letter to his old comrade Patton began with a formal salutation, "My dear General Patton," and offered, "my sincere congratulations for your outstanding success. . . . My good wishes are delayed, but none the less sincere." Allen went on to describe the work the 104th was doing with provisional truck companies. "We hope that by handling these necessary SOS 'chores' with the utmost efficiency, we may be released for an early combat assignment; at least that is the attitude of our units."

"I believe this division is really hot. They are well disciplined—are thoroughly trained—are tougher than hell physically—and have an intensive [sic] belief in themselves. They are eager for combat, and I hope will soon be permitted to show what they can do. [There was no poll of the troops to indicate their alleged eagerness to come under fire.]"

In the letter to "My dear General Bradley," Allen conveyed his felicitations on Bradley's elevation to lieutenant general with command of the 12th Army Group. Allen then repeated what he had written to Patton. "Our division is eager to 'do its stuff' in combat. They were well disciplined—are thoroughly trained—are tougher than hell physically—and have an intensive belief in themselves and their division." It is not happenstance, of course, that he assured both Patton and Bradley his troops were "well disciplined."

During the first week of October, Allen issued a memorandum for all units in the division concerning the right to vote in the 1944 federal elections. The directive began, "Soldier voting is of paramount importance." It then spelled out the requirements and procedures. Allen, himself, admitted after World War II that he had never cast a ballot before that.

The moment came when even the frenetic Red Ball Express could no longer satisfy the voracious appetite of the Third Army's drive, and Patton's units—out so far in front—threatened to expose their flanks. Eisenhower called a halt. That signaled an opportunity for Allen to bring his division to battle.

"Since Patton wasn't moving any more," said Williamson, "he could take care of himself. We got a letter from First Army telling us to turn in the 150 trucks. From my experience in the States, I knew that supplies were supposed to be delivered by the army but they rarely got to places where they were needed. That was in the U.S. where we weren't in combat. In Europe we were going to have trucks hit mines, be blown up by shells. Yet, we wouldn't get new ones to replace them and soon we'd run out of trucks. I told the CO of the ordnance company, 'Keith [Smith], I want your men to look over these 150 trucks and pick out the 60 best ones. Turn in the other 90 to Army as directed. Army is so confused, they'll never miss them.'

"We got the 60 best trucks and put them in a little pool in our ordnance company. That meant we had to find 60 drivers and we only had

150 people in the company. When we went into combat, we'd have to be able to move these trucks along with everything else. But the fellows were just tickled to death to have the vehicles and we got the drivers. Sure enough, we went into combat and one of our trucks hit a mine. It was destroyed. We filled out the papers, sent them to Army and asked them to please replace it. To this day [48 years later] we never got the truck. So we just took one of our extra ones and issued it to the infantry.

"When the war ended, we were the only division not to be missing a single truck. We were very careful; every time we lost a truck, we filled out the papers and sent them in. Otherwise, Army might have gotten nosy and asked how come these people aren't worried about the trucks. We made the requests for replacements but never received a single one. Gen. Allen was a pretty smart cookie. Nobody pulled the wool over his eyes. He knew there was something fishy about us being the only division on the front that had all of its trucks and the rest of them were crying their eyes out because they didn't have enough. But he never asked any questions. He kept his word."

With the Red Ball Express suspended and their own gear on hand, in late October the 104th traveled from France to Belgium for the baptism of fire. On 20 October, Allen met with all unit commanders and his staff officers at an ancient Belgian castle. He revealed, "Our mission is to be prepared to relieve elements of the 49th Infantry Division [British] within the next few days." The 104th was temporarily attached to the First Canadian Army, which was struggling to secure the port of Antwerp—threatened by the Germans, who held the northern approaches to the Scheldt Estuary, the gateway to Antwerp. In September, Operation Market Garden, a coup planned by Montgomery to gain the disputed ground, and which depended heavily upon airborne British and American troops, had been repulsed with serious losses.

In the early hours of 23 October, the 413th Regimental Combat Team, in relief of a British brigade, took up positions in the vicinity of Wuestwezel. The first action amounted to patrols, spurts of rifle and machine-gun fire, and a few artillery shells. The first of the German buzz bombs crashed and exploded, causing some fright but no casualties. That night, however, Pvt. Hubert L. Merritt of Company A, 413th, became the first KIA of the 104th.

Field Marshal Montgomery, commander of the 21st Allied Army Group—to which the Canadian First Army and the 104th belonged—convened the top officers of the Timberwolves to disclose his strategy.

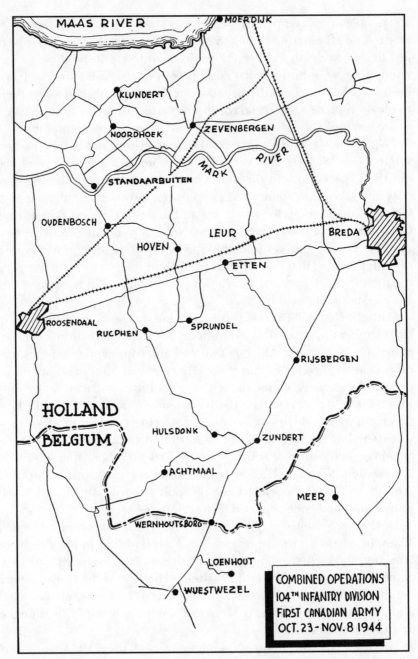

In late October 1944, the 104th Division under Terry Allen was attached to the First Canadian Army battling to clear German control of the approaches to the Belgian port of Antwerp.

The 104th was assigned to secure a line just north of the Belgium-Holland frontier. A photograph of the gathering, with Allen and Montgomery in the foreground, shows the American wearing an overseas cap, while the Briton sports his usual black beret and a sheepskin jacket. Montgomery had no dress code like that so vigorously enforced by the Americans during the earlier campaigns.

Hayden Bower, as a lieutenant with Company K of the 413th Regiment, remembered a sobering moment shortly before the division came under fire. Allen in one of his talks to the troops said, "I will never promise you anything but a wet ball on a muddy field, but I will be there with you." How much comfort that gave the men cannot be measured, for however much the general empathized, it would be the GIs who would bleed and die while they carried out the missions he ordered.

A rifleman with Company G of the 414th, Bob Bilinsky, recalled, "We were standing on the outskirts of one of those seemingly nameless little farm hamlets that dot the Belgium/Holland countryside. Although our immediate surroundings seemed peaceful enough, an occasional artillery explosion off in the distance contributed to a bit of uneasiness among us. The overcast sky didn't help matters much either since it seemed to further increase the concern of what might lie ahead for G Company. We were preparing to move into our first-ever frontline positions. None of us knew exactly what to expect. Were the 'front lines' something like the trench warfare of WW I, or would it be more like the 'gung ho' warfare depicted by the John Wayne movies?

"The 104th Infantry Division Headquarters had directed us to replace a Scottish unit that had been holding frontline positions for an extended period of time. As we prepared to move into those positions we tried our best to hide those uneasy feelings. Ammunition was checked and rechecked and so were the M-1 rifles, grenades and backpacks. As a rifleman in the 2d platoon I was acutely aware of an enormous change in the prevailing attitude of our platoon. Conversation was hushed. Efforts were made to avoid noise. Even the order to move out was given in an uncharacteristic, 'O.K., let's move our men' . . . completely counter to what the 2d platoon had become accustomed to in Camp Carson.

"Circling around a peaceful looking farmhouse, G Company moved into a dirt lane and then out into an open area which seemed to stretch forever towards what we assumed to be the German position. We expected gunfire to erupt at any minute but thus far, German guns remained silent. Each member of the Scottish unit was glad to see us and eagerly hopped out of their foxholes. As each Scot abandoned a foxhole,

G Company riflemen, like squirrels sensing danger, quickly scampered to its safety. From our hunkered-down positions we watched with a certain amount of envy the departing Scottish unit assemble in that dirt lane. Some of us were amazed at the complete disdain they seemed to have for the fact they presented an easy target for German gunfire.

"Suddenly it happened. The silence was shattered. Not by gunfire but by the loud strains of the Scottish bagpiper as the unit marched away in a swaying but perfect cadence to the pulsating beat of the music. At that moment the thoughts of war, and perhaps imminent enemy gunfire, diminished as we listened to the delightful bagpipe sounds that echoed about us. The members of G Company perhaps owe that bagpiper a 'Thank you' for helping us lose just a little of the nervous edge we had built up on our first assignment to frontline duty."

But that relief from tension must have been brief. On 25 October, all three infantry regiments jumped off in the morning and advanced, meeting increasing volumes of automatic weapons and artillery. By nightfall, the 104th troops essentially occupied the line designated on maps. A discussion among Allen, Montgomery, and the British I Corps's Lt. Gen. John A. Crocker led to a plan for the division to press the Germans with a night attack, to the satisfaction of Allen.

The heavens were clouded over and dark when the 413th began to move out. While division artillery peppered known enemy installations, the GIs filtered forward. They had gained less than one thousand yards before they contacted well-dug-in defenders. Battalions from the two other regiments also tried to gain ground. Soldiers from the 415th Regiment sloshed through marshy terrain and over diked four-foot-deep ditches filled with water. The men were soaked up to their armpits; they carried their rations and ammunition forward by extending their hands above the water.

Robert Wood toted a BAR (Browning automatic rifle) for Company E of the 414th Regiment in that night assault. "My rifle squad, with four men in front of me, led the whole attack. We started from a large farmhouse and moved out in a column of twos across fields or pastures. We expected to spread out in a skirmish line on a broad front before we reached the enemy positions. However, long before we were ready to spread out, we were fired upon by a German machine gun, just as our two scouts had cut a fence by a small ditch. The gun was located almost in front of us, just a few yards beyond the fence. The four men in front of me—the two scouts, the platoon leader and my squad sergeant—were probably killed in the first burst.

"I hit the ground and remained motionless, expecting someone from the rear of the column to sneak up and take out the gun, in accordance with our training. Everything was quiet for some time and I don't remember any kind of activity or grenade explosions. Later, I was told the machine gun positions had been covered with some kind of netting which prevented our grenades from knocking out the gun.

"After a while, I realized that there were four guns firing on us, rather than just one. I suspect that the Germans realized they had pinned down more than just a small patrol. They then moved two guns up along our right flank to box us in, and proceeded to lay down traversing fire over the entire area. Fortunately for most of us, they kept their fire about 12 to 14 inches above the ground, which allowed us to lie flat on the ground without being hit. This was pretty scary because you can see the streaks made by bullets passing over you, especially at night.

"I decided to try and find some cover, because lying out in the middle of a cow pasture did not provide much protection. I belly-crawled up to the ditch but there was no room for me. Apparently many other men had the same idea and the ditch was full of what I thought were dead bodies. While I was debating what to do next, the enemy gunner in front of me started to fire into the ground at the next fence post to my left. He then traversed the gun towards me, with the bullets hitting the ground directly under the fence. I knew that the little four-inch fence post I was hiding behind would not protect me. I expected to die momentarily with a bullet in the face. I have never been more terrified in my life than I was at that moment.

"However, for some reason the gunner stopped firing when the bullets were hitting the ground less than a foot from my left shoulder. There was no further question about what to do, just get away from there. Quickly I turned around, only to discover there did not seem to be anyone in the field behind me. I assumed that everyone had already bugged out. My only thought was to get back to the farmhouse where we had started. I began to crawl out, dropping all my equipment except my BAR and ammunition belt. I didn't ever try to see if anyone needed help.

"Back at our original jump-off position, I learned that John Dubelko had been shot through both legs but there was no information about my other BAR team member, Harold Scatterday. Later we were notified he had been wounded and lost some fingers. The next morning, after the terror of the night had passed, I was very glad to be one of the few men from E Company that showed up for breakfast, maybe 50 out of about

200. None of us had a mess kit to use; they either had holes in them or had been abandoned during the night."

Dick Jones, another automatic rifleman with the 414th's Company E, who was in the deluge from automatic weapons, quoted the regimental history. "The second Battalion withdrew under heavy enemy fire to its line of departure and reorganized." From his personal recollection, "It was a poorly organized beginning and after being pinned down by the heavy fire it was total chaos. Myself and several others did not find our unit for several days. Later night attacks were better planned and organized and were not as crazy as the first one."

Allen's recruit from the 1st Division, Lt. Col. Gerald Kelleher, led several jeeps bearing members of the 415th's 3d Battalion Headquarters Company. Parley "Pop" Allred, a radio operator in the third vehicle of the convoy, recalled stopping at a crossroads. "While sitting there I received a message that the Germans had the crossroad zeroed in and would soon open fire. I sent the message up to Col. Kelleher and just about that time all hell broke loose. We sure didn't waste much time in getting out of there. They were shelling us with 88s, mortars, machine guns and everything but the kitchen sink. You knew that you were alive if you heard the sound of an 88 coming in because the speed of the shell was faster than that of sound. You heard the explosion first.

"From the crossroad we traveled on to the town of Oudenbosch, about a mile and a half away. Col. Kelleher stopped in the middle of town and went into a building to talk to someone there who was working in the underground. He came running back out and shouted that the Germans had pulled out and were going to start shelling the town in ten minutes. They didn't wait that long. Starting at each end of the street and meeting at the center of town, they really peppered that road at ten minute intervals. We immediately hit the gutters and crawled into any available cover we could find. Just as the gray light of dawn started to appear, we heard quite a distance back down the road, the high pitched whine of a Heinie motorcycle coming wide open. When the rider passed me he was leaning just as low to the bike as he could and still steer it. I know he was praying to God for safe passage and must have gotten it. Cause I know that everyone of those GIs laying in the gutters on each side of the street took at least one shot and maybe more and didn't even touch him."

Allred mentioned Kelleher's contact with the Dutch underground. Subsequently, Kelleher entered the village of Achtenwaal, as part of the advance guard of his battalion. The lieutenant colonel thought the town deserted until, "At the main intersection, a uniformed man came out to meet us. He identified himself as a Dutch police officer and asked for the senior Allied commander. When I made myself known, he asked me for identification and then showed me [his identification] for the Dutch underground. He then brought me into a house. In the living room . . . he shoved back a stove which hung on a hinge. Where the stove had been was a concrete slab. This he removed and brought out a large neatly wrapped bundle of papers which had been given to him by a Dutch underground operator . . . with orders to turn them over to the first Allied officer he met. I immediately sent these back to the Division."

Allen and his intelligence officers were thus enabled to inspect two bulky volumes of maps, overlays, and logistical data for the German defenses in the towns in Holland. The material was quickly forwarded to the First Canadian Army, which relied upon it for the remainder of the campaign in the region.

To retain control of the estuary, the German Fifteenth Army had woven trenches, bunkers, field fortifications, machine guns, and 20mm flak guns—all well concealed and camouflaged—into defenses in depth, with overlapping fields of fire. The strongpoints mutually supported one another. To overcome such stalwart obstacles to an advance, British Churchill tanks aided the infantrymen from the 104th.

Charles Dodd, a Company L soldier from the 413th, remembered marching a distance of five miles while the British troops on the other side of the road headed for the rear. He was struck by the sight of "every fifth or sixth man [with] a teapot tied to the side of his pack." Dodd became half of a two-man team, uneasily manning a .50-caliber machine gun on a road near Brecht, Belgium. "I had never before been that close to one of those things, much less fired one but the other man seemed to know what we were supposed to do. He seemed to know what to do until we saw men coming down the road toward us. We couldn't tell whether they were our patrol or a German patrol. We both were undecided whether we should open fire or wait for the signal the returning patrol was supposed to give. We waited, and thank goodness, the patrol gave the prearranged signal.

"On 26 October we left Brecht about dark and moved up until about 2330 when we were told to dig in for the night. The hole we dug that night was more for comfort than protection. I think it was about seven feet square and only about 18 inches or a little more deep. We found some straw to line the hole and had just settled in when word came we were moving out. I have no idea how far we walked before we stopped, and when we did we were right in the middle of the war. Shells exploding and tracers everywhere. I can still hear the medic call out that Sgt. [Albert] Knorr was dead, shot right through the heart by a stray bullet, our first casualty."

Dodd's platoon, under orders, crawled forward; then, in a skirmish line, they ran through a pine grove, falling every few yards, with groups firing—while comrades advanced in similar fashion through the small grove. They reached cleared ground swept by enemy guns and mortars. Pinned down, nearly out of ammunition, they were about to fix bayonets when the rumble of tanks sounded. "I heard later," said Dodd, "that the Brits didn't get there earlier because they had to finish their tea. The Germans had started coming our way. Two Churchill tanks pulled up side by side and Captain [Marshall B.] Garth with a phone, from the tanks, on each ear, directed their fire and broke up the counterattack."

Casualties mounted, but after repelling several counterattacks, the GIs finally crunched across the border to establish a line inside Holland. Private Beverly Tipton from the 413th's Company G earned the 104th's first Distinguished Service Cross. After his squad's lead scout was killed, Tipton assumed that post, took a BAR, and—shooting from the hip—wiped out an enemy machine-gun crew while three separate snipers tried to eliminate him.

An Associated Press dispatch quoted Allen, saying, "So far everything has gone according to schedule. I can't ask for anything more at this point. I cannot say too much in praise of the Canadian units and the British who are supporting us with tanks and artillery."

After several changes in direction as higher-ups shifted their interests, the division marched toward the Mark River, which ran roughly east-west in the sector. The 414th and 415th Regiments, accompanied by British armor, reconnaissance units, and artillery battalions, advanced on the objective while the 413th stayed in reserve at Zundert. When the 3d Battalion of the 415th halted under a storm of German artillery and mortars, Gerald Kelleher ran to the head of the column to rally his GIs. As he personally led the advance, an enemy patrol of about ten men approached. Armed only with his pistol, the battalion leader chased them off and even captured a pair. When the column moved ahead, a shell wounded his executive officer. Kelleher exposed himself to fire, as he rushed to the fallen man and then carried him to shelter in a building. For all of these endeavors, Kelleher received a DSC.

Despite the defenders' stubborn resistance, the Americans cleared them south of the Mark and on 30 October closed on the objective. On the left flank, the British 49th Division—now returned to the fray— neared the river, while the 1st Polish Armored Division on the right also approached the stream. Reconnaissance revealed the bridges in the 414th's zone too damaged for use and it fell to the 1st Battalion of the 415th to cross and create a bridgehead.

George Roxandich, a rifleman from Company B, recalled embarking with a boat that he had been told would carry his group (he had been given the boat's number): "We arrived at a field that had a lot of large rowboats. We picked up our numbered boat and started walking with it, about eight to a boat. It wasn't until we started to get sniper fire that we realized we were going to make a river cross under fire.

"We crossed without too much fire. The company held up a short time on the bank of the river and then we went over a road toward a farm-house. I went past the house and dug a foxhole across a ditch. A short time later, while relieving myself, a couple of shells started hitting around my position. I was able to see a German tank 50 to 70 yards from our po-sition. One of the shots hit in back of me on the other side of the ditch. The concussion knocked me out."

Roxandich said he recovered quickly and jumped back into his fox-hole. "I had three rifle grenades. I lobbed them and hit him with one. Since it hit [the tank] in the front, it did not do much to him [but] he backed up between two farmhouses and shelled us from there, at least 100 yards away. I could see men running across the area. I kept firing at them. I saw one climb on the tank and he must have been talking to the men inside. I fired a shot at him. It happened to be a tracer bullet. It went right between him and the tank. I kept firing at them until I ran out of shells. The only ammo I had left were three hand grenades.

"It got quiet for a while. The tank did not fire anymore. After dark, I just stayed in my foxhole and waited to see what was happening. I was not in touch with anyone. I don't know how much later it was, but I heard rumbling to the rear. In silhouette I saws three tanks and some infantry. I thought they were GIs. I was going to tell them there was a tank up front until I heard them talking. I realized it was not in English. I got down in my foxhole and hoped they would pass. Instead, they parked right next to me, only about 15 feet away.

"I kept down and waited. They were in a couple of groups with one in front of the tanks, another between them, and two right beside the tank across the ditch from my hole. They did not seem to notice my hole at first. They stopped talking and one of them looked over my way, got up on his toes to get a better look. The only thing I thought to do was pull the pin on one of the grenades and toss it at them. When the handle let go I heard one of them say, 'Vas ist das?' I don't know what happened to them because I pulled the pin of the other two grenades and tossed them at the other groups and started running.

"I was hit by a piece of shrapnel as I was running. I realized that two other GIs were coming from the side of me. One did not have a rifle. We ran into two German infantrymen. The Germans had encircled us. One of them said, 'Hands up!' Since I was out of ammo and the other guy had no rifle, there wasn't much we could do. But the one guy with us said, 'No!' and shot one of them in the stomach. He went down screaming but the other German shot the GI and he just dropped. The German held the gun on us while he bent down at his buddy. He kept screaming 'Hans! Hans!'

"Others came along and took us back to their headquarters. I was in a field hospital for a while where they operated on my arm. They cut away the loose skin and flesh without any anesthetic. From there I was sent to a hospital. Later I went to a prison camp."

Only a portion of the 415th had actually succeeded in reaching the north bank of the Mark. The plan had been for the 2d Battalion to follow; but, so many boats had been destroyed and the hostile gunnery directed at the river so effective that a further crossing was postponed. With only riflemen on the other side of the Mark, and artillery or air support unavailable because of wretched visibility, the I British Corps directed the 1st Battalion to withdraw to the south side of the river.

A relief party of several hundred managed to achieve the north banks and evacuate wounded. Lieutenant William C. Tufts from Company C volunteered to lead a patrol that included antitank weapons and would aid men forward. The group forced a wedge through the German lines, enabling most of the battalion to retreat. Unknown to higher headquarters, a band of sixty-five to seventy men had dug in one thousand yards north of the dike, cut off by German tanks. They held out for three days until the Americans regrouped and swept back across the Mark.

In a renewed effort to gain the objective, the 413th Infantry planned to strike out from the left of a small village, Standaarbuiten, while the 415th's surviving battalions would jump off from the town, which actually straddled the Mark. The attack would begin at nightfall. A concentrated artillery barrage preceded the attack, and the entire affair was co-ordinated with the advance of the British and Polish organizations.

Charles Dodd of Company L in the 413th, and whose unit had been saved by the timely arrival of British tanks a few days earlier, recalled assembling behind a levee close to twenty feet high at the edge of the Mark. Engineers had built a footbridge about eighteen inches wide. "They had neglected to install a handrail," said Dodd. "The current was not very fast but it did sweep the bridge downstream until the anchor lines were taut, and then the bridge slowly swept back up stream. Under normal conditions this would not pose much of a problem but I was loaded with gear: a bazooka and three rockets, M-1 rifle with 220 rounds of ammo, 45 caliber pistol with 50 rounds, two hand grenades, steel helmet, entrenching [shovel], overcoat, field jacket, raincoat, wool shirt and pants, long underwear, leggings, shoes and a couple of K rations tucked in somewhere, besides cigarettes and other personal items. Without all this extra gear I weighed about 135 pounds. With it, I may have been close to 200. Carrying it was not the problem; stepping off the bridge [into the water] would have been but it did not happen. On the far bank, about 300 to 400 yards from the river, the small village of Standaarbuiten was already in flames when we made the crossing and headed for those burning buildings."

Other men from the division crossed in assault boats while the artillery doused the ground ahead of them with waves of shells. Despite the cascade of lethality from the artillery, the enemy still peppered the advancing soldiers with small-arms fire. The Germans fought hard from the shattered houses of the village and from behind the canals that soaked those traversing them and that had been artfully furnished with barbed wire to add a degree of difficulty.

Lieutenant Cecil H. Bolton, weapons platoon leader of Company E in the 413th, brought mortar fire to bear when a pair of machine guns pinned down his unit immediately after they crossed the Mark. He directed fire on the enemy positions, until he was severely wounded in his legs and temporarily rendered unconscious by a shell. When he regained his senses, he crawled ahead and then led a two-man bazooka team through chest-deep, bone-chilling ditch water toward one of the machine guns. While the bazooka team covered his progress, he maneuvered to fifteen yards of the emplacement. Not stopped by his injured legs, he sprinted the distance and used grenades to destroy the enemy gunners who were located in the shell of a house.

Bolton guided his companions over open ground toward the second machine gun. They shot down a sniper en route, and Bolton then killed a member of the gun crew with his carbine while his associates accounted for the remainder. The trio of Americans next headed toward an 88 that was pounding the troops by the river. The lieutenant directed bazooka rockets that knocked out the artillery piece. Returning to the Company E lines, Bolton incurred another wound before he collapsed. For these achievements he received the division's first Medal of Honor, to which in subsequent action he added a Silver Star.

During this period, recalled Albert Schwartz, "One of the regiments had a tough canal crossing. The division quartermaster hadn't really done his job right and Allen sent word from his command post that he wanted extra blankets and socks for the regiment. I went to a hospital unit and traded one of our trucks for blankets. Later the quartermaster colonel complained to Allen about what I did. I explained, 'You told me to take care of the men.' Allen fired the colonel."

The relentless pressure all along the Mark forced the Germans to fall back. They skillfully employed all of their weaponry and tactical prowess for an orderly retreat. The net result, however, was that the 104th was able to advance to the banks of the next substantial natural barrier, the Maas River—which, as it flows farther south in Belgium and France, becomes the Meuse. A final assault by the Canadian First Army would clear the enemy from the area where they were preventing the use of the Scheldt Estuary, passageway to the vital port of Antwerp.

But the 104th was not part of the final blow. On 5 November, a dispatch from the U.S. First Army directed the division to move as soon as possible to the vicinity of Aachen, inside Germany itself. As the last elements of the Timberwolves disengaged from combat while being relieved by British Tommies, Allen forwarded to the commanding officers of all units Montgomery's thanks for "the splendid work they have done." A pat on the back also came from the head of the First Canadian Army. Lieutenant General Courtney Hodges, of the American First Army, and Maj. Gen. J. Lawton Collins, commander of the VII Corps, welcomed the 104th, acknowledging its significant contributions to its previous masters.

Allen himself issued his own commendation "To All Timberwolves." After paying tribute to the entire organization, he concluded with what had become a mantra, adapted from his days with the Big Red One, "NOTHING IN HELL MUST STOP THE TIMBERWOLVES."

16: To the Roer

The swift requisition of the 104th from the First Canadian Army came at a moment when the Allied juggernaut across Europe had slowed perceptibly. Having advanced to the border of Germany, under Hodges the American First Army faced the redoubts of the Westwall, or Siegfried, line—a thick and sometimes two-layered series of huge cement bunkers, tank defenses, and traps. The hint of winter hovered over the front and the Third Reich had girded itself for an all-out defense of the homeland. Eisenhower hoped he could push his forces to the Rhine before frigid temperatures and snow would halt operations. The "to the Rhine" strategy required the presence of the 104th, along with other organizations new to Europe.

In what was probably the most misguided venture of the European campaign, Hodges, with the approval of Bradley (12th Army group commander), had already tried twice to penetrate the Westwall through the dense Hürtgen Forest. The 9th Infantry Division had made small advances at heavy costs before relinquishing the responsibility to the 28th Division—which was all but destroyed during its plunge into the evergreen fastness of the Hürtgen. The stalemate in the forest, which eventually chewed up four more American divisions, would eliminate any chance of gaining the Rhine objective before winter.

In the pause between the 104th's work in the lowlands and its shipment to the front facing the Westwall, Allen dropped a letter to his son, now at N.M.M.I. "The division has been fighting hard for several weeks and so far has had rather marked success. I only hope we can keep it up and that our training and skillful use of maneuver will help to keep down casualties. This is a nasty business, but must be done well.

"Mother has written you're doing well. Congratulations!!!

"Don't worry about me, old top, I'm too lucky to get hurt."

On 8 and 9 November, the 104th relieved Allen's former command by moving into the positions of the 1st Division in its eight-mile-wide sector. Bill McIlvaine, as a member of the 413th Infantry's Company A, said, "We had been told that General Allen was extremely proud of our performance in Holland and I am quite sure he was even more proud when we relieved the 1st Division in the pillboxes outside Aachen."

Kenneth Downs (an Allen aide) wrote in a piece for the *Saturday Evening Post,* "The veteran division, like an All American welcoming the kid brother into his first big game, outdid itself to make the relief smooth. The first man wearing 'the Big Red 1' to spot General Allen was big, egg-shaped Sergeant Ferry of the MPs, who was directing traffic at a sensitive crossroads when Allen's jeep approached.

"'Jeez, there's Terry Allen!' he yelled. Ferry, a former semipro football player from Pennsylvania and a crack shot, had been the general's bodyguard in the ticklish early days in Tunisia. . . . The general asks how the hell Ferry is, and Ferry says he is fine. A short pause.

"Then Ferry says, 'Well, General, I see you're still wearing those same boots, sir.'"

Hugh Daly, a private in the intelligence and reconnaissance platoon of the 415th's Headquarters Company, said, "When we took over the positions of the 1st Infantry Division, so many veteran soldiers of the Big Red One remarked how lucky we Timberwolves were to have Terry Allen as our commander."

Meanwhile, Allen's former command had struggled with an obstinate defense at Aachen, a city renowned as the coronation site for the Holy Roman Empire and Charlemagne's capital. Aachen not only anchored the most massive stretch of the Westwall fortifications, but it offered an easier avenue through difficult terrain. It also had the symbolic value of being the first German city vulnerable to capture. Aachen finally yielded on 21 October, but the 1st Division barely resembled the outfit Allen had commanded. The losses at Omaha Beach, and then in Normandy, and now the bloody battle for Aachen, had emptied it of most of the men who had fought in North Africa and Sicily. It would be further depleted when the division would be hurled into the Hürtgen Forest in mid-November. Still the 1st remained one of the premier fighting organizations, and Huebner is credited with having maintained its proficiency. He was well aware of having a different relationship with the troops than they had under Allen. Huebner remarked, "The men respected me, but they loved Terry Allen."

Before the Rhine lay another formidable natural obstacle, the Roer River. The defenders in the Hürtgen had blocked any advance by brother divisions through that sector to that river. The first offensive within Germany by the 104th would concentrate upon the Roer. The Timberwolves were scheduled to commence an attack on 11 November, World War I's Armistice Day.

According to Downs, "General Eisenhower and Gen. Omar Bradley came up to tell General Allen it was imperative, for reasons of morale, that the 104th score with all possible drive and dash in its first operation. They explained that a quick success by this new division would have a heartening effect on the other units, some of which had been in the line since D Day in Normandy, and would be evidence of the kind of help promised them."

The 104th's offense opened against the objective of Stolberg, a small industrial city overlooked by Hill 287, a steep highland observation mount appropriately protected by concrete fortifications and dugouts bristling with lethality. Working with the 104th was the 3d Armored Division commanded by Maj. Gen. Maurice Rose. Beyond Stolberg lay other heavily fortified towns, Eschweiler, Weisweiler, and Lucherberg.

The 104th actually was part of a massive VII Corps drive, but the kick-off was delayed five days while fog, rain, and overcast skies grounded both the U.S. air forces and the RAF. When the weather finally cleared, twenty-four hundred heavy and medium bombers from England showered thousands of tons of explosives all along the front. Simultaneously, some one thousand cannons blasted specific targets.

In typical fashion, the 414th Regiment began the march toward Stolberg on a pitch-black night. They tramped through streets of rough cobblestone and slick pavement in a steady rain and penetrated the first few miles into German territory. They arrived in the village of Bushbach by dawn—able to enjoy the sight of the hundreds upon hundreds of bombers overhead.

Shortly before one in the afternoon, the 414th infantry launched itself at Hill 287. To the dismay of the troops, the Germans appeared lit-

tle damaged by the onslaught from the air and artillery. The enemy
manned its weapons and deluged the GIs with small- and large-caliber
gunfire. The gains for nearly twelve hours of savage combat advanced
the front only from four hundred to nine hundred yards. While the
Americans rousted the Germans from a pair of pillboxes, the topmost
one continued to spew deadly fire.

Louis Belsky (with the communications platoon of the 414th's 3d Battalion) said he watched the aerial strike on Hill 287: "The pillboxes
slowed the battalion down about two days. I saw Gen. Allen and the 414th
Regimental Colonel come up front discussing this situation. It was rare
for high officers to be in a battalion area while the action was on."

A single house served as a command post for both the battalion and
elements of the 3d Armored. The proximity of attackers and defenders
was so close that when a ten-man patrol left the command post, two machine guns ambushed it before the group had traveled two hundred
yards. Company I soldiers burrowed into the earth. For ten hours,
minute-by-minute artillery and mortar shells pounded the ground about
them. The men slipped back several hundred yards, under a blanket of
darkness, to comparative safety.

Wes Gaab, a machine gunner in Company M of the 414th, recalled,
"We were in support of K and L Companies. The battle was gigantic and
one of confusion, noise, death and the smell of decaying German soldiers left on the battlefield. We did not take Hill 287 that day.

"The attack resumed early in the morning of the 17th. Through heavy
fire, countless mines and booby traps, a small group of GIs somehow
made it to the top of the hill. We found refuge under a knocked-out Tiger
tank which the Germans had used as a pillbox. There were two dead Germans still inside the tank. We were less than 100 yards to the left of the
bunker. The dirt under the tank had been excavated and provided just
enough room for the five of us.

"It was about midday when we finally got to the top. Then something
strange occurred. We suddenly realized that all was quiet. The shooting
on both sides had stopped. We assumed the 2d Battalion had taken Hill
287. We even cracked out the K-rations to celebrate. But if the 2d battalion had taken the hill, why were there only five of us here—where were
the others? We learned later that they had pulled back to a row of battered houses at the foot of the hill.

"I was at the end of our under-tank fortress, so I was elected to go out
and take a look around. I borrowed an M-1 from someone since my

sidearm was a .45 and we didn't even have the machine gun set up. I crawled over to what looked like a low coop that could have housed chickens or rabbits. I rested the M-1 on the top and looked around. There was no one to be seen, until a head slowly appeared above the top of the bunker. He was a German soldier, using binoculars. He wasn't looking at us to his right but down the hill in the direction from which we had come. I shot him.

"Within minutes I saw Germans pouring out of the rear of the bunker. They were in a trench with only their heads and shoulders showing above ground. I fired on them with the M-1 and the heads would disappear, only to reappear in a matter of seconds. They were in a big hurry to get out of there. When the last had left the bunker, I returned to the tank and told the other four what had happened. We were sure it was all over for us. We waited for the Germans to surround us, but they never came. What did come was even more frightening. The clanking rumbling sound of a tank coming up behind us. He put two rounds into our tank at point blank range. Miraculously we weren't even scratched. He didn't do the two dead Germans in the tank any good. We then heard him back down the hill and all was quiet again.

"We remained under the tank for the rest of the day with infrequent trips out to see if we could locate any of our buddies, but there were none to be seen. We didn't realize it at the time, but we five GIs had taken and held Stolberg Hill 287. We decided to wait until darkness and go back down the hill to our own lines. Tiptoeing through a minefield at night can get the heart beating faster, but going down from shell crater to shell crater we managed to get down safely. Well almost—we didn't know the password and nearly got shot by our own guys who thought we were a German patrol. We finally convinced them that we were one of them and they let us in, one at a time.

"We reported to a lieutenant that the Germans had vacated the bunker, but he gave us a 'Ya, sure they did.' The next morning, November 18th, the Battalion once again charged the hill only to find it abandoned."

Parley E. "Pop" Allred, the radio operator with the 3d Battalion's Headquarters Company, remembered an initial position at Brand, just in front of the Westwall's "Dragon's Teeth"—the antitank barriers. "[We were] facing Stolberg and close enough to the German forward observation post that if we turned up the volume on our radios, we could hear each other's programs, which we did quite often. It was kind of a gentlemen's agreement between us and the Germans that we would pick up brickets to keep us warm from the same coal pile. We got ours in the daytime and they at night. One night the I & R came in and said, 'The Germans have trucks over there and are hauling the coal away.' That to us was a violation of our gentlemen's agreement. So we proceeded to call in artillery fire on them and that rectified the problem."

The battle for Stolberg ravaged the city—shot, shell, and bomb pulverized the tall chimneys, factories, and houses—with the foe tenaciously fighting from amid the rubble. Pole and satchel charges, and other demolition, often with self-propelled guns, reduced bricks, mortar, and stone to dust. Hand-to-hand combat, attacks, and counterattacks eroded the strength of the defenders. Stolberg finally fell on 19 November after three days of ferocious combat.

Allred said, "Our division began trying to get through the Dragon's Teeth without much success. One night Colonel Kelleher came by and said, 'We have never been beaten before, but this time we have. Get ready to pull back. I'm sending the I & R [intelligence and reconnaissance] platoon to find out what the Germans are doing and then we will retreat.' When the platoon came back, Sgt. Wells said, 'They beat us to it; the Germans have all pulled back.' Since we were all ready to move someplace, we moved forward through the Dragon's Teeth and into the town of Eschweiler."

That well-defended city northwest of Stolberg was besieged by all three regiments of the 104th. At 3 A.M. on 22 November, two companies from the 1st Battalion of the 415th silently slipped through the blacked-out streets, surprised the sleeping Germans, and swiftly bagged key objectives. Because Eschweiler sat on the banks of the Inde River, engineers constructed a bridge for further advance.

Albert E. Siklosi, as a member of Company C, 329th Engineer Battalion, on 2 December rode a truck to Weisweiler. "At the edge of town we parked the trucks, dismounted and prepared to enter the town. We could hear sounds of firing and explosions in the distance and knew the infantry were having a busy time. What we didn't know was who owned Weisweiler at our time of entry. Henry Gram and I were designated as point men and sent in to find out. We found the town unoccupied.

"Our assignment was to put a footbridge across the Inde River at the west end of town. The infantry needed ammunition resupply and were anxious to get their wounded back to aid stations. When we reached the river we found an American tank had attempted to ford the stream and had become bogged down. The tankers left it there. The tank looked like it would be useful as a means of anchoring the footbridge midstream as we assembled it.

"Herbert Meyring and I were detailed to enter the river and lash a guy-line to the tank to serve as a safety line for the work. The water was ice cold, had a strong current, about chest deep with an uneven bottom. We had climbed onto the turret when enemy shells started coming in. We lifted the hatch cover, jumped in and closed the hatch. The tankers had left two flashlights in holders on the underside of the hatch so we were not completely in the dark.

"When the shelling ceased we opened the hatch and waded back to shore, well soaked. The bridging equipment was being unloaded by most of the other men and we were standing on the bank filling in the platoon leader on river life. He seemed preoccupied, then asked us if we had seen any sign of Henry Gram. He had sent him separately to determine the status of a culvert across on a side stream feeding into the Inde. It was between us and the factory outside Lamersdorf where the infantry were battling the Germans.

"I offered to go look for Henry and also find out what shape the culvert was in and how strong it would be. He warned me that just before the culvert, his map showed a fork in the road to the right and that as far as he knew was enemy territory. I went back into the water and crossed to the far side, hunkered down and made for the culvert along the road to the factory. I saw the fork to the right, just before reaching the culvert.

"By now I was starting to hear bullets whistling around so I dropped and crawled the rest of the way. Crawling under the culvert I felt a lot safer and made a thorough inspection finding the culvert as solid as could be. All this while I had seen nobody, including Henry, so I figured he must have taken the forbidden fork to the right. Henry had always had a quiet determination to do things his own way. In Stolberg, he had gone out sniping at German infantry as if this were his mission, not building bridges.

"I returned to the fork and took the road to the right at a slow crouch softly calling his name. I hoped I wouldn't have to go too far. I didn't go much further eastward before I found him, semiconscious under several dead German medics. Gram had been hit and the medics had come to give him first aid, bandaging a head wound. Then German shells had hit the group, killing the German medics and further wounding Henry in the hand and thigh. He had lost some fingers, but managed to wrap his hand and control the bleeding. To protect himself, he had partially covered his body with the dead German medics.

"Since he was in no condition to travel I told him to stay put and I would go back for a stretcher and help. I dogtrotted hunched over, pausing when the moon shone too brightly, until I reached the river, waded back to the west shore and told the lieutenant the situation. Then I led Doc Kilgore with his stretcher, Dave Phillips and John Kasarda back across the river to Gram. We loaded him on the stretcher and began crawling back, making an awful big target as a group of five. Since progress was so slow and Hank was almost unconscious, we took him from the stretcher and half-dragged, half-carried him to the river. There we formed a chain and splashing and stumbling along finally got him to the other bank where the rest of the platoon dragged us out to safety. It was a cold, wet, exhausting experience, but we had brought our own back safely."

During this drive, word came that some wounded GIs had been cut off on a hill. Allen's "Brooklyn," George O'Connor, led a patrol that extricated the injured men. For this deed he received a Silver Star.

Newsweek complimented, "By the third week of the big push, it became apparent that Terry Allen had trained a very good division indeed. . . . Allen taught his Timberwolves some new tricks along with the old, for as the Germans on their sector have discovered, the 104th is a body of night-fighting specialists."

Don Whitehead, the Associated Press correspondent on the scene wrote, "Even in the short time they have been in action with the First Army, the Timberwolves proved themselves to be an outstanding Division as they drove to Eschweiler. Allen often was at the front personally directing the operations and giving instructions to battalion and regimental commanders—and company commanders."

Bill McIlvaine noted, "*Stars and Stripes* reported that Axis Sally said we were unfair by fighting at night when the poor German soldiers were sleeping and we shouldn't be sneaking in under cover of darkness."

Lucherberg, a village of only four hundred inhabitants across the Inde River, fell after being severely battered by concentrated fire that came from all of the division's artillery units, along with some from attached and adjoining organizations. Intelligence sources indicated as many as five hundred to six hundred in the Lucherberg garrison, with tanks support close by. Just before midnight on 2 December, two companies, E and

G from the 415th—holding rifles, bayonets, and grenades overhead—waded the icy, waist-deep Inde to assault the defenders.

While men from the 2d Battalion clung to their positions, the 415th's 3d Battalion troops also joined the assault. At midnight, led by Lt. John Olsen, Company I crossed the Inde over a railroad bridge and climbed a steep hill in front of the town, hoping to surprise the defenders through this approach. A barbed-wire fence halted the lead elements, and when the GIs stooped to slide under the strands, rifles and machine guns opened up on them. Olsen, responding to the enemy's awareness of their presence, shouted, "I'm making a rush to the town. Come if you like, or stay and be wiped out by artillery fire in the morning." He and two platoons charged up the ground and drove off a tank with bazooka rounds. The Americans managed to gain possession of several houses before the lieutenant was mortally wounded.

In one desperate fight, a group of Americans holed up in the basement of a house while enemy troops occupied nearby buildings and the streets. Lieutenant Arthur Ulmer, a forward observer of the 929th Field Artillery, and Lt. John D. Shipley, from Company I of the 415th, called down their own artillery and 81mm mortars to hammer the sector. United Press war correspondent Boyd Lewis said in his story, "They believed that the Germans were more exposed and would suffer greater losses than the Americans would. They got most of their men into a heavy basement which had thick, fortress-like walls, posted riflemen at slits picked out of the brick walls.

"Then Ulmer radioed his artillery to crash down on the town with everything available." For seven hours, the ground rocked with explosions. Boyd continued, "But toward the end of the day German resistance collapsed while Ulmer was still calling for more fire. By 1615, Company I—what was left of it—was able to mop up the town with virtually no difficulty. Some 200 Germans lay dead in the streets." A summary of the artillery activity for the critical twenty-four hours required to subjugate Lucherberg showed that the division plus attached artillery (but excluding guns from the VII Corps or other divisions) had fired 370 missions with a total of 18,950 rounds.

Radio operator Parley Allred at 3d Battalion, 415th Regimental headquarters, recalled, "General Allen did come down and he brought all the fixings for a victory celebration including a citation and lots of praise. What actually took place at that party I can't rightfully know. But I do know that General Allen couldn't get into his jeep under his own power after it was all over."

VII Corps commander, Lt. Gen. Joseph Lawton Collins, sent a message to Allen, "Congratulations to the 104th Division on its superb performance in capturing Lucherberg."

Lucherberg lay but a short distance from the Roer River. But control of the western banks sector, allotted to the 104th, required capture of three final barriers: the villages of Pier, Schophoven, and Merken. Active reconnaissance by troops from the 414th and 415th found the enemy holed up in prepared positions within Pier; and only a rolling barrage of artillery enabled the infantrymen from the 414th to advance over twelve hundred yards of open ground to come to grips with the enemy. Within Pier, house-to-house fighting again saw men from both sides occasionally occupying adjacent rooms in a building. Once armor from the 750th Tank Battalion stormed into Pier, the remaining Germans were killed, captured, or routed.

Merken, a town of some one hundred stone and brick houses, ideal for defenders, sat behind open ground—killing fields for automatic weapons. The only way to avoid horrendous casualties was to approach in darkness. On 11 December at 4 A.M., the 1st Battalion of the 415th, behind a wall of artillery fire, overran the outposts and then overpowered a large portion of the confused garrison. Yet another house-to-house fight ensued, but by nightfall the body count showed 160 prisoners and 100 enemy casualties, with only three GIs lost.

The last stronghold of the Germans was Schophoven. As troops from the 104th wrested control at Pier and Merken, others assaulted Schophoven. The ancient Mullenark Castle, surrounded by a moat, presented a particularly hard nut. Again dangerous open ground stretched between the oncoming Americans and their target. To lessen the opportunities for a devastating reception, Company F set out on an approach march before daylight. Staff Sergeant Frank Perozzi remembered, "We were loaded with bandoleers, grenades and various types of ammunition which did not ease our way through the darkness, ankle deep mud and water-filled craters. Anyone who fell in the deep mud required the assistance of two men to set him back on his feet. Since the chateau was surrounded by a moat, we had cross[ed] the line of departure carrying an eighteen-foot plank to span the water barrier. It was impossible to keep the plank moving with the company, forcing the carrying party to either rid themselves of the plank or get lost. The heavy beam sank into the thick mud.

"It was 0630 when the artillery barrage opened up, together with H Company's mortars and overhead heavy machine gun fire. We would wait ten minutes before starting across the open plain. The barrage was a spectacle, beautiful but devastating—the flashes of our 'automatic artillery' would race in two seconds time from one flank of our objective to another.

"Jerry had been awakened by the terrific barrage and was now throwing in 'searching' mortar shells. He did not know from what direction infantry were advancing if at all. We moved as fast and as quietly as possible, stumbling over the turnips and sugar beets of the rain-flooded fields. We kept visual contact with our squads only by dropping low and silhouetting the men against the sky.

"We were approximately 300 yards from our objective when our artillery lifted—a little too soon for the majority of us. Our only concern now was not to be caught in the open by enemy low trajectory fire—we had to reach our objective but quick! We would never be able to defend ourselves if trapped in these fields. To fall under enemy fire at this moment would have made retreat hopeless, for dawn and its light was nearing.

"Dawn broke as the men of the first and second squads alternately slid into the cold, chest-high water. Luckily, the moat was at 'lo' tide; we had expected a depth of eight feet. Enemy snipers were picking away at us from windows of Mullenark and were zeroing in their mortars. The second squad was pinned where it stood, forcing the men to dig in on the spot. The first squad managed to maneuver around the pond and set up on the dike. Men paid the price of one enemy slug toward them with each shovelful of dirt from the life-saving foxholes. Men were drenched and cold and lay in water, unable to sit up and afraid to smoke a sneaked cigarette. Men tore off overshoes and untied shoes to lessen the pain on water-soaked feet. Men were wounded; there were no medics. Those attempting to locate medical help never came back. Our own artillery was firing again; air bursts too close for comfort! From upper windows, Jerry rifle grenades were easily dropped against our parapets. The second squad BAR man lessened enemy resistance by knocking out a machine gun in a tower to the rear of Mullenark.

"The third squad had gone too far to turn back and miraculously made its way to a one-room, ground level shelter behind the chateau. The six-

man squad had twelve prisoners before Heinie mortars began to fall outside the entrance. With each mortar round or machine gun burst at the
doorway, Jerries and Americans would simultaneously hit the straw floor
in one grand mix-up. Eventually, two of the men were able to contact a
tank from Schophoven and, with covering fire from the tank, the rest of
the third squad maneuvered into town. Schophoven had fallen by 1030.

"The 2d Platoon was dug in on the chateau bank of the moat and bore
the brunt of enemy mortar fire. Many casualties were the result of tree
bursts that sent whistling shrapnel into their water-filled holes."

The murderous fire continued until early the next morning, but the
castle was isolated by the troops that seized Schophoven. According to
Perozzi, a combat patrol of sixteen men—all that remained of two platoons normally numbering about 80—buttressed by salvos from tanks,
broke through the main entrance of the castle. Painstakingly they cleared
the building but captured only four prisoners; the other defenders
somehow had slipped away.

The drumfire of criticism of Allen by the likes of Bradley was absent
during the great November offensive. Perhaps that's attributable to better behavior by Allen, but judging from Allred's statements, Allen continued to party with enthusiasm when circumstances permitted. More important, the context in which he functioned had changed enormously.
In North Africa and Sicily, the 1st Division and its commander dominated
the drama—it was a more intimate war. During that period, only a handful of other American organizations strode the stage compared to the
vast cast involved in the European theater. Here, the size of the stage and
the number of actors reduced everyone to the level of a supporting
player. While it was expected that everyone would play his part, individuals were dwarfed by the sheer mass of military. Gone was the competitive nature of the earlier campaigns, where commanders felt obliged to
outdo their allies and to "look good." While Montgomery continued to
rile his allies, Eisenhower and Bradley were totally in charge; rivalry with
a prickly Sir Harold Alexander was over.

In Whitehead's Associated Press story, he reported the presence of
Allen at regimental, battalion, and even company headquarters during
the campaign to the Roer. Although constantly in contact with his subordinates, Allen was probably not quite that ubiquitous. Only a handful
of the enlisted men recall seeing him up close, and—more often than
not—these were chance encounters while on the way to their positions.
Bill Bracey, a member of an 81mm mortar section for H Company of the

414th, recalled, "During one of the times we were in Eschweiler, there was basically a stalemate. We were not moving forward as usually was the case. General Allen came striding up the middle of the cobblestone street in the middle of the day, wearing his famous Swedish boots, in the company of a small group of men. He continued to walk further towards the very front lines and the next day at the latest we began to move forward."

The huge numbers of men that were involved along the front required a coordinated effort to prevent chaos, and that limited the kind of freewheeling actions Allen indulged in during the earlier campaigns. Certainly Allen directed units of the 104th against specific objectives, selecting which regiment to hit where and, of course, insisting upon his signature nocturnal attacks. He could order the division artillery to support the infantry or request from First Army additional cannon power and air aid. But the actual tactics against targets were the responsibility of his lessers, who relied not only on division intelligence, but also on regimental and battalion resources, along with company patrols. One of Allen's major roles, which was played by the other divisional leaders as well, was to push and encourage the troops. It meant exposing them to destruction; yet, it is a mark of his effectiveness that so many of the men believed he would not sacrifice them needlessly. In the 104th, as in the 1st Division when he led it, the men never expressed the "*Our* blood and *his* guts" tag that was hung on Patton.

If Allen no longer felt himself threatened by the displeasure of his superiors, he still labored under great stress. Foremost probably was his awareness of the growing casualty list. He had taken to writing letters to the kin of the dead. To be sure, the letters became a kind of form message typed by a clerk. But often the bereaved wrote back to Allen, and he then responded. One typical example was a request from a mother for more information about her son who was killed in action in Holland. Allen wrote, "Battle casualties are saddening indeed, particularly to the loved ones at home and I can appreciate your desire for accurate information which apparently you have not received.

"I have referred your letter to our Division Chaplain, who makes a special study of these matters, and who I assure you will give you all the information possible, just as soon as he can possibly ascertain the same. . . . Again assuring you of my deep sympathy and assuring you that your request will be attended to as soon as possible. . . ."

Allen also dealt with the problems and the fears of those at home. In one notable incident, a wife complained that she had not heard from her husband in months. After a quick investigation through a chaplain, Allen concocted an explanation. He advised the woman that her husband had been out of touch because he had been on a secret assignment but could now resume contact with those at home. He then made certain that the GI wrote to his spouse.

Some of the Timberwolves appear to have communicated their affection for their commander to the folks back home. Allen received a note from Mrs. E. G. Green, then a resident of Colorado Springs, saying, "My husband is in the 104th Division, Hq. Co. 415th Inf. We have a son 4 mos. old that he has never seen. I heard him talk so much about you I named him Terry Allen." Several other babies became similar namesakes, including one sired by Allen's former orderly, Joe Pennisi.

Personal matters also weighed upon Allen. In December 1944, as the 104th dug in along the western banks of the Roer, he dealt with his perennial financial problems. He wrote to Maurice Schwartz, the father of his quartermaster company commander, Albert, about "a very confidential matter." The general explained, "Prior to my departure from the United States, I had cleared up practically all of my obligations except a long-standing loan of $1,800 which I had borrowed on my life insurance company. . . . I had borrowed this amount . . . at that time to take care of an emergency need. However, I reassured the complete protection of my family by increasing the amount of my insurance at the same time by $2,500."

He told Schwartz that he had instructed his bank to begin paying off this loan at the rate of fifty dollars a month from his personal account. But he had not heard from the institution and "I hesitate to bother Mary Frances about this matter, and I would appreciate your confidentially . . . checking up on this matter for me personally.

"I see Albert frequently—in fact, nearly every day. He is very busy with his Quartermaster Company, and in these critical times is performing an invaluable service to the country and to the division. He is one of the most thoroughly dependable and reliable young officers that I know."

Another letter on the same date to a friend at Fort Bliss whom he addressed as "Pop" without further identification began with thanks for a pair of gloves and then went on to say, "The division is still slugging its way along, and is still attaining all objectives per schedule. Adjoining units have been relieved, but the Timberwolves are still clawing their way through after more than 50 days of continuous day and night attacking.

"The balance of this letter, Pop, is quite confidential and I know you will treat it as such. I appreciate greatly your attending to that item regarding Terry, Jr.'s tuition costs at New Mexico Military Institute. Please withhold the check I gave you dated December 30 for an additional six weeks. I am chagrined indeed to ask this but I am sure you will understand the reason. By that time, my account will be in such shape that the items can be handled with much greater convenience. . . ."

"The division is still in fairly good shape and will always be in good heart. Losses have been saddening, but are not excessive considering the accomplishments. . . ."

Terry junior had entered N.M.M.I. in 1944 with the expectation that he would graduate its high school in 1948 (N.M.M.I. at the time also had a two-year college program that would briefly be expanded to a full four years). In his letter to Schwartz, Allen mentioned his son's attendance at the school and commented that he was doing well, "I am delighted indeed with the progress he is making in his studies and in his work."

Despite the general's troubles at the U.S.M.A., there seems to have been no doubt that his goal was for Terry junior to matriculate at West Point. Even though a possible appointment was at least three years off, Allen dropped a note to Texas senator Tom Connolly asking him to consider his son as a 1947 nominee. Allen had also approached others: A copy of a 26 December 1944 letter from Col. Harry Vaughn, liaison from the War Department, to Vice Pres. Harry S. Truman, advises an otherwise unidentified "Bob" that his letter sent through army channels took fifty days to reach Truman. However, Vaughn wrote, "You may be sure that we will take care of Terry Allen's boy. That is if we haven't revised West Point and Annapolis by then. We are working on a plan to eliminate political appointment."

A much more depressing family concern centered on his younger sister, Mary. Allen wrote to Maj. Gen. Norman T. Kirk, army surgeon general, noting this was a personal matter for which he would appreciate "the urgency of my request." Allen continued, "My sister . . . Second Lieutenant ANC has been in the Army Nurse Corps for the past three and one-half years. She has been very happy in her chosen profession and I understand she was doing well up to the past few months. She went to France with the 2nd Evacuation Hospital, one of the first medical units to land, and was evacuated therefrom for return to England, about June 29 [three weeks after D day].

"She wrote me that her case was initially classified as a mental case. I believe it was alleged that she had been adversely affected by service close to the front, whereas she frankly contended to me that she had fared no ill effects from the strain of serving with a front-line unit. . . .

"Her case was never clearly defined, nor had she ever been informed what the diagnosis was in her case."

Whatever her problem, Mary de la Mesa Allen, after hospitalization in England, was sent back to the States to a series of medical facilities. But, apparently no cure for whatever ailed her had been proposed.

"This has been very distressing to my sister and causes her no end of worry. She contends that she has always been in excellent health and that her nervous system was never affected in any way. I am greatly worried over her present status.

"I know my sister, Mary, exceedingly well, as we have always been very close to each other. She is a woman of excellent character, with very high ideals. She is devoted to her chosen profession of nursing. She has worked very hard to attain her commission in the Army Nurse Corps and has always been very proud of her efforts. All of this was done on her own initiative and through her own unaided effort. She has many fine qualities, but she is very diffident and reticent in many ways. And thus it is not easy for others to appreciate her fine qualities as well as I do. My sister is particularly worried regarding her future status in the Army Nurse Corps as she is greatly anxious to continue therein permanently. Her needs have only recently been brought to my attention, as our letters have been greatly delayed in transmittal since I have been overseas."

In a short paragraph Allen summarized his division's role in the campaign and then continued, "My sister has accumulated several months' leave. I request that she be given a short leave to visit my mother, who is now living in Washington, D.C. I also request that she be afforded an opportunity to consult with Miss Blanchfield, the Chief of the Army Nurse Corps, regarding the details of her case, her capabilities and her urgent desire for continued service in the Army Nurse Corps." He concluded with assurances of gratitude for whatever could be done on behalf of his sister. But, for all of her brother's concern and efforts, Mary de la Mesa's problems would worsen.

As he indicated to the Surgeon General, Allen's widowed mother now made her home in Washington, D.C. Allen kept up a desultory correspondence with her, counseling her on repairs to the house that she lived in and superficial details about his experiences in Europe, in contrast to the more detailed information supplied while he was a bachelor during World War I. According to family members, Mary Frances and her mother-in-law were not on the best of terms, which may account for the absence of more intimate letters.

A few weeks after the 104th firmly established itself on the banks of the Roer, Lt. Gen. J. Lawton Collins, commander of the VII Corps, sent a "Dear Terry" letter, expressing his admiration and appreciation of "the magnificent work you did for the VII Corps." After paying tribute for the success during the first phase of the campaign, Eschweiler-Weisweiler-Stolberg, Collins continued, "The second phase involving the crossing of the Inde River and the advance to the Roer was even more difficult, but with characteristic skill and dash, in a series of brilliant night attacks, the 104th Division forced a crossing of the Inde and in a few days had cleared the entire sector to the Roer River. I regard the operation which involved the seizure of Lamersdorf-Inden-Lucherberg as one of the finest pieces of work accomplished by any unit of the VII Corps since D-day."

Allen circulated the statement throughout the division with his own congratulations: "There will be other rivers to cross and more objectives to take before final victory is attained. Our standards of discipline, training and physical toughness must be maintained. We must *all* be imbued with the fighting spirit of our Division and an intensive belief in our units." He closed with his customary "NOTHING IN HELL MUST STOP THE TIMBERWOLVES."

17: Over the Roer

The 104th had hardly settled in along the banks of the Roer before the first patrols ventured over the river preliminary to a crossing that would renew the drive to the Rhine. But on 16 December, the Germans surprised the U.S. First Army with an attack through the American front stretched across the Ardennes, a patch of craggy hills, swift-flowing streams, and gorges south of the 104th. Omar Bradley—like other Allied commanders including Montgomery and Eisenhower—had believed the Nazi forces were so badly hurt that they could at best manage only a defensive campaign. "I had greatly underestimated the enemy's offensive capabilities," Bradley later confessed. To actualize the strategy of a breakthrough in the Westwall through the Aachen-Stolberg corridor and the Hürtgen Forest, Bradley and his associates had deployed the 104th along with a number of other organizations, gambling that the weakened foe could not exploit the thin lines manning the forward positions in the Ardennes.

The penetration through that area wreaked havoc on all of the Allied plans. Thousands of American soldiers were ground up in the maw of a panzer-led juggernaut that penetrated sixty miles into the solar plexus of the U.S. Twelfth Army Group. Any notions of further advance beyond the Roer by the likes of the 104th Division vanished. All American units north and south of the bulge created by the German onslaught assumed defensive stances. To protect the sector, the Timberwolves relieved elements of both the 9th and 83d Divisions, both of which had absorbed a beating in the Hürtgen Forest approach to the Roer. From 17 December through most of February, the basic area occupied by the division covered a nine-mile front along the Roer, from Merken to south of the city of Düren.

Albert Schwartz remembered a conversation he had with the general during this period of inactivity after Allen drew compliments for the performances of his men on the way to the Roer. "I said to him, you really ought to be a corps commander. He said, 'Albert, don't be naive. I failed at West Point, I'm a Catholic and I passed over a lot of colonels when I became a general. I am not ever going to be a corps commander. Besides, I like what I do.'"

Although the fierce action of the early part of December had abated, casualties continued to erode the manpower. Addison Austin, who drove a truck for Headquarters Company, 1st Battalion of the 414th, recalled, "I had picked up about a dozen replacements who'd spent Christmas at home. By the 16th of January, all but two of them were dead." From his experience with the 1st Division, Allen had realized that survival under combat conditions required additional training for replacements arriving in Europe. Under his direction, the veterans gave a two-week course to newcomers. He personally welcomed each group enrolled in the program, which used a renovated German barracks in Eschweiler. His appearances were all tailored to fit his notion that troops responded better if they knew who led them. By the time the war in Europe ended, some three thousand soldiers who joined the 104th had received this advance instruction. Other divisions—on their own, or taking their cue from Allen—also began to teach replacements the lessons that could mean the difference between life and death.

Jim Williamson, as Allen's ordnance specialist, also learned something about his responsibility. " I never realized until I got to Europe and combat how much the infantry depended on those BARS [Browning automatic rifles]. Next to their food they'd have given up anything before they'd give up their BARS. It was an automatic weapon. You could hold down the trigger and it would go Boom! Boom! Boom! just like a machine gun but you carried it in your hand. They just loved those weapons. But due to General Allen's night fighting, unfortunately, infantrymen had a tendency to lose these weapons in mud and in the dark. [The BAR and its ammunition magazines were considerably heavier than the M1 rifle.] Pretty soon they wound up with practically none. It was just like the trucks. You could ask army to replace the ones you lost but you never got any. They were always 'very sorry, very, but we don't have 'em. If we did we'd give them to you.'

"I was a lieutenant colonel and the regimental commanders were all full colonels, regular army, some West Pointers. They would come into my office with almost tears in their eyes, and say, 'Williamson, don't you realize how important these BARs are to our people? And you're not gettin' them for us. We're short. We need 'em.' All I could say was, 'Colonel, I know what you need. I've been down to army headquarters. I've done everything I can. I've made the requisitions. I've gone in and asked for them and their story is always the same. 'If we had 'em we'd give 'em to you but we just don't have them.'

"The whole problem was a matter of distribution which I was well aware of. There were plenty of BARS in Europe but they were sitting in a warehouse in France, and not up to the front where they were needed. My supply officer, Lt. Marchant, had been a supply sergeant before he got his commission. He knew all the angles, all the ropes, the tricks to be played. He came to me, 'Colonel, you give me a jeep and a trailer and a driver and about three days or four days off. Don't ask me no questions but I'll get your BARS.' I said, 'Marchant, it's a deal.' I could guess what was going to happen. For some strange reason we couldn't get BARS but we could get pistols. We had all the pistols we could have wanted. In division, there were extra ones laying around in supply.

"Everybody loved their pistols, everybody wanted one, take home an extra. People back at warehouses in France had to have a signed order to account for every pistol, every BAR, every rifle. In combat there was no accountability. If they lost them in dark, had them shot up, they did not have to account for them. We didn't have to account for all those .45 caliber pistols we had. I knew Marchant was going to get some of these extra pistols, load [them] up in [a] jeep, and see some sergeant back at warehouse and say I'll give you some pistols, you give me BARS. They would be tickled to death to be given a pistol to take home. Marchant took along the paperwork showing we required 200–300 BARS we didn't have. I signed the sheet so he could give that to the sergeant who would issue the BARS.

"In due time here comes Marchant back to the 804th Ordnance Co. with a trailer loaded clear to [the] top with brand new BARS. We had all we needed. I never asked any questions. I'm sure we traded pistols for BARS. I don't suppose they lasted too long, they would get lost. But for a time we were the only division on the front who had all their BARS." And certainly Allen never questioned the influx of weapons.

As commander of the quartermaster company, Albert Schwartz marched to the same drumbeat. "Allen made you aware that little things like the comfort of his men were greatly appreciated. There is nothing more miserable than wet socks, even if boots are dry. He believed in doing everything he could for the guys. He instilled that attitude throughout division. If more ammo was needed than the men were supposed to have, ordnance people got it. If they needed more telephones, we didn't worry about what the rules of the game were, we just got more telephones. They called it midnight requisitioning. You'd be surprised what a sergeant can do. We were a quartermaster company and we ate as well as anybody. It was scratch my back, I'll scratch yours. This went all the way back to the U.S. All kinds of illegal stuff was loot. A German Lugar [pistol] would bring all kinds of whiskey. A colonel wanted a jeep, not a command car. We went out and got him a jeep. We had a hot car shop; we painted some numbers on the front bumper and back bumper, repainted everything. There was no way you could tell it came from a division on our right flank."

During the worst winter in European memory, the last days of December 1944 slid into the new year. Snow now covered the shattered towns and blasted fields. For all of the blankets and extra socks Schwartz and company could requisition, borrow, or steal, GIs huddled in their foxholes or the cellars of buildings—trying, not always successfully, to stay warm and dry. Some scrounged lumber to create ceilings, walls, and even bunks in the rubble. Old newspapers served as insulation. Others took refuge in concrete storage bins. The World War I scourge, trench foot, disabled more and more soldiers. Allen issued a memorandum detailing measures to prevent that malady, as well as some other matters concerning the "Health of the Command."

He gave these instructions to the commanding officer of the 413th Infantry, Col. Welcome P. Waltz: "Leaders down to and including squad leaders are responsible for making an immediate inspection of enlisted men to insure that clothing, shoes and socks are adequate and that all men are inspected prior to exposure to the elements and are dressed accordingly. A system will be instituted, if possible, and if not already in operation, for supplying patrols, outpost guards and men rotated from forward areas with a warm dry place where wet clothes may be exchanged or dried and where hot coffee is available if practicable. Leaders of all echelons will direct attention to the comfort and health of their men."

Allen turned his attention to another growing problem. "Unit commanders and surgeons will coordinate closely to prevent evacuation of malingerers and men with minor complaints who multiply their troubles in order to avoid hazardous duty. Fifty-five (55) men were evacuated as combat exhaustion cases during January, a month of relatively little battle activity. Some of these are reinforcements who merely state that they 'can't take it' or they are 'afraid,' and the responsibility is shifted to medical channels. Every effort will be made to maintain an unsympathetic attitude toward this type of man in order to maintain morale." As much as he empathized with the combat soldier, Allen was unwilling to condone shirkers.

Allen also used the lull in action to argue for a change in weaponry. To Maj. Gen. Charles Corlett, CG of the XIX Corps (part of the Ninth Army led by Lt. Gen. William H. Simpson), Allen drafted a request that his 692d Tank Destroyer Battalion be equipped with 90mm self-propelled guns, known as M36s, to replace the three-inch towed guns called M5s. He faulted the M5 because it could not be deployed due to its lack of mobility and vulnerability to small-arms and mortar fire. He observed that it had limited maneuverability and was inferior to the M36 in respect to armor penetration, range, and capability against fortified positions. Allen had come a considerable distance from his casual attitude to ordnance and gunnery at West Point.

During January, some units of the 104th made their home in Eschweiler, setting up housekeeping in some wrecked buildings beside a bombed-out steel mill. Jim Williamson said, " I had my ordnance company about a mile away, still in the town of Eschweiler. There was about four inches of snow on [the] ground and the sun was shining brightly. We were doing nothing because [there was] nothing we could do. All at once we heard airplanes coming toward the west. That was not unusual, it usually occurred at night. We'd be trying to sleep and we'd hear these planes going over from England to bomb eastern Germany. It seemed like it would take forever; there were hundred and hundreds of them to fly over. Then you'd go back to sleep; then they'd wake you up when they were on their way back to England. That went on night after night.

"On January 10, there had been a daylight raid. The B-17s had gone over and now they were headed back for England. Being a bunch of country boys we grabbed our field glasses to have a look at these planes. We were standing out there looking up in the sky and as they approached Eschweiler we saw the bomb bay doors start to open. That was completely out of this world, not supposed to happen. The planes presumably had finished their bombing mission and were on their way to their home bases in England. The bomb bay doors opened all the way and the bombs started to fall. These were B-17s, American planes. They proceeded to bomb this steel mill about a mile from us. They did a real job; they knew what they were doing. They never missed a thing.

"Unfortunately, on the outside of this steel mill there were some brick buildings and we had some soldiers sleeping in them. The bombs killed 45 of our men in those buildings [the official toll was 24 dead, 28 wounded]. Gen. Allen and the headquarters were in the air raid shelter underneath the bombed-out steel mill. They were so far underground that they felt the explosions but nobody down there was affected. One of my officers, a second lieutenant, had his field glasses up and he was the only person in the division who had the foresight to write down the numbers under the wings of these planes. The numbers identified what unit they were. He reported that to Gen. Allen. Gen. Allen got in touch with the Air Force in England and told them what had happened.

"The next day, much to our surprise, here comes a three-star general for a visit. He was Gen. Jimmy Doolittle. He apologized for all the people killed. He gave Gen. Allen an excuse we couldn't accept. He said the Rhine and the Roer were parallel, and only a few miles apart. We were beside the Roer and they thought they were bombing a target on the Rhine. Anybody who couldn't tell the difference between the big enormous Rhine River and this little dinky Roer River shouldn't have been flying a plane. Doolittle had to make some sort of an excuse but that was [the] best he could come up with."

Doolittle followed up his meeting with Allen with a letter of explanation that differed from what he originally said. "It has been determined . . . that the low squadron of the 92d Bombardment Group, composed of 12 B-17s, dropped 38 100-lb. bombs in that area. The Squadron Leader had started a visual run on the primary target, but during the run his aircraft was hit by flak, causing it to leave the formation. At this point the Deputy Squadron Leader took over but, due to great difficulty encountered from the intense contrails and intense, accurate flak, was unable to properly identify the target. He thereafter picked up, as a target of opportunity, an industrial town which he felt sure was Duren [on the east side of the Roer]. In this he was in error, as you too well know.

"This bombing error was made in violation of existing SOPs [standard operating procedures] in that crews of this Air Force have all been briefed repeatedly that secondary or last-resort targets will not be bombed unless they are *positively* identified.

"As a result of this regrettable incident, I have relieved the command pilot, navigator and bombardier concerned of lead status and am investigating further to see if disciplinary action is in order. In this case, while the lead crew was definitely in error, they were trying hard to do their job and I am most anxious not to take any action that will tend to make the Eighth Air Force crews less eager to serve the Ground Forces. We are trying at all times to increase our proficiency without detriment to 'eagerness.'"

To Allen, it must have been a less-than-reassuring mea culpa. The terrible mistake, interestingly, never appeared in Kenneth Downs's magazine piece on the 104th. However frustrated and angered it may have left Allen and his men, they prepared to resume the final campaign against the Third Reich.

Four days after the B-17s struck the men of the 104th, Allen wrote his wife, beginning with his usual apology for dilatory correspondence, and then continuing, "I have temporarily been laid up with a touch of flu . . . that left me feeling pretty lousy for a day or so. Was ordered back to a rear headquarters in France on the 6th and while there had a chance to go into Paris for two or three days between meetings.

"Tried to get you some decent presents, but could not get many things that I thought you might like. However, did managed to get 7 bottles of Chanel #5, an evening bag that I thought you might like and some scarfs [*sic*]. Prices on dresses and things were out of sight, 20,000 francs or more for anything. And francs for the Army cost 50 per dollar whereas in the black market for civilians one could get about 300 francs per dollar.

"The billeting officer put Eastman and I up at the Ritz Hotel and it did seem fun to be warm and comfortable for a few days. I saw Lee [Lt. Gen. John C., head of Service of Supply] and Ike and many others that I knew.

"The situation on our front seems fairly well established now and there probably is little danger of another German breakthrough. During all the turmoil and excitement of the breakthrough, the 104th was sitting tight on secured positions, on objectives we had attained on the Roer River.

"After 3 months of hard fighting now, our division has attained all its objectives on schedule, has *never* given ground, and furthermore our casualties have been far less than in other divisions.

"Of course by this time I realize what the set-up is and know that many others are probably already lined up for better jobs.

"But nevertheless it is something to have commanded and trained the acknowledged best of *both* the old and the new divisions." There is a wisp of disappointment here that conflicts with his retort to Schwartz concerning a possibility of a corps command.

"We are fairly comfortably fixed in our CP now in the basement of an old demolished factory. It is a bit chilly but not at all bad.

"Our CP got bombed the other day, but I was away at the time. It was pretty bad for a while." That was all Allen said about the unfortunate raid. In fact, none of the letters that exist contain any details of the carnage. Because he frequently mentioned what a "nasty" business the war was, probably he avoided describing the grim scenes, or incidents such as the bombing of the 104th's GIs, to spare Mary Fran's feelings.

". . . I manage to get a work out with medicine balls and my old Indian clubs nearly every day. That with some sort of bucket bath keeps me from going too stale.

"It is pretty cold and dreary right now but we do have good rations and strange to say a liberal whiskey ration."

A week later he sent off another letter to Mary Fran. He devoted a portion to a recitation of the 104th's achievements and its deflection of German counterattacks. "In the drive to the Roer, we were in the First Army and operated under Joe Collins in the VII Corps. . . . Joe Collins, by the way, is the finest commander I have served under. He is a square shooter, is absolutely honest, is highly efficient and it would be a pleasure indeed to always work under such a commander.

"Joe was appreciative of our efforts under his command. It later developed that their optimistic estimate of our capabilities was to take Stolberg and Eschweiler in 17 days, whereas both were taken and mopped up in 6 days. Also we were to have then 'punched out' for rest and recuperation, while the 1st and 4th continued on to the river. But actually the 104th never 'punched out' and led the way in the VII Corps all the way to the Roer.

"It was a remarkable coincidence that we relieved the old 1st Division, on entering the lines in this sector, and that we fought beside them. There was hardly a day went by that we did not get an encouraging message from the old 'Fighting First' or from one of their units. They were generous indeed and seemed to get a big kick out of the fact that our new Timberwolf Division was setting the pace.

"Huebner who followed me in command of the 1st Division is now promoted to command a Corps [V Corps] and Clif Andrus is commanding the division. Both are thoroughly deserving. . . . Have a new tank battalion now attached to the division (colored). They call themselves the Black Timberwolves."

In the midst of this chatty letter, Allen suddenly referred to a negative story about him. "Can readily understand your worries about this latest newspaper propaganda of Drew Pearson's. But it is all too absolutely ridiculous to worry about. *Drew Pearson is a damned liar anyway.* His alleged publicized statement that I was relieved in North Africa by Ike because of happenings at the Kasserine Pass just simply does not make sense.

"It is a matter of recorded history that the 1st Division (less certain detachments) was brought hurriedly from Ousseltia Valley to counterattack at the Kasserine and that their counterattack and the stand of the 18th Infantry (also of the 1st Div) at Sbiba were largely responsible for causing the German withdrawal.

"It is true that many things might possibly have been handled to better advantage in both North Africa and Sicily. Yet nevertheless they cannot deny that we never 'lost a round' in combat.

"Am sure that Ike is too really fine and generous to permit anyone to be *unjustly* slandered. He has been very cordial to me over here.

"Please do not let it worry you, and above all do not let the press to ever persuade you to make any statements in any form whatsoever.

"At times over here it has been necessary to give the press certain information in accordance with their prerogatives and in accordance with instructions. I have been very careful to always restrict this to a bare, factual statement of our missions and accomplishments and have specifically refused to be quoted or to express any opinions whatsoever.

"After all, if you can't be quoted, you cannot be misquoted.

"No one realizes more than I, the terrible harm that malicious gossip can do. Therefore, I have been very careful to avoid any drinking parties or gatherings; have very few intimates and have . . . strictly minded my own business.

"Don't let this business worry you. My careless confidence in many so-called friends may have been embarrassing in the least, but I've learned my lesson in that respect.

"Have been disillusioned about many things, but still have an intensive belief in our soldiers and their capabilities and get a lot of 'kick' out of now having what is being acknowledged as the best of the new divisions.

"Don't worry about [what] you hear and don't pay any attention to that bird Pearson. . . . I did want to give you the dope and caution you are not to worry about Drew Pearson or any other liars and scandal mongers. After all your true friends need no explanations and others should be *totally* ignored."

The Pearson story obviously was bogus, but Allen generally drew favorable notices in the press, although his letter implies considerable suspicion about the media of the day. He told Mary Fran that he avoided situations where he might be tempted to voice opinions about his contemporaries. Even his intimate correspondence contains no criticisms of other military figures.

He was considerably more upbeat a few days later when he wrote to his wife a brief note saying, "It has been necessary to put on a raid in our sector to get Boche prisoners. . . . This time we used the good old Cavalry Reconnaissance Troops commanded by [Arthur] Laundon and a new lieutenant just promoted from sergeant.

"Under terrific fire support, they made a dash across the river, exacted Boche casualties and brought back prisoners that gave us information that is intensely valuable."

"I just returned from up forward to see them return and check off the prisoners. *We had no losses.* It's that sort of stuff that keeps our Timberwolves from being surprised."

He also wrote Terry junior. He "was delighted" with the latest reports from the school, which indicated the youth was studying. "It will give you a background in your basic subjects that will be tremendously helpful to you when the time comes to try to get into West Point and to pass the course there. Above all, try to learn your daily lessons without too much strain or undue effort, and learn to relax in your final examinations so as to do the most justice to yourself and get used to the strain of taking examinations.

". . . I know you are trying hard and I am completely satisfied with your efforts. I gather . . . you are still playing on the first team in polo. Do all you can to practice your stick work and keep up with your horsemanship. Also interested to know that you are developing a new pony. That's a fine thing to do. . . .

"You must write to your mother frequently and let her know what you are doing. She gets very lonely with both of us being away. Try to have her come up to see you as often as you can, and give her what time you can when she is able to come and see you. You must do all you can to keep her in a cheerful frame of mind."

In mid-February, as plans jelled for the inevitable Roer River crossing, Allen paused to write another letter to Maurice Schwartz. "I have just heard from Mary Frances and from Albert of the death of Sam's boy, 'JM' who was killed in action in the Philippine Islands." He was referring to the son of Maurice's brother and enclosed a copy of a note he sent to the father expressing his deep sympathy. "I realize that there is little that one can say to the parents of these fine boys who are killed in action."

After reporting that Maurice's son Albert was still "in fine shape and doing well," and observing that Mary Frances was "quite lonely with Sonny and me both away and is rather forlorn," the general wrote, "You asked me if there was anything that you might do for me. It seems that Mary Frances would like to be able to get a little special gasoline to make a trip to visit Roswell [home of N.M.M.I.] now and then to see Sonny. Would it be possible to arrange for her to get some special gas coupons on some Red Cross pretext or something of that kind?" Gasoline for civilian purposes was rationed during World War II, but a black market was thriving aside from what might come through a Red Cross request.

Allen also spoke of his finances: "Since coming overseas I have paid that company [his insurance loan] $1,000 in postal money orders . . . and the bank has been paying $50 per month since the first of December. . . . This loan . . . I am thankful to say is now my last outstanding debt." He asked Schwartz to find out whether his assumptions were correct.

During the long lull in offensive maneuvers, the 104th had aggressively patrolled the far side of the Roer. Sergeant Bill M. McIlvaine of Company A, 413th Infantry (the former Fordham University ASTP student), volunteered along with others for a reconnaissance mission. With three other soldiers, he studied some aerial photographs and determined a route of approach that would take advantage of concealment behind dikes and in a small wooded area. An artillery barrage would harass the enemy, throwing a veil over the patrol's movements.

"We decided to travel as light as possible," said McIlvaine. "For weapons, we had three automatic carbines and a Thompson sub. Ammunition was one thing we had in abundance. A flashlight to signal the boat on our return, two carrier pigeons for communication, a pair of wire cutters and a couple of K rations apiece completed our gear."

Engineers rowed them across about ten o'clock at night. "In less time than it takes to tell, we were on the enemy side of the river and the boat had started back. With its disappearance we all felt a personal loss. We turned and started up the bank but were stopped by a barbed wire fence. The wire cutters fixed that.

"We crossed a small ditch, all of us soaked to the skin but did not notice the cold in our excitement. After creeping and crawling, slipped and sliding through the muck, we became so tired and exhausted we had no sense of time or feeling. All we knew was to follow—at the time the thought of capture seemed a relief. Suddenly Sergeant Flores [TSgt. Isable M., leader of the quartet] called us quietly to him. There, only a few feet from us lay a German sleeping in his foxhole. Leaving Pfc. [Frederick] McCain with a knife at the throat of the unsuspecting foe, we crept softly away. McCain followed. The sleeping enemy was left unmolested— under different conditions he would never have seen another sunrise.

"The next half hour was just a matter of going forward, inch by inch, wondering what might happen the next second. Then, one of our worst fears was realized. Sergeant Flores, being extremely careful, saw antipersonnel mines. We retreated a few yards and planned our next move. At last, we decided to give the area a wide berth. But from there on we lived with the dread that with the next step we might activate a mine.

"After we had passed the minefields, we breathed a little more easily and began to feel as if everything would go off without a hitch. In single file we started for the house we had picked for our command post. Our thoughts of a house were short-lived, however, as we reached the place and saw a crack of light from one of the windows and heard singing from inside. It sounded as though a party were in progress. We had left our formal attire with our buddies, so we retreated to a not-so-cozy shell hole a hundred yards away. The holes were wet, our field jackets were soaked and night was passed in a series of chills. We lay there freezing, thinking of the nice warm room we had left of our own free will for a place like this. We lay shivering, blaming ourselves for our sad plight, and waiting for morning to bring us relief from the cold and dampness.

"At last it grew light, but instead of a warm sun, we received a cold, dismal sky. We released one of the pigeons, then waited breathlessly until he flew out of sight. A little later in the morning, our unknowing hosts began to move again. We felt safe in our holes and if we had been more comfortable would have enjoyed spying on the unsuspecting foes. It was easy to tell that they had profound respect for our artillery. They exposed themselves as little as possible and did all of their work on the double.

"Our artillery gave us a few anxious moments also. Since we were not in the designated house, we were exposed to the very fire that had been scheduled to give us added protection. During the barrages we laid low. However, we did discover the approximate strength and location of German troops in the vicinity of Duren.

"The longest day of my life finally ended and we started to release the second pigeon, but he had grown weary of his gas mask cage and flown the coop. We then wearily but eagerly returned to the river. We had a few anxious moments when a burp gun opened up but after a brief hesitation, we decided it was just harassing fire and went on to the river. We signaled the boat with our light and in a few minutes were on our way back to what we had commonly referred to as paradise. The coffee we were given when we reached the 1st Battalion command post never tasted so good.

"A day or two after the patrol, General Allen came to the front. Our entire battalion was assembled in the town square. General Allen pinned a Silver Star Medal on each of us. Don't think too many of the guys were happy about that and frankly I was more concerned standing there at attention while we received the Silver Star than I was during the patrol. We were only a hundred yards or less from the Roer with the Germans right on the other side. We were well within range of mortar fire and only General Allen seemed unconcerned."

The division conducted more than six hundred patrols of this nature prior to the assault across the Roer. During this period, assault boat training and practice river crossings were conducted at the Inde River. With various watercraft, the engineers experimented on the most expeditious use of small boats. Communications specialists tested various devices such as rockets and grenade launchers as means to shoot wire over the water.

The VII Corps dubbed the offensive Operation Grenade, with the 104th Division assigned to occupy the high ground, the northern part of Düren, before advancing on the major German city of Cologne—while the 8th Division on the right flank would also attack Düren. The actual date to begin operations was delayed several times because the Germans, who controlled the massive Schwammenauel Dam—which controlled the flow and depth of the Roer—released thousands of tons of water disrupting the plans.

In addition to all of the intelligence gathered by the patrols, Hayden Bower, the CO of Company K of the 413th, recalled, "We had studied mockup models of the enemy's position across the Roer River for weeks so that each soldier could study what and where he would be making his efforts when we crossed the river and landed on the enemy shore."

Chief of Staff George Marshall later would say, "I myself dreaded the crossing of the Roer and the advance to the Rhine more than any other operation during the war. The terrain there was very difficult. In fact, I dreaded crossing of the Roer more than the cross-Channel attack. I was certain that we would get across the Channel."

In the pitch-black night of 23 February, the skies erupted in jagged flashes of light as a thunderous barrage from every piece of artillery and mortars—augmented by heavy machine guns, rockets, and shells from tank and tank-destroyer battalions along the front—blasted the far shores. For forty-five minutes, the cannonade drenched the enemy positions. While devastation rained down on the Germans, the American infantrymen gathered near the river with their engineer boat crews. At 3 A.M., Hayden Bower said, "We had already formed up in our canvas and wood-ribbed boat parties of ten men plus two engineers to each boat. It

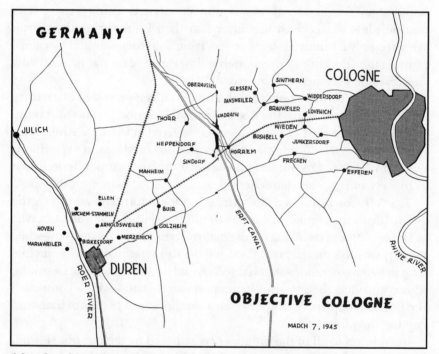

After breaking through the West Wall at Stolberg, the 104th successfully crossed the Roer River at Duren and advanced beyond the Erft Canal to attack Cologne on the Rhine River.

would take about four boats each to get a platoon across, plus two more for Company headquarters or 16 to 18 boats for the whole company. We started forward and found we had to carry the boats over 300 yards to reach the actual banks of the river, all over flat terrain which was muddy and slippery so we were pretty tired when we got there, but we managed to launch our boat.

"Besides a runner and myself, our boat held the company communications sergeant with his 48-pound radio strapped to his back and my first sergeant, making up my command party. In addition to my regular 358th Field Artillery Battalion Forward Observer who would radio corrections back to his firing batteries, we had three other F.A. Observers from the heavy artillery who would be supporting us.

"The engineers had assured us the river on our side was about six-feet deep but on the German side was only three to four feet deep, making for an easy landing. We struggled furiously with our wooden paddles as we tried to hold our boat against the rapid current fearing that we would be twisted around and maybe overturned. We knew we would be forced downstream with its six to 12 mph current. It was very hairy indeed. I didn't know if we would make it but all you could do was to pray and paddle like mad. Other outfits were having it as rough as we were. Many boats were overturned with the men being tossed into the river, screaming and struggling to try to swim to the riverbank. Many drowned as their equipment helped to drag them down in spite of our little waist life belts. Lt. [William] Ault lost most of his boat party when it capsized. Lt. Ault, however, had managed to struggle and reach the bank only to be killed by German machine gun fire as he climbed up. Two of his sergeants struggled to get what was left of the 2d platoon out of the river and they stumbled up the bank to rejoin the rest of the company."

"We thought we had anticipated how far we would drift downstream and where we would land. When we finally reached the other bank, I jumped out of the boat first and went into the water up to my chin. The engineers were misinformed as to the depth of the river on the German side. It was certainly more than three or four feet deep.

"The engineers were trying to land us and return for more men, but so many boats were lost in trying to cross the river that only eight were left. After our crossing, the engineers had been assigned to put a footbridge across the river to allow the rest of the battalion to cross. Still later, a steel Bailey bridge would be put across so tanks and trucks would cross to support us and exploit our success.

"Company I lost its 1st Sgt. [Milton] Barshop who had said before that he could not swim and was very nervous and worried that his small life belt could not save him. How prophetic this was. One of the men in another company had his arm below the elbow blown off by a low burst from our own antiaircraft battalion's .50 caliber machine guns. They were an all black battalion and they enthusiastically gave us support by firing their quad .50s over our heads.

"Once on land I moved ahead up the bank. I saw a German soldier in his foxhole who was in complete shock, unable to function due to the heavy volume of fire from our artillery preparation. My party followed me as we unknowingly walked right through a minefield. My runner, Jimmy, had his right foot blown off and all we could do for him was use his pants belt as a tourniquet and move on. He later recovered in the States. One of the artillery observers was also hit by shrapnel but not too seriously.

"I realized I was lost because the smoke screen blinded us on the riverbank, although we had looked across and studied this enemy shore for weeks. If it had not been for a burning haystack I never would have found my way to our initial objective which was the factory. We were all soaking wet and most of the men we saw were without the rifles or other equipment. But where was the rest of my Company? As we pushed on through the smoke towards the factory we began to pick up some other boatloads of men. I ran into two of my lieutenants with their 1st platoon and weapons platoon and most of their men. We moved into the factory. All this time the artillery had continued their supporting fires, silencing any returning German fire. The lieutenants, along with Sgt. [Travis] Harper drove the Germans out of the factory and more of the Company K men showed up. First Sergeant [Henry] Logan estimated that we had lost about eight or nine men in the river alone."

For others the Roer was at least as severe an ordeal. William Ecuyer from Company C of the 329th Engineer Battalion, as a member of a three-man crew that ferried ten foot soldiers and a large reel of telephone wire, attempted to gain the far shore. Disaster struck as they pushed off. The soldier assigned to man a rudder in the rear fell off the boat. "As we approached the center of the river, the current starts to take us and the boat spins on itself. It rotates and spins and the wire drags and it's a heck of a job to get straightened out. After much trouble, we finally reach the other side. In knee deep water, the infantry leave Miller and me in the boat, taking with them the giant reel of wire.

"Miller and I turn the boat around and push off as best we could with just the two of us. Again the current takes us and we approach an area where the green tracers are right above the water. Green tracers are from German machine guns. Miller jumps over the side and hangs on the edge of the boat. I remember how cold the water is, chose to lay in the bottom of the boat. After we pass this area of fire, I help Miller back in the boat."

Helpless jetsam in the swift-running river, the two engineers and their craft drifted near a sunken autobahn bridge, demolished by the retreating Germans. A soldier standing atop a platform left by the wreckage shouted for them to jump as the boat was about to smash into the remains of the autobahn. The pair scrambled to safety. The GI who warned them explained that he was the only survivor from thirteen who had been sucked beneath the water created by an undertow rampaging about the ruined bridge. The trio retrieved the assault boat. Wet, cold, and thoroughly frightened, they managed to make their way safely to the western side of the Roer.

Lawrence Peterson from Company I of the 413th said, "As we shoved off, the current seemed to grab our boat. Even though we paddled furiously and almost reached the opposite shore, the current won out and swept us downstream. Soon our boat was swirling around and we could not see either shore. We went over a small waterfall—almost capsized—waves came over the side and our boat sank beneath our feet.

"There were cries for help from the darkness. After a moment of panic, I realized that my inflated life belt was keeping my head above water. I desperately tried to swim to shore, but could not make any progress. It was a weird and helpless feeling to be floating down a raging river between two battling armies. About 1,000 yards downstream I was swept into shallower water. However, I could not stand up—my legs were numb from the cold. Two GIs from another outfit pulled me out to the American side."

Anthony Manzella, another engineer from the 329th, was aboard a boat that foundered. "I was in the rear when the boat struck a blown-out bridge. The other soldiers came back on me and pushed me below the steel rods hanging from the bridge. These rods were used in the concrete reinforcement of the structure. As I was pushed under, I was unaware of the condition of the other soldiers. Later I discovered that 11 of them had perished. I went under the current which carried me about a mile or more down the river. A German fired a parachute flare and upon spotting me started shooting. I went under water for cover. Daylight approached and I swam to the American side of the river."

Manzella evaded more fire from the enemy and staggered through a burned-out factory until he collapsed in a road. An American jeep picked him up and carried him to an aid station.

For all of the horror stories of those who set out on the Roer that night, enough had made their way across to engage in battle. Company K's CO Bower said, "Lt. Col. William Summers, our battalion commander, who had crossed the river in a later boat, came up to me and said, 'Hayden, I want you to continue the attack.' I said, 'Hell, no! I don't have all my company together yet and many men have no weapons or ammo.' Col. Summers assured me that he would see that my men were resupplied and rearmed and he would get all the artillery support to go up that hill and seize the objective complex on its top." The object of Summers's desire was commonly known to Americans as "the asylum" but it was actually the "Health and Welfare Institute" of Düren, atop a 140-foot-high hill.

After Summers made good on his promises of equipment, Bower plotted his assault. "I decided to attack in a column of platoons up a line of houses as fast as we could follow the artillery barrage—just 50 yards behind it. We were that confident of our gunners!" The timetable called for the artillery to fire at 2:15 P.M. and capture of the two-story building forty-five minutes later.

Private First Class Glen Lytle, of Company K—one of the GIs whose engineer boatmen had brought him over to a dry landing—participated in the scramble toward the asylum. "Lt. John Cook took the 1st platoon along the scenic route up the road with some cover, whereas the 3d platoon, led by Lt. Harold Coffin, took a direct route up the hill following some aiding artillery fire. Fortunately, the open field was very lightly dusted with snow—making the S-mines visible, and we were able to step through the minefields without setting off every one. We actually double-timed most of the way."

According to Bower, "Through powerful twin artillery telescopes, from the three-story . . . creamery building on our side of the river, . . . Gen. [J. Lawton, VII Corps Commander] Collins and Terry Allen would keep constant watch on our every move. K Company men were well trained in how to follow an artillery rolling barrage but we reminded them again just how important it was to hug the advancing fire as close as possible in our attack. The line of our artillery fire was perpendicular to our advance and the sight of the shell rounds landing and bursting

in front of us was very unnerving! We could see the shells land and ex-
plode, their shrapnel screaming up and out from each burst. One's natural desire was to hold back for fear of being hit by its shrapnel, but we
had to hug the line of fire for the protection it gave us from enemy resistance and counter-fire. Lt. Jones, my 385th Field Artillery Forward Observer, was at my side, constantly on his radio, making the adjustments
needed to run up the hill.

"The 385th did a magnificent job of moving the barrage ahead of us.
We were running as fast as we could behind their fire. I anxiously anticipated that flying shrapnel would fall short and hit some of our men and
they would drop to the ground, dead or in agony. Later, Sgt. MacBride
said, 'We didn't have time to clear out the houses along the way or we'd
have fallen behind our artillery barrage, so we just ran by and riddled
them with our fire as we went.'

"My two headquarters men began to lag behind me. I realized that the
48-pound radio made it rough on the younger man and the other one
was 40 years old. But I knew we had to keep up the pace. We ducked in
and out of houses as we moved on. Later, Col. Summers said Generals
Collins and Allen remarked that I was worth a Silver Star Medal as they
watched me brandishing my pistol in the air, in the middle of the road,
as I urged my men forward, for I was worried that my men might fall behind and get caught by German counter-fires.

"My command group continued to fall behind. I remembered that I
had once heard that anger can sometimes make a man give the extra effort needed. So I said, 'Come on you S.O.B.s, if I can keep up so can you.'
I knew they were both angry with me and I really had a high regard for
them. But what was important right then was that they had to keep trying and making a last effort even though our legs seemed like lead and
our lungs were on fire. We finally made it! We reached the asylum successfully." Bower said he immediately contacted Summer with news of
the success, "The asylum is ours, on to Cologne."

Lytle noted, "When we entered the campus-like setting at the top of
the hill, Paul Groop spotted a lady disappearing down the other side of
the hill pushing a baby buggy. There was cognac and food on the tables
and some of the candles were still burning in the buildings. [Our] 80
men captured our objective by 1453 and Captain Bower called the
colonel to report we had completed the task seven minutes early. This
was accomplished without a casualty, except for a large hole torn in the
left arm of my field jacket by a tree burst from a mortar shell just as we

arrived at the first building. We buttoned up for the night, just to the east and endured a heavy counter-attack early the next morning, and being surrounded on three sides. It was another night without rest."

In fact, the Germans doused the new American positions with concentrated bombardments that rained as many as forty rounds per minute. They tried on three separate occasions to oust the GIs. Men from Company I had moved in alongside of Company K. When Lt. Peter Branton and two soldiers attempted to contact the 8th Division on the right flank, they were unable to find them. The troops from the 8th had been delayed because of problems with the outboard motors hooked onto their boats. A party of German soldiers captured Branton and his companions and they spent the remainder of the war in a prison camp.

The 413th's S-2 (intelligence officer), Sam Koster, said, "The river was pretty big because of the spring rains and the flooding from the dams. We were in houses on one side and the Germans were in houses on the other, although they had all been smashed by artillery." Koster led the 2d Battalion of the 413th across the Roer during the night. "Once on the other side, we moved out in single file. It was the only way we could keep control at night. But the men had their different objectives and they would peel off at the right place." The operation proceeded so well that Allen decorated Koster with a Silver Star.

Two days later, the first units from the 3d Armored Division began to pass through the positions of the 104th. Meanwhile, Allen made good on the Silver Star he promised for Bower.

18: To the Elbe and Peace

Traffic flowed freely over five bridges thrown across the Roer by engineers, although the remnants of the German air force occasionally harassed the passages. Allen and his staff created a paddock-like system. To avoid gridlock, after each vehicle was scheduled to reach the front, it would move into the "paddock," as at a race track. At the appropriate moment it motored to the river and crossed without delay.

The Allies continued the drive toward the Rhine. In the 104th's sector, the flat terrain held a number of villages before the principal target of Cologne and was interrupted by the Erft Canals, three barriers about three feet deep and from twelve to thirty feet wide. The fast-moving troops rolled through the towns and hamlets as enemy soldiers surrendered in increasing numbers, as many as three thousand a day.

When the 1st Battalion of the 414th Infantry captured the town of Sindorf, near the Erft Canals, a patrol sifted forward after dark. Although all of the bridges had been destroyed, they brought back word that the remains of a railroad crossing could be planked to allow dry-footed passage. Others would make their way beyond the canals by means of boats and bridges constructed by engineers.

On the eve of the venture across the Erft, Col. Anthony Touart, commander of the 414th, tossed a small dinner at an ancient German farmhouse. Allen attended, along with the new assistant division commander, Brig. Gen. George A. Smith Jr., who replaced Brig. Gen. Bryant E. Moore, just chosen to head up the 8th Division. Kenneth Downs wrote,

"Handsome, debonair Tony Touart, the idol of his regiment, was a delightful host. The roast liberated chicken was excellent, and when the party broke up [about 8:30 P.M.] the officers were in fine spirits."

At 3 A.M., the attack across the Erft was to start. Allen stationed himself at the forward command post of the 414th located in a factory on the edge of Sindorf, while Touart and Smith—after conferring with Allen—left for the 2d Battalion forward observation post. A torrent of American artillery shells fell across the Erft with only a desultory response from the Germans. But in the redoubt occupied by Allen, a message by telephone advised that one of the German guns scored a direct hit on the 2d Battalion forward observation post about two hundred yards from where Allen waited for the attack to begin. He had expected to move up to that position shortly.

According to Downs, Allen asked, "How bad is it?"

Major Fred Flette, the regimental S-3 answered, "Pretty bad, sir, I'm afraid. They are digging them out." It was a military catastrophe. Just as the troops had begun to engage the enemy in the darkness, they lost those responsible for overall command and control. Touart and Smith, who had been with the 104th only two days, were both dead along with the CO of the 2d Battalion, Lt. Col. Joseph M. Cummins Jr. Other key personnel were seriously wounded or stunned.

Allen instantly issued orders to repair the damage. He directed Gerald Kelleher, the CO of the 415th's 3d Battalion, to take over the regiment. He contacted Col. Welcome Waltz of the 413th and told him, "There's been an accident over here. Impel your attack with all possible aggressiveness, and be prepared to help on your right, if necessary."

Downs remembered, "The outside door opened and Lt. Manfred Schnier, dazed and covered with brick dust and blood, stood framed there for a moment. . . . He staggered and blurted, 'General Smith and Colonel Touart are dead.' He burst into racking sobs. General Allen was at his side in a flash, and with an arm about his shoulders, got him gently but quickly out of the room." Schnier would be KIA within a few weeks.

Kelleher arrived at the factory CP. "The general," said Downs, "who seemed to be everywhere at once, caught him before he went in, and briefed him. 'Now go in there, cheerful,' he said, punching him fiercely in the shoulder for emphasis. 'God help you if I catch you with a long face today, Jerry. Go in there smiling now.'

"I was awestruck. I knew so well how the death of soldiers he didn't even know tore the general to pieces inside and here he was, after losing some very dear personal friends, counseling cheer. But it worked. For in this heavy hour, the 414th went smoothly ahead, hardly missing a beat in the rhythm of the attack."

Lieutenant Colonel Cummins Jr., leader of the 414th's 2d Battalion, was a 1934 graduate of the U.S.M.A. and the son of one of Allen's friends, retired Maj. Gen. Joseph M. Cummins. Allen wrote to the father, "I would have written you sooner except that we are not permitted to do so until the official War Department notification has been received.

"There is little that I can say to properly express my sympathy. Joe was a gallant and a very capable soldier and one of our outstanding battalion commanders. He was a tremendous asset to his regiment because of his earnest leadership and his combat effectiveness. I had great respect for Joe and always hoped that he would survive the hard fighting which the division has undergone continuously since October 23."

Allen supplied brief details of what happened and said, "We notified all battalions that Colonel Touart and Joe had been killed and that Lieutenant Colonel Leon Rouge, the other battalion commander, had been wounded, and that they must carry on without their leaders. You will be proud to know that they did so, thanks to the fighting spirit that Colonel Touart and Joe had instilled in their units." It was a soldier's letter of condolence, intuitively offering whatever comfort might be derived from an appreciation of the dead by someone of Allen's stature.

Another letter went to an acquaintance in New York, a Mrs. J. F. McDonnell. "I have been intending to write you for some time to thank you for the numerous boxes of candy, the Christmas box, etc., that you have been so good as to send me. Murray [her son] tells me that you are sending me one of those special pairs of field boots from Abercrombie and Fitch that you were good enough to order for me. . . . I am particularly grateful for this. . . .

"I see Murray very frequently and I know that you and Mr. McDonnell will be delighted to know that he has been doing a swell job, is a truly fine combat soldier and is a distinct asset to his combat engineer battalion. I saw him just the other night when his engineer company was supporting one of our infantry regiments in the crossing of the Erft Canal during one of our major night attacks. He was well and happy, in fine physical shape. . . .

"Murray is at present in a field hospital for a few days, *but I do want to assure you that he is quite all right, and has not been injured* [his italics]. It is merely the result of a considerable shock which his system received when he happened to be in one of the buildings where the CP was located which had received a heavy bombardment. A very sad thing happened the other night which is one of the regrettable instances connected with the somber aspects of warfare which is part of the cost that must be paid when spearheading a major offensive effort." He followed up the rather clumsy sentence with a brief account of what had happened at the forward command post of the 414th and which included a bit about how he had escaped injury.

"I happened to be taking a brief nap for an hour when they went forward to this OP or I would have accompanied them. In fact, I would have been with them had they wakened me as I intended for them to do." Allen then noted that "Murray was with them at the time. In fact, he was in the same building when this occurred. As near as I can find out, he did not receive a scratch, but his system received quite a physical shock, which is perfectly normal, and frequently happens.

"I arranged through my aide, Captain Eastman, to have him immediately evacuated to the field hospital for a brief rest of a few days where he might properly recuperate. Of course, he very violently objected, but the unit Surgeon said it was a necessary evacuation for his continuing welfare. He will rejoin us in a few days as well—if not better—than ever.

". . . I have tried to send a personal note over my signature which the Chaplain's staff prepares, to the next of kin of every officer and soldier killed in our division. The courageous tone of the replies received I think is quite indicative of the courageous attitude of those at home."

He remarked that Mary Frances remained in El Paso, lonely for him and their boy. "Sonny is doing well at the New Mexico Military Institute. Am hoping to get him to West Point in 1947 or 1948 and hope that he may get in a year of college before going. Hope he improves upon my record when I was a cadet, which was not much good."

The 104th drove forward, and although the *Luftwaffe* now flashed its fleet jet fighters, the company reached the outskirts of Cologne. The 3d Armored on the left flank and the 8th Division on the right joined in the siege of the Rhine River city. (3d Armored fought under Maj. Gen. Maurice Rose, a veteran of North Africa, and 8th Division was led by the 104th's former deputy commander Brig. Gen. Bryant Moore.) The Americans relentlessly purged Cologne, block by block, house by house. By 4 March, the Timberwolves had advanced four thousand yards into the heart of the city—and two days later, white flags hung from every building.

Albert Schwartz remembered, "When we got to the Rhine River, we were in a barracks that had been used by the SS in Cologne. We were sitting on our side, the Germans were sitting on their side, there was a little sniping back and forth going on. All the bridges were down, except one bridge still standing at Remagen, south of us and not in our divisional area." The demolition charges on that bridge had only damaged it, and it would become a gateway for the first American advances over the Rhine.

For the moment, the 104th awaited means for it to get across the river. Said Schwartz, "In that SS building, a division commanders' meeting had been called. I went up there because in the army you don't want to be late. I was early and talking to a bunch of the guys. We weren't fighting, we were licking our wounds, getting replacements, doing all things you do between battles, meeting some of the new guys. In the basement of this building, where division headquarters was, they set up office by stringing GI blankets in what was an open space.

"Gen. Allen had more GI blankets around his office than anyone else and Gen. Bradley had come for a visit. Both of them were a little deaf and both of them had sort of high voices, especially when they were excited. We were all gathered outside of these offices and you could hear anything said, if you wanted to listen.

"Here were the two generals talking. Bradley said, 'Terry, I just want to tell you this 104th infantry division of yours, they're ranked with the 1st and the 9th divisions as the finest combat divisions in the ETO [European theater of war].' The 1st and the 9th were pretty damn good outfits but instead of saying, 'Oh thank you, general, what a nice compliment,' as a lot of guys would have politely done, Allen said, 'Brad, the 1st and the 9th are in damn fast company.' Everybody out there just hollered. We all yelled, 'You tell 'em, General.' That was just typical of Terry Allen. He didn't take anything from anybody. He believed in his unit and felt we were the best damn division in the United States Army. He had told me that in El Paso, Texas, when he said you want to go with me and he hadn't even joined the division."

Schwartz asserted that Allen had a knack for instilling this same confidence throughout the organization, down to the lowest soldier. "The guys just loved him. You'd hear them yell, 'Hi, Terry,' when they saw him passing. There wasn't a whole helluva lot of saluting in that area. He didn't stand on that kind of protocol. He would be up front with them, he'd be in regimental headquarters in a battle, go down to battalion HQ, sometimes would even get up to company HQ. Major generals aren't supposed to do that. They are supposed to be more valuable than us punk kids who were out there as cannon fodder."

Certainly, he continued to connect with the individual GI even as the war wound down. Truck driver Addison Austin, shuttling between various depots and headquarters, recalled, "They were moving some tanks up and I had to stay and wait for them to pass. Here comes a guy with stars on his shirt. When he saw us he said to one of us, 'You've got mud in your eye, soldier.' He was always up front, taking charge of everything, making decisions."

Edwin Krieger, a former member of the ASTP, was a member of the 413th Regiment; while savoring a respite from combat in the southern suburbs of Cologne, he said, "I was notified by my platoon leader that I was going to be taken to division headquarters to see the general. No explanation was given for this highly unusual order. All I could think of was that I was going to be court-martialed for fraternizing with a German girl, which was strictly against orders at the time, although violated by many GIs. I was really worried.

"When I went into Gen. Allen's quarters, he immediately put me at ease by having me sit down, and in a very relaxed, friendly and informal way asked me a number of questions regarding how I was getting along. At one point he even inquired if there was anything I wanted to ask him about the 104th and its role in the war. He stated that he was required to check up on former ASTP students and my name had come up at random.

"When I returned home in July 1945, I found out that this whole incident occurred because my father had written to Terry Allen, asking about my welfare. It seems that my Dad had not received any mail from me in a long time. Bear in mind Terry Allen did not know either of us. The general sent my father a letter describing this meeting. How many other division commanders would have bothered to act on a request of this nature?"

Indeed, Allen's files hold a copy of his letter to the elder Krieger. It says, "I can readily understand your worry regarding him and your anxiety to secure accurate information regarding his welfare. I have just sent for your son, have talked to him and find he is in fine shape and doing well. The division has been fighting hard since October 23 and so far have had marked success without excessive losses when their accomplishments are considered. Your son and the other boys like him have been largely responsible for the combat success of the division. . . . Your son has been through some of the toughest fighting but it does not seem to have affected him physically or otherwise."

Allen noted that Edwin had asked if the meeting was because his parents had written to Allen. The general had written his father that to protect the son from any adverse comment by fellow soldiers he had concocted the fib of checking on former members of the ASTP.

In his pamphlet on leadership, Allen spoke of the requirement that a commander know the needs and capabilities of his men and that the commander must set "an example of cheerfulness and fortitude even after prolonged exposure to hardship, danger and fatigue." In his case, the tenderness toward his "boys" was not only a demonstration of leadership but seems to have emanated from an innate affection for those with whom he served. They must have been surrogates for his beloved Sonny.

In the midst of his concern for the fortunes of the 104th, he received a disquieting answer from Surgeon General Norman T. Kirk on his sister Mary's problems. "I have checked into your sister's hospitalization, disability and other things concerning her service. I found that the diagnosis made was Dementia Praecox, simple type; that she appeared before a Retiring Board on 13 March, and this Board recommended her retirement." Dementia praecox now goes under the label of schizophrenia.

Kirk continued that the disability was "considered in line of duty and incident to the service. They also felt that she could be released from military control without danger to herself and others and that she is competent to take care of herself from a legal standpoint." The surgeon general expressed regrets that he could not, as Allen had hoped, keep her in the service. "It would neither be fair to her nor the patients whom she was detailed to treat to keep her on active duty." The separation of Mary Allen from the Army Nurse Corps set her on a sad course that troubled her brother for years.

The Remagen Bridge over the Rhine was captured by the 9th Armored Division and exploited for a bridgehead across the river by 9th Infantry Division soldiers, but it collapsed after ten days. With American forces occupying a chunk of the east bank, however, engineers had erected a number of pontoon causeways. A convoy of trucks hauled the 104th across and VII Corps instructed the division to enlarge the bridgehead. Timberwolf units worked in concert with the 3d Armored Division.

The steady advance—first over the Roer, and then beyond the Rhine— could not hide the losses, particularly of infantrymen. As far back as De-

Beyond Cologne, the Timberwolves captured Paderborn, crossed the Weser River, and liberated the concentration camp at Nordhausen. After capturing Halle, the division met the Soviet armies at Torgau as the war ended.

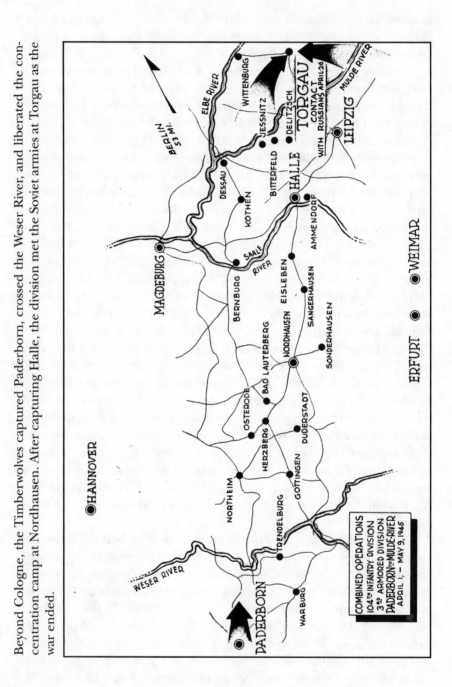

cember, Eisenhower and his staff recognized that they were facing a critical shortage of an essential figure of World War II combat, the rifleman. Replacement camps in the States churned out foot soldiers with thirteen to seventeen weeks of instruction in the rudiments of their craft. A surplus of qualified flight personnel enabled the personnel managers to shift air cadets into ground pounders. And, the latest draftees almost always embarked for the infantry training camps. When the Battle of the Bulge further seriously depleted the ranks of riflemen, the army reluctantly turned to those previously denied the right to fight in combat, the African Americans.

In the segregated U.S. military, the army had fielded two all-Black infantry divisions, the 92d and 93d, with White officers above the company level. The 93d, shipped to the Pacific, soon was changed into a service and supply organization. In Italy, the 92d fought under White commanders. Except for one fighter-plane group and a few isolated units, these were the only men of color shooting and being shot at. But as in past wars, scarcity required the services of more Blacks on the firing line. A call went out for men in quartermaster and other service organizations to volunteer. Those who stepped forward lost their stripes while being admitted to the fraternity of the combat soldier.

About five thousand volunteered and of these half underwent a retraining program, although many had gone through basic training. They were packaged as all-Black platoons and assigned to various divisions where White noncoms and officers would command them. When the contingents for the 104th arrived, they received the benefit of Allen's prescribed course. Kenneth Downs reported, "Among the proudest graduates of the battle school were the 'Black Timberwolves,' three platoons of Negro combat troops sent to the division. As he doled out their shoulder insignia, General Allen told them, 'You are Black Timberwolves now and we expect big things from you.'"

Joe DeVaux, himself a White replacement in the 413th, remembered, "On March 21, 1945, a platoon of black soldiers was assigned to our Company G and I understand there were three such platoons, one for each regiment. They were in combat the last six weeks of the war and distinguished themselves as good soldiers. One of them, Pvt. Willy James of our company, was awarded the Congressional Medal of Honor but not until I believe 1998 when it was recognized that Pvt. James and a few others had not received proper recognition for their heroic actions. The 'colored' soldiers as they were referred to in those days pretty much hung out together. But there were many times we mingled with them and we all got along and enjoyed their friendship."

Hugh Daly and two fellow intelligence scouts, Jimmy Sprouse and Tuffy Nabors, from the 415th Regiment, were working with the 3d Armored Division as it encircled thousands of German soldiers trapped in the Ruhr Valley pocket. Daly said, "Some distance beyond Marburg, we were on a rest break, sitting just off the road on the steps of a farmhouse. Two jeeps, one going east, the other west, stopped by the side of the road. From one came General Maurice Rose, commanding general of the 3d and from the other, our beloved General Terry Allen. We couldn't believe our eyes.

"As they chatted, General Allen beckoned to us, asking if we had a light. He steadied my hands as I lit his cigarette and said, 'Thank you soldiers. You all take care of yourselves.'

"What a thrill for us, such a distinguished person treating us lowly privates as peers, like his family.

"That evening, the wonderful General Rose was killed in an ambush."

Actually, Rose—intent on directing an assault on Paderborn—had ridden forward in his jeep, when suddenly four Tiger tanks from a training center loomed in the fading light of the afternoon. Rose told his driver to accelerate past them, but his vehicle sideswiped one and was pinned to a tree. Rose and his aide and his driver prepared to surrender; but, a German soldier misinterpreted his moves as offensive and fatally wounded him.

The Allies were chewing up miles of Third Reich ground and bagging tens of thousands of prisoners. In eight days, from 25 March to 1 April, the 414th Regiment overran the defenses for more than two hundred miles. The infantrymen, often riding atop 3d Division tanks, knocked out a series of strongholds as the entire U.S. First Army penetrated ever deeper into the Third Reich. One of the more intense firefights centered around Paderborn, where trainees from an SS replacement camp mustered a fanatical resistance.

According to Downs, one of the African American platoons distinguished itself in an attack on a hill in the Hardshausen Forest, south of Paderborn. "One of these platoons went in singing a ribald song about the Fuhrer and killed or captured eighty-seven SS troops, for a loss of eight of their own."

Anxious to maintain the pressure on the crumbling Nazi forces, Allen directed his people to force crossings over another substantial natural barrier, the Weser River. Assault boats ferried men from the 413th and 415th Regiments across, beginning in the dark hours of the morning. The success enabled the 3d Division to rumble east as the spearhead for further advance. Infantrymen on tanks, in some cases aboard captured German vehicles as well as their own trucks, and on foot headed farther east toward the Harz Mountains—the last natural defensive site in their path into the northern German plain.

They reached Nordhausen on 12 April. Leon Karolokian with the 104th Signal Company remembered, "As battered towns go, Nordhausen resembled the others with its share of dead cows, horses and an occasional human caught in the open by an artillery burst. Yet there was a difference, for Nordhausen was to provide a ghastly traumatic experience never to be forgotten by those who passed through it. The existence of concentration camps and hints of atrocities were long a subject of rumor. But here in town, what seeming was a series of warehouses, we uncovered what aptly could be called a death factory.

"On the grounds laid out in neat rows were an estimated thousand decaying corpses ranging from the near skeletal to the newly dead. In the buildings, bedded on straw, side by side, in indescribable filth lay the emaciated living, too weak to move away from the dead. Nordhausen was not a major concentration camp. It did not have the huge inmate population of Auschwitz. Nor did it have gas chambers . . . a refinement apparently reserved for Jewish victims who were on the bottom of the insane Nazi scale of values. Its crematory, though small, was able to convert one hundred of yesterday's men to heaps of ashes each day.

"The three thousand victims here, dead and alive, were predominantly Polish slave workers, with some French, conscripted to turn out in enormous underground factories the deadly supersonic V-2 rockets that were taking a heavy toll of lives and property in London. . . .

"The full medical resources of the division and from other units did all that was possible for the living. Some would be fed like infants and live to relate their experiences. Others according to health officers were too far gone and indeed many did not survive the next several days. The very few walking skeletons able to stand wandered about dazedly in the now-familiar striped uniforms, bodies shrunken, white faces, blood-drained, reaching for the hand of their liberators as they shed their tears. Battle-hardened men of the 104th wept too."

Albert Schwartz noted, "We killed some of the people in the camp by accident. We gave them candy bars, but they were so starved and dehydrated, they couldn't handle the food. They needed to be brought along slowly. When Gen. Allen heard about those camps he wanted as many of his men as possible to see them. We were on another mission, to catch up with the retreating Germans, before they could dig in for another stand. We didn't have but a few hours, some of us stayed for only a day. But he wanted everyone to see the place, to see the kind of cruel, unjust treatment that human beings could inflict on other human beings. In the civilized world it was unbelievable."

According to Leon Karolokian, "Town residents and officials claimed ignorance of what was transpiring so close at hand. Whether this was true or not never will be known but skepticism was the prevailing opinion among us. Able-bodied male citizens were not plentiful, but enough were rounded up for the distasteful work that had to be done. Mass graves were dug on the city outskirts. Bodies were carried by hand to the burial sites." Undoubtedly the work was mandated by Allen.

Leaving the camp inmates to be handled by rear echelon troops, the Timberwolves trekked deeper into the Harz area. On 13 April they liberated another camp. This one, at Duderstadt, held Americans captured earlier in the war. The procedure of the army was to make up a roster and then ship groups to tent cities where the men would recover from their ordeal before leaving for the States. One of those freed was a medical officer from the 106th Division. He and several companions had confiscated a Mercedes (a German staff automobile) and felt themselves healthy enough to avoid waiting in an encampment for transportation home. He recounted, "We all met General Terry Allen who took time out from directing the chase against the fleeing German army to entertain us with a memorable steak dinner. In conversation after dinner, he informed us that there was a fuel operation being carried out at an airfield near Gottingen. He suggested that we seek out the officer running the show and persuade him to smuggle us aboard a plane heading back to England. . . .

"Moreover, he invited us to follow along as his 104th moved northward. To facilitate our movements, he also sent us over to his motor pool where the mechanics painted 104th identification numbers on the Mercedes so later we were never stopped by the ubiquitous MPs."

Three days later, the former POWs traded their car to a major in charge of fuel depot operations who placed them on the manifest of a C-47 bound for England.

Some fifty miles east of Nordhausen lay Halle, the tenth largest city in Germany with a population of 210,000. Miraculously unscathed by Allied air raids, Halle housed historic buildings, Gothic churches, and other cultural assets, along with a fanatically recalcitrant, 4,000-strong garrison. Allen created Task Force Kelleher—composed of two battalions from the 414th, augmented by tanks, tank destroyers, engineers, field artillery, a reconnaissance troop, and a chemical battalion with its heavy mortars. It would lead the division assault. Employing a three-pronged approach, they dug into the city's outskirts, breaking through roadblocks and fending off flak guns, *panzerfausts* (hand-held antitank rocket weapons), and concentrated small-arms fire.

Intelligence learned that the civilians of Halle, aware of the devastation visited upon other cities where the *Wehrmacht* refused to yield, begged the German army commander to declare an open city. He adamantly refused, and a deluge of leaflets from U.S. planes warning of inevitable death and destruction dropped by air did not change his mind. For four days, house-to-house combat raged through Halle.

On 16 April, Count Felix von Luckner, a celebrity from his World War I days as captain of a sea raider for the German navy, entered the American lines to negotiate. Allied policy dictated only unconditional surrender, and the German military commander would not agree to that because he feared the consequences to his family. Through von Luckner, a bargain was struck for the military forces to evacuate the northern sections of Halle and confine their battle to the southern third. Three days later, the GIs routed the last vestiges of resistance, taking more than twenty-five hundred prisoners. Von Luckner inscribed a photograph of himself for the general, with praise for Allen's "humanity."

When Allen dropped a few lines to his wife on 20 April, he made no mention of the horrific discoveries at Nordhausen. Instead, he recited the swift passage of the troops as well as hitchhiking on tanks, trucks, and captured German vehicles. He remarked on the approach of the "Russians . . . only 18 miles from our division."

Beyond Halle lay the Mulde River, a tributary of the Elbe. Orders from headquarters halted the 104th just west of the Mulde while Soviet forces on the other side of the Elbe advanced on that river. About twenty thousand German soldiers wandered in between the American and Soviet forces—they were the disintegrated remnants of *Wehrmacht* units. Mixed in with them were Allied prisoners liberated from prison camps, thousands of civilians fleeing the oncoming Soviets, and displaced persons escaping concentration camps or forced labor.

Artillery spotter planes dropped leaflets with instructions in German for surrendering, and patrols negotiated with small groups of soldiers to disarm them and dispatch them to holding pens. GIs from the 69th Division, adjoining the 104th, met a Red Army column on 25 April. On the following day, Lt. Harland Shank, Sgt. Jack Adler, Cpl. Bob Gilfillan, and Cpl. Sam Stanovich, accompanied by a Soviet lieutenant who had been freed from a POW camp, rode a jeep that crossed the Mulde on a barge. Their mission was to contact the ally coming from the east.

According to Gilfillan, a few miles beyond the river, they learned from a civilian that some six hundred German soldiers were in the next town. When they entered the village, they discovered them to be hospital patients who gladly accepted pamphlets with information on how to surrender. Motoring ahead, they met a German officer. Gilfillan related, "During the conversation, the colonel told us of 1,200 troops which were under his command just outside of town. I soon found myself saluting beaucoup German brass. We did hit luck, however, for the colonel could speak good English which helped the delicate bargaining along. Our conversation was about how we wanted to aid the German soldier and he seemed to like it. We mounted our jeep and followed the German officer about two kilometers outside of town, and there coming down the road was a breathtaking sight. Here we saw wagons loaded with guns and ammunition; troops on foot and bicycles coming toward us; these men were the colonel's command. Some waved, others looked at us as though they were ready to do the Fuehrer another favor."

The patrol parted from the colonel without hostile action and continued forward. (The enemy troops they left offered no resistance to the Timberwolves who advanced behind the patrol.) They saw a number of German soldiers, and while at least one apparent threat was made, none of the foe showed any genuine inclination to fight. Most were happy to accept word on how to give themselves up to Americans.

As they neared the Elbe with an American flag hanging from the front end of their jeep, they were advised the Russians were in the vicinity of Pretsch, a town up ahead. "I think we were a little more afraid of the Russians than of the Germans because we were not sure they would recognize us. The jeep slowed down, all eyes covering 360 degrees. Halfway through the town and no Russkis; the other side of town and still no Russkis. The jeep was nearing the top of a hill just outside of Pretsch and there over the crest came four heads—very slowly at first, and then a loud cheer, and the American flag had come through again.

"I have seen men that have not shaved for months, but they had nothing on these boys. Either they lost their razors or forgot how to use them, because I really felt the bristles scrape my face like sandpaper when they gave us that good old kiss on both cheeks. For about fifteen minutes, we, as well as the Russians, were never so happy—the world had been waiting for this for a long while."

The small band of Americans continued their journey, meeting more and more Red Army people. They floated to the other side of the Elbe over a pontoon barge hauled by a cable. "As we drove towards the headquarters of the 118th Russian Infantry Division of Marshal Ivan Konev's First Ukrainian Army, more cheers rose and the only Russian word I could understand was 'Amerikanski.' Greeting the general was quite an honor, for I got the feeling that I myself was tying a bond that signified the end."

Gilfillan and his four companions dined with Soviet officers and wobbled through a long evening of vodka-driven toasts. It was the first of a number of such festive occasions for members of the 104th and Red Army units. Captain Charles Gensler, from Headquarters Company of the 413th, accompanied several soldiers from a Soviet patrol back to their headquarters—where the colonel in command held a banquet, with "an endless supply of vodka" in their honor. Gensler told how "the Russians were particularly emotional about the recent death of President Roosevelt [April 12], and of course the meeting of the armies, the approach of the Nazi surrender. Halfway through the meal, the Russian Colonel gave me a photo of his son who had been a junior officer and been killed in the battle of Stalingrad. He then asked me for a photo of General Terry Allen. I told him I was sorry I had none with me but would attempt to send one to him when I returned to American lines."

Gensler instantly sensed a coolness, as if his hosts thought he was holding out on them. In an inspired moment, he brought out pictures of an infant son, born the day he sailed. "I offered this to the colonel and asked my interpreter to tell him that I had not yet seen my own son, since I was fighting a war, but he was as precious to me as the colonel's son and I hoped he would grow up to be as great a hero as the colonel's." The assembled Soviets relaxed, and the atmosphere of bonhomie returned.

On 28 April, Major General Sohanow, commandant of the 118th Russian Infantry, was flown in American artillery planes from Annaberg to Delitzsch, where Allen formally received his opposite number. The American appointed his guest an honorary Timberwolf, removing his own shoulder patch in order to place it on Sohanow's sleeve. Allen solved the problem of how to affix the insignia by loosening his pants buckle, reaching inside for a safety pin on his underwear, and then using it to attach the Timberwolf patch. The era of good feeling bubbled with celebratory toasts.

Albert Schwartz missed the parties. He and his quartermaster company were bedded down in a sugar beet factory. However, he heard that "Gen. Allen went over there [and] crossed the line to meet with the Russians. He and a general from the Russians and they had a big night. They tried to drink each other under the table. I think Terry beat him." As part of the mutual admiration society, Soviet marshal I Konev hung the Order of Suvorov II upon the American. All along the line, Americans met their ally between the Elbe and the Mulde.

On 7 May, Allen received word at division headquarters that a representative of the German high command had signed the unconditional surrender of all of the German forces in Europe—including those opposing the Western democracies and the Soviet forces in the East. The following morning brought the official V-E Day.

19: Home and Terry Junior

Initially after V-E Day, the Timberwolves—as dictated by higher authorities—pulled back until once again they were on the west banks of the Mulde. Traffic between the Soviet and the American armed forces flowed more and more in countercurrents of displaced persons. Some headed toward the Communist-controlled territory, while others sought their homelands in the West. The 104th alone processed more than forty-one thousand civilians. The division also attended to substantial numbers of prisoners who were taken during the final days of the war.

On 12 May, Allen was advised by the VII Corps that the 104th would be among the first divisions to be redeployed to the Pacific, where the war against Japan still raged. Travel plans scheduled the Timberwolves to depart from Germany around 1 June; they would sail home for a thirty-day furlough. For the record, the 104th had cleared eight thousand square miles of Europe, captured 51,724 prisoners, and inflicted an estimated 18,000 casualties. The 104th's KIA had been 1,447 comrades, with 4,776 wounded and 76 missing. The final tally of medals showed 2 medals of honor, including that issued in 1997 to a Black soldier, 24 Distinguished Service Crosses, 1 Distinguished Service Medal (awarded to Allen), almost 600 Silver Stars, and 2 Croix de Guerre from the French. Some 3,600 men, including Allen, pinned on Bronze Stars, and 1,996 Purple Hearts for wounds in action were recorded.

While Allen shifted his attention toward matters of redeployment, the difficulties of his sister Mary had not abated. On 20 May, Allen wrote to her, "As you may remember, I told you that I would do all in my power to help secure some sort of employment for you [he had already provided letters of recommendation] which would be congenial to you and suitable for your needs.

"A fortunate thing happened the other day, which may help bring this about. The division was recently visited by Mrs. Anna M. Rosenberg, who is particularly interested in the civilian re-employment of our military personnel.

"Mrs. Rosenberg, who is a very influential, understanding and capable woman . . . was confidential advisor to our former president, Franklin Roosevelt [she was an assistant secretary of war]. She is now a confidential advisor to our present president Mr. Harry Truman in matters connected with labor and the re-employment of military personnel." After a few further respectful comments on Mrs. Rosenberg's qualities, Allen said he had discussed Mary's situation "most confidentially." He reported, "She felt quite confident in being able to assist you to secure some form of suitable and congenial employment. She asked for your address and said she would communicate with you soon after her return."

The general suggested the best possibilities might lie in a state or municipal position because that would permit her to draw her retirement benefits (three-quarters of her pay as a nurse), something she could not do if she found a place with the federal government.

Evidently his sister had complained of her treatment by the administrators of the Army Nurse Corps, for Allen warned, "I must ask you not to mention to her your personal feelings regarding the background or causes of your retirement, whatever your feelings or my feelings may be in the matter. Because Mrs. Rosenberg is connected with the White House, and it would not be possible for her to become involved in the decisions of an Army Retiring Board or any other government agency."

Another unpleasant duty involved one of the men from an African American platoon of Company G, 413th Infantry: Pvt. Raymond Collins had been convicted by a court-martial of raping a sixteen-year-old German girl, and he was sentenced to be executed by a firing squad. Collins did not testify, and according to the court record, the evidence against him was not contradicted. Collins's company commander then asked Allen to make an "intensive, informal investigation of the circumstances connected with [Collins's] trial." As part of this activity, Allen met with the condemned man.

The general then prepared a written statement that began, "I am recording this memorandum at the request of and in the presence of Private Collins and his squad leader, Sergeant Leonard Brown . . . who is an outstanding member of the colored platoon attached to Company G, 413th Infantry.

"Pvt. Collins requested permission to talk to me confidentially and privately. I authorized him to do so and he discussed with me the circumstances connected with his trial by general court-martial. Private Collins told me that he thought his trial had been conducted with complete fairness and justice. He further informed me that he had been properly represented by proper counsel. He further informed me that he considered that the members of his special platoon and he himself had been treated with complete fairness as American soldiers in this division. Private Collins asked me if it was possible for me to commute his sentence to a prison term, rather than the death penalty which was adjudged. I told him that it was impossible for me to do so, because I was not empowered to reduce this sentence of a general court-martial convened in the division. I further informed him that it was my duty to forward the court-martial proceedings with the sentence as adjudged, without remark. . . ."

At Allen's request, the adjutant general of the 104th, Lt. Col. Melvin M. Kernan, forwarded his statement to Brig. Gen. Benjamin O. Davis, the first of his race to achieve the rank of general, and who served as a special advisor to the War Department on Black soldiers. Kernan noted, "This was the first general court-martial case involving a colored soldier attached to this Division. . . ." Apparently Allen did not or could not make any plea for mercy. He was a product of a southern culture as well as the army. Rape in the 1940s was a capital crime in many states and also in the military; and if the perpetrator was Black, a death sentence was frequently mandated. However, with the shooting war in Europe over, the death sentence for Collins was commuted.

The army resumed its policy of strict segregation shortly after V-E Day. The three African American platoons attached to the 104th said farewell. Allen publicly expressed his appreciation for their combat record. He decorated two men with Silver Stars and ten with Bronze Stars. The Medal of Honor would go to Pfc. Willy F. James fifty-two years later.

The Anna Rosenberg visit was one of several by Washington-based civilians. Robert P. Patterson, Undersecretary of War, was touring the American encampments and met with Allen. Later, he dropped Allen a note complimenting the organization, which said, "The Timberwolf Division has made a great record. The American people are proud of it and I know you are proud of it." Allen distributed copies of the commendation, noting that Patterson was a former distinguished infantry officer in World War I, and concluded with his usual slogan about the unstoppable division.

Toward the end of May, Allen wrote to Lt. Gen. Joseph Stilwell, who after being recalled from China at the demand of that country's Generalissimo Chiang Kai-shek, now held the chair of commander of U.S. Army ground forces. Allen included a summary of what the division had accomplished and commented, "The men are delighted at that prospect [departure for the United States] and are not worried about the expected redeployment." (This was a highly questionable assumption, but pro forma for a commander.)

Allen referred to the division's effective combat procedures and stressed the night attacks made possible by intensive prior training. He expressed hope that the 555th Antiaircraft Battalion (which he used as ground support), the 917th Tank Destroyer Battalion, and the 87th Chemical Mortar Battalion might all remain attached to the 104th when it shifted its operations to the Pacific. The Timberwolf leader gently suggested the preferability of "a western training area where the climatic conditions will be helpful to the health of the troops." He observed that Camp Carson had been ideal.

He had already sketched out a program for eight weeks of training. Allen allotted sixteen hours to discipline—covering the salute, military courtesy, and close-order drill. The troops would be honed to combat readiness through forty-eight hours of intensive exertion—five-mile marches, hand-to-hand exercises, obstacle courses, and bayonet drill. He specified time devoted to instruction in sanitation, booby traps and mines care, and also cleaning of weapons. Special effort would be given to security, because the Japanese were expert at infiltration. And, of course, there would be lessons on night operations.

As the 104th prepared to travel to Camp Lucky Strike, a site some twenty-five miles from Le Havre—from where they would load onto ships—Allen devoted thought to his family. He wrote to his mother, whose health was declining, "I have just heard recently from Mary that you have been returned to Walter Reed Hospital for continued treatment. I hope that things are not too serious with you and you will soon be quite all right. I was quite worried as I had not heard from you for some time.

"... I was glad to hear from Mary that you have several tenants in the house of a sort that seem quite desirable, instructors and students from the University. I think it is a good idea, because it brings in a little income to the house and provides certain protection for the premises. . . . Mary writes me that she intends having a bathroom installed on the first floor in order that you may live more comfortably there and not be forced to go up and down stairs. Please send me the bill for this. I will be glad to pay it, myself." The offer indicates that Allen's financial woes were finally over.

Allen was more realistic with a remark that the troops, while happy to be going home, "are philosophical about being redeployed for combat." He promised to visit once the 104th would reach the United States. And, he closed with, "Again, please let me know if there is anything I can possibly do for you. You will never know, Mama, how much I admire your courage and fortitude, and I only wish I could make things easier and better for you."

He continued to seek to ensure an appointment to the U.S.M.A. for his son. A bread-and-butter letter to the "Honorable R. E. Thomason" in the House of Representatives mentions Terry junior and his 83 percent average at N.M.M.I. and that he played position number one on the polo team. (The best players usually were in the two and three slots.) "It's straightforward guys like you and he [Dewey Short] (even if you are politicians) who keep our army on an even keel."

In a letter to "Dear Sonny" he wrote the boy that he had bought a saddle in Europe that would be sent to Abercrombie and Fitch for cleaning and then forwarded to him. Additional gifts would include a "fancy necktie," white flannel trousers for tennis, a Russian general's pistol, and "a check for 15 bucks."

On 20 June, after the division had ridden to Camp Lucky Strike on the venerable "40 and 8s," Allen sent a long message to Mary Fran. He told her he expected to sail on the *Monterey* before the week was out and would arrive after a voyage of "six or seven days."

It was apparent that he had acquired a cornucopia of souvenirs: ". . . They have finally authorized me to take this British caravan, as they call it, along with me. This caravan is one of those fitted-out Command Post trucks, which includes bunk, wash room, desk and quite a little baggage space. It was given to me by the First Canadian Army as my personal property after our drive in Holland and as an expression of good will from the British. I lived in it a good part of the time during our various campaigns and movements. Maybe Sonny would like to have it for fishing trips. The caravan is pretty well loaded down just at present with various boxes and all sorts of junk that I could not have brought home otherwise."

Attached was a memorandum that listed the contents of a series of boxes. "The radio set referred to is a very fine German Army Radio which is manufactured in Holland and would be very difficult to get at home. The Scotch and Gin referred to were gotten without cost from the British. The assorted liquers [sic] referred to were captured liquers which are the finest sort. In the rug roll there is one particularly fine Persian rug which is supposed to be very fine. In the box of war souvenirs there are several German battle flags which we picked up en route and about a dozen German daggers of various sorts. I am also bringing home a German pistol which I promised to Mr. Thomasson. I also have a Russian pistol with a silver engraving given to me by a Russian general which I am giving Sonny. The blanket roll in Box No. 5 includes the six pure wool heavy white blankets with a red stripe. I believe they are pure wool and they are very similar to Hudson Bay blankets. . . ."

He explained that the troops would go from the ships directly to either Camp Kilmer or Fort Dix, New Jersey, before their thirty-day furloughs would begin. "It is quite likely that I will be given a thirty-day leave at the same time. . . . We can spend the leave together with Sonny wherever you want to be. I should like to be around New York with you for a while, and then go wherever you wish. Any place will suit me so long as I am with you and Sonny." He noted that his mother was at Walter Reed Army Medical Center in Washington, D.C., and he did plan to see her for a day or so, but had no plans beyond that.

The general remarked on the atmosphere of joy emanating from the prospect of going home. He reiterated the comment he had made to his mother. "They are philosophical about being redeployed for combat." He added, "Frankly, they are not glory hunters who are seeking more combat, as they know how tough it is, having spearheaded five major operations, and have been outstandingly successful in every single combat operation. However, Okinawa having just fallen and with the prospect of the Japs being bombed out of existence [the first A-bomb was still six weeks away] I frankly feel that resistance in the Pacific area may fold up more rapidly than is generally thought. I have talked to every company and separate unit in the division and find that they are ready for whatever may be forthcoming for the division. I told them possibly the Japs would fold up completely when they hear the Timberwolves are coming.

"Having already made two landings, Africa and Sicily, and having had more combat and all of it successful, than any other Division Commander, I am not seeking any more combat just to be doing it but I do feel a terrific obligation to the Timberwolf Division since they have supported me in every possible way, and I believe it is more than my duty to stick by them." It is possible to read into the statement that Allen was growing weary of the stress of his job or it may be he was simply trying to forestall any plea from his wife that he request a noncombat post.

He rattled on, "I am also bringing home in a caravan a box of various gifts, and a little trinket for Mary Harris, Charlotte and Mrs. McDonnell. I think with this last load of stuff . . . you will have enough Channel No. 5 to start a perfume shop of your own.

"There is not much to do here, as we are camped out in the lonely wastes of Normandy, champing at the bit and waiting for embarkation. I manage to get a workout with Sgt. Watts nearly every day and jog a couple of miles and get in my daily exercise. There is nothing much to do except sleep and eat and attend to the many bothersome details connected with our embarkation."

Allen paid tribute to some of his subordinates: "Old John Cochran [CO of the 415th] proved to be one of our outstanding combat soldiers. He and Gerry Kelleher were our two best combat leaders. Neither of them ever failed to get the job done and with minimum casualties. [Allen never forgot how painful a price could be paid for an operation.] It is strange that two of such opposite types should both do so well. . . ."

Three days later, he advised her he was still "sitting around the Normandy sand dunes" awaiting a ship, the SS *Monterey*. He included his Bronze Star citation and letters of commendation from Montgomery, Sir John Crocker (the British corps commander in Holland), and Lt. Gen. Guy Simonds (the Canadian general under whom he served).

He mentioned an anniversary present he had arranged for Maurice Schwartz to give her and bragged, "I got four new uniforms while overseas *and all free of cost.* Three better-grade issue uniforms of the new type and one tailor-made uniform from the best tailor in Paris, a favor only supposed to be done for the army commanders. But my friends in the QM [quartermaster corps] were looking out for me.

"I do hope you will like the things I brought you. Also want to do some shopping for you in New York, as I saved up some of my pay to do that for you.

"Am delighted over the reception given Ike as he deserved all he got. . . .

"Tell Sonny not to get any shoes or ties as I have some for him. Am crazy to see him.

"After much wrangling and persuasion in Paris I finally managed to scrape up about 6 or 7 more bottles of Chanel #5 for you."

After claiming that everyone agreed his was the best of the new divisions in Europe, Allen added, "Of course I have been definitely passed up for a corps command or for promotion but they can't possibly deny the record for accomplishment."

Both Mary Fran and Terry junior had come to New York several days earlier in hopes he would arrive ahead of schedule. Allen reported he was unable to get permission to fly home, however, because all of the other general officers with divisions had preceded him in advance detachments.

On 3 July, the *Monterey* arrived with him on it, and for a week the family held a reunion. Allen made a side trip to Washington to visit his hospitalized mother, but he was back in New York City on 11 July as the second ship, the SS *Ericsson,* docked with the remainder of the 104th. Albert Schwartz was on the *Ericsson,* and related, "When we finally came in, here came Terry Allen in a tugboat, a fast-moving one. He met us in the harbor, and swung aboard like a trapeze artist on a rope. I got a call, to come up and see him. He said, 'Albert, your Daddy is sick. I want you to go home.' I said, 'General, I got to get these guys unloaded and then go with them to the camp.' He said in his own inimitable way, 'Go home.' I turned my duties over to my executive officer. I got home earlier than expected. My Daddy wasn't gravely ill, but he was pretty sick. I missed a long train ride because I managed to get on an airplane to go on back. That was typical of Terry Allen, he did nice things for people. He didn't have to do that. He only did it because he was a friend of my Dad, a friend of mine, who wanted me to get home in case it was serious. I missed the parade in New York City."

Along with the three other infantry divisions rotated back to the United States, the 104th received a thirty-day furlough. At that time, the GIs also drew orders to report to Camp San Luis Obispo in California. But as their month-long leaves ended and they trickled into their new home, the atomic bombs exploded first over Hiroshima and then Nagasaki. Before they could even begin intensive preparations for the seaborne assault— scheduled for November—the Japanese surrendered. "Instead of gathering up steam, girding our loins for another battle," said Schwartz, "the Timberwolves were disbanded."

Deactivation was not immediate: Not until Douglas MacArthur found that he had enough troops on hand for occupation duty was the fate of the 104th settled. A system that awarded points on the basis of time served, overseas assignments, medals, and family responsibilities quickly separated men from military service in all units including the 104th. On ceremonial occasions, the division paraded on the West Coast, marking time before its dissolution. As the high-point soldiers left Camp San Luis Obispo, Allen was awarded a bronze oak-leaf cluster for his DSM.

According to George O'Connor, still with the division, the soldiers who saw their separation from the service imminent became "unruly." Allen summoned him to his offices and addressed him, "Brooklyn, you're flat-footed and Irish. That's a cop. From now on you are the provost marshal [the officer responsible for policing the division]."

On 15 September, the third birthday for the 104th, it performed a final review for Allen. In his speech, Allen detailed the division's accomplishments, concluding with his rousing paraphrase of the battle slogan, "Nothing in hell *did* stop the Timberwolves." The official inactivation date was set for 20 December 1945. Allen and a small cadre presided over the required paperwork.

In early 1946, after thirty-three years of active service, as well as four years as a cadet, Terry Allen retired. His official list of honors included Distinguished Service Cross; Distinguished Service Medal with an oak-leaf cluster; Silver Star; Bronze Star; Legion of Merit; French Legion of Honor; Croix de Guerre with Palm; Most Honorable Order of the Bath; Order of the British Empire; and the Order of Suvorov from the Soviets.

The Allens settled in El Paso, where Terry senior attempted, with partners, to obtain a license for a radio station. When that came to naught, he signed on as a representative of the Lincoln National Life Insurance Company. As a celebrity in El Paso and the surrounding area, Allen had easy access to people of means. No one thought of him as a salesman, but instead he could open doors for others who could then present insurance policies to the best advantage. He and Mary Fran moved into a comfortable house in an affluent neighborhood about a mile from Fort Bliss. His mother, at age eighty-three, had died at Washington's Walter Reed Army Medical Center.

Allen was a regular at the Fort Bliss officers' club, where he was a welcome visitor to the socializing retirees like himself as well as much younger men who were still on active duty or hoping to make a career. He persuaded the commandant to retain a field for polo; and although he now reluctantly gave up play, he served as an umpire. He continued to work out with his Indian clubs and to jog and play tennis.

Bob Kane, a 1946 graduate of West Point—assigned to Fort Bliss as a second lieutenant in the artillery—recalled meeting Allen: "On a tennis court at the post in 1947, I was practicing serving by myself on a hot day. After a while, I noticed this 'old' man standing on the side. As I went to retrieve the balls I had hit to the other side, he asked me if I was waiting for a tennis date. I replied in the negative and invited him to join me. I was surprised and somewhat terrified to hear him say, 'Hello, young man. I'm Terry Allen.' I stammered out my name and rank, wondering if I would kill the old codger in the blistering heat. After all, second lieutenants had few chances to play tennis with a war hero, one old enough to be my grandfather.

"I needn't have feared. General Allen ran my backside around the court for three sets, winning all of them. Each time I made a good shot, he praised me, although dumb luck was responsible for most of them. By the end of the match, he was unruffled, while I was dripping sweat and totally exhausted. He then said, 'Lieutenant, let's go the bar and I'll buy you a beer. I think you need it.' I of course accepted and we had a friendly short visit together.

"I didn't see him again, because of an overseas tour, but back at Fort Bliss I attended the annual West Point anniversary party in March 1951. Terry was there, having the grandest kind of time with some of my classmates. Toward the end of the evening, he and one of my classmates (we were captains by this time) both skunk drunk, decided to bombard each other from opposite sides of the room at the officers' club with full drinks. Allen would bellow, 'On the way' and classmate Dan would respond, 'Bombs away.' It took much effort to break up this friendly war, but fortunately, Dan didn't get into any trouble. After all, Terry Allen was the senior officer egging him on."

Albert Schwartz, now busy with his father's store, spoke of a visible change in his old commander: "Gen. Allen was the kind of a guy who should always have worn a uniform. He wore it as it should be, standing tall and strong. When he retired and took it off, I couldn't believe the difference. The effect was not good, so far as I was concerned. He didn't look like Maj. Gen. Terry de la Mesa Allen in civilian dress. He wore tweeds, maybe with a leather patch at the elbow, a kind of disreputable tweed hat but he didn't carry himself as proudly as before."

Bill and Bebe (Genevieve) Coonly were good friends of the Allens. Bebe had grown up in El Paso. And her husband—a native of Buffalo who joined the army as a common soldier before Pearl Harbor—had won a commission in the field artillery and served in North Africa, among other campaigns. She remembered Mary Fran as "old school, very feminine, with a steel backbone. She wore big hats, was dressed and groomed immaculately, had great dignity. She told me she kept coloring her hair because 'Terry wouldn't have it any other way.'" In contrast, "Terry always looked as if he slept in his suit and sat on his hat."

Bill Coonly, who observed from his experiences in North Africa that "the 1st Division looked a lot sloppier than the rest of the soldiers," after V-J Day served as an aide to Gen. John Homer, the Fort Bliss post commander and U.S.M.A. 1911 graduate, who knew Allen from those days. Coonly recalled that Allen in his frequent appearances at the bar would invite people to join him. "He called the chaplain 'the devil chaser.' Occasionally, he would offer a toast to fallen comrades—then throw his glass into the fireplace. When Omar Bradley as Chief of Staff came to Fort Bliss, Gen. Homer gave me instructions, 'Don't let Terry Allen get anywhere near him.' I spent the whole night trying to keep Terry away."

While Allen and Mary Fran had a full social life, it was Terry junior's future that most involved the father. In June 1944, before the 104th ventured overseas, Allen—who had been in close contact with the faculty at N.M.M.I.—drafted a proposed course of study for his son in the coming school year.

"It is desired that he complete his high school course in June 1946, if it is possible to do so without crowding him too much. It is desired that his future course of instruction be based on qualifying him as well as possible for entry to the United States Military Academy in 1947 or 1948. Prior to such entry, I should like to have him complete at least one college term and to have included in his curriculum as much as possible of his first year course of study at West Point. I wish to have particular attention paid to a *sound basic foundation* in mathematics, a *sound course* in English and History and a *fair basic proficiency* in one language."

What Allen was proposing was hardly out of the ordinary, and even today schools that prep candidates for the military academies try not only to help them pass the entrance examinations but also give them a leg up on the first year's academics upon which many a cadet or midshipman founders. Allen noted that following consultation with his boy's teacher, he considered it advisable for Terry junior to repeat plane geometry I, because he was barely proficient in the subject and required a strong foundation in that course. He remarked that during the summer his son would be taking a six-week review of algebra under a high school teacher in Colorado Springs. Furthermore, the father observed that his son would need help in Spanish II because he was weak in languages. It seems quite apparent that Terry junior was academically a chip off the old block, one who would have difficulty making it through the mills of West Point classrooms.

Born in 1929, Terry junior had grown up mostly in El Paso. His early years were unexceptional: They included the customary childhood diseases and an early proficiency in the saddle, having learned to ride at two. At age six, he won the children's riding contest at Fort Riley. Patricia Rogers, a contemporary, remembered him from when they were occasional playmates as a "very nice boy." "He liked sports, and there never seemed to be any question that he would follow in his father's footsteps." As others noted later in his life, she remarked that he never sought to trade on his father's fame.

Albert Schwartz caught glimpses of the youngster in El Paso and when Mary Fran and Terry junior followed the general to the desert training in Arizona. "I saw a good bit of him during that time. He seemed like a neat kid, a good boy. He reminded me a lot of his Dad."

Unlike his father, he did not become a traveling army brat. There were sojourns in Florida and Colorado Springs, but the bulk of his education before he entered N.M.M.I. was in El Paso. There he completed a year at Austin High School and played a year as a quarterback.

At N.M.M.I., while he delighted his father with a position on the polo team, he labored in his studies. In 1946–1947, he finished with Cs in chemistry, algebra, English, and drawing. He flunked analytic geometry and repeated the course. Only in "Military Science and Tactics," an ROTC feature, did he do well—receiving a numerical score of 84.79.

The following year he improved somewhat, recording an A in Physics 7, a slide-rule study, and Bs in English, world history, and his second shot at analytical geometry. For American history and psychology he earned Cs.

One of his instructors in mathematics, Paul Mount Campbell, wrote, "He is concerned about not doing as good as others and this feeling has been a handicap in the past. But believe he has developed a great amount in overcoming the complex."

Other faculty members described him as "well coordinated," gave him better than average ratings for his "initiative," "personal magnetism," "common sense," and "physical coordination and stamina." Colonel Robert W. Strong, the ROTC cavalry professor, noted, "This young man is rather quiet, of excellent character and personal standards. At this institution he has shown a healthy progressive development."

His grades were not those ordinarily acceptable for nomination to the
U.S.M.A. According to Coonly, Allen once got into a conversation with
General Homer on the difficulty of getting his boy into West Point. Allen
remarked, "Jack, he's a great, great athlete, captain of the polo team."
When Homer mentioned the scholastic requirements, Allen answered,
"Not everyone is a student." Homer snapped, "He might do better
pounding a book up his ass instead of a saddle." In pursuit of the ap-
pointment, Allen traveled to Washington, D.C., and through Pres. Harry
Truman, Terry junior won a nomination by Sen. Carl Hatch of New Mexico in March of 1948 to the Class of 1952.

His classmates at N.M.M.I. liked him. Ruben W. Evans, who attended
the school from 1945–1948, said, "He was a very good cadet. He was not
an outstanding polo player but very steady. When we had games, his father would show up, and sometimes we went to El Paso to visit. His father of course had a great deal of charisma; Terry was calmer."

Cliff Feder was several years ahead of Terry junior at N.M.M.I. and recalled how impressed everyone was when the general and his wife first
appeared after the division returned from Europe. "On one occasion he
played a polo game with the local players. Terry junior was a nice kid who
never got into trouble. We had the feeling that it was a very, very happy
family."

Tom Cole was another classmate of Terry junior. He, too, played polo
at the school and recalled that the squad was seeded number one among
collegiate teams, winning the national championship one year. "I don't
think he had a problem of having to try to live up to his father. He was
very down to earth, and if you knew Terry, you trusted him. There was
nobody who knew him who didn't like him."

Terry junior and Tom Cole both traveled to El Paso from N.M.M.I. to
take the examinations that would qualify them for admission to West
Point. "General and Mrs. Allen took us to the officers club at Fort Bliss.
The only restriction he placed on us was not to play the slot machines.
When we were the only people left, we looked around for the General.
Mrs. Allen said, 'I know where he is,' and it was in the bar."

Both the younger Allen and Cole passed the academic test. "The night
before we reported to West Point," recalled Cole, "we spent the night bar-
hopping in New York City. Riding up in the train, then walking up the
hill [from the station to the academy], Terry was deathly ill. He said he
wanted to die."

20: Third Generation

Terry Allen Jr.'s introduction to life at West Point was through the traditional Beast Barracks, the one-month ordeal that plebes underwent upon arrival. Carl Guess (a native of Temple, Texas, who met him during the summer of 1948) told, "Unlike many of us who entered the academy just out of high school, and had not been more than a couple of hundred miles from home, Terry's whole life had been spent around the army—and it showed. He took BB all in stride."

Because of his years at N.M.M.I., he was far more prepared for the style of discipline exerted at the U.S.M.A. than his father had been, and in this respect, Terry junior fit into the life at West Point far more smoothly than Terry senior had. The younger Terry would rack up some demerits during his four years there, but he fell well short of approaching the totals earned by the general.

Guess said that at the end of a plebe hike in August, Terry junior—who had been assigned to the same company as he was for the 1948 academic year—asked him to be one of his roommates. "I readily agreed! He seemed to be one of the few cool heads around in that sea of chaos."

Wallace Hastings Jr., whose father had graduated in 1924, was another plebe with the younger Allen. He too was impressed by his aplomb. "He was the first guy my age that I ever saw smoking cigars." It was to Hastings that the younger Allen confided that the chief villain in the general's downfall in North Africa and Sicily had been Beetle Smith.

Bill Reilly, another member of 1952 (appointed from Wyoming), said, "I had done pretty well academically the first two years, so I was assigned to room with Carl Guess and Terry Allen Cow Year [third, or junior, year at the academy] to help them along. They were both great 'Wives' [West Point slang for roommates] and I enjoyed being with them very much." (Bill Reilly ended up graduating 8th out of 527.)

"Terry was very outgoing and personable, and he did like to party although that wasn't much of an option during those years at West Point. He did study hard, but it didn't come easily to him. Terry had a signature greeting, like a loud cattle call—shades of his time at NMMI and his love of the cavalry and horses. I don't recall that he got significantly more demerits than average, but he did enjoy company and a good time. Through his father's 1st Division contacts—a well-known movie producer, Sam Fuller, was a member of the 1st Division Association and produced *The Big Red One*—he enjoyed entry into some very nice spots in Manhattan. Through the same connections he dated a Hollywood starlet, Terry Moore."

Guess recalled, "Terry was a very outgoing person, even as a plebe, who enjoyed barracks bull sessions, was a good storyteller [a trait inherited from his father], and with a receptive audience would regale us with tales of the 'old army.' He could be reserved also, even aloof among strangers (but he knew so many people). As a cadet, Terry was pretty straight-arrow and while he occasionally directed his somewhat sardonic sense of humor at the tactical department, he had a very professional viewpoint about it.

"My remembrance was that Gen. Allen's advice to Terry junior may well have been that some of his own cadet adventures were silly and that Terry should avoid the old man's errors. There was an undertone to a lot of Gen. Allen's talk about his cadet days/Army career indicating that the authorities breathed a collective sigh of relief when he left W. P. for good and this followed him throughout his army career. He told me during June Week 1952, when Terry junior's graduation was in question, that 'they' were out to get Terry junior just like they had Terry senior. I don't remember any pattern to the demerits that Terry junior received, but there was nothing remarkable in them I'm sure.

"When I think of Gen. Allen, several impressions come to mind: one as a prototypical Irishman—gregarious, boisterous, somewhat belligerent in a very agreeable way, preferring the company of men but a perfect gentleman in the presence of ladies. My wife, an Army brat herself, was absolutely charmed by him. I cannot listen to the strains of Gary Owen, the 7th Cavalry anthem [one of Allen's units], without thinking of Gen. Allen, because Terry junior would often sing it."

His image of Mary Fran matched that of the Coonlys. He described, "Mrs. Allen was very gracious, typically old army (according to my wife who grew up in the army). She was tall, stately, a fine-looking woman, every inch a lady, somewhat reserved; but most people probably appeared reserved in the presence of the general. Sometimes when he got carried away and let out a 'hell' or 'damn,' she would remind him to tone down his language—and he did."

Carl Guess starred on the U.S.M.A. football team. This was the era of Coach Earl Blaik, and gridiron talent was enthusiastically recruited and, some say, pampered. According to Guess, Terry Allen Sr. personally recruited high school athletes for the academy. In 1951, scandal swept the academy when it was revealed that a substantial number of cadets—particularly members of the football team—had violated the honor code by cheating in their studies. That would lead to profound changes in the functioning of the athletic department and the supervision of cadets, but it did not significantly affect Terry junior.

Although he was an enthusiastic rooter for the football team and, said Guess, "very supportive of my endeavors in Army football," he did not play any major or minor intercollegiate sports. He was actively involved, however, in a number of intramural activities: lacrosse, squash, tennis, wrestling, soccer, and boxing (at the 145-pound weight). West Point did not field a polo team. According to Wallace Hastings, "There were no horses at all at West Point"—the mounted cavalry had become extinct. On the nonphysical side, Terry junior was a member of the Spanish Club and the Catholic Acolytes.

"To my recollection," Carl Guess said, "Terry would never introduce a story about his dad by saying, 'Gen. Allen said or did . . . ' but if something came up, he might relate an incident in Gen. Allen's cadet days that was similar. These were often very humorous and would involve some of the general's schoolmates with familiar names, such as Walton H. Walker [who, like Allen senior, originally was a member of 1911 but turned back and did graduate in 1912].

"It is probable that all the 'Army Brats' at W.P. were aware of who Terry's father was, but the awareness level among the 'dumbjohns' was too low to register much. This was not the kind of thing that was talked about a lot except in 'Brat' circles. In fact it was not wise to call up your military background too often. Even 50 years later I am still discovering classmates whose dads were graduates."

That was the same sense that Bill Reilly had. "Terry adored his father but he never flaunted the relationship in front of people. He also adored his mother, a very gracious lady."

The restrictions upon social life that Samuel Allen and also Terry senior experienced while in residence at the academy had dramatically lessened by the post–World War II era. Roommate Guess reported, "Terry junior was a ladies' man—not much question about that!—definitely not shy around women, who seemed to like him. We double-dated a few times at W.P. and in New York City and when the class was in Ft. Bliss for summer training or when I would visit Terry there. He also visited me in Temple a couple of times, and I got him dates with Temple girls."

However sophisticated he may have appeared, it was quickly apparent that, as with his father, the classrooms at West Point threatened his survival. "Like me," said Guess, "Terry's academic interest was in the social sciences, especially those that had a military orientation, such as geography, military arts/engineering, military history, etc." But the curriculum was far broader than in his father's era, and the demands much greater.

"Math and science subjects were our (almost) undoing," said Guess. "Terry was conscientious in his studies, generally, while I was not at all in math/science (I had a typical 'jock' attitude about them) but [we were] relatively dedicated to studies in history, government, etc." The cadets studied chemistry, physics, math, English, a foreign language (Spanish in his case), and such vocational items as topography, military hygiene, and military psychology. At the end of his first year, Terry junior ranked toward the bottom of his 608-member class. His grades ranged from 2.5 to a low of 2.008. He continued to perform below average academically in the following years: ranking 560th as a third classman and 530th as a second classman (the 1952 group had shrunken to 578).

Although Reilly had been assigned to room with Guess and Allen in the hope that he could help them academically, Guess recalled that Reilly was taken aback when the pair were suddenly placed in his world history section, which was reorganized monthly in accordance with the grades from the previous month. "He wouldn't talk to us two 'goats' [designation for those ranked lowest in the class] for the next month (this is only a slight exaggeration)."

But Reilly and others did try to help. Guess explained, "We would attend various department review sessions or get tutoring from classmates like Reilly, as well as study individually. We would sometimes go to the library to avoid interfering with roommates' free time.

"Terry was very methodical and tended to outline or write out notes to assist in his study, while I mostly just re-worked problems. Terry liked to quote George Patton's line that W.P. offered a five-year course (we would often add 'in subjects we didn't hold with') which some people finish in four."

Terry junior did not improve his grades during his final year. He did his best in law, military art, military psychology, and physical education. He barely scraped by in his father's nemesis, ordnance, but he and two others—George A. Grayeb Jr. and Charles Yarborough—failed the final examination in engineering. Bill Reilly said, "The Department decided they had not exerted enough effort and had not taken the exams seriously enough."

The general and Mary Fran had actually come to West Point to attend the commencement ceremonies only to discover their son was confined and facing being turned back. Allen senior appealed to higher authorities in Washington, D.C., and the trio took a make-up exam: All three passed.

On 26 June 1952, three weeks after everyone else in the class, Terry junior received a belated commission, ranking dead-last among the 529 who completed the four years. Reilly remembered, "Terry was proud that they [his father and he] were both 'Goats' and wore that status with pride." (Technically, the senior Allen was not worthy of that appellation because he never graduated.) The new lieutenant had chosen infantry for his branch of service. He quickly completed additional training in that field and then qualified as a paratrooper and underwent Ranger training.

"In the fall of 1955," recalled Bill Reilly, "I reported to Fort Benning for Ranger School and Terry was stationed there. I contacted him to arrange a meeting at the Officers Club after duty one afternoon. As I walked into the darkened room, and while my eyes were still adjusting to the dim light, I was loudly greeted by his signature cattle call. Seems that George Grayeb, aide to the commanding general of the XVIII Airborne Corps, had just flown into Benning, and the two of them were well into a joyous, libation-filled reunion of the Class of 26 June, with two-thirds of the class present."

After a stint as a platoon leader with the 504th Airborne Infantry Regiment, the younger Allen traveled to Korea to serve with the 5th Infantry Regiment. Upon his return from that tour, he commanded a rifle company, earning accolades from his superiors. During the late 1950s, over a period of three years, he was first an aide to the head of the Continental Army command and then under Lt. Gen. Charles Hart, commander of the U.S. Army Air Defense, which was based in Colorado Springs.

Bill Coonly also was on Hart's staff, and he and his wife had become very close to the younger Allen. "We considered him part of our family," said Bebe. Bill Coonly remembered Terry junior banging on his door one morning at 3 A.M.. to say, "My father said never drink alone. So here I am."

"When Terry junior's tour with General Hart ended," recounted Bebe, "there was a party at Colorado Springs. Everyone was having such a great time that when the band was finished someone asked if we could afford to pay them for another hour. Terry said, 'Why go second class, when for another nickel you can go first class.' He wanted to splurge for a party that would go longer than an hour."

He was home on leave when his mother suggested he pay a call on neighbors three houses away who had a very handsome daughter, Jean Ponder. She was only nineteen, a niece of Bebe Coonly, a graduate of local Catholic schools, and a student of English literature at the University of Texas at El Paso. "I had never seen Terry Allen Jr. before he walked up to the house. It was a quick courtship. He sent me white roses regularly, and three months later we were married at St. Patrick's Cathedral in New York. It was not a big wedding because it was out of town. This was deliberate. I wanted a small wedding which would have been difficult to do in El Paso."

Jean Allen, whose parents were divorced, entered an entirely different world from the one in which she grew up. "Terry adored his father and with good reason. He was a remarkable man. He wore his accomplishments and greatness with humility. When he would talk about events in World War II, wonderful stories, he always mentioned 'the man upstairs' and praised the enlisted men. His gratitude and belief in a divine creator never wavered. He possessed an amazing freedom which enabled him to be himself among the great and not so great. He was so secure in himself that he could be authentic and genuine, more than anyone I ever met. There was nothing fake; he didn't know how to pretend.

"He and his wife were very close to each other. She adored him and he had the utmost respect for her. They worked together very well. Mary Frances understood Terry senior had his realm and she respected it.

"He was very close to his son. He watched over Terry junior's career very closely. Terry junior was different. He was much more introspective, more scholarly, even though he had not focused on his formal education. He loved history and reading about it, was knowledgeable and liked to talk about history. If he had been in another context, I think he would have pursued liberal arts.

"I wasn't aware of this when I first married him. I realize now that a famous parent puts a tremendous burden on an offspring. Not that his father demanded anything of him, but Terry lived to please him."

Captain Allen received orders that sent the couple to Europe, where he joined the 8th Infantry Division and then the 1st Battalion of the 70th Armored in the 24th Infantry Division. While they were in Germany, their first daughter, Consuelo, was born. According to her, when the grandfather asked the source for the name, his son had answered, "After your mother." The general said, "But her name was Concepcion." Told it was too late to make a change, Terry senior admitted, "I always hated the name Concepcion."

The senior Allens visited the young marrieds and their child in Germany. Tom Cole (Terry junior's former schoolmate at N.M.M.I., then with the 14th Cavalry, an armored unit) remembered the general coming to their station at Fulda: "The 14th Cavalry had been his outfit on the Mexican border and he talked about the old days. He sat on the pool table in the rec hall and he kept 150 soldiers spellbound with his stories. He mentioned how he had been part of the last cavalry charge by the U.S. Army in the Mexican expedition."

Jean Allen said she and her husband savored their time in Europe. "I loved travel and to live in other places. Terry and I did what we could do to live in the culture of Europe, while some of the others [in the military community] did not."

In fact, Jean Allen never quite fit into that rather tight-knit society. Her daughter Consuelo remarked, "She was not a person to sit around drinking and playing canasta." The life of an officer's mate can be quite stressful—frequently, the wife is left behind for long periods while the mate is stationed elsewhere, even overseas. The single parent often must run the permanent household, handle the chores of moving, and raise the children. It is even more difficult in wartime. Even a supposedly steel-spined woman like Mary Fran buckled a bit during World War II. Some drink, some become unfaithful, some manage to stick it out. Said Jean Allen, "I've grown to appreciate people who can do it [cope] and do it well."

Jean also had to deal with a generational component. She was only nineteen when she married; her husband was thirty-two, and the wives of his contemporaries were older than she was. "I had some friends but in the service friendships are lateral, based on rank." By the time Terry and Jean returned to the United States and settled down, they had two more daughters, Alice Genevieve (nicknamed Bebe) and Mary Frances. And the Vietnam War had begun to swallow up the country.

Terry junior received a staff position with the U.S. Strike Command at Tampa, Florida. While it enabled him to demonstrate additional talents, it was obvious that any officer who hoped to rise in the ranks needed a tour in Vietnam. "When Terry told me he volunteered for Vietnam," said Jean, "it was not a big shock. I knew that for future advance you had to have a role in combat. We had discussed it and I did not try to persuade him not to go. My reaction really was 'Wow!' This is what he needs to do for his career. This is what my country is doing and my husband needs to go, okay. Both of us were very naive about the war. We thought it was another World War II."

After he informed his father, the general sought out, among others, Bill Coonly. The latter remembered, "General Allen called me on a Sunday morning and asked me to come and talk with him. Terry had written his parents, mentioning volunteering. The general asked me what did I think of the idea. I said, 'I don't believe in the Vietnam War. If I got orders, I would go. Otherwise I'd tell 'em to stuff it.' Everybody in Texas knew Lyndon Johnson was full of bullshit. The general was noncommittal. But I understood why Terry junior felt he had to go."

It was February 1967 and Terry Allen junior had arrived in Vietnam. He was assigned to the 28th Infantry Regiment, as the operations officer for the 2d Battalion of the Black Lions. During World War I when the U.S. Army fielded "square" divisions, the 28th had been the fourth regiment in the 1st Infantry Division. When the army changed to "triangular" divisions with just three regiments, the 28th became part of the 8th Infantry Division. In Vietnam, however, the 28th was part of the 1st Division, the organization his father had commanded in the Mediterranean theater.

As countless reports and histories have demonstrated, the war in Vietnam was a brutal and often frustrating business. While the Americans and the Republic of Vietnam soldiers possessed far superior firepower and controlled the skies, the rebels of South Vietnam, the Viet Cong (VC), and the troops from North Vietnam were well equipped with small arms, dedicated to their cause, and able to fade into the jungles, paddies, and general population. General Terry Allen's maxim, "Find 'em, fix 'em and fight 'em," was extremely difficult to fulfill.

In 1966, the 2d Battalion of the 28th Infantry had earned a valorous-unit award for "extraordinary heroism" when it fought off a "vastly superior Viet Cong Force" that attacked the unit while they were engaged in operations designed to block a VC supply route. The official account claimed 450 of the enemy dead with only 26 "friendly" casualties.

The Black Lions picked up a second citation for Operation Manhattan, a two-week search-and-destroy mission in a "vast logistical and staging area" known as the Iron Triangle. A series of hit-and-run battles cost the Americans four dead and sixty wounded, while the VC left behind sixteen bodies before helicopters evacuated the GIs on 8 May 1967.

Terry Allen Jr. had been part of Manhattan and now moved on to the post of Deputy G-3 (Plans and Operations) for the division. His replacement with the 2d Battalion was Jim Shelton, a graduate of the University of Delaware in 1957, who was called up because of his ROTC courses. "I liked the Army," said Shelton, "and my wife convinced me to stay in. Her father has been a career military man."

Shelton had served in Korea, completed a tour with the 82d Airborne, and was giving advanced infantry training when he received his orders to Vietnam. "I felt it was a just cause. I had been a general's aide in 1961 and was exposed to a lot of intelligence reports the general got. They were infiltrating south in sampans and I thought, 'What the hell! How can we put up with this. We can't let the Communists take over the south. We've got to draw a line.'"

When he reached Vietnam in July 1967, he said, "I spent one night in a base camp and then I was assigned to the Black Lions, the 2d Battalion of the 28th. I met the XO [executive officer] and asked, 'Where's the battalion?' He told me it was out in the field. I flew out at night to the location and the first guy I met was the S-3, Terry. He was wearing horn-rimmed glasses and he asked me, 'How're you doing?' I was very apprehensive that first night, which was miserable. I didn't have a hole. Terry was busy as hell. He had two days to teach me everything he knew. He introduced me to everybody, including the clerks and the radio operator, in a way that I could see this guy has respect for the troops.

"I was struck by what a good guy he was. I didn't realize, even with the junior tacked onto his name, that he was the son of the greatest infantry soldier I had ever heard of. I was at Fort Benning when John Corley told a story about how Terry Allen was the greatest soldier; and later again when I was a general's aide, he named Allen as the best. Later, when I went to reunions of the 104th I couldn't believe the cult of Terry Allen.

"Young Terry and I would talk every night. He would say, 'My Dad just couldn't take Bradley. He couldn't figure out why Bradley was where he was.' Terry junior was quieter than his father and he'd have only an occasional beer [the Vietnam experiences may well have dampened the younger Allen's thirst for spirits]."

Shelton settled into his job—which he discovered actually required him to unofficially run the battalion because the nominal CO was incompetent. "I was up there in a helicopter with our battalion commander as the troops were moving out, and he looks down and says, 'Those guys are moving too slow.' They were up to their waists in water but he insisted they needed PT [physical training] to get in shape. The battalion commander was an asshole and he was relieved."

Promoted to lieutenant colonel, Allen returned to the 2d Battalion to take over command. Shelton described, "When Terry came back, 45 days after he had left, it was almost dark. I had set up a perimeter and he came up to me. I shook his hand, 'Great to have you, sir.' I gave him a quick rundown on the situation. We were in a hole in the ground and he said, 'Jim, I'm now the battalion commander of this fucking outfit, not you. You're the S-3.' I laughed and said, 'Great.' He was telling me 'Back off, Jack,' and I understood.

"He never made a lot of noise or commotion and rarely raised his voice, but he had a commanding presence when he was among his subordinates. He impressed me with his helpfulness and forthrightness, as well as the way he treated the soldiers around him with dignity and respect. He was not party to the posturing and puffery that are exhibited by some officers—men who are so carried away with having been designated 'officers and gentlemen' that they feel they must impress everyone around them.

"He enjoyed talking about a wide variety of subjects, and both of us expressed our opinions that although we had spent some good years in the military, we could also have done well in another profession."

According to Shelton, the 1st Division commanders "had fostered a cult of forceful personality and dynamism," building upon the reputation and traditions of the organization. "Esprit de Corps is admirable," remarked Shelton, "but in modern warfare—particularly at battalion level and above—it can be an invitation to disaster. . . . They had to prevail; defeat could not be considered a possibility."

Neither Shelton nor Terry Allen accepted one aspect of the 1st Division command style: "Neither of us really agreed with the 'ass-chewing' mode of correction prevalent in the Big Red One, but he was better than I was at taking it without passing it along," said Shelton. That style of course was incompatible with Maj. Gen. Allen's way when he led the 1st.

Back home, the younger Allen's relationship with Jean had been challenged. Although the antiwar partisans were a small minority in the city with its massive military orientation, they had attracted support. According to Jean, "The media had a big influence on me. It brought the war home in a way I had never anticipated. We were living in El Paso, and I got involved somewhat in the counterculture movement."

The biggest change in her life, however, was an infatuation with a performer at a local radio station. She wrote to Terry what in World War II was known as a Dear John letter. She said she was in love with someone and wanted to divorce. "I lived with him," said Jean. "I wasn't doing it in secret."

Bebe Allen, their daughter born in 1963, blamed a number of factors: "Jean was brought up a princess and never learned to cook. They moved around so often, and I think she may have had postpartum depression after the last child. Her mother was dying, and six months after she died, Terry went to Vietnam. I think she felt abandoned."

According to Jean, her mother's illness had been personally devastating. "She fought a long battle with cancer and I traveled back and forth from Florida to El Paso many times before she finally died."

Upon receiving the letter from his wife, the distraught husband procured a two-week emergency leave and flew home. From San Francisco, he telephoned Bebe and Bill Coonly, who invited him to have lunch as soon as he reached El Paso. "We were grief-stricken," said Bebe. "He didn't know how to tell his parents. I said, 'I'll tell them and you can stay with us.'" She called Mary Fran and informed her, but no one said a word to Terry senior.

Attempts by the husband to effect a reconciliation failed. Jean said she was convinced their marriage was over. "When he talked about the war, he told me it was not the kind of situation he had imagined. Morale was low; the chain of command broken down. People questioned what they were doing and made it difficult to operate. He said he had made up his mind to get out when he finished his tour."

During this interval, Terry junior also talked about his experiences in Vietnam with Bill Coonly. "My Dad couldn't exist in today's army. You wouldn't believe how things are done. The unit commander is down with the troops while the battalion commander is flying overhead in a helicopter, and he's in constant contact with both the troops and the regimental commander, and they try to run the whole damn thing by radio calls." He confided that he would retire when he came home from Vietnam. "He had every intention of returning," remembered Coonly. "He talked endlessly about how he really wanted 'to get back to my little girls and bring them up.'"

When it came time for him to return to the war, his oldest daughter Consuelo, then five, clung to his leg, sobbing, "You're going to die." Bebe, a year younger, was crying. Mary Frances, only three at the time, cannot recall the departure.

Back in Vietnam with the 2d Battalion, Terry junior spoke to Jim Shelton of the future. "I think I can patch this up with my wife. You gotta understand, she doesn't understand the military, why I was going to Vietnam." Although Jean in 2001 insisted the marriage was over and that she accepted his need to go to war, he appears to have hoped to restore the marriage and rationalized the reasons for her infidelity. And he talked of the distinct possibility that he would leave the army after the war. "He said he wanted to try something else, completely different," remembered Shelton. "He certainly did not have his eyes on being a general."

From 18 to 21 August 1967, Allen ran Operation Rochester. The Black Lions were airlifted into an area where intelligence reported the presence of components of the 9th VC Division. For three days the Americans scoured the area. They discovered hooches, a company-size bunker and firing positions—all abandoned. At the end, Rochester found negligible resistance, with no losses to either themselves or the enemy. It was another abortive exercise.

The attrition through ambushes, the occasional full-scale battle, disease, the inability to prevent the enemy from pursuing his ends, and the growth of the antiwar movement in the States all contributed to a climate of frustration at the American headquarters in Vietnam. The desire for decisive actions led to a large-scale offensive into the major jungle areas to the west and north of Highway 13, the north-south highway that ran north from Saigon to Loc Ninh. In the target area, large elements of the Viet Cong moved under cover of the jungle canopy and from bases established in Cambodia.

Typically, the American forces choppered into the zone battalion-size forces, such as in Rochester, in an attempt to confront enemy troops. On 6 October, the 1st Battalion of the 18th Infantry engaged in a battle that produced a body count of an estimated sixty VC. Five days later, the Americans, under Lt. Col. Richard E. Cavazos, prepared to carry out a planned maneuver. On the night before the soldiers were to move out, a scout dog began barking and would not stop. Cavazos prudently ordered a "reconnaissance by fire" and it provoked a thunderous barrage from the nearby enemy. Instead of being ambushed or caught in the open, the 18th Regiment soldiers were able to fight off the VC.

Jim Shelton reported that on 8 October, Allen's 2d Battalion of the 28th Infantry had been airlifted into the jungle northwest of Cavazos's GIs to wall off what intelligence thought was a full regiment of VC. The soldiers from the 2d Battalion began looking in several directions for the enemy. After the insertion in the zone, the 2-28th Infantry Battalion had conducted daily search-and-destroy missions. Normally, the battalion reconnaissance platoon and two rifle companies would patrol their assigned turf, rotating the third rifle company in position to secure the battalion's mortars, command post, command and control elements, and supplies. They detected ominous signs of extreme danger with the enemy in strong defensive positions, willing and able to exchange fire.

After a conference with Brig. Gen. Bill Coleman (the assistant division CG) and Col. George Newman (the division's 1st Brigade commander), to carry out the objectives of what was dubbed Operation Shenandoah II, Allen expected to drive deeper into the area. Both of the senior officers were experienced field leaders. But no one knew the numbers and disposition of the enemy.

First Lieutenant Alfred Welch had enlisted at seventeen right out of high school, and after serving with the U.S. Army Special Forces–Green Berets, he'd applied for and received a direct commission. He began with the 2d Battalion as a recon platoon leader, and then—after considerable combat experience—took command of Company D, which was added as a fourth rifle outfit. According to Shelton, because of Welch's background, he was very savvy about the ambience in a combat zone. Welch, who overheard the briefing, said, "The plan that Allen presented to brigade and division headquarters was a good one. Artillery would pound the area into which we would advance. But later, when Allen came to the company commanders to brief them, the plan for some reason had changed. There would be no artillery accompanying us." Who altered the original plan is unknown.

The area was marked by heavy jungle on relatively flat ground, with small open areas along streams, recalled Welch. Although considered the dry season, the temperature ran above 90 degrees during the day, with high humidity and afternoon showers. Intelligence believed enemy forces included two battalions and a controlling headquarters—three hundred to four hundred soldiers. Identified as part of the 271st Viet Cong Regiment, they were combat experienced and in a base camp, recovering from previous encounters that severely bloodied them. While perhaps short on rations, they were well armed, with AK-47 assault rifles, light machine guns, captured U.S. .50-caliber heavy machine guns, automatic weapons of Chinese manufacture, abundant claymore mines, and even rocket-propelled grenade launchers.

Welch and his Company D had already engaged them in a firefight on 16 October. On that day, with Company B in trail, D advanced into the thick overgrowth. Suddenly, Welch spotted the Viet Cong, and he immediately deployed his people. An intense firefight followed. Welch claimed at least thirty of the enemy were killed by the outpouring of small-arms, machine-gun, mortar, and artillery fire. He personally accounted for five or six of the dead with his own weapon. Only nine Americans from the two companies were wounded, but the captain who was assigned as a U.S. advisor to the attached provincial Vietnamese unit was killed. As night fell, Allen directed Welch to break off contact and return to the battalion's night defensive position (NDP).

When Allen broached his plan for 17 October, Welch suggested extreme caution. Shelton reported that Welch said, "We shouldn't be going back there. We barely got our asses out. Those guys are good. They know what they're doing. We need more artillery." However, reported Shelton, "For some reason, Allen refused to listen, accusing Welch of being gun-shy."

Listed as the Battle of Ong Thanh, it began with Company A, with 65 GIs in the lead. Normally, a full-strength infantry company in Vietnam numbered 125. An 11-man ambush patrol that had fought the previous day was left behind to rest. The 75 to 85 men in Welch's Company D trailed. Welch noted that a 25-man mortar section had also remained in base camp along with half a dozen soldiers scheduled for rest and recuperation. Allen was on the ground as part of the command group, which consisted of himself, battalion Cmd. Sgt. Maj. Francis Dowling, the battalion intelligence captain, the operations sergeant, a combat photographer, and four radio operators. The group traveled with Company D. One company from the battalion had been left in reserve at the base camp, while another was engaged about ten miles away. Shelton—who two weeks earlier had been transferred to division headquarters as an operations officer—was at a radio, monitoring the stream of reports. Contrary to some reports, when the action began there were no helicopters with senior command people present. Although, on other occasions they would be; and to the chagrin of those on the ground, they would attempt to micromanage an operation.

The GIs advanced cautiously—it took two hours for them to travel less than a mile. Small patrols to the front and flanks preceded the main body. Nonetheless, they were caught by surprise. A Company A scout reported a group of enemy troops crossing the front. It was between 9:30 and 10 in the morning. Captain Jim George, a onetime ministerial student, whose ROTC participation brought him to Vietnam as A Company commander, advised Allen in his command group and hastily organized an ambush. As soon as Welch heard the radio message, he deployed his men in defensive positions, spoke to Allen, and then moved forward with his own artillery observer.

If anything, the first sighting of Viet Cong triggered a savage response, because as soon as the Americans reacted, a deadly, heavy volume of accurate enemy fire ripped through the ranks of Company A. Said Welch, "A Company was not so much surprised by the enemy fire as overwhelmed by it." Captain George became the first casualty, knocked down, blinded, and deafened by the explosion of a claymore mine. First Sergeant Jose Valdez rushed to aid George and then led him away from the action. While that saved George, Company A was now leaderless as two of its platoon leaders were killed almost immediately. The remnants of the unit struggled to defend themselves. Within ten minutes, Company A was reduced to a handful of able-bodied. Too few survived that first few minutes' onslaught to protect or care for the wounded. "Many A Company soldiers performed incredible acts of individual heroism and sacrifice," said Welch, "but within minutes, A Company was no longer an effective fighting force."

Company D, in a defensive stance, reinforced the connecting link with Company A and also formed a perimeter to cover the command group with Allen. The first burst of enemy fire destroyed Allen's communications with Company A. The Viet Cong—sighting the many radios, antennas, smoke, markers, and maps—seem to have recognized the command group for what it was and now focused its fire upon it. Battalion intelligence officer, Capt. Jim Blackwell, was badly wounded. Later, tales were told of members of the command group who threw their bodies atop Allen to protect him; but Welch tersely dismisses that as "bullshit."

Allen's clothes were bloody; however, Welch attributes that to those around the battalion commander who had been struck.

Welch brought two of his company medics forward to treat the wounded from the command group and those stumbling backward from Company A. As a furious fusillade of sniper fire from trees, assault rifles, rocket-propelled grenades, claymores, and machine guns ravaged the Americans scrambling for cover, Allen asked Welch to go forward and check the status of Company A.

During his foray, Welch was able to offer some direction and encouragement to his own GIs as he tried to find what was left of the brother unit. He personally killed a treed sniper and shot down another Viet Cong. While his people hugged the ground, Welch exposed himself as he left cover in an attempt to pinpoint enemy positions. He was hit twice, a bullet in the chest and shrapnel in the face and body.

He realized there was no one left to direct supporting artillery fire, a duty for Company A. Welch summoned his own forward observer, Lt. Harold "Pinky" Durham, to take control and bring the weight of supporting artillery down upon the enemy. Durham's radioman had been wounded while getting into position and his radios destroyed. Welch turned over his own radios to Durham, who had been struck several times by enemy rifle fire. Despite his wounds, Durham began bringing effective artillery fire into the enemy. It was a difficult job, because the opposing forces were so close and many of the Company A wounded lay along the front.

Welch made his way back to the command group and apprised Allen of the desperate situation for Company A. Most of the wounded—on their own or with the aid of medics—had begun working their way to the east, away from the fighting, but also outside the perimeter created by Company D. He told Allen that his forward observer was now directing the artillery fire, which was exploding close but with effective results.

Durham, in fact, was protecting the artillery radio net with his body, while operating his radio handset with the stump of his wrist. His hand had been blown off by enemy fire. Although mortally wounded, he smiled when he saw Welch on one of his trips forward and yelled to him.

A pair of Viet Cong suddenly charged, penetrating the perimeter. Durham, first to spot them, could not fire his own weapon, but he shouted and pointed. Welch and Sergeant Barrow shot down both of the enemy.

Almost alone among the command group, Allen miraculously still had not yet been hit. By radio he was requesting immediate air strikes and additional artillery. Welch reverted to his role as Company D commander—moving about while under almost constant fire to urge on his men, direct their weapons to where they would be most lethal, encourage the wounded to hang on, and assist them to more protected places. The steady rain of shot and shell from the other side advised Welch that the Viet Cong had surrounded his perimeter, intent on wiping out the Americans with the command group.

Welch absorbed two additional wounds, including a bullet from a machine gun that blew off the bicep of his left arm, which now hung uselessly at his side. He saw an enemy rocket-propelled grenade gunner launch a projectile at the command group. It killed Cmd. Sgt. Maj. Francis Dowling, and the explosion knocked Welch down. He recovered enough to run toward the VC and shoot him down with his .45-caliber pistol.

Welch's own small command group had fared poorly. Lieutenant Durham and his radio operator, Sgt. Jim Gilliam, had both been critically wounded; Durham would die of his injuries. The two radiomen with Welch had both been struck and their equipment demolished. The company communications sergeant and the company medic had both been killed. No ranking leaders remained; two platoon leaders and two platoon sergeants were dead. His first sergeant, Clarence A. Barrow, had been knocked down, having been hit in the back and legs. Yet, he continued to battle on with an M60 machine gun and shouted encouragement to those still able to man a weapon. Barrow watched Welch sprint from man to man, trying to keep them in the fight even as he cared for the wounded and dying, distributed ammunition and water, and directed the resistance.

In considerable pain from his wounds and despite the withering spray of fire from the enemy, Welch stood up to get a better look at the foe's movements and positions. He arranged for a machine gunner to shift to a better field of fire. Barrow yelled to him, "Get down! The fire is too heavy."

Welch replied, "If I die, I'll die on my feet," and he continued to seek out his troops, aid those who needed help, and increase the effectiveness of the survivors.

The torrent of explosives and small arms shredded the jungle canopy, ripping away from both sides the cover of vegetation. While Company D still had enough ammunition and weapons, the visibility and the growing number of casualties denied any possibilities of tactical maneuver or even an orderly withdrawal. Allen continued to plead for air strikes. Hugging the dirt, Welch heard the aircraft come in and then some distant explosions. But the close quarters restricted the effectiveness of aid from the air. The artillery directed by the badly hurt Durham could mark a finer line, avoiding ground where American wounded lay. It kept the enemy at bay. Barrow saw Welch drag several of the fallen GIs to relative safety behind the Company D perimeter.

The Company D commander ran and crawled to Allen, who continued to report to higher headquarters, asking for more artillery support and for troops that might assist what remained of his battalion. To this day, Welch does not understand why Company B was not dispatched to aid the remnants of the outfit. "Bravo Company never moved," complains Welch. Allen ordered Welch to withdraw his people back along the route they had come to the night defensive position established earlier. But Welch estimated that he had too many badly wounded or dead from both companies to be able to move out. Intense and accurate enemy fire continued to rake the area. Anyone who moved was immediately a target for concentrated attention. On his own, Welch, without informing Allen, decided to ignore the order to attempt a withdrawal.

A few minutes after their conversation, a bullet struck Allen in the forehead, killing him instantly. There was nothing the lieutenant could do for his commander.

Helicopters with 1st Division senior officers aboard now hovered over the scene. They were able to coordinate artillery fire to much greater effectiveness. The Americans on the ground remained under siege, but the enemy attack slackened. Welch said he had little knowledge of the flow of the battle, but he continued to offer succor to the wounded, working with a medic to administer the last supplies of morphine to them.

Welch was lapsing into unconsciousness from his own injuries as he crawled toward First Sergeant Barrow. The latter yelled that a pair of VC were moving among the downed GIs, killing them. Welch pulled himself upright and killed the two interlopers. He fell to the ground and slumped against a tree, while trying to seal a sucking chest wound. He drifted in and out of consciousness, and then awakened suddenly as he felt jerks on his shoulder harness. To his horror he saw Barrow aim his M60 machine gun directly at him and open fire. It was his last memory of the day.

Later, in a hospital in Japan, he met Barrow who was also recuperating. Welch asked why the sergeant had turned his machine gun on him. Barrow explained, "Sir, a VC had you by the harness. He was standing behind you trying to pick you up, and the belt and harness pulled up over your chest, and you were still on the ground. I cut him in half with the M60."

The firefight at Ong Thanh that cost Terry Allen junior his life actually lasted only about two hours. But the survivors, such as Welch, were not evacuated until about 4:30 in the afternoon as darkness approached. The effort was confused by the presence of the survivors of Company A who had escaped to the east—the evacuation teams thought their location was the site of the battle.

In fact, the zone where Welch and the others lay was not hospitable to helicopters, and it was feared that any rescuers might be endangered. The battalion I&R (intelligence and reconnaissance) team had come forward and landed nearby, but the fearful commander remained at the base. Platoon sergeant Mark Smith disregarded orders, however, and led his men into the now-quiet battlefield. They picked up the wounded and carried or dragged them to a place where helicopters could carry them to a medical facility. Smith himself carried Welch to safety.

Division had sent forward more people to help organize the defense. Among them was a celebrated U.S.M.A. football star, Maj. Don Holleder. When he left his helicopter, he was, said Welch, "apparently the one person in his little group who was aware that a considerable number of U.S. troops were still in the woods. The door gunner heard him say, 'I'm going to rescue Americans.' Others in his group chose to head for the base camp. Holleder traveled about 50 feet before a single bullet from the tree line cut him down."

When the Americans finally extricated themselves, they had lost 58 dead—including 22 bodies they could not recover—plus 61 wounded. The official figures for enemy dead were set at 102 but that could have been only a guess. The 2d Battalion of the 28th itself was a casualty, no longer fit for duty.

Some in the 1st Division either downplayed the event or even tried to make the Battle of Ong Thanh a victory, but said Shelton, "We got our asses kicked." It was a stunning defeat, one of the earliest instances where the enemy, instead of operating in a hit-and-run attack or a simple ambush, in the words of Gen. William Westmoreland, the head of U.S. forces in Vietnam, "stood and fought to a greater degree. . . ."

Welch believes that Terry Allen junior, like everyone in the battalion, was near exhaustion. The battalion commander was further stressed because of the breakup of his marriage and because, due to circumstances, he had no one with whom he could discuss or work out his problems: Welch remarked that the operations officer was not very effective and the executive officer was off on another assignment. The age and rank gap between Lieutenant Colonel Allen and the lesser officers—lieutenants like Welch—was too great to permit easy sharing of concerns.

Why Terry Allen junior chose to disregard the counsel of the more experienced Welch became the subject of an article written by Shelton for *Vietnam* in 1994. Now a retired brigadier general, Shelton attributed the disaster to attitudes of those in command, from the top, down through Allen himself. Referring to the division leadership, Shelton noted that the division commander, Maj. Gen. John H. Hay, "was a very cautious commander. He did not like to take calculated risks, although operations were full of them. He always wanted the upper hand before the fight started. What happened to the 2d Battalion . . . was an absolute aberration to his way of thinking." But Hay was in Saigon when his assistant division commander, the brigade leader, and their staff plotted the operation.

Shelton concluded, "There were no villains in the battle, no obvious flaws in the leadership. So what went wrong? Ironically, the same thing went wrong at the tactical level on the battlefield that had gone wrong at the strategic level in Washington." He quoted from Gen. Bruce Palmer's book *The Twenty-Five Year War:* "The only explanation of [the failure of the Joint Chiefs of Staff] is that the chiefs were imbued with the 'can do' spirit and could not admit the possibility of failure." It was the reassertion of what Maj. Gen. Terry Allen had claimed for his divisions, "Nothing can stop . . . " Korea had been the first war in which the United States had been stopped. That conflict had ended in a stalemate; but neither the politicians in Washington nor the military leaders seemed willing to consider that the results in Vietnam might replicate Korea. Intoxication with American military power, and the concept of victory as the only acceptable end, befuddled those in charge.

In Terry Allen junior's case, Shelton pondered why, although Terry junior was "a first class soldier and officer . . . when Welch voiced his concern . . . Allen was not in a listening mood. He may have been tired and looking forward to the opportunity of finally getting into some decisive action. He may never have considered the possibility that the VC might get the upper hand. . . . Allen did not take into account that his lead company commander might be knocked out . . . he might lose control over the entire company. He did not realize that air and artillery fire would be useless to him . . . as the enemy closed in on his unit. He did not visualize the Big Red One, the great division of his father and his source of strength and confidence, as being incapable of helping. . . . He did not visualize that his enemy force might be, pound for pound, better trained, better conditioned, better armed for jungle battle, and at least the size of his own."

The *Vietnam* magazine dissection of what went wrong does not consider the matter of motivation among the Americans and their opponents. No one can definitively state what influences drove the younger Allen to exceed the bounds of prudence. While analyzing Terry Allen junior's potential failings, Shelton focused on strategy and tactics rather than why he was where he was when killed. In conversations with the author, Shelton—who has nominated Alfred Welch for a Medal of Honor—has remarked that Terry junior had an undistinguished career before he came to Vietnam. "Being a battalion commander was his last chance. You were either successful at it or it's all over."

In Vietnam, it was unlikely that an officer would be highly rated if he adopted a defensive stance. There was no substitute for winning. That had been true in World War II; Maj. Gen. Terry Allen stood out because he was aggressive, wanted to fight. Those who showed less inclination to attack lost their commands. Washington and the command in Saigon wanted triumphs: A battalion commander who was deemed not offensive-minded would soon lose his position. Allen, as the son of a legendary warrior, must have felt the pressure to attack.

Terry Allen Sr. had never required that his boy emulate him; but perhaps because he was so loving and asked nothing more than effort, Terry junior had gone into the military without ever considering any other profession. Although he never tried to trade upon his father's achievements, he could not have escaped the idea that people expected him to be like his father. Jean recognized the pressure upon her late husband. She said, "Terry lived to please his father, even though he was not demanding."

After he was killed, some people speculated that Terry Allen junior, distraught over the collapse of his marriage, acted in a suicidal mode. That hardly squares with Allen's statement to Bill Coonly that he expected to return and raise his daughters. Shelton squelches the allegation: "In my opinion his marital problems had no effect on his mental state or on his feelings and responsibility for the battalion. He felt sad, of course, but it certainly did not preoccupy him or interfere with his ability to command. He was mature and level-headed about the situation. He was too good a soldier to lead his people into a massacre."

21 : Taps

The first information about Terry junior that was flashed by phone from Vietnam to the next of kin listed him as missing in action. "I knew he was dead," said Jean.

Mary Fran called the Coonlys and reported the terrible news, "Terry is lost." The couple immediately went to the Allens' home and remained overnight. Bebe Coonly recalled the following morning, when she, "was with Mrs. Allen when she looked out the window and saw three chaplains coming up the walk. She screamed. The general said only, 'The Lord giveth and the Lord taketh away.' I have never seen anything like the letters and flowers that poured into the house." The general, who had signed so many messages of regret to the parents of those killed in battle, was now the recipient of condolences.

The funeral ceremony was held at Fort Bliss. Albert Schwartz attended the ceremonies and said, "The general was handed the American flag from the coffin. He stood tall and proud once again. It was the first time in a long while—and the last time—that I saw him show that kind of spirit.

"It was reflected when we went to their home after the funeral. It wasn't like a lot of homes where there has been quiet and respect for those in mourning. The Allens had sandwiches, booze and beer for everyone. Terry went around shaking hands, popping people in the chin with his left hook, darn near floored me. He wasn't happy, but I quote him: 'Let there be no tears in this house; this is the house of an infantryman.' That damn near broke me up. It showed how tough he could be. I don't think he meant it; and, I'm sure when he was by himself and certain nobody could see him, he shed some tears, because Terry junior was his pride and joy.

"He just faded after his death. I don't think he sold a whole lot more insurance after that. He didn't look good in his clothes. His carriage was round shouldered; he bore a heavy, heavy load. It was something that was painful to see. He had been disappointed that Terry junior's marriage didn't work out—that his wife was contemplating very seriously a divorce." Others insist that the father was unaware of the situation between his son and his wife, that had the general heard she was living with another man, "he would have chased him out of town or shot him."

According to Allen's granddaughters, the general was very gentle and playful with them. For a time he continued to visit Fort Bliss, where he would hand out his pamphlets on subjects such as night attacks and advise, "Soldier, this is going to save your life." During the years that followed, Terry senior's wife, Mary Fran, never talked about the near-divorce nor was she vitriolic toward Jean.

Gossip about the breakup of the marriage slithered through the military community and those associated with it. It is not difficult to imagine the outrage of those in uniform when they heard that the wife of a man under fire had been unfaithful. Bebe Coonly remembered a dance some months after Terry junior's death when someone shouted, "How's the whore in your family?" She said she could not attend a party without hearing remarks of that nature.

Jean Allen's affair crumbled and she remained in El Paso, trying to raise her three daughters. Mary Fran helped, but the atmosphere between her and her daughter-in-law, said Jean, "was strained. I was not in touch with the army people. I didn't have any friends at Fort Bliss; if people said evil things about me, I never heard them."

The general's health declined swiftly after his son's demise. He developed a heart condition that made it difficult for him to climb the stairs of his two-story home. Several small strokes eroded his memory. "He was going in and out of reality," said Consuelo. "He sometimes thought that I was my Dad."

On 12 September 1969, Terry Allen Sr. died of natural causes and was buried alongside his son in the Fort Bliss National Cemetery. As Mary Fran, relatives, friends, and dignitaries—a crowd of three hundred—

looked on, a thirteen-gun salute boomed out in his honor. Schwartz said, "Lieutenant General Richard Cassiday, who was commander of Fort Bliss, gave him an old-fashioned cavalryman's funeral, complete with the riderless horse and boots turned backward. We walked from the chapel to the cemetery and he was given every honor in his death that any dignitary could have imagined. It was a hard thing to realize that someone like Terry Allen was gone, but really he'd been gone for a while. I guess I sort of hoped that he and Terry junior got together afterwards."

Major General Samuel Koster, the former member of the 104th Division and now superintendent of the U.S.M.A., eulogized, "Those of us who were Timberwolves saw firsthand the miraculous leadership capabilities of Terry Allen. His professionalism and wisdom are legendary and will never be forgotten by the soldiers who served for him." From Vietnam, the commanding general of the 1st Division also sent a tribute.

In the years that followed, the granddaughters were invited and welcomed to reunions held by the National Timberwolf Association, the 104th Infantry Division Association. Bebe Allen (christened Alice Genevieve) said, "Men in their seventies would line up and tell us, 'I had a cup of coffee with your grandfather.' 'I treated your grandfather's sinuses.' They wanted us to know how much they revered him."

The comrades of their father who had been with him when he was killed also met with them and spoke of Lt. Col. Allen as a fine soldier who was considerate of his troops. Jim Shelton became a family friend.

"We knew all about our grandfather and father," said Terry junior's daughter Bebe. "There were photographs of them and things connected to them all around the house." As a widow, Mary Fran continued to live in the house on Cumberland Circle in El Paso. "She was a very visible presence in our lives," said granddaughter Bebe. "We called her Franny; she did not want to be referred to as 'grandmother.' She was always very proper, well dressed, like the image of a steel magnolia. One of us would stay at her house every weekend. It was exciting, a treat. She would take us to restaurants and she was very particular about how we ordered and the service. Our home life was kind of turbulent and she gave us a sense of calm and security. She was supportive, would compliment us if we did anything, like writing letters. We knew she was deeply wounded by what had happened to Dad; but, while she was cool and distant to our mother, Franny never made any vitriolic comments in or out of her presence."

But the loss of both her son and then her husband sapped the life force within Mary Fran. "Gradually," said Bebe, "she stopped eating and became reclusive. She broke a hip in 1977 and after that she seemed to have lost her desire to live." She died a year later at age sixty-seven, with no apparent heart disease or other malady. "I think she really died of a broken heart," said Bebe, "and just wanted to go." She was buried in the Fort Bliss plot.

In the following years, the three girls all attended Boston University and established their own careers. Consuelo acted in theatrical productions and settled in Austin where she has a catering business and is an environmental activist. Her sister Mary Fran, married to a lawyer, is an executive with an El Paso customs brokerage company. Bebe, living in Austin, became a bride in 2001 and works for an organization that promotes safety at railroad crossings through presentations at schools and organizations such as the Boy Scouts.

Suddenly, in 1986, Terry Allen's granddaughters heard from the family of their grandfather's sister, Ethel McGovern. Terry Allen's oldest sister had married James Cadmus McGovern—who held the rank of major during World War II. The McGoverns made their home in Los Angeles and had a son, Terry Allen McGovern, who in World War II served in the navy as a Boatswain's Mate, 2d Class, and earned a Bronze Star.

Ethel McGovern outlived her brother by seven years before she passed away at age eighty-nine in 1976. The McGovern branch of the Allens had become involved with the care of the youngest of the general's siblings, Mary, who had alternated between wandering the streets of Washington and institutions for the emotionally troubled. In 1984, at a Veterans Administration hospital in Virginia, she died of pneumonia as a consequence of Alzheimer's disease. In a note discovered by the McGoverns in an old copy of *Time*, Mary left each of her grandnieces five thousand dollars.

With her children independent, Jean Allen entered into two more marriages—which also failed. She moved to the West Coast, where in 2001 she pursued a doctoral degree in theology, writing a dissertation on the relationship of spirituality, ethics, and sexuality.

The Allen military line had come to an end, but not before it had served its country so valiantly. Of the three professional soldier Allens, only the middle one rose high enough and held sufficient command to have left a military legacy. Two respected generals from World War II, John Corley and Don Clayman, had called him "the greatest soldier." That's not the same as saying Allen was the best general. To compare the achievements of Allen with those of say Eisenhower, Bradley, Patton,

MacArthur, or other senior commanders would be nonsensical. The responsibilities and the jobs were so different as to defy comparisons. But "the greatest soldier" is another matter. In terms of understanding the strengths and weaknesses of his troops, in exerting leadership and teaching that quality to his subordinates, in strategizing and implementing the tactics to realize plans, and in getting the best efforts from his people at the least cost to them—it would be hard to argue against Allen's superiority.

When the United States went to war in 1941, Terry Allen, who had led a battalion in France during WWI, was one of the very few senior officers who had combat command experience. Patton and MacArthur were among the handful of others. Admittedly, a working knowledge of 20th Century warfare dating back almost a quarter century meant that Allen still had much to learn on the job. On the other hand, both Eisenhower and Bradley lacked anything resembling Allen's background and his contemporaries, Courtney Hodges, the First Army Commander in Europe, Mark Clark the Fifth Army Commander and Beetle Smith, Eisenhower's deputy, during WWI served only as junior officers, below the level responsible for strategy and tactics. In contrast, the Axis commanders who confronted the United States had already engaged in modern war. The German generals, however, suffered from the interference of Hitler, a former corporal during WWI.

As a rule, defensive strategy requires less imagination than other offensive warfare. It was in this dodgy aspect of combat that Allen brought something to the table. His talent and understanding of how to take the initative was married to his personality, pugnacious, outspoken and a willingness to risk going beyond the accepted bounds. Patton had much the same in his character but unlike him, Allen had a genuine feeling and understanding of human cost.

While it's unlikely there would be a place for a freewheeling Terry de la Mesa Allen in today's army, his understanding and experience as a leader should still resonate. In *The Face of Battle,* John Keegan mused about what sustains those in battle: "The behavior of men struggling to reconcile their instinct for self preservation, their sense of honor and the achievement of some aim over which other men are ready to kill them." He pointed out that coercion has always been a means for those in command to push their subordinates. However, the ancient courage stiffeners—drink and prayer—that had been involved before the twentieth century were less important during the world wars. For the most part, combat troops did not enjoy alcoholic drinks before battles, although the kamikaze pilots were plied with wine before taking off. Religion in the Allied forces was not used to spur soldiers to fight, but rather to help them deal with their fears.

Keegan remarked, "The personal bond between leader and follower lies at the root of all explanations of what does and does not happen in battle." He dated this back to the presence of the king during late medieval conflicts. Allen intuitively grasped the potential of his persona, endeavoring to create bonds by his interactions with the men and by making himself as accessible to the battlefield as possible. In his officers he sought that same engagement. But Allen's approach was by no means Machiavellian. His humility and modesty were genuine; his affection and concern for his troops was instinctive.

The author of *The Face of Battle,* after listing a number of elements such as fear, courage, leadership, and compulsion noted, "it is always a study of solidarity and usually of disintegration of human groups . . ." In Tunisia, Allen vociferously voiced his belief in unit integrity; arguing against splitting up men who trained together and had bonded, the keystone of Keegan's prized "solidarity." Few in combat would claim that they hung in because they did not want to sully the honor of the Big Red One or the Timberwolves. But by boosting his organizations, Allen provided the framework for what most agree is the true source of a combat soldier's grit: his loyalty to his comrades. Soldier after soldier has explained he persevered because he did not want to look bad or let down his closest associates. By welding a strong sense of unit, Allen nurtured that affinity the men in his outfits had for one another.

War in the twenty-first century differs from that of the past; yet, as long as people are required to put their bodies in harm's way, Terry de la Mesa Allen remains a model of the soldier's general.

Bibliography

Allen, Terry de la Mesa. *A Factual Situation and Operations Report on the Combat Operations of the 1st Infantry Division During Its Campaigns in North Africa and Sicily.* Unpublished, undated, typed paper, Eisenhower Library, Abilene, Kans.

——. Personal Papers. Eisenhower Library, Abilene, Kans.

——. Personal Papers. Special Collections, University of Texas at El Paso, Tex.

——. Personal Papers. Archives, U.S. Army War College Library, Carlisle, Pa.

Ambrose, Stephen E. *Duty Honor Country.* Baltimore: Johns Hopkins University Press, 1966.

Blumenson, Martin. *The Patton Papers, 1940–45.* Boston: Houghton Mifflin, 1974.

——. *Kasserine Pass.* New York: Cooper Square, 2000.

Bradley, Omar N. *A Soldier's Story.* New York: Henry Holt and Co., 1951.

Bradley, Omar, and Clay Blair. *A General's Life.* New York: Simon and Schuster, 1983.

Clendenen, Clarence C. *Blood on the Border.* New York: Macmillan [Toronto CM Sec. 15.157], 1969.

Coffman, Edward M. *The War to End All Wars.* New York: Oxford University Press, 1968.

Denno, Bryce F. "Allen and Huebner: Contrast in Command," *Army,* June 1984.

D'Este, Carlo. *Bitter Victory.* New York: E. P. Dutton, 1988.

———. *Patton: A Genius for War.* New York: HarperCollins, 1995.

Downs, Kenneth. "Nothing Stopped the Timberwolves," *Saturday Evening Post,* 17 August 1946.

Eisenhower, David. *Eisenhower at War 1943–1945.* New York: Random House, 1986.

Eisenhower, Dwight D. *Crusade in Europe.* New York: Doubleday and Co., 1948.

Ellis, Joseph, and Robert Moore. *School for Soldiers.* New York: Oxford University Press, 1974.

Farago, Ladislas. *Patton: Ordeal and Triumph.* New York: Ivan Obolensky, 1964.

Fleming, Thomas J. *West Point.* New York: William Morrow, 1969.

Gavin, James M. *On to Berlin.* New York: Viking, 1978.

Heintges, John. Oral History. U.S. Army War College Library, Carlisle, Pa. [n.d.].

Herr, John K., and Edward S. Wallace. *The Story of the United States Cavalry.* Boston: Little, Brown and Co., 1953.

Hoyt, Edwin P. *The GI's War: American Soldiers in Europe During World War II,* New York: Cooper Square Press, 2000.

Keegan, John. *The Face of Battle.* New York: Penguin Books, 1976.

Liebling, A. J. "Find 'Em, Fix 'Em and Fight 'Em," *New Yorker,* 16 and 23 April 1943. [installments].

National Timberwolf Association. *Timberwolf Tracks.* Wichita, Kans: [National Timberwolf Association,] 1999.

Palmer, Gen. Bruce. *The Twenty-Five Year War: America's Military Role in Vietnam,* Lexington, Ky.: University Press of Kentucky, 1984.

Pappas, George S. *To the Point: The United States Military Academy 1802–1902.* Westport, Conn.: Praeger, 1993.

Pogue, Forrest C. *George C. Marshall: Ordeal and Hope 1939–1942.* New York: Viking, 1965.

Porter, Robert. Oral History. U.S. Army War College Library, Carlisle, Pa., 1981.

Pyle, Ernie. *Here Is Your War.* New York: Henry Holt, 1943.

Rapp, Kenneth W. *West Point.*: North River Press, 1978.

Shelton, James E. "The Battle of Ong Thanh," *Vietnam,* August 1994.

Time. "The Infantry with the Dirt Behind Their Ears," 23 August 1943.
Weigley, Russell F. *History of the United States Army.* New York: Macmillan, 1967.
———. *Eisenhower's Lieutenants.* Bloomington, Ind.: Indiana University Press, 1977.

Index

About the Author

GERALD ASTOR is a critically acclaimed military historian and author of such books as *Wings of Gold, The Mighty Eighth, A Blood-Dimmed Tide, The Right to Fight, The Greatest War,* and *Bloody Forest.* He lives near New York City.